Law, State
and the Working Class
in Tanzania

Books in African Studies

HISTORY

T. O. Ranger *Peasant Consciousness & Guerrilla War in Zimbabwe*

Cased 0-85255-000-6
Paper 0-85255-001-4

Robert Shenton *The Development of Capitalism in Northern Nigeria*

Cased 0-85255-002-2
Paper 0-85255-003-0

Donald Crummey (editor) *Banditry, Rebellion and Social Protest in Africa*

Cased 0-85255-004-9
Paper 0-85255-005-7

Jan Vansina *Oral Tradition as History*

Cased 0-85255-006-5
Paper 0-85255-007-3

Ralph Austen *African Economic History**

Cased 0-85255-008-1
Paper 0-85255-009-X

J. D. Omer-Cooper *History of Southern Africa**

Cased 0-85255-010-3
Paper 0-85255-011-1

William Beinart & Colin Bundy *Hidden Struggles in Rural South Africa**

Cased 0-85255-012-X
Paper 0-85255-013-8

ECONOMICS

C. George Kahama, T. Luta Maliyamkono & Stuart Wells *The Challenge for Tanzania's Economy*

Cased 0-85255-100-2
Paper 0-85255-101-0

Allan Low *Agricultural Development in Southern Africa*

Cased 0-85255-102-9

SOCIO-ANTHROPOLOGY

David Lan *Guns & Rain: Guerrillas & Spirit Mediums in Zimbabwe*

Cased 0-85255-200-9
Paper 0-85255-201-7

GOVERNMENT, POLITICS AND LAW

Roger Tangri *Politics in Sub-Saharan Africa*

Paper 0-85255-300-5

Philip Ndegwa *Africa's Development Crisis*

Paper 0-85255-306-4

Issa G. Shivji *Law, State and the Working Class in Tanzania*

Cased 0-85255-302-1
Paper 0-85255-303-X

Julie Frederikse *South Africa: A Different Kind of War*

Paper 0-85255-301-3

Peter Lawrence (editor) *World Recession & the Food Crisis in Africa**

Paper 0-85255-304-8

Joseph Hanlon *Apartheid Power in Southern Africa**

Cased 0-85255-307-2
Paper 0-85255-305-6

LITERARY CRITICISM

Eldred Jones & Eustace Palmer (editors) *Women Writers in African Literature Today**

Paper 0-85255-500-8

Ngugi wa Thiong'o *Decolonising the Mind**

Paper 0-85255-501-6

Georg M. Gugelberger (editor) *Marxism and African Literature*

Paper 0-85255-502-4

*in preparation

James Currey
54b Thornhill Square · Islington · London N1 1BE

Law, State and the Working Class in Tanzania

c. 1920–1964

Issa G. Shivji
Associate Professor of Law
University of Dar es Salaam

James Currey
LONDON

Heinemann
PORTSMOUTH N.H.

Tanzania Publishing House
DAR ES SALAAM

James Currey Ltd
54b Thornhill Square, Islington, London N1 1BE

Tanzania Publishing House
Independence Avenue, PO Box 2138, Dar es Salaam

Heinemann Educational Books Inc
70 Court Street, Portsmouth, New Hampshire 03801, USA

© Issa G. Shivji 1986
First published 1986

British Library Cataloguing in Publication Data

Shivji, Issa G.
  Law, state and the working class in Tanzania: c. 1920–1964.
  1. Labor and laboring classes——Tanzania——Political activity
  I. Title
  322'.2'09678   HD8797

  ISBN 0-85255-302-1
  ISBN 0-85255-303-X pbk

Library of Congress Cataloging in Publication Data

Shivji, Issa G.
  Law, state, and the working class in Tanzania.
  Bibliography: p.
  Includes index.
  1. Labor laws and legislation——Tanzania——History. 2. Trade-unions——Law
and legislation——Tanzania——History. 3. Labor and laboring classes——
Tanzania——History. 4. Law and socialism——History. I. Title.
  LAW   344.678'01'09   85-24949
  ISBN 0-435-08013-X (Heinemann) 346.7804109

Typeset in 10/11 pt Plantin by Colset Pte Ltd, Singapore
Printed in Great Britain

Contents

v

Tables

Abbreviations

AC	Appeal Cases (UK)
ACEA	African Commercial Employees' Association
AFL–CIO	American Federation of Labour–Congress of Industrial Organizations
ANC	African National Congress
ARLD	Annual Reports of the Labour Department
CJC	Central Joint Council (sisal industry)
CO	Colonial Office (Records in Public Record Office, London: below, p. 255)
CS	Chief Secretary
DC	District Commissioner
DMT	Dar es Salaam Municipal Transport Company
DOAG	Deutsch-Ostafrikanische Gesselschaft (German East Africa Company)
EA	East African Law Reports
EACA	East African Court of Appeal (Reports)
EACSO	East African Common Services Organization
EAF	East Africana (University of Dar es Salaam Library)
EO	Employment Ordinance
FCB	Fabian Colonial Bureau (below, p. 255)
ICFTU	International Confederation of Free Trade Unions
ILO	International Labour Organization
ISIC	International Standard Industrial Classification
LC	Labour Commissioner
LRT	Law Reports of Tanzania
KB	King's Bench (UK)
MLH	Ministry of Labour and Social Welfare, Headquarters (Records in Dar es Salaam Office, below, p. 255)
M & NSO	Master and Native Servants Ordinance
NPLUB	Northern Province Labour Utilization Board
NUPTE	National Union of Post and Telecommunications Employees
NUTA	National Union of Tanganyika Workers
PC	Provincial Commissioner
RH	Rhodes House, Oxford (below, p. 255)

SEA	Security of Employment Act
SILABU	Sisal Labour Bureau of TSGA
SS	Secretary of State
TAA	Tanganyika African Association
TAGSA	Tanganyika African Government Servants' Association
TALGWU	Tanganyika African Local Government Workers' Union
TANU	Tanganyika African National Union
TFL	Tanganyika Federation of Labour
TGWU	Transport and General Workers' Union
TLR	Tanganyika Law Reports
TNA	Tanzania National Archives (below, p. 253)
TNR	*Tanzania Notes and Records*
TPWU	Tanganyika Plantation Workers' Union
TRAU	Tanganyika Railway African Union
TSGA	Tanganyika Sisal Growers' Association
TUC	Trade Union Congress (British)
TUPE	Tanganyika Union of Public Employees
WFTU	World Federation of Trade Unions

Principal Legislation

1922   Hut and Poll Tax Ordinance, No. 12
Involuntary Servitude (Abolition) Ordinance, No. 13
House Tax Ordinance, No. 26

1923   Master and Native Servants Ordinance, No. 32

1926   Master and Native Servants Ordinance, No. 11
Native Authority Ordinance, No. 18

1927   Master and Native Servants (Amendment) Ordinance, No. 9

1931   Master and Native Servants (Amendment) Ordinance, No. 35

1932   Trade Union Ordinance, No. 32
Shop Assistants Employment Ordinance, No. 33

1934   Native Tax Ordinance, No. 20

1935   Identification Ordinance, No. 13

1938   Employment of Women Ordinance, No. 14

1939   Trade Union (Amendment) Ordinance, No. 7
Minimum Wage Ordinance, No. 19

1940   Employment of Women and Young Persons Ordinance, No. 5
Compulsory Service Ordinance, No. 23

1941   Trade Union (Amendment) Ordinance, No. 30

1942   Master and Native Servants (Written Contracts) Ordinance, No. 28

1943   Employment of Women and Young Persons (Amendment) Ordinance, No. 4

1945   Sisal Industry Ordinance, No. 15
Shop Hours Ordinance; No. 25

1947   Labour Utilization Ordinance, No. 2
Trade Disputes (Arbitration and Enquiry) Ordinance, No. 11
Minimum Wages (Amendment) Ordinance, No. 14

Subsidiary Legislation

Selected Cases

1. *R.* v. *Mathew bin Condala & Anor*, Tabora Criminal Sessions Case No. 124 of 1939 (unreported).
2. *R.* v. *Pandosi Kuhekera*, Criminal Revision No. 213 of 1937 (unreported).
3. *Drossopoulos* v. *R.*, Criminal Appeal No. 39 of 1930 (unreported).
4. *R.* v. *Haji Abdurasul*, Criminal Case No. 73 of 1957, District Court, Dodoma (unreported).
5. *R.* v. *H. Milde*, 1 TLR (R) 215.
6. *R.* v. *M.K.A.* Uberle 1 TLR (R) 672.
7. *R.* v. *Kirumba*, Criminal Case No. 48 of 1938, 1st Class Subordinate Court, Tanga (unreported).
8. *R.* v. *Hemedi*, Criminal Case No. 49 of 1938, 1st Class Subordinate Court, Tanga (unreported).
9. *R.* v. *Mrs Fredeal Schimidz & Gustav Wreker*, Criminal Case No. 4 of 1936, 1st Class Subordinate Court, Morogoro (unreported).
10. *Kitundu Sisal Estate* v. *Shingo and Others* (1970), EA 557.
11. *Mishi Sefu* v. *Massawe* (1978), LRT n. 13.
12. *Attorney General* v. *Patel Farmers*, Criminal Appeal No. 108 of 1957 (unreported).
13. *Rajabali Meghji Visram* v. *R.* (1956), EACA 428.
14. *R.* v. *Valambia* (1963), EA 12.

English cases

1. *Horwood* v. *Millar's Timber and Trading Co. Ltd* (1917), 1 KB 305.
2. *Amalgamated Society of Railway Servants* v. *Osborne* (1910), AC 87.

Glossary

askari	An African soldier or policeman
'boys'	Commonly used during colonial times to describe workers
bwana	Master
fungu	Heap, pile, or portion: common measure by which vegetables, etc., are sold in markets
kaniki	A black or dark blue calico worn by women in the same way as *khanga* but used for work
kanzu	Long-sleeved robe or gown worn especially by Muslim men
karai	Big metal bowl often used to carry stones and concrete on a worker's head at construction sites
khanga	Piece of printed cloth worn by women
kibaba	A common dry measure, about a pint, or 1½ lb of grain
kikapu	A small basket
kipande	A labour ticket with thirty empty spaces to record attendance at work
mafungu	Plural of *fungu*
marekani	Literally American. Refers to white coarse cloth often used to make prisoners' uniforms
manamba	Literally plural for *namba* (number). Swahili slang for contract labour.
mtama	Sorghum
panga	A long knife
posho	Ration given to labourers on plantations. Also refers to coarse yellow maize flour
sembe	White maize flour
shamba	Field
'toto'	Colonial-settler slang meaning *watoto*
wanyapara	Headmen, supervisors
watoto	Children
wazee	Old or elderly persons

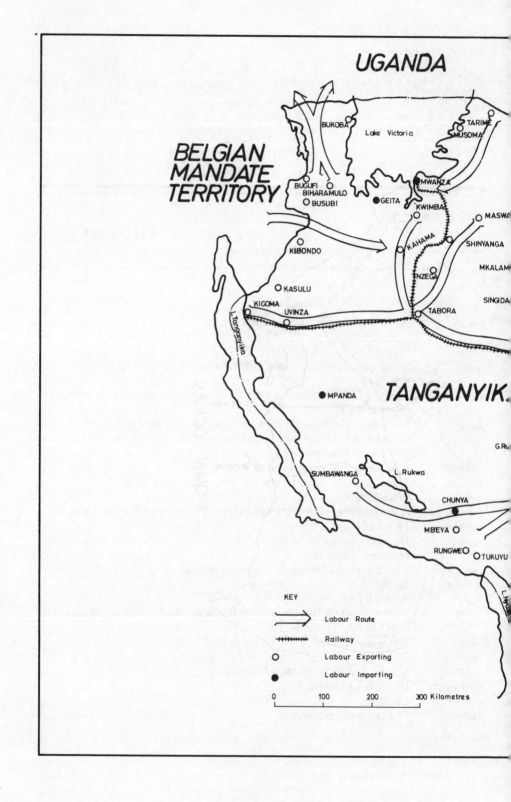

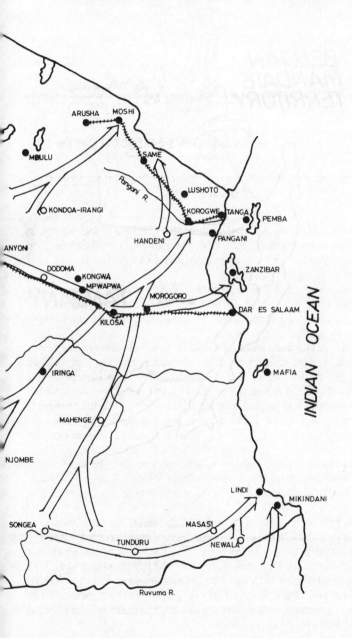

LABOUR IMPORTING AND LABOUR EXPORTING AREAS AND PRINCIPAL LABOUR ROUTES

Acknowledgements

This work was spread over a fairly long period of time and involved the assistance of many individuals and several institutions. The University of Dar es Salaam assisted with research grants which enabled me to carry out research in Great Britain and visit factories in Tanzania. To them all I am grateful.

I would also like to thank the staff of Public Records Office, London; Rhodes House Library, Oxford; the Tanzania National Archives, Dar es Salaam; the Ministry of Labour and Social Welfare, Dar es Salaam; and the University of Dar es Salaam Library for their assistance and co-operation.

Several friends read parts of the draft and made useful comments. Professors Abdul Sherrif and Umesh Kumar, my supervisors, scrupulously scrutinized the draft of each chapter and helped me greatly in ironing out contradictions and inconsistencies. I would like to record in particular the great care, concern and dedication with which Abdul Sherrif went about his task of supervising an argumentative candidate. Ernest Wamba, George Hadjivyanis and Zinnat Bader made useful comments and helped me morally with words of encouragement. B. B. Pande, Wilbert Kapinga, Chris Peter and Mike Wambali took the completion of this work to their heart and prodded me along during the last few weeks with friendly advice and encouragement. In particular I cannot forget Wilbert's assistance which was always forthcoming without hesitation. Without the inspiration of all these friends, I would have probably faltered and failed to . complete the task.

A. Mchulupete, A. Kitiwili, T. S. Mangumbuli and Mohammedi Kaonda undertook the task of typing and mimeographing the original manuscript within record time.

Lastly, I must mention two people who bore the heaviest brunt of the work and tolerated the eccentricities and idiosyncracies of its author. Parin's involvement with this work is as old as her involvement with me. She did all the transcription, tolerated long hours of sleeplessness and finally ensured its completion at the expense of her health. To her, I am deeply indebted. And finally my mother's concern helped to boost my morale and overcome moments of hopelessness.

Preface

Wavuja-jasho – meaning those who bleed sweat – is how the Tanzanian working class describes itself. It is also an apt summing-up of the history of its development and conditions. For that history has been written in sweat and blood, groans and tears. Truly the working class makes its own history which intellectuals only author from different standpoints. In this study, the development of the Tanzanian (mainland) working class is recorded, described and analysed in its relation to labour law and state from the standpoint of the working class.

Although the study was submitted to the University of Dar es Salaam for a PhD, we have not found it necessary to change its format substantially, nor to revise and abridge it. Some detail and description herein may mar readability but then, we believe, much of this information is being printed for the first time. The material we discovered in the course of our research was so new and enticing that we could not resist the temptation to make it available to a wider readership. It is our hope that this work will stimulate future Tanzanian researchers to dig even deeper in the several areas and issues thrown up by this study. The least that committed Tanzanian intellectuals owe to the working class is constantly to research into and present its history and current struggles in all its expanse and depth. This is one way of debunking ruling bourgeois ideologies which belittle and ceaselessly slander the role and place of the working people in our society.

This is not a traditional legal study and therefore non-lawyers need not be put off. We have consciously tried to avoid legal formalism and technical jargon, for one of the main tasks of our work was to lift the halo and mystery that surrounds bourgeois law. Yet law occupies a central and significant place in bourgeois state organization and capitalist social relations. It needs to be studied and dissected ceaselessly. When we first thought of embarking on this research a decade or so ago, our original conception was to do a straight history of the working class. 'Why waste time with bourgeois law?' we then argued. But the late Walter Rodney, himself a historian, advised otherwise. He said something to this effect: 'Use your skills as a lawyer to expose the oppressive and mystifactory role of law. Some of us trained in non-law bourgeois disciplines may not be able to do the same effectively.' We would like to think that this has been a worthy response to that advice.

*To
the makers of history
authored herein
and to
Ma and Pili*

INTRODUCTION

Law, State and Society

*There is no history of politics,
law, science etc., of art, religion.*
Marx/Engels[1]

Law does not have a history of its own. What goes under the name of legal history is often a recounting of successive laws locating their cause and effect within the inner contradictions of law itself. The illusion that law has history and that legal development can be explained within law itself is created specifically with the emergence of the division of labour wherein occupations assume independent existence. The rise of the ideologists, lawyers and jurists, nurtures such an illusion. The material relations of life, in a lawyer's mind, become fossilized concepts, which, he believes, explain the *development* of law. 'In consciousness – in jurisprudence, politics, etc. – relations become concepts; since they do not go beyond these relations, the concepts of the relations also become fixed concepts in their mind. The judge, for example, applies the code, he therefore regards legislation as the real, active driving force.'[2] The ideologist turns everything upside down, the shadow is taken for the substance.

Engels elucidates these arguments succinctly in the following passage:

It is indeed among professional politicians, theorists of public law and jurists of private law that the connection with economic facts gets lost for fair. Since in each particular case the economic facts must assume the form of juristic motives in order to receive legal sanction; and since, in so doing, consideration of course has to be given to the whole legal system already in operation, the juristic form is, in consequence, made everything and the economic content nothing. Public law and private law are treated as independent spheres, each having its own independent historical development, each being capable of and needing a systematic presentation by the consistent elimination of all inner contradictions.[3]

Thus to understand the movement and development of law we have to locate it within the general movement of the material conditions of life, that is, within social history.

In the present study we have attempted to analyse the development of labour laws in mainland Tanzania in its interconnections with the origin and development of wage-labour. The focus has been on the two-fold characteristics of law: on the one hand as a reflection of the movement of wage-labour and on the other as an instrument to secure the conditions of its development. The underlying theme which informs the study as a

1

whole is the relation between law, state and society. In this connection, the basic propositions of historical materialism form the general guiding threads of our study.

The analysis of the character of productive forces and relations of production form the basis for explaining and understanding the broad movement of the development of wage-labour. The most crucial aspect in this respect is the fact that the genesis and subsequent development of wage-labour was located within imperialist domination. The sway of capital[4] and its invasion of pre-capitalist relations in Tanzania was a process which imparted specific characteristics to wage-labour.

The study covers the broad period from approximately 1920 to 1964. The approach is thematic rather than chronological. Nevertheless, two broad phases may be distinguished. The first phase until about the end of 1930s was dominated by semi-proletarian labour. Chapter 1 discusses the development of this type of labour and Chapter 2 gives its conditions. Both these aspects are analysed in the context of the relation between capital and labour, the dominant fraction of capital being finance capital.

Chapter 3 gives the character and organization of capital and its relations with the colonial state. It is argued that whereas capital was well organized and to a large extent managed to minimize inter-capital contradictions, the semi-proletarian character of labour militated against collective organization and resistance of labour.

During the period when semi-proletarian labour dominated, the central piece of legislation was the Master and Native Servants Ordinance. Its main purpose was to facilitate the procurement of labour for capital and regulate its recruitment and repatriation. This legislation and the regulations made thereunder are discussed and analysed in the context of the contradictions of the system of semi-proletarian labour.

The second broad phase of the development of wage-labour begins in the early 1940s with the struggles of the dockworkers. Chapter 4 deals in detail with the development of permanent wage-labour, in particular the industrial, agrarian and mining proletariat. The conditions of the proletariat, especially those pertaining to industrial accidents and safety, are discussed at length in this chapter and such legislation as the Factories Ordinance, the Workmen's Compensation Ordinance and the Employment Ordinance are analysed closely.

Chapter 5 concentrates on the struggles of the dockworkers and goes into a detailed discussion of the four major strikes during the decade of the 1940s. Dockworkers have painted a brilliant picture of militant working-class struggles. It was in the wake of their struggles that for the first time the labour law scene began to change with the introduction of Minimum Wage legislation, Factories Ordinance and so on.

Once the workers had embarked on a collective struggle and collective organization (trade unions), the state came to the rescue of capital by introducing legislation to control and supervise working-class organizations; hence trade union legislation. Chapter 6 discusses the complex class struggles of the 1950s in the fire of which the most important trade unions of the Tanzanian working class were born and matured. It was again during this period that the most important outlines of legislation on trade disputes were worked out.

In spite of its phenomenal successes during the 1950s, the trade union movement was not to last. With the coming of independence, it fell victim to inter-petty-bourgeois struggles. The emerging bureaucratic bourgeoisie threw the weight of its neo-colonial state behind its own interests and those of foreign capital. The trade union movement was rapidly smashed and laws were hurriedly passed making strikes illegal and establishing a single trade union which in substance became part of the state machinery. This is analysed in Chapter 7.

As noted earlier, the underlying thread that runs through this study is the interconnection between law, state and society. Law and state are intimately connected. In law, the ruling class expresses its generalized will which is determined by definite material conditions.[5] Both law and state in the final analysis serve the interests of the ruling/dominating class as is borne out by this study. In some cases law is used as a direct instrument, tool, of the ruling class and serves its immediate interests without mediations of intermediate links. This we term as the *instrumentalist* character or aspect of law. The bloody legislation in Western Europe of the late fifteenth century and the whole of the sixteenth, which assisted the expropriation of the peasantry[6] from the soil, may be said to be predominantly of instrumentalist character. But at times, particular pieces of legislation may also exhibit a *political* characteristic. By political characteristic we refer to that aspect of law which encapsulates or embodies either the results of class struggle or is meant to control class struggle. Here, too, it is *ultimately* the interests of the ruling/dominating class that are served. Yet they are mediated through and do embody certain partial successes and gains made by the ruled/dominated classes. Laws on trade unions and trade-disputes settlement machinery may be said to be of this type.

The third aspect of law is its *ideological* characteristic. By ideology we refer to that form of social consciousness which *mystifies* and *disguises* real relations of life.[7] This is not to say that ideology is purely and simply false consciousness, although this too may be true in case of certain types and at certain levels of ideology. Nevertheless, to the extent that ideology is class-based, at best it reflects only *partially* the real relations of life. We would suggest that the ideological content of law is of a lower order than, say, philosophy or religion; that is, it is least removed from the material conditions of life.[8] This is because law – as opposed to jurisprudence which is the philosophy of law – has to *regulate* real relations on earth, albeit relations as perceived by and in the interest of the ruling class.

Which particular aspect or characteristic of law is dominant would differ from society to society and with different types of legislation and within the same society in different historical periods. Among other things, it will depend on the stage of development, the conjuncture of class struggle and the historical and cultural factors pertaining to legal consciousness as a whole. This is not a place to go into details of these different aspects of law. Suffice is to mention that in this study, at specific points, we have attempted to draw attention to these different characteristics of law in the context of close interconnections between law, state and society.

NOTES

1. Marx, K. and Engels, F., *The German Ideology*, in Marx, K. and Engels F., *Collected Works*, Vol. V (Moscow: Progress Publishers, 1976), p. 92.
2. ibid.
3. Engels, F., *Ludwig Feuerbach and the End of Classical German Philosophy*, in Marx, K. and Engels, F., *Selected Works*, Vol. III (Moscow: Progress Publishers, 1970), p. 371.
4. See, generally, Lenin, V. I., *Imperialism, the Highest Stage of Capitalism*, in Lenin, V. I. *Collected Works*, Vol. 22 (Moscow: Progress Publishers, 1964), pp. 185ff. For a theoretical treatment of imperialism in relation to Africa see Khamis, L., *Imperialism Today* (Dar es Salaam: Tanzania Publishing House, 1983).
5. 'The individuals who rule in these conditions . . . have to give their will, which is determined by these definite conditions, a universal expression as the will of the state, as law, an expression whose content is always determined by the relations of this class, as the civil and criminal

law demonstrates in the clearest possible way' (Marx, K. and Engels, F., *The German Ideology*, op. cit., p. 329).

6. For an analysis of this legislation see Marx, K., *Capital*, Vol. I (Moscow: Progress Publishers, n.d.), Ch. XXVIII.

7. For an elaborate discussion of ideology see generally Sumner, C., *Reading Ideologies: an investigation into the Marxist theory of Ideology and Law* (London: Academic Press, 1979). We may observe in passing that Sumner has expanded the meaning of ideology so wide as to embrace virtually all forms of consciousness; there is therefore a danger of it losing meaning altogether (see Sumner, C., op. cit., p. 20).

8. See Engels, F., *Ludwig Feuerbach*, op. cit., pp. 371–2.

The Development of
Semi-Proletarian Labour

Pre-colonial commodity exchange

One of the prerequisites of wage labour and one of the historic conditions for capital is free labour and the exchange of free labour against money, in order to reproduce money and to convert it into values, in order to be consumed by money, not as use value for enjoyment, but as use value for money. Another prerequisite is the separation of free labour from the objective conditions of its realization — from the means and material of labour. This means above all that the worker must be separated from the land, which functions as his natural laboratory. This means the dissolution both of free petty land ownership and of communal landed property, based on the oriental commune.[1]

The two prerequisites of wage-labour that Marx mentions are that there is a considerable development of commodity economy and that labour power itself has been converted into a commodity. But the latter is predicated on the existence of *free labour*. The separation of the producer from his means of production is therefore the second prerequisite of wage-labour. In pre-colonial Tanganyika, while there was some development of commodity exchange there was hardly any existence of free labour. Let us examine each one of these in turn.

There were two main types of exchanges in nineteenth-century Tanganyika. One was based on the exchange of surplus agricultural products and the other on the exchange of specialized craft, mineral and natural products. There is little doubt that almost everywhere the level of technology used in agriculture was low. Therefore higher yields and the possible production of surpluses depended on such factors as higher fertility of certain areas and the possibility of irrigation. The Rufiji flood plains are one such example. Warufiji had devised ingenious agricultural practices whereby, by making use of annual floods, it was possible for them to become independent of rainfall and have several harvests in a year.

The rich alluvial deposits of the lower Rufiji valley enabled the growth of maize, rice, millet, ground-nuts and peas. Inland, along the Rufiji tributary system, the rich alluvial soil of the Great Ruaha River made this area 'one of the most fertile spots in Africa'.[2] Wamahenge, who then lived along the Great Ruaha, extensively cultivated rice, millet and maize in this area. Rice-growing was also important higher up along the Ulanga/Kilombero River. These areas together produced significant amounts of surpluses.

5

Kjekshus observes that it is possible that 'the grain surpluses from these areas were eventually included in the regional trading network and made places like Mgunda, Kondoa/Kilosa and Morore important provisioning stations along the central trade routes'.[3]

The other group of commodities involved products of handicraftsmen. Karagwe, Bukoba, Uha, Ufipa and Unyamwezi were some of the important areas of iron-smelting in Tanganyika. They produced iron hoes which were variously exchanged for food and other products along the caravan routes.[4] Besides, iron was also an important item in the regional trading network. The Pare smelters supplied Wachagga and Masai in the north-east. Wafipa in the south-west exchanged theirs for cloth from Rukwa valley, and so on.

Salt mined for centuries in Uvinza and pots made by, among others, Kisi women of the Nyasa lakeshore were other items in the regional trading network.[5]

Thus there was a fair amount of commodity exchange before even the beginnings of the long-distance Arab caravan trade. Nevertheless, this commodity exchange was small in terms of the volume of products involved and still at a very elementary stage of its development. Almost all the Tanganyikan societies involved in exchange at this time were at the stage of the production of use-values. It was the surpluses of these use-values which were then exchanged. The commodity exchange was peripheral and occasional, confined to border exchanges, like those between Wachagga and Masai in Chaggaland, or the traditional women's food markets.[6] The most developed trade was undoubtedly that based on the products of specialized craftsmen who were already detached from food production and depended on bartering their products against food.[7]

The low level of commodity exchange is further reflected in two interrelated phenomena. First, none of the societies appears to have reached the stage of using a 'universal equivalent' in their exchanges. The system of exchange was essentially based on barter. Secondly, with a few exceptions, for example the Yao traders, the Tanganyikan societies had not as yet developed a specialized group of middlemen or professional traders.[8] As Kjekshus puts it:

The importance of the traditional market rested, however, in the fact that women met as partners in a total economy to equalize through exchange the differences arising from individual production methods. In addition, the exchange provided variety in the diet and disposed of perishable surpluses. Thus, the traditional food market was oriented to distribution, not to profit.[9]

We are thus dealing with societies which were very little specialized, and where private property had yet to develop. The division of labour was between sexes[10] although, as we have seen above, in some places there were beginnings of the separation between handicraft and agriculture. The lack of middlemen and profit motive that Kjekshus mentions reflected the mode of production based essentially on the production of use-values.

If the development of commodity economy was still at an elementary stage, the development of labour power as a commodity was hardly known in pre-colonial Tanganyika. Although the producer had varying and differentiated rights to the use of land depending on his age-group, clan membership and so on, the fact was that the producer was not separated from land, his 'natural laboratory'.

The introduction of wage-labour into Tanganyika was one of the most important innovations of the coastal/Zanzibar-based long-distance trade carried out by the Arabs and a few Indians. The caravan trade, as it has come to be recognized in history, expanded the existing commodity exchanges and introduced even some completely new commodity trade, especially that in ivory and slaves, not to speak of guns. This new form of long-distance trade no doubt provided the decisive external conditions for exacerbating the internal contradictions of the Tanganyikan societies. But most important of all, for the first time, it introduced a completely new form of commodity exchange, the exchange of labour power.

The caravan traders employed large numbers of porters.[11] These were mainly temporary workers, mostly from Unyamwezi, the inland centre of the caravan routes. They were usually paid in kind rather than money,[12] worked for anything between one and three months with the caravans and then probably returned to the land. These were the first hesitant steps in the development of wage-labour in Tanganyika.

In spite of the important impact of the long-distance trade on the internal order of the Tanganyikan societies, it was not until the German invasion towards the end of the century that these societies can be said to have been firmly integrated in the world-wide capitalist system, the system based on wage-labour. Such integration required the combined economic might of finance capital and the colossal political will of an imperialist state, both of which came in the form of the German colonization of Tanganyika.

The aim of colonization, as one of their leading spokesmen put it, consisted 'in the utilization of the soil, its products, and its men, for the economic profit of the colonizing nation'.[13] One of the forms by which the 'colonizing nation' set about utilizing Tanganyika's men was through the system of wage-labour. The next section analyses the various methods used by the German, and later the British, colonialists, to create wage-labour in Tanganyika.

The creation of wage-labour

Three main methods were used by the colonialists to separate the producer from his means of production and to force him to labour for capital. These were: forced labour, taxation and recruitment. Although the intensity of each differed from period to period, all of these methods survived until the later part of the colonial period. We propose to discuss them in some detail.

Forced labour

Use of direct force was much more marked during the German than the British period although, as we shall see, the latter was not free from it. Slavery, the early form of forced labour introduced in the days of caravan trade, survived until the end of the German period. Although the slave trade had been abolished the Germans were pretty lax about the use of slaves on plantations. The Germans issued some 52,313 certificates of freedom but there were still several thousand slaves until the system was completely abolished after the First World War.[14] The British enacted the abolition of slavery in the Involuntary Servitude (Abolition) Ordinance[15] passed in 1922.

Another system of forced labour very common during the German period was to allocate a number of villages to a settler. The headmen of these villages were obliged to provide the settler with a fixed quota of workers every day.[16] Use of force was so common and vicious during the German period that it is said to have been one of the causes of the great Maji-Maji uprising of 1905.[17] The uprising was brutally put down at an estimated loss of some 120,000 lives.[18] Meanwhile, the system of forced labour continued and besides paying their taxes workers had also to pay almost half of their wages as war damages for the uprising.[19]

The British were much shrewder and more sophisticated in the use of force to obtain labour. Restrained by the mandate provisions which forbade use of compulsory labour except for 'essential public works and services',[20] and later the ILO Convention,[21] they had constantly to provide rationalizations for the use of force. The so-called 'communal labour' or 'tribal turnouts', the tax-defaulters' labour and conscription were the three main forms of forced labour during the British period.

The so-called 'communal labour' referred to the requisitioning of labour of the villagers for a definite period once or twice in a year. The practice began as early as 1921[22] and was later given legal recognition in the Native Authority Ordinance[23] of 1926. Section 8 of that Ordinance empowered a native authority to issue orders to 'natives' to, among other things, provide labour 'for the purpose of exterminating or preventing the spread of tsetse fly'. Paragraph (q) made a blanket provision that 'natives' could be ordered for the purpose of 'prohibiting, restricting, regulating, or requiring to be done any matter or thing which the native authority, by virtue of any native law or custom for the time being in force and not repugnant to morality or justice, has power to prohibit, restrict, regulate, or require to be done . . .' The power to issue orders under this section was not the prerogative of only the native authorities, for a provincial commissioner or administrative officer could in fact require a native authority to issue orders if he thought it expedient to do so.[24] Thus the native authorities were really the 'front men', the cannon fodder, behind which the real holders of power attempted to hide.

Thousands of people were employed under this system to work for anything between ten and twenty days per year: clearing roads, clearing bush for eliminating tsetse, building dams and doing other works which were considered by the colonial officials as being in the interest of the community. Colonial officials argued that this was not forced labour: that in fact it was voluntary labour and had its sanction in the local tribal customs. They rationalized this practice as being in continuation of the old custom where subjects were obliged to give free labour to their chief to maintain certain public facilities in the villages.[25] Hence in theory this work was supposed to be confined to only village roads, although in practice the distinction between village roads and district roads often got blurred.[26] The villagers used their own tools and were not paid any remuneration except some beer and meat ration. Although communal labour was supposed to be voluntary, the governor's authority was invariably sought to make a statutory order allowing punishment of those who would not turn up for such work. The maximum penalty of a Shs. 200 fine or an imprisonment not exceeding two months was prescribed for disobeying the orders of a native authority.[27]

The practice of forced labour in the form of so-called 'tribal turn-outs' was very widespread geographically as well as in its intensity.[28] To cite but one example, the Provincial Commissioner of the Central Province proposed to call out some 40,000 people in 1948,[29] some 24,000 in 1951[30] and some 67,000 in 1954[31] to work for anything between ten and twenty days on such works as the up-keep of roads, bush clearing and building dams, wells and contour banks. The numbers involved are a clear testimony to the amount of virtually free labour that was deployed by the colonial state to build the necessary infrastructure in the interest of capital.

Another form of widely used forced labour was that of tax-defaulters. The system of taxation, as we shall see in the next section, was used by the colonial state to flush out labour for capital. It would have therefore served little purpose if the non-payment of tax was simply treated as a civil breach where the tax would be recovered by a civil suit.

Under the Hut and Poll Tax Ordinance of 1922, and later the House Tax Ordinance,[32] a 'native' liable to pay tax could discharge his obligation by providing the equivalent amount of labour on any government undertaking or on any 'essential public works and services authorized by the Government'. Even under the ILO Convention on Forced Labour, in spite of its various exceptions, this was considered forced labour. The colonial officials, however, continued to insist that it was necessary in the 'primitive' conditions of Tanganyika at the time. In the words of Governor Byatt:

It is impossible to apply to primitive social systems such as those of the native tribes in this territory social principles and political ideals which have been evolved by and accepted as suitable for peoples in an advanced stage of civilization and it is no exaggeration that the European who penetrates to the interior of tropical Africa steps back 2,000 years or so in the history of human progress, the circumstance which is often not realized by the philanthropist who has no personal knowledge and experience of primitive Negro communities . . . I can state definitely that the natives of this territory as a whole are both willing and anxious to discharge their obligations to the government, even when unable to do so — they constantly consult political officers as to where or how they can obtain money for the purpose: but there is, of course, a proportion of wilful defaulters and it is essential that the government should have the means of dealing effectively with this people. If the power to do so is lacking, the news will spread with surprising rapidity that the government takes no action against the evader and it is easy to foresee that the proceeds of native taxation, the most prolific of all sources of government revenue, will shrink in a very short time, to the point of disappearance.[33]

The capitalist civilization that Governor Byatt represented required the extraction of every ounce of labour in the interest of capital. And if the concrete conditions demanded force, the civilized representatives had no qualms in using it. Thus this form of forced labour continued to exist in Tanganyika until 1951[34] when the very development of commodity economy and wage-labour had made it an anachronism.[35]

Nevertheless, during the period in which it existed forced labour of tax-defaulters built the sinews and arteries, the infrastructure of the colonial economy. This was not simply the labour of a few recalcitrant tax-defaulters but of thousands of men who had nothing but labour to discharge the obligations imposed on them by the state. Hundreds of miles of roads were cut, tens of buildings were built and maintained, dams were constructed and agricultural works carried out by the sweat and blood of these so-called tax-defaulters. At its peak, between 1933 and 1942, an average of some 25,000 tax-defaulters were put to work annually. Taking the average of thirty-six man-days worked by each tax-defaulter in 1935 as typical, this would amount to some 900,000 man-days of work annually.[36] There is no doubt that these figures, calculated from the official sources, are deflated since colonial officials deliberately under-stated the number of tax-defaulters so as to avoid criticism in the Mandates Commission.[37] Even then they show that this form of forced labour played no small part in the colonial economy.

The third form of forced labour which reached gigantic proportions during the Second World War was conscription. The powers granted to native authorities were used to requisition labour before the war. Under that law a native authority or a provincial commissioner through a native authority[38] could require a native to engage in paid labour for 'essential public works and services' for a period of not longer than sixty days per year. Much of the labour that was requisitioned was used for porterage to carry loads of administrative officers, tax money and so on. In the early period of colonialism, lack of motor transport meant that even the heads, let alone hands, of the colonized were pressed into work. This was the notorious head-transport. In 1927 more than 15,000 people were requisitioned for this purpose.[39] The numbers fell somewhat during the 1940s to an annual average of some 9,000 between 1940 and 1950.[40] Porters were remunerated at the going rate of wages: in 1935, this meant some 30–50 cents a day.[41] Besides porterage, requisitioned labour was also used for occasional repairs of roads, bush clearing and so on. Conscription, however, became very significant during the war.

The colonized people were not only drafted to bear arms in the fight amongst imperialists, but they were also forced into production to sustain the economies of the warring countries while the masters resolved their contradictions on the battle-field. Complete figures for the numbers forced into military service are not available. Official figures have it that from 1940 to 31 July 1943 some 67,000 Tanganyika Africans were taken into military service. However, we have a fuller picture of conscription for civilian works, which began in earnest in 1942. Conscription for military service, lack of availability of commodities and therefore incentive to earn wages, and the colonial state's campaign to produce more, all meant that private employers felt an acute shortage of labour during the war period. They pressed on the colonial state to provide them with compulsory labour. The distinction between private and public was no longer maintained, for the warring 'united nations' needed certain strategic raw materials and food and the colonies were assigned to shoulder this burden of feeding the imperialists and their industries. After the fall of the Far East the allies lost important sources of hard fibre, manila hemp from the Philippines and sisal from Java, not to speak of the loss of rubber from Malaya. They began to rely on their colonies in East Africa to supply sisal and also food for their troops in the Middle East.[42] The production of food, sisal and rubber was declared 'essential production' for the war, for which labour could be conscripted under the powers given to the governor by the Compulsory Service Ordinance of 1940.[43]

These, then, were the three important sectors where conscripted labour was employed. In the sisal industry conscripted labour constituted over 10 per cent of the total labour force at the end of 1944; in the case of rubber over 35 per cent were conscripted whereas the respective figure for essential foodstuffs was around 25 per cent.[44] Over 60 per cent of the conscripted labour was employed by private capital. A total of 86,000 workers were conscripted between 1942 and 1945 for essential production.[45] Table 1.1 gives a summary of conscripted labour in employment.

Table 1.1   *Conscripted labour, 1941–5*

Date	No. in employment	Essential public services	Foodstuffs, pyrethrum	Rubber	Sisal
1.1.41	100	100	—	—	—
1.1.42	400	400	—	—	—
1.1.43	6 525	1 843	3 705	977	—
1.1.44	12 386	112	4 315	5 061	2 898
1.1.45	26 256	535	6 429	7 476	11 816

Source: Orde-Brown, G., *Labour Conditions in East Africa* (London: HMSO, 1946), p. 10.

The compulsory service was for anything between three and six months in the case of essential foodstuffs, and nine and twelve months in the sisal and rubber plantations. Conscripts were remunerated at the going market rates and were supervised under strict military discipline. Therefore the rate of desertion tended to be high, as much as 10 per cent.[46]

One of the important features of conscription was that in some cases it forcefully introduced a completely unaccustomed people to wage-labour for the first time. This was especially the case with the Wagogo from the Central Province. Many of them were conscripted to work on rubber plantations in the Tanga Province. Not used to wage-labour as such, but also because of the tough conditions of tapping rubber, considerable numbers deserted — some 468 between April and December 1943. But the colonial state was determined to drive home the discipline of wage-labour and deter desertions. Those arrested were given prison sentences of up to two years with hard labour. No wonder, as one colonial official put it, the 'prison sentences had an immediate effect in checking the flood of desertions'.[47] It was thus that the all-important rubber was produced by the Wagogo, whom one colonial described as 'unsophisticated natives with a deepseated fear of the unknown'.[48] If the unknown was the brutal violence of the colonial prison, the fear was undoubtedly justified.

Two broad conclusions may be drawn from our preceding discussion of the use of forced labour during the colonial period. First, there is no doubt that this type of labour was a significant component of the total labour force and fulfilled the immediate need for labour. It was an important portion of the labour that built the basic infrastructure of the colonial economy. The colonial state which employed much of this labour was almost exclusively responsible for laying the infrastructure to enable the pentration of private capital.[49] It must be emphasized that the cost of building this infrastructure, which was in the ultimate interest of finance capital, was wholly borne by the colonized people.

Secondly, the long-term effect of forced labour was to instil the habits and conditions of wage-labour in the producers who had never known it before. This the colonial official themselves realized quite well. Answering the arguments of the Northern Province private employers who complained that 'communal turn-outs' interfered with their supply of labour, the District Commissioners of Singida and Kondoa argued that 'the Native Authorities' efforts to organize communal labour turn-outs in their Chief-doms are usually the indirect cause of large numbers of Africans proceeding to Arusha in search of work in as much as the communal work is not paid for in cash'.[50] Similar opinion was expressed by the governor's deputy on the question of conscript labour: 'The compulsory system also has the effect of bringing considerable numbers of natives into contact with non-native enterprise and of forming wage earning habits which would not otherwise have occurred. This may lead to more men offering themselves voluntarily for work later on when they have become accustomed to the idea, and provide sources of supply hitherto hardly touched.'[51]

Forced labour thus played an important role in the creation of wage labour. We now turn to the second method.

Taxation

Taxation was one of the important instruments in the colonial state's arsenal for creating wage labour. Both the Germans and the British used it extensively. The Germans imposed a generalized system of taxation as early as 1898[52] and systematized it as a hut and poll tax in their House and Poll Tax Ordinance of 1912. As a matter of fact, under the German law, a collective tax could be imposed in any district in lieu of individual poll tax. This mechanism was often used to mobilize a particular district to provide labour.[53] In a number of revolts against the colonialists, resistance to taxation constituted an important element. For example, in 1894 Machemba, a Yao chief, led a tax protest. It was crushed in 1899. The chief fled to Mozambique while his followers were imprisoned. In 1902 Mpoto from Kitangari was hanged for leading a tax protest.[54] As late as 1928, the Wanyakyusa migrated to Nyasaland in protest against the tax on 'plural wives'.[55] In spite of these protests the colonial state did not lessen its drive for taxation, as this formed a key element in its pursuit of extracting labour.

The British colonial state inherited and developed the system of hut and poll tax introduced by the Germans. Under the Hut and Poll Tax Ordinance of 1922 every owner and occupier of a hut was jointly and severally liable to pay His Majesty a tax prescribed by the governor from time to time. The hut was defined to mean 'any hut building, or structure of a description commonly used by natives as a dwelling'.[56] Where a person had more than one wife housed in the same hut he had to pay an additional hut tax for each wife after the first.[57] This was the notorious tax on 'plural wives' that the Wanyakyusa protested against.

Where a person did not own a hut he had to pay a tax for his mere existence, the so-called poll or head tax. 'Every able-bodied male native of the apparent age of sixteen years or over . . . shall pay annually a poll tax of such amount as the Governor . . . may prescribe.'[58] Unlike the tax system of advanced capitalism where taxation is predominantly a system to earn revenue, the 'hut and poll tax' was primarily a system aimed at extracting labour.[59] The colonialists knew this and consciously used it for the purpose. New migrations of labour were stimulated by imposing or increasing taxation.[60] It was thus that the Wanyakyusa and the Wangoni of Southern Tanganyika,[61] the Wabena of Njombe[62] and the Waha of the Kigoma were brought into the labour market.[63] In many cases the district administration actually planned their tax drives so as to flush out labour during periods when the employers needed it most.[64] So, although it is true that once the people had been integrated in the money-economy certain of their necessities (such as salt, sugar and oil) and even social obligations (for example, bridewealth) could be discharged only by earning cash, payment of tax in cash continued to be an important stimulant to hiring out one's labour.

The character of hut and poll tax as essentially a labour tax is further borne out by examining the following important features of the legislation itself.

First, it applied only to the indigenous population, the most important source of labour. Secondly, certain groups of people who fell within the definition of 'native' were exempted from paying the hut and poll tax. These were mainly the military and police personnel who had already offered their labour in the repressive apparatus of the state: the 'Chiefs, Liwalis and Jumbes' who had opted to work as the agents of the state in the latter's stystem of 'indirect rule', and the destitute and disabled persons who could not offer their labour in any case.[65] A destitute or a disabled person was explicitly defined as someone 'without means to pay hut and poll tax and is *unable to obtain employment by reason of age or infirmity'*.[66] The governor could also exempt certain huts situated in urban areas from hut and poll tax and make them liable to house tax.[67] House tax applied mainly to urban areas and was based on the value of the house rather than simply its existence. Presumably the owner and occupiers of 'huts' in urban areas were already involved in the commodity economy as traders, wage-labourers or in other money-earning occupations, and therefore there was no need to subject them to the labour tax of the hut and poll tax kind.

Thirdly, both the hut and poll tax were fixed without regard to the value of the hut or the income of a person. As long as a person was an able-bodied adult, that is, over 16 years old and therefore capable of work, he had to pay the poll tax regardless of whether or not he had an income. As we have already seen, a person liable to tax could be required to provide labour instead. So there was no alternative but to provide labour: whether as a peasant growing cash crop, as a wage-labourer or as a tax-defaulter.

The Hut and Poll Tax Ordinance was revoked in 1934 but the new law virtually retained the important provisions of the hut and poll tax except for raising the age of liability to 18 years. In addition, it introduced two new forms of taxation for Africans:

the graduated personal tax and communal tax. The graduated personal tax was a recognition of the differentiation and the resultant differences of wealth that had begun to take place in some areas.[68] However, both these new forms remained long on the statute book before being actually applied. For the large majority of the people, the most important incidence of taxation continued to be the hut (now called the house) and poll tax.[69] If, therefore, they found themselves in the labour reservoir areas they had no alternative but to sell their labour power to earn the necessary cash to pay their taxes.

This indirect method of forced labour was not covered by the ILO Convention on Forced Labour. To be sure, the ILO did *recommend* to its members to avoid 'indirect means of artificially increasing the economic pressure upon populations to seek wage-earning employment, and particularly such means as imposing such taxation upon populations as would have the effect of compelling them to seek wage-earning employment with private undertakings . . .'[70] The typical response of the colonial state to this recommendation, as we have seen, was to put the graduated personal tax on the statute book without applying it in practice.

It is also important to note that this indirect compulsion in many cases became direct force in practice for the colonial state took the collection of hut and poll tax very seriously. As a matter of fact, the tax collector, besides the police and the administrator, was the most important representative of the colonial state and was so identified in the minds of the colonized. The tax ticket was like an 'identification card' and the 'native' had to carry it wherever he went because non-production of a tax receipt on demand was a *prima facie* evidence of the non-payment of tax.[71] The few scandal stories that reached the records of the colonial office suggest that the use of force in collecting tax was not uncommon.[72] A letter written to the Secretary of State by a white sympathizer in 1936 mentioned an incidence of death resulting from severe beating of an African by a government tax collector. 'It is a long sad story how this tax is collected from mere defenceless creatures. Sometimes it's their womenfolk who are pinched sometimes their cattle, goats and sheep.'[73] No wonder people hid in caves[74] and left village settlements[75] to avoid tax collectors or offered themselves to the recruiters of labour, the slave-masters of the colonial era.

Recruitment

Recruitment referred to all those operations engaged in by an employer or his agent or a professional person so as to obtain labour that did not offer itself spontaneously at the place of work. Shortage and irregular supply of labour continued to haunt colonial employers and therefore they had to resort to recruiting to obtain necessary supplies.

Around 1905 an attempt had been made by the League of German East African Plantations to form a central recruiting agency but owing to contradictions between the big and small employers it failed. Governor Rechenberg's efforts in the same direction also did not bear fruit although later in 1909 he tried to put recruitment on a more systematic basis by issuing the 1909 Ordinance. But under this Ordinance and its successor, the 1913 Ordinance, a person who wished to recruit had to obtain a licence from the governor. A recruiting licence was issued for a particular district and for a definite period, supposedly to allow the state to control the activities of the professional recruiters.[76]

The system continued under the British and was regulated by the Master and Native Servants Ordinance[77] and the regulations made thereunder. Although the government officials were involved in issuing permits to the recruiters, examining and attesting contracts, they did not directly participate in the recruiting exercise. This would obviously have smacked of the use of force and would have been in breach of the ILO Convention.

The recruiters consisted of basically two types: private professional recruiters and agents employed by the employers themselves. The former of course charged fees and were interested in making profits. This inevitably led to numerous abuses. In theory the recruiter was supposed to enter into a contract with a person voluntarily offering himself. In practice, to maximize the number of people recruited and therefore his profits, the private professional recruiter resorted to all sorts of means — from cajoling and deceiving to outright force — to coerce unwilling people to sign contracts.[78] The case of the Usukuma Labour Agency which reached scandalous proportions illustrates this and other points.

The Usukuma Labour Agency[79] was owned by two Englishmen, T. H. Henry and M. G. Rees. It was the first agency to operate in the Bukoba area, recruiting mainly the Warundi and Warwanda filtering into Bukoba from the then Belgian mandated territory. In 1929, the Bukoba Provincial Commissioner sent in a report with bulky evidence against the Usukuma Labour Agency. Various sections — the chiefs, missionaries and the recruited workers — complained that the agency represented itself as recruiting for the government and used inhuman methods and force to enlist people. The following testimony of one Balitoye from Bugufi, who was recruited by the Agency, is typical of the evidence that was collected:

I came to Bukoba District two months ago to find work. I engaged myself to Joseph of Katoke to hoe his shamba. Joseph gave me and my four companions a hut in which to sleep. Joseph slept in another hut. During the night a native named Shabani came and broke into the hut and told us that a European had given out an order that all 'Bashuti'[80] were to be taken to go and work for a European. We were taken to Kamachumu and put in a house to sleep. During the day we were kept in a compound. I as the leader amongst my friends was told to see that no one ran away. At night the room in which we slept was locked with a padlock. There was another man, a native of Ruanda also appointed as headman to look after his batch. There were 22 of us. I was there six days. Wood and water was obtained by two men taken under guard by one headman whilst the other remained with the rest. The chief of Ibuga came with a European officer and his wife when we made our complaint and were told to come to Bukoba.[81]

Similar stories were narrated by the missionaries and others who testified. In spite of this evidence the Labour Commissioner, Major Orde-Browne, continued supporting the Usukuma Labour Agency which openly boasted of its friendship with the major. The agency was not censured until a year later when it was involved in another scandal, having recruited unfit persons, a number of whom died on arrival at the plantations.

The Usukuma Labour Agency episode probably illustrates in an extreme form the gruesome methods that were often employed by professional recruiters to fulfil their contracts. Thus recruitment really hid procuring of, in many cases, involuntary labour which would have squarely fallen under the ILO Convention on Forced Labour. A later petition from the Chagga Cultural Association of Tanganyika to the United Nations Trusteeship Council could well be a summary of the feelings of the victims:

This Association strongly objects to the Labour Utilization Board and calls for its dissolution. This Board, a government creation, is more of a slave market than a centralization of manpower. Africans are recruited from all over the Territory by means which are far from being voluntary. These unfortunate Africans are transported as far from their homes as 800 miles in such a way that would make one's blood run cold. Cattle are better treated than these prospective labourers.[82]

The Northern Province Labour Utilization Board, referred to in the above quote, was an attempt by the colonial state to centralize recruiting of labour for the Northern Province employers following the successful experience of centralized recruiting during the war. The Tanganyika Sisal Growers' Association had formed their own central recruiting agency in 1944 called the Sisal Labour Bureau (SILABU). The chairman of the Growers' Association boasted about the achievements of SILABU at the passing of a resolution in 1968 to dissolve the association: 'From the commencement of operations in August 1944 up to the closure of the Labour Bureau in March 1965 over 463,500 adult male employees had been brought into the Industry: in addition about 442,000 persons had been repatriated. Together with overheads the total net expenditure of the Labour Bureau during the 20 years of its existence was some £2,639,400.'[83]

Employment centres, labour reservoirs and the sectoral distribution of wage-labour

Uneven development, an important characteristic of capitalist penetration, asserted itself in an even more exacerbated form in the colonies. It expressed itself at various levels of the social economy but that which concerns us here directly is the development of the employment centres and the labour reservoirs.

Following the pacification, the Germans established themselves on the coast. German settlers moved to the most accessible and climatically suitable area, the highlands of the Usambara. It was thus that the north-east — the coast of Tanga and the valley of the River Pangani — became the stronghold of capitalist enterprise and continued to be so throughout the colonial period. The railway from Dar es Salaam going further north to Moshi and Arusha and the harbour of Tanga provided the essential transport system, a decisive factor in the further development of the area.[84] Tanga Province eventually became the home of the most important crop, sisal, which dominated the export economy of the country for more than five decades. Tanga Province and particularly the areas around Tanga, Pangani and Korogwe were the most important centres of plantation employment. Between 1935 and 1965 Tanga Province produced 50–60 per cent of the total sisal crop[85] and in 1949 employed close to 25 per cent of the total wage-labour force.[86]

Sisal was also the most important industrial crop around Dar es Salaam, Morogoro and Kilosa in the Eastern Province, Lindi and Mikindani in the Southern Province and Moshi and Arusha in the Northern Province. But the Eastern Province was the second most important producer after Tanga as well as an important employment centre. The geographical distribution of sisal went hand in hand with the transport network since a cheap means of transport was a crucial factor in the transport and export of the bulky sisal fibre. All the important sisal areas were well served either by rail or sea ports, Morogoro and Kilosa being on the central railway line and Lindi and Mikindani being on the coast. Table 1.2 gives the distribution of wage-labour by provinces.

The Northern Province (principally Arusha, Moshi and Mbulu) constituted another important concentration of wage-labour. After reaching West Usambara, the settlers had naturally pushed west-wards to the Kilimanjaro and Meru mountains and appropriated fertile land of the Wachagga. Here also later settled the Afrikaner refugees from the Boer War. Besides coffee as the chief export crop, the settlers grew a variety of essential foodstuffs such as maize, wheat, beans, seed beans and oil seeds. This stronghold of white settlement during colonial times was an important supplier of food to the

Table 1.2 *Distribution of wage labour by province, 1949 and 1952*

Province	1949		1952	
	No.	%	No.	%
Tanga	115 292	25.2	127 490	28.7
Eastern	100 805	22.0	106 195	23.9
Northern	56 591	12.4	51 979	11.7
Southern	47 002	10.3	41 050	9.3
Southern Highlands	43 948	9.6	33 925	7.6
Western	38 498	8.4	30 219	6.8
Lake	34 329	7.5	34 358	7.7
Central	20 756	4.5	18 381	4.1
Total	457 221[a]	100.0	443 597	100.0

Note: [a] Does not include Overseas Food Corporation employees.
Source: Tanganyika Labour Enumeration, 1949 and 1952, as reported in *EA Statistical Bulletin*, June 1950 and July 1953 (Tabl s VIII and I respectively).

plantation workers of Tanga and Eastern Provinces and acted as a food granary of no small significance during the war, supplying essential foodstuffs to the Allied army in the Middle East.

The three provinces of Tanga, Eastern and Northern, constituting roughly one-fourth of the total land mass of the country and occupied by less than one-third of the total population (1948),[87] had two-thirds of the country's total wage-labour (see Table 1.2 above). The north-eastern area of the country was the most important employment centre and labour-importing region of the country, as shown in the map on page xvi.

In the other five provinces, there were pockets of some concentration of wage-labour depending on particular economic activities. The discovery of gold resulting in the upsurge of mining activity made areas like Iringa, Mbeya and Chunya in the Southern Highland Province and Musoma and Geita in the Western Province important pockets of wage-labour. In its heyday, around 1935, the Lupa gold-fields of Iringa employed some 18–20,000 workers[88] while some 10,000 worked in the Musoma, Geita and Sekenke gold-fields.[89] Later, the development of some plantation agriculture in the Southern Highlands Province (tea, tobacco, maize and so on) was also an important absorber of wage-labour.

In addition to being employed within the territorial boundaries, a substantial number of Tanganyikan Africans also migrated to work in the copper mines of Rhodesia, the diamond mines of South Africa, the coffee farms of Uganda and the clove plantations of Zanzibar. In 1954, according to Gulliver, some 21,000 were employed in Rhodesia and South Africa and some 8,000 in Uganda.[90] An unknown number also worked in Zanzibar and Kenya. The recruitment of labour for outside the territory was regulated by the Master and Native Servants Ordinances and related legislation.[91] After allowing some official recruiting in the early 1920s when the local supply exceeded the demand, recruiting by foreign professional recruiters was generally prohibited. However the official policy was to put no restriction on the voluntary movement of labour to the surrounding countries.[92]

Having seen the main regions of wage-labour in the country, we now consider the sources which supplied this wage-labour. It is natural that in the initial period the employers should have turned to their surrounding areas for labour. During the German times the settler plantations along the River Pangani were consciously interspersed with 'native reserves' to supply labour.[93] In spite of this it was difficult to get local labour, for the very existence of the plantations, and therefore the food market, provided a source of cash income to Wabondei who consequently did not have to sell their labour.[94] This was probably also the case with Waluguru, who never became an important source of supply of labour for the sisal plantations of Morogoro. Elsewhere, the local people surrounding the employment centre themselves took to cultivation of cash crops and thereby satisfied their cash needs. This was especially true of Wachagga and Waarusha. To be sure, thousands of Wachagga women and children from poor peasant families did offer their labour as coffee pickers during harvesting seasons[95] but this was obviously not adequate and the Northern Province planters had to look outside their province for labour. The net result was that a large portion of the wage-labour in the employment centres was not composed of the local people but of people from other distant areas where there were neither opportunities for growing cash crops nor markets for food. These areas became what has been called the 'labour reservoirs', specializing in the export of labour.

The pattern of labour-exporting and labour-importing areas and regions around 1950 would probably have resembled that illustrated in the map on page xvi.[96] Excepting a few pockets of employment, virtually the whole of the western, southern, south-western and central regions of the country were potential sources of labour. To be sure, not all the nationalities living in these areas were affected to the same extent.

In the south and south-west the Wanyakyusa, Wangoni, Wayao, Wamakua, Wamakonde, Wapangwa, Wabena and Wafipa were some of the main suppliers of labour. Gulliver estimated that some 5,000 Wangoni from Songea, some 100 Wanyasa and nearly 8,000 Wabena, Wakinga and Wapangwa sought outside employment in 1953.[97] 'By the end of the war, 45 per cent of Wabena, 50 per cent of the Wakinga and 40 per cent of the Wapangwa men were absent, at any given time, from the [Njombe] district.'[98]

The Western and Lake Provinces constituted another main source of labour. The Wanyamwezi and Wasukuma, who had been caravan porters during the days of the long-distance trade, took easily to wage-labour in the plantations.[99] Tabora District, the home of the Wanyamwezi, had been so much drained of its adult male population as a result of labour emigration that it could not hold out against the invasion of tsetse fly and had to be closed to recruiting in the 1930s.[100] The Wasukuma, on the other hand, eventually escaped wage-labour only with the development of cotton in their area. The other significant supplier of labour from western Tanganyika were the Wahangaza from around Bugufi and Busubi, Warusubi from Biharamulo, Waha from around Kigoma and Wasumbwa from Kahama. The 1953–4 Annual Report of the Lake Province estimated that over one-third of the male population of Biharamulo and Ngara Districts was absent working on the coffee farms of Uganda.[101] Uha, on the other hand, provided labour to the sisal plantations of the Tanga and Eastern Provinces. The combination of taxation and lack of any alternative source of cash income forced the Waha into wage-labour.[102] Since the middle of 1920s they in fact became one of the most important single suppliers of sisal labour.

The Wanyaturu, Wairamba and Wasandawe of the Central Province from around Singida and Kondoa Irangi trekked in their thousands every year to the plantations of the Northern Province.

From Kondoa, some 2,000 Warangi and Wasandawe go out annually to the Northern Province for work on plantations and return to their homes in time for the planting season. It is estimated that about 3,000 to 4,000 Warangi and Wasandawe are permanently settled as squatters on farms in the Northern Province . . . The number [of potential labourers] for Singida is roughly 12,000.

Of that total, about 4,000 work on the mines in that district and about 8,000 are available for hired labour — some proceed in search of work on their own account but a large portion offers itself as recruited labour.[103]

In the late 1940s more than 70 per cent of the recruited labour for Northern Province came from Singida District.[104] The Wagogo from Dodoma, Manyoni and Mpwapwa were not affected to the same extent although even they were not left out in the all-out conscription during the war. In fact the Central Province was considered an exclusive labour reservoir of the white planters of Moshi, Arusha and Mbulu.

The last but not the least important source of labour for the colonial employers was the immigrants from neighbouring countries, the most important being the then Belgian mandated territories of Rwanda and Burundi in the west and Portuguese East Africa (Mozambique) in the south. The heavy taxation imposed by the Belgian authorities on top of the dues and tributes extracted by their feudal lords left the 'Bashuti' (poor peasants) of Rwanda and Burundi no alternative but to seek refuge in neighbouring countries. Thousands of them worked on the coffee plantations and were recruited by the sisal plantations of Tanga and Eastern Provinces. The Mawiha from Mozambique surreptitiously crossed the Ruvuma and after walking hundreds of miles reached Morogoro and Tanga.[105] Together with the Warwanda, they were an essential component of the sisal cutters. Gulliver estimated that in 1953 some 10 per cent of the territorial wage labour or 36,500 men were immigrants. Of these, slightly more than half came from Rwanda, Burundi and Mozambique, while the rest were mainly from Kenya, Northern Rhodesia and Nyasaland.[106]

The areas of labour reservoir that we have just discussed were also areas of 'economic backwardness and stagnation' within the generally backward colonial economy. Unlike the employment centres which were integrated in the international capitalist economy as producers of cash crops, the main export of the labour reservoirs was labour itself. It was also the former which benefited from whatever little infrastructural construction that took place during colonial times.

The employment centres and the labour reservoirs were hundreds of miles apart, which meant that workers had to travel long distances to reach their destinations. This gave rise to the gruesome journeys undertaken by thousands of people every year, on foot, in motor-lorries, and packed like cattle in train wagons. We shall have occasion in a subsequent chapter to discuss the conditions under which these journeys were under-taken. Suffice it to say that they involved enormous wastage of manpower and productive forces which none but a colonial economy based on extremely cheap labour could afford.

Having seen the creation of employment centres and labour reservoirs, we now turn our attention to the sectoral distribution of labour, which was a direct reflection of the character of the economy. The chief interest of both German and British finance capital was to obtain cheap raw materials. The Tanganyikan economy was a textbook example of a colonial economy based on export of raw materials and import of manufactured goods. The interests of finance capital in obtaining cheap raw materials set the pattern and the local capitals followed suit.

Capital investment before the Second World War was almost exclusively in the agricultural export sector. Other sectors of the economy were tied up with and responded to the needs of the export sector. Thus the construction of the infrastructure to facilitate agricultural exports was the second most important sector. The distribution of wage-labour faithfully followed this sectoral distribution. Table 1.3 (p. 20) vividly illustrates the point. The main employing sectors were agriculture and mining while manufacturing was almost non-existent. In fact, much of the employment in the manufacturing sector before the Second World War was concentrated in processing sisal fibre and cotton for export, and elementary processing of food like flour, rice and oil mills.[107] This period has been rightly dubbed as the period of 'non-industrialization'.[108] Before 1946, out of some hundred manufacturing establishments about 50 per cent were involved in sisal decortication and cotton ginning, while around 15 per cent were concerned in food manufacture.[109] The 1949 Colonial Report summarized the state of manufacturing industry thus:

Sisal is decorticated, cotton is ginned, rice, flour, maize flour, sugar and timber are milled, oil of groundnut, coconut and sesame is expressed, tea is processed, coffee is hulled but exported in the bean, tobacco is cured but exported in the leaf, papain is extracted from pawpaw and ghee and clarified butter is separated from milk. Soap made from local coconut oil and imported caustic soda has the largest market. There is also a brewery, furniture establishments as well as leather goods, shoes and boots establishments.[110]

We can see that wage-labour was concentrated in primary and export-oriented economic activities: agriculture, mining and laying of infrastructure.* There was hardly much of the industrial proletariat to speak of. It was this *primary* character of production which enabled much of the wage-labour to be semi-permanent and migrant. Before we discuss the conditions that underlay the existence of semi-proletarian labour we briefly touch on the type of labour in the next section.

Types of labour

As we have already seen, colonial employers could not obtain all their labour supply from the adjacent areas and therefore had to employ long-distance migrant labour. It is extremely difficult to assess with any accuracy the proportions of migrant and local labour in the total labour force. The 1947 labour census, analysed in Table A.1 in the Appendix, shows that in the private sector the migrant and local labour were almost equally divided. Although substantial, these figures probably underestimate the significance of migrant labour. Local labour in these figures appears to include those from faraway districts but who had settled in the surrounding areas. This is brought out by our earlier examination of the nationalities which supplied labour where we noted that the nationalities near the employment centres did not figure as the main suppliers of labour. The extent of settlement of 'alien' nationalities in the employment areas is seen in the population figures for Tanga Province. In the Tanga and Pangani Districts around 1935, out of an adult male population of some 54,000 over 50 per cent were of alien nationalities, the majority being Wanyamwezi, Wanyasa, Wasukuma,

---

* There is evidence that with the development of export cash crops among the peasantry in areas like Kilimanjaro and Bukoba, differentiation had already begun to take place even during the colonial period. It is difficult to estimate with any precision the extent to which labour was employed by the rich peasantry in those areas. Iliffe thinks that wage-labour was more common in Buhaya than Chagga since the former was surrounded by impoverished and overpopulated areas like Bugufi, Biharamulo and Karagwe, not to mention the Belgian mandated territory of Burundi. By 1924, some 20,000 of the poor peasants — *bashuti* — from these areas worked in the coffee farms for as low a wage as four shillings a month.[111] Many long-distance migrants from Burundi and Rwanda on their way to sisal employment areas of Uganda put in a few days' work at these coffee farms for food.[112]

These were the first hesitant steps in the beginning of capitalism within the peasantry. In terms of wage-employment, the number of workers in the peasant sector was far overwhelmed by that in the plantations.

Table 1.3 Sectoral distribution of wage employment, 1926-42

	1926		1928		1930		1932		1934		1936		1938		1940		1942	
	No. (000s)	%	No. (000s)	%	No. (000s)	%	No. (000s)	%	No. (000s)	%	No. (000s)	%	No. (000s)	%	No. (000s)	%	No. (000s)	%
Agriculture	140	51	170	67	140	59	110	56	110	50	124	49	125	47	125	46	133	49
Mining	7	3	7	3	4	2	4	2	24	11	32	13	32[a]	12	24[a]	9	24	9
Infrastructure construction & maintenance (incl. transport)	106	38	47	18	62	26	49	25	52	24	57	23	45	17	60	22	47	17
Manufacturing	3	1	6	2	6	3	5	3	7	3	10	4	20	8	20	7	16[b]	6
Domestic service	20	7	25	10	24	10	18	9	18	8	20	8	30	11	30	11	35	13
Miscellaneous (uncategorized)	—	—	—	—	—	—	10	5	10	5	10	4	12	5	12	4	15	6
Total	276	100	255	100	236	100	196	100	221	100	253	100	264	100	271	100	270	100
of which: Government employment	—	—	—	—	23	10	23	12	26	12	37	15	27	10	41	15	37	14

Notes: Corrected to nearest round figure. The reliability of the Blue Book figures is somewhat doubtful. At best, they may be considered close estimates.
[a] Estimated. [b] Includes trade.
Source: Annual Blue Books.

Wamanyema, Wafipa and Waha.[113] In the Northern Province the employment of local labour was even less than in Tanga and Eastern Provinces. One estimate for 1949/50 showed that out of a total wage employment of some 42,000 in the Northern Province, only 7,000 or 17 per cent belonged to the local nationalities.[114] While it is difficult therefore to gauge accurately the proportion of migrant labour, there is little doubt that it was more than 50 per cent, and it would not be an exaggeration to put it at about two-thirds of the total wage-labour. Sabot estimates about 70 per cent of all wage-employees to have been long-distance migrants.[115]

The migrant labour may be further divided into four categories. Using Dr Wilson's terminology, these were: attested labour, temporary alien labour, resident alien labour and non-resident alien labour.[116] Let us examine these together with local labour in some detail.

Attested labour

In the colonial literature this was commonly known as contract or recruited labour or *manamba* (the Swahilized plural of the English 'number' since it was by numbers and not names that the recruitees were identified!). It referred to those usually from the labour reservoirs recruited by professional recruiters. Their terms of employment were governed by sections 3, 4, 8, 11 and 12 of the Master and Native Servants Ordinance, 1923: 'A contract of service to be performed within the Territory but outside the district in which the servant is engaged shall not be binding on the servant unless it is in writing and signed by the parties thereto' (s. 3(3)). Besides being in writing, such contract had also to be attested before an administrative officer who was required to read over and explain the contract to a worker who was illiterate (s. 4(1)). Breach of such a contract on the part of a worker was a criminal offence punishable by fine and/or imprisonment (s. 41(1)). Among other things, it was required that the contract should specify 'the nature and duration of the service' (s. 7(a)). This gave rise to an interesting practice, the origin of which probably lay in the German times. Faced with a shortage of labour and having no compunction in using compulsion, the district authorities in West Usambara issued the following regulation in 1910. Each Shambala was given a labour card: 'The cards are valid for four months. Whoever works for thirty days within this period for a European or coloured . . . is exempted from public road construction. Others will be enlisted for this for those days up to thirty which they have not worked. They will receive only food.'[117] This system of working a number of days within a larger number of specified days spread to other areas and was even carried over to the British period albeit in a different form. Although there was nothing in the original Master and Native Servants Ordinance sanctioning the practice beyond specifying the maximum duration of a written contract, a typical written contract of service indicated the duration of service as, say, 'two hundred and seventy working days to be completed within one year'.[118] The method of recording was by giving a labour card, called *kipande* in Kiswahili, to a worker. Each day that the worker turned up for work was recorded in one of the thirty blank spaces on the card. The practice was judicially approved in the case of *R.v. Pandosi Kuhekera*[119] and later statutorily recognized.[120] In Kuhekera's case the High Court ruled: 'That as the servant had only bound himself to work for one hundred and eighty days during a period of nine calendar months there was no duty on him to work on the particular day in question and his refusal to do so involved no criminal liability.' In fact the *kipande* system, as we shall see below, was actually prescribed by statute in the case of non-attested and local labour. It was a recognition of the impermanent and irregular nature of semi-proletarian labour.

The maximum duration of a written contract of service provided by law was two years[121] although in practice contracts tended to be of 180–270 working days to be completed within one year. At the expiry of the specified period the employer was obliged to repatriate a recruited worker on written contract to his place of engagement if the worker so wished (s. 14).

The incidence of attested or contract labour on written contracts was not very high but it filled an important gap in the demand for labour. Its greater regularity helped to maintain constant production. It was certainly absolutely necessary for some estates whose notoriety in respect of conditions of work would not attract 'voluntary' labour. Attested labour varied between 10 and 15 per cent of the total wage-labour and at no time exceeded 30 per cent.[122] The Tanga and Northern Provinces (20 and 15 per cent respectively in 1947)[123] relied more heavily on contract labour than the Eastern Province.

Temporary alien labour

Known variously as 'voluntary' (as opposed to contract), 'non-attested' or 'migrant' labour, this category was the most numerous section of the migrants. In addition to those recruited by professional recruiters, thousands of others left their home areas on their own to 'find their tax', as the neighbours would say in reply to queries about migrants.[124] One estimate in 1927 put those leaving on their own to find work as being four times the number of those who went on contract.[125] The rest camp statistics in Table 1.4 bear out the fact that the number was very large. 'In 1947, 135,000 people, nearly 8 per cent of the entire adult male population of the territory, moved from one rural area to another in pursuit of employment.'[126] They chose their own employers and were welcomed by the latter since by employing them the employers saved recruiting and transport expenses. Like the attested labourers, they usually came without their families and lived in camps on the estates. Dr Wilson estimated that around 1940 this category formed as much as 40–45 per cent of the total labour force in the sisal estates of Eastern and Tanga Provinces and as much as 60 per cent in the Southern Province.[127]

Table 1.4 *Numbers of migrant wage-labourers using government rest camps, 1927–47*

Year	Estimated no. (000s)
1927	72
1929	98
1930	80
1940	110
1947	135

Source: Sabot, R. H., *Economic Development and Urban Migration: Tanzania 1900–1971* (Oxford: Oxford University Press, 1979), p. 18.

They entered into what was known as 'oral' contract of service. Contract of service within the district of engagement where the *specified number of working days did not exceed thirty*, did not require to be in writing.[128] However, the employer was obliged to give to the servant a labour card upon which he was required to enter certain particulars like name, address, nature of employment, rate of remuneration and so on, and 'a notification of each day upon which a day's work is performed by the servant' (s. 6(1)(g)). This was then the legal basis of the well-known *kipande* system. The legal provisions regulating the system have been well summarized by the committee which was appointed to look into the question of supply and welfare of labour. We can do no better than quote them at some length.

The employer supplies the employee with a card showing the man's name, rate of pay, nature of work, etc., etc., and thirty blank spaces for days worked; as the employee completes his daily task a space is filled in and when all the spaces are filled, the wages due are paid. The employee is allowed double the number of working days specified in which to complete the contract and, similarly, the employer is allowed double the number of days specified in which to offer work. If the employee absents himself from work for six successive days without reasonable excuse or the consent of the employer, he is liable to prosecution. At the end of the period of double the number of working days specified, the contract becomes voidable; if the employee has failed to perform the specified number of working days by reason of his own default he is entitled to receive pay for the number of days work actually performed, while if the employer has not offered a sufficient number of days work to allow the contract to be completed, the employee is entitled to receive the wages due for the full contract.[129]

It is clear that this law recognizes a maximum of 50 per cent turn-out and this in fact reflected the objective practice. Extremely low wages and bad conditions of work simply did not allow a person to turn up for work every day of the week. He would either be sick or else would be cultivating food on land allocated by the estate. Only thus could he survive. Neither the employer nor the law expected regular attendance from semi-proletarian labour.

Although in the case of non-attested migrant labour the duration of contract was only thirty working days, many of them would do six or so *kipandes* so as to save enough cash for tax and to buy other necessities.[130] They too, like the contract workers, returned home after a spell of a few months of employment.

It is important to note at this juncture that both the attested and non-attested migrant labour were impermanent workers. Their divorce from their means of production was only temporary and partial. The reasons for this lay in the very pattern of colonial production and the character of dominating capital, which we shall discuss in the next section. Suffice it to emphasize that this is really semi-proletarian rather than fully fledged proletarian labour.

Resident alien labour

A small portion of the migrant labourers were encouraged by the estate owners to settle on the estates. These were the squatters. Their number was restricted by limited availability of free land on the estate for cultivation. Without cultivation they and their families could hardly subsist on the small wages given. A small section of the squatter labour provided the semi-skilled and white-collar workers of the estates: factory hands, mechanics, masons, drivers, clerks and headmen. They occupied more permanent structures on the estate camps and formed the nucleus of permanent labour. It is difficult to estimate the number of squatters although it appears that the number was not very large. In 1947/48, they constituted only about 8 per cent of the total labour force in the Northern Province which probably had more squatter labour than any other province.[131]

Non-resident alien labour

This refers to those from afar who had settled in the villages in the vicinity of the employment areas. For all practical purposes they were like local labour but probably depended more on wage-labour than the latter since they did not have sufficient land of their own for cultivation. The figures for Tanga Province already quoted (see above, p. 19) show that the incidence of this type of labour was quite high here.

Local labour

Although not to the same extent, the 'indigenous' nationalities of the employment areas too were affected by wage labour. Dr Wilson estimated the local labour in the thirty-five sisal estates that he visited at less than 30 per cent of the total. In the Southern Province it constituted a larger portion than in Eastern, Tanga and Northern Provinces. Moreover, they worked only casually and intermittently, maybe finishing two to three *kipandes* at a time. They did work like clearing and hoeing on the estates but rarely involved themselves in sisal cutting. 'Such labourers usually reside in their own homes and have considerable distances to travel to work in most cases, they therefore only undertake work such as clearing, in which the tasks are small and the rates of pay correspondingly low.'[132]

It is clear that local labour really came from surrounding peasantry who had to hire themselves out temporarily for particular cash needs but whose main means of sustenance was their own land. Thus they too were semi-proletarians still retaining their own means of production.

One broad conclusion may be drawn from our foregoing investigation of the types of labour. Except for a very small portion of the labour force who worked as semi-skilled or white-collar workers, the labour force was either temporarily employed, as in the case of migrant labour, or intermittently and casually employed as in the case of local labour. In neither case were wage-labourers completely divorced from their means of production. They were therefore semi-proletarians rather than proletarians completely dependent on wage-labour for their subsistence. In the next section we investigate the forces which generated and reproduced the semi-proletarian type of wage-labour.

The main features of semi-proletarian labour

The thirst for super-profits[133] by the dominating finance capital dictated profitability rates in the colonial economy. The *raison d'etre* of finance capital that was actually physically invested in the colonies was *super-profits* and it would not be satisfied with anything less than that. On the other hand, the local colonial capital had to *share* their profits with finance capital which dominated the international polity and economy. At the level of international markets, on which the export-oriented production of the local enterprises so heavily depended, local capital had very little bargaining power and was virtually a price-taker.[134] The most important way in which finance capital could get its super-profits (and not only average profits) while leaving an adequate return to local capital was through the maximization of *super-exploitation* of labour. In the case of wage-labour this was done in two ways: one, by transferring the reproduction of labour power to the pre-capitalist peasant economy and, two, by cutting into the necessary consumption of a worker.

The concrete manifestation of super-exploitation was the system of *bachelor wages* that dominated the colonial wage economy until the late 1940s. Cash wages, housing on the estates and food rations, where they were provided, were all supposed to be just enough to satisfy the bare minimum needs of a single adult male worker. The worker's family was meanwhile supposed to subsist 'on the produce of their fields'.[135] This was a decisive factor in providing extremely cheap labour to capital. Although his ideological orientation made him interchange cause and effect, Orde-Browne clearly recognized this fact when he said: 'the fact that the worker has an alternative means of support for his family is a constant factor in keeping wages at a low figure'.[136]

The other element which made low wages possible was that they did not adequately provide for a humane subsistence of even a single worker, let alone a family. This comes out again and again in various investigations and reports of the colonial officials. Let us examine one or two pieces of evidence to illustrate our foregoing discussion.

Much of the computation of the budgets of necessities that was often done by colonial officials was based on the concept of 'Poverty Datum Line' (PDL) developed by Dr Batson of the University of Cape Town. This involved computing the lowest retail cost of a budget of what a colonial official thought was necessary for an African worker.[137] One such example, slightly simplified, may be taken from F. Longland's report on labour on sisal estates which he wrote in 1936.[138] The following is a budget of necessities of a family of four of a local labourer in a sisal plantation near Tanga, assuming that everything was to be bought for cash:

Expenses for a family of four for foodstuffs for 30 days/month

	Shs.
10 days' raw cassava: 4 *mafungu* per day (approx. 2½ lb) @ 6 cents per *fungu*	2.40
10 days' dry cassava: 8 *mafungu* per day (approx. 1½ lb) @ 6 cents per *fungu*	4.80
10 days' dry maize or *sembe*; 1½ lb per day @ Sh. 1 per *kikapu or* 25 cents per day	2.50
Meat: ½ kg per week @ 24 cents	0.96
Vegetables: spinach, potatoes leaves, tomatoes: 3½ lb per week @ 3 cents per *fungu*	0.36
Coconuts: 10 a week @ 2 cents each	0.80
Salt: 8 oz per week @ 2 cents	0.08
Cost of feeding per month for a family of 4, approx.	11.90
Cost of feeding per year for a family of 4, approx.	142.80

Expenses for a family of four for clothing and miscellaneous household effects, for a year

Clothing		Shs.
Man:	2 shirts @ Sh. 1	2.00
	2 loincloths @ Sh. 1	2.00
	2 *kanzu* @ Shs. 2.50	5.00
	1 hat @ Sh. 1	1.00
	1 belt (lasts 2 years)	0.30
	1 blanket	2.00
		12.30
Wife:	4 *khangas* @ Shs. 1.25	5.00
	2 *kaniki* @ 80 cents	1.60
	(Uses husband's blanket)	
		6.60
Boy (aged 10):	2 shirts @ 60 cents	1.20
	2 loincloths @ 60 cents	1.20
	(Generally uses loincloth as blanket)	
		2.40
Girl (aged 5):	2 *khangas* @ Sh. 1	2.00
	Total (for clothing)	23.30

Summary		
	Foodstuffs per year	142.80
	Clothing per year	23.30
	Household effects per year	38.94
	Total expenditure per year	204.84
	Cost of living for a family of 4 per month:	Shs. 17.08

Even on this starvation diet and rags as clothing costing Shs. 17.08, a family of a worker getting around Shs. 10–12 per month could not subsist. The budget itself, as is very clear, is below what one would consider necessary consumption to provide for the physical and psychological needs of a worker. Batson himself made the following comment on the computation of PDL:

Such standard is perhaps more remarkable for what it omits than for what it includes. It does not allow a penny for amusement, for sport, for medicine, for education, for saving, for hire purchase, for holidays, for odd bus rides ... It does not allow a penny for replacements of blankets, furniture or crockery. It is not a 'humane' standard of living.[139]

He himself suggested that 50 per cent should be added to PDL to bring it to an 'effective minimum level'. If that was done to Longland's budget the cost of living of a family of four would fall short of income by over 50 per cent. In fact, Longland's own figures indicate that even a single man could not permanently rely on these low wages to lead a decent humane life. The point need not be belaboured. Suffice it to quote from a 1940 study on 'The Nutrition of Sisal Labour', which put it thus:

Under present conditions the sisal cutter if he turns out to work every day receives 34.3 cents cash and 14.91 cents in food each day including Sundays. The estimated cost of the additional food he should obtain for himself and his family purchased *at the cheapest rate available to the employer*[original emphasis] is 37.78 cents. It is quite evident that if he spent the whole of his remaining money on food the family would still be malnourished unless the family can cultivate for themselves an appreciable quantity of additional food.[140]

In the next chapter we present detailed evidence on wages, housing, food and other conditions of work of semi-proletarian labour. This evidence shows that the remuneration of labour fell far short of what could be considered necessary consumption of a worker even in the historical conditions of colonial times. This, then, was the basis of the super-profits of imperialist capital in its colonial form. In Marx's argument, the existence of an industrial reserve army on the one hand and strong trade organizations on the other more or less ensures that the wages of labour fluctuate around the value of labour power. Both these factors were absent in the colonial system of wage-labour. The impermanent and irregular nature of wage-labour made it difficult, if not impossible, for the emergence of workers' organizations. At the same time, the fact that wage-labour was only partially proletarianized and continued to keep its link with the means of production was the basis of the virtual non-existence of an industrial reserve army. These factors then allowed capital, assisted by the state, to pursue a policy of cheap labour, the blatant manifestation of which was the so-called 'bachelor wage'. The system of bachelor wage in turn ensured that wage-labour would continue to be migrant.

The migrant character of much of the labour force was the second important feature of the colonial wage-labour. We have already seen the methods by which capital flushed out labour from labour reservoirs. The system of bachelor wages in turn meant that labour in the employment areas could not be permanent; that it had to return to the labour reservoirs after spending a few months in employment. This form of migration was, we suggest, a specific feature of the invasion of pre-capitalist formations in colonized countries by finance capital. The process of proletarianization so initiated should not therefore simply be likened to the process of primitive accumulation. The term 'primitive accumulation' used by Marx to describe the historical process 'which takes away from the labourer the possession of his means of production; a process that transforms, on the one hand, the social means of subsistence and of production into capital, on the other, the immediate producers into wage-labourers'[141] does not capture the double specificity of the penetration of capital into colonies. This double specificity lay in (a) the temporary separation of the producer from his means of production and (b) the specific character of the capital involved in the process: that is, finance capital representing imperialism, the highest stage of capitalism (Lenin).

The long-distance migrant labourer was not completely 'freed' from his means of production nor from his peasant social milieu. His family continued to reproduce itself within the peasant economy to which he too eventually returned. It was a temporary migration of male adults.[142]

Local labour, on the other hand, came from the surrounding peasantry. This too had its means of production on which it mainly relied and worked for short periods as wage-labourers to satisfy its particular cash needs. We use the term semi-proletarian to signify the *partial* and temporary separation of a labourer from his means of production which was the case with both these categories of colonial wage-labour.

To be sure, this system of wage-labour had certain advantages to colonial capital. These were summarized succinctly by P. E. Mitchell, the then Secretary for Native Affairs:

(i) simplicity and cheapness, especially of organization, for types of work which will not stand any but the lowest scale of wages; (ii) the absence of any need for elaborate housing arrangements, medical organization, and so on, due to the natural and, therefore, comparatively healthy living conditions of a great part of the labour force, conditions which include the possibility and very generally the practice of a normal family life; (iii) the relief of industry from the necessity of unemployed pay and many other factors of a fully organized labour force dependent entirely on wages; (iv) the slowing if not indeed the prevention, of the process commonly described as detribalization [i.e. proletarianisation], and, perhaps most important (v) the contentment of the labourers who work in conditions which to them are generally satisfactory.[143]

Ignoring the last part and (ii) above, which is an exercise in self-deception by a colonial official, this is an accurate summary of the advantages that the colonial capital reaped out of this system of wage-labour. Mitchell's first point in fact refers to the important question of the low level of productive forces in the colonial economy. The semi-proletarian labour not only reflected but also perpetuated the low level of productive forces.

The question of the level of productive forces may be discussed with respect to its three main elements: (1) organization of the labour process; (2) the level of development of instruments of labour, that is, what goes under the name of technology; and (3) the subjective aspect of the productive forces, that is, the skill, training and capability of the worker himself. All three are interconnected in their development of an economic formation. As we have already seen, the main economic activity in the colonial social economy was essentially primary production for export, this being in Tanganyika's case agricultural raw materials, food and mining. The other main activity — infrastructure construction and maintenance — was to serve the needs and requirements of the export sector.

The division and social organization of labour in plantation agriculture and even mining were simple and elementary. General lack of mechanization and very little use of complex technology meant that there was a virtual absence of *detailed* division of labour. The example of sisal plantations illustrates the point. The cutting of sisal, which was the most important activity on the plantation, was done exclusively by the use of labour. The only instrument used was a sharp, long knife (*panga*). The five main operations involved in the cutting of sisal are:

1   *Bush cutting*: this involves removal of troublesome weeds and other overgrowth which has strayed into the sisal;
2   *Cutting*: 1–3 leaves of sisal are cut off consecutively, their tips are removed and the leaves are thrown haphazardly on to the path between the rows;
3   *Bundling*: this involves counting 30 leaves, putting them on 1 or 2 strings and then binding them together;
4   *Carrying*: 3–6 bundles are then carried to the side of the road or a rail line;
5   *Piling*: the bundles are piled in the shape of a box near the road or the line.[144]

All these five operations were done by one man — the sisal cutter — through sheer use of his muscle-power. There was no mechanical tool used besides a knife.

The sisal was transported by lorries or locomotives to the decorticating factory, which processed it into fibre. The comment made in 1946 by one Eric Rigby-Jones of Irish Ropes Ltd on the decorticating machines gives an idea of the technology involved in this process.

The great bulk of production now comes from corona decorticators built by Krupps and supplemented by a few British and Dutch machines . . . It is inconceivable that the decortication equipment of the industry will be radically altered within a life time: but the outsider is likely to be impressed by the paucity of modifications to a machine on which little advance has been made over the past thirty years . . . [Yet] it should not be beyond the wit of modern engineering to devise some automatic decorticator feed and to increase productivity by maintaining an always full but never overloaded feed belt.[145]

(As late as 1968 there were only two estates in Kenya and probably none in Tanganyika using semi-automatic feeding of leaf.) The drying of fibre too was done naturally and in 1948 there were only two estates in East Africa using machines for drying.[146] The meagre use of machinery can be further gauged from the figures for Northern Province, which probably had much more agricultural machinery than anywhere else in the country. In 1950, when something like 86,000 acres were under cultivation in the plantation (settler) sector, the following machinery was employed: 245 tractors, 360 ploughs, 314 harrows, 36 planters, 32 drills, 18 shellers, 101 cultivators, 35 combine harvesters, 3 winnowers, 5 mowers, 4 thrashers, 17 bean-sorters and 2 stubble-shavers.[147] As for mining, the Chief Inspector of Mines noted in 1935 that there was gross wastage of labour because there had been no attempt by the mining properties to mechanize: 'It is the case that as a rule 6 to 12 men are doing the work which should and must be done by one machine.'[148]

If the technology was meagre and antiquated, the skills and training of the labour force were still worse. In 1952, only 15 per cent of the wage-employees were skilled or semi-skilled while in agriculture over 90 per cent of the wage-labour force was unskilled.[149] The category of skilled and semi-skilled included such occupations as carpenter, mason, mechanic, fitter and driver, and white-collar workers like clerks and supervisors. In 1949, in the whole country there were about 6,800 carpenters, some 7,300 drivers, some 10,300 masons and bricklayers and only about 7,500 mechanics and fitters.[150] Given the kind of economic activity in which much of the labour force was involved, there was not much need of skilled labour power. The impermanent nature of the wage-labour in turn discouraged employers from making investment in the training of the labour force. The development of a skilled proletariat, the most important index of economic development, was thus hindered. 'As long as the instability of the wage earners reduced the rate of return on employers' investment in human capital, attempts to raise the level of productivity in the wage sector and to develop a modern industrial sector, which requires a disciplined and moderately trained labour force were seriously hampered.'[151] No wonder that the low productivity and inefficiency of the colonial labour force became legendary. The efficiency of an African worker was estimated to be half that of a white worker engaged on the same job.[152] And lack of technical skill was only one factor responsible for low efficiency; the other factor was the general bad health and undernourishment of an African worker subsisting on starvation wages. 'There is no doubt that all labour in the Territory works at a very low pressure and one of the main causes of this state of affairs is inherently poor physique and malnutrition.'[153] The undernourishment and malnutrition of the labour force under colonialism was literally a wastage of the most important productive force of the country, the worker himself.

Finally, we turn to the last important feature of semi-proletarian labour and that is the use of the instrument of law by the colonial state to regulate relations between capital and labour. At the outset let us note that the state played a central role in the penetration and development of capitalism in the colonies. It is true that in the developed capitalist social formations as well the state played an important role in the transformation of the feudal mode to the capitalist mode of production. Nevertheless, the *conditions* for capitalist development already existed and had matured within the womb of the feudal mode. The state only facilitated and accelerated its development. In the colonial situation the imperialist state had to disarticulate the existing modes, destroy the self-sufficiency of the producer and integrate him in the commodity-circuits of the metropolitan capitalist system. This specific role of the state was distinctly manifested in the *political coercion* which marked the birth of both the commodity economy and the system of wage-labour in Tanganyika. To use Marx's clinical metaphors, here the state was not simply midwife at the birth of capitalist relations, but actually father to it.

One of the manifestations of the use of state force in the realm of wage-labour was a resort to penal sanctions in regulating essentially *civil* relations between master and servants. The use of penal sanctions in what would be a contractual relation under advanced capitalism was a reflection of the semi-proletarian character of labour.

Penal sanctions were embodied in the various Master and Native Servants Ordinances. This piece of labour legislation applied only to Africans, the main source of semi-proletarian labour. 'Servant' meant 'any native employed for hire, wages or other remuneration as a labourer, herdsman, clerk, artisan, domestic servant, sailor, boatman, porter, messenger, or in any employment of a like nature to any of the foregoing . . .' (s. 2). Once a few Africans began to obtain some white-collar jobs, especially as clerks, and there was a proposal to form an African civil service, the definition was promptly amended to exclude them from the purview of the Master and Native Servants Ordinance.[154]

Probably the most interesting piece of legislation which tried to draw a clear distinction between a semi-proletarian worker and a permanent one was the proposed Labour Ordinance drafted some time in the middle of 1930s. The Labour Ordinance removed the racial criterion and instead defined 'servant' to mean anyone earning less than Shs. 150 per month. This was a piece of sophistry to hoodwink international opinion since in practice very few non-Africans fell within this wage category, and a few, like shop assistants, who would have fallen within this wage bracket were excluded by paragraph (a) of the definition of 'servant'.[155] The other thing it did was to draw a distinction between a 'labourer' and a 'servant'. 'Labourer' meant 'any servant employed to perform unskilled manual labour in or upon any estate, mines, factory, wharf, road or railway construction or maintenance or other works of a like nature', and 'servant' meant:

any person under agreement or a contract of service with an employer whose hire, wages or remuneration however expressed, and whether payable daily, weekly or monthly, do not exceed a rate equal to Shs. 150 in the month but does not include:
  (a) any clerk, accountant, shop assistant or person employed in any occupation of a like nature; or
  (b) any person on the permanent establishment of the government service.[156]

The penal sanctions under this Ordinance were to apply only to 'labourers' and not 'servants' which meant in effect only to the semi-proletariat since all the categories of skilled, semi-skilled and/or permanent labour would fall outside the definition of 'labourer'. However, as the war intervened, the draft was shelved.

The penal sanctions were otherwise contained in the Master and Native Servant Ordinance, 1923, as amended from time to time. In Tables 1.5 and 1.6 we have tried to group the offences by employees and employers in a few main categories and give a sample data of convictions. The main categories of offences by employees were desertion, absenteeism, disciplinary and those against employer's person or property. As can be seen, desertion accounted for almost two-thirds of the total convictions. As a matter of fact, desertion continued to be a major problem of the colonial employer and administrator. Under the law of advanced capitalism desertion would be a breach of contractual obligation resulting in a civil liability. Under the colonial labour law, it was a major criminal offence. In the absence of a possibility of *collective* resistance, desertion was essentially a form of *individual* resistance on the part of a worker, a point which we shall discuss at length in Chapter 3.

Table 1.5 *Categorization of offences by employees*

Offence	No. of convictions					
	1925	1926	1928	1929	1930	1931
Desertion	387	268	524	247	316	196
(ss. 41(e) & 45)	(59%)	(55%)	(65%)	(60%)	(64%)	(49%)
Absenteeism	—	—	7	34	9	6
(s. 18(1))			(0.9%)	(8%)	(2%)	(2%)
Offences relating to work-discipline	243	181	250	116	146	139
(ss. 40(a), (b), (c), (d), (g))	(37%)	(37%)	(31%)	(28%)	(30%)	(35%)
Offences against employers' person or property	25	38	23	17	19	57
(ss. 40(e), (f); 41(a), (b), (c), (d))	(4%)	(8%)	(3%)	(4%)	(4%)	(14%)
Miscellaneous offences	—	—	3	1	—	—
(ss. 39, 40(h))			(0.4%)	(0.2%)		
Total	655	487	807	415	490	398
	(100%)	(100%)	(100%)	(100%)	(100%)	(100%)

Source: Mitchell, P. E., *Notes on Labour in Tanganyika* (Dar es Salaam: Government Printer, 1933), p. 20, for 1928–31 figures; and CO 691/89/18189/10 and CO 691/90/18318/56 for 1925 and 1926 figures.

Absenteeism was another chronic headache of the colonial employer. Irregularity and high turnover were the hallmark of colonial labour force, as we shall see in the next section. Thus this too was made a criminal offence.

Another set of offences related to the problem of discipline. Discipline born of a permanent break from one's means of production, complete dependence on wages for subsistence and the complex social organization of labour, which is the characteristic of an industrial proletariat, was lacking in the colonial semi-proletariat. The employer tried to get around this problem by imitating somewhat the work-pattern of peasant production — for example, a task-oriented rather than time-oriented work schedule — and by employing overseers and headmen as supervisory staff. The breach of work-discipline, however, does not appear to have been a big problem because the very *labour process* and the low level of productive forces did not require labour discipline of the kind necessary in, say, a modern factory.

Table 1.6 *Categorization of offences by employers*

Offences	No. of convictions					
	1925	1926	1928	1929	1930	1931
Withholding wages	31	44	63	54	324	105
(s. 47(a))	(79%)	(73%)	(71%)	(68%)	(87%)	(77%)
Offences relating to obtaining of labour	6	13	9	20	20	7
(ss. 10, 16, 27, 33, 34, 35, 37)	(15%)	(22%)	(10%)	(25%)	(5%)	(5%)
Offences relating to care and welfare of labour	1	2	12	2	16	18
(ss. 24, 25, 26, 28, 29, 47(c), 47(d))	(3%)	(3%)	(13%)	(3%)	(4%)	(13%)
Miscellaneous offences	1	1	5	3	11	7
(ss. 6, 20, 47(b))	(3%)	(2%)	(6%)	(4%)	(3%)	(5%)
Total	39	60	89	79	371	137
	(100%)	(100%)	(100%)	(100%)	(100%)	(100%)

Source: Mitchell, P. E., *Notes on Labour in Tanganyika* (Dar es Salaam: Government Printer, 1933), p. 20, for 1928–31 figures; and CO 691/89/18189/10 and CO 691/90/18318/56 for 1925 and 1926 figures.

As far as the offences against employers were concerned, most of these related to either 'care and welfare' obligations or were directed against fellow employers rather than servants. The main offence which directly related to contractual obligation was the offence of withholding wages. This also accounted for the highest proportion of convictions. It appears that the majority of culprits in this respect used to be small employers: sub-contractors on railway building works,[157] small-time mining prospectors out to make a quick fortune[158] and small agricultural employers. In 1935 some forty-three employers were charged with the offence of withholding wages in the Tanga Province while in the Northern Province the number convicted, for the same year for the same offence, was sixteen.[159] Even in these cases prosecution was instituted as a last resort. 'The policy has been to enforce payment where possible without instituting legal proceedings and a demand for payment is usually sufficient.'[160] 'As a general rule, there is no more to be gained by criminal prosecutions of employers who are financially embarrassed and cannot pay their labour than of any kind of debtor; and, normally, such proceedings are only suitable in the few cases . . . of complete recklessness and fraud.'[161]

This generosity shown to the employers in the case of the most important penal offence against them illustrates the important fact that the use of penal sanctions in the civil relation was directed mainly against the servant rather than the master. The point is further evidenced in the administration and enforcement of penal sanctions. To save the employers from trouble and facilitate quick disposal of prosecutions against workers, some labour officers were given magisterial powers of subordinate courts with power to sentence the accused for minor offences.[162] In theory, a labour officer could try an employer as well but in practice this hardly mattered since his powers of fining were often restricted. In addition, the employers even when convicted could often be acquitted in the higher courts on some legal technicality. There was, for example, the case of a Greek employer (*R.* v. *Drossopoulos*) who had been charged with 'withholding wages' of some £730 from 139 of his labourers. The lower court convicted him but the High Court allowed his appeal on the ground that an employer could not be said to have 'withheld' wages if in fact he did not have the funds wherewith to pay.[163] As a result of this case section 47 of the Master and Native Servants Ordinance was amended in 1931 to read 'failure to pay wages' instead of 'withholding wages'.[164]

Finally, as would be expected in the case of employers, a relatively smaller proportion of those charged were convicted. For the years 1925 and 1926, for instance, only 32 per cent and 44 per cent respectively of the employers charged were convicted compared to some 88 and 79 per cent respectively of the employees.[165] This is of course a reflection of the built-in biases in a legal system manned by the members of the dominant class and governed by the ideology and morality of that very class.

Some contradictions of the system of semi-proletarian labour

If the system of semi-proletarian labour had certain advantages to the employer, it also had its other side: the problems. It was riddled with contradictions. In this section we discuss three main contradictions of this 'system'.

The first one was what in the colonial literature was categorized as the problem of 'low daily turn-out' or high rate of absenteeism. In 1929, it was estimated that the daily turn-out in the Tanga Province was 74 per cent for contract labour, 64 per cent for squatter labour and 50 per cent for local labour.[166] In 1934 in the sisal plantations in Tanga the daily turn-out ranged from 52 per cent for non-attested labour to 67 per cent for contract labour, the average daily turn-out for all categories of labour being around 50 per cent. In mining concerns the picture was the same: daily turn-out being 50–60 per cent. The problem of the irregularity or absenteeism of labour continuously haunted the colonial employer. 'At one mine a total of 258 natives are entered on the labour roll of the mine. On October 29th, 96 reported for work, the next day there were 84. At a small mine the register has from 52 to 58 names. The daily rate is from 32 to 47. This then is the difficulty: uncertainty of the labour, a difficulty which is shared with other industries.'[167] That quote from Longland's report of 1935 is typical, and various other reports repeated the problem *ad infinitum*.

The short-term solution adopted by the colonial employer was to employ double the labour he wanted at work every day. Thus there was a great wastage of manpower but the employer could afford it, given the extremely cheapness of labour.

The cause of this malaise was obvious and well known. The below-subsistence wages and deplorable conditions of health made it impossible for an undernourished worker to turn up for work every day of the week. He would inevitably either be cultivating his food or be sick in bed. The eye-witness account of a doctor carrying out a medical survey of sisal estates illustrates this condition dramatically:

I saw a Ruanda Native with signs of malnutrition, who had not drawn rations for two days. I saw him at the end of the second day, in the course of a camp inspection: he had then finished his work for that day. He had stood off the previous day and drawn no ration; and to the best of my belief he had not then drawn rations in respect of the second day. The reason for his having failed to do so I do not know, but the reason for his having missed a day's work may well have been disinclination for it on physical grounds.[168]

As the Southern Province Provincial Commissioner's report of 1942 reminded its readers: 'It must not be presumed because a man is absent from his work that he is necessarily idling in his village: he may be ill, more likely he is working in his own fields on the production of food for himself and others or of crops for export.'[169] An article in the *Tanganyikan Standard* correctly summarized the situation:

Where conditions amount to malarial saturation, where sanitation is defective, where diet is poor and food values unstudied, where reasonable thought and care of the native labour is absent and where housing is the poorest, it is not surprising that the tasks accomplished on some estates are one-sixth of those accomplished by Asiatic labourers, or that it is necessary to carry a labour force many times in excess of requirements.[170]

As we have already seen the *kipande* system gave both a legal and a practical recognition to the irregular nature of semi-proletarian labour. A worker was allowed sixty days within which to complete his thirty days of work. It was the pressure of war and the intense need for labour which made the colonial state reduce this period to forty-two days. During the war the state provided conscripted labour to private employers and also imposed greater regularity on labour by law.[171] Coupled with this, it took inspection of labour conditions rather more seriously. Thus in the post-war period the daily turn-out showed some improvement. It was around an average of 70–75 per cent in 1947[172] although even then it fell short of 83 per cent which was required by native labour regulations.[173]

Low wages and bad conditions were responsible not only for irregularity but also for the short working hours that prevailed on the sisal estates, especially. Sisal cutting was based on task work. Experienced sisal cutters could complete one task, which was equivalent to cutting some 2,000 sisal leaves, in about five to six hours.[174] But even then less than 10 per cent of labour volunteered for a double task.[175] One commentator even constructed a rule that 'if a man does do more than one task in a day, he does no work on the following day, or if he does double work for several days, he sooner or later takes some days off'.[176] Closely related to the problem of irregularity was the incidence of inefficiency, low productivity and indiscipline, discussed in the foregoing sections.

Probably the other most important contradiction that bedevilled the colonial system of labour almost throughout the whole period was the question of supply of labour. First the Germans and later the British constantly complained of shortage of labour. With the exception of brief periods immediately after the First World War and during the depression, the shortage of labour persisted throughout the colonial period.[177]

To be able to theorize the practical problem of the shortage of labour in the colonial period, we have to appreciate the role of 'industrial reserve army' in the capitalist mode of production. In Marx's theory, the process of capital accumulation is accompanied by a progressive change in the organic composition of capital. Marx showed that in the capitalist mode of production there is a tendency for constant capital to rise faster than variable capital, resulting in the displacement of a portion of the employed wage-labour. This may be picturesquely summarized as the expulsion of workers by machines. The workers so displaced constitute the relative surplus population of the industrial reserve army.

'But', Marx said, 'if a surplus labouring population is a necessary product of accumulation or of the development of wealth on a capitalist basis, this surplus-population becomes, conversely, the lever of capitalistic accumulation, say a condition of existence of the capitalist mode of production.'[178] The industrial reserve army becomes the 'lever of capitalistic accumulation' in two important ways: one, by providing the ready source of labour whenever the expansion of existing capital or new investments require it and, two, by acting as a constant check on the rise of wages over and above the value of labour power. We know that capitalist development takes place in fits and starts. The cycles of 'periods of average activity, production at high pressure, crisis and stagnation' (Marx) are themselves interrupted by smaller oscillations of expansion and contraction, of capital. These changes in capitalist activity continually require fresh supplies of labour during expansion as they in turn 'set free' a part of the labourers during contraction. But expansion would be impossible 'without disposable human material' (Marx), without an industrial reserve army. Secondly, without an industrial reserve army, a greater demand of labour than its supply could raise wages and cut into the surplus-value thereby destroying the very rationale of the capitalist system. Thus we can see that the law of supply and demand in so far as it regulates the fluctuations of wages around the value of labour power is predicated on the existence of an industrial reserve army. Naturally, if the industrial reserve army acts as a check on the upward movement of wages, the collective organization of the workers acts as a check on its downward movement.

It is clear that Marx's theory of the industrial reserve army is based on the fundamental assumption of full proletarianization, that is, a labouring population which has been completely divorced from its means of production and is fully dependent on wages. In the colonial system of semi-proletarian labour, as we have seen, this assumption did not hold. Until about the end of 1940s, an industrial reserve army in the Marxist sense could not be identified. We suggest that the non-existence of an industrial reserve army was the basis of the problem of shortage of labour. At the same time the non-existence of an industrial reserve army was a logical outcome of the system of semi-proletarian labour.

The problem of shortage of labour manifested itself in the form of various conflicts, such as competition between peasant and plantation production, the question of excessive depopulation of labour reservoirs, and the question of length of contract. We examine some of these below.

We have shown that the extraction of super-profits by finance capital was based on the system of semi-proletarian labour as far as wage-labour was concerned. The other important source of its super-profits was the exploitation of peasant labour which does not concern us directly in this work. In the case of Tanganyika the collective capitalist, the colonial state, was responsible as the foremost representative of imperialism for ensuring production in both these spheres. However, in practice this so-called 'dual policy' was not easy to maintain. One of the most important areas of conflict was the question of labour. In the colonial literature this question is often referred to as competition between peasant economy and the plantation sector. It is true that much of the labour for the capitalist sector came from the labour reservoirs which were not important cash-crop growing areas. But even from these areas the colonial state could not allow unrestricted flushing out of labour. Unlike individual capitalists, the state as a collective capitalist had the foresight to see that excessive depopulation of such areas would result in undermining the cultivation of food on which depended the reproduction of the workers in so far as their families continued to rely on the peasant sector. Besides, some of the most important labour reservoirs like the Western Province were under constant threat of invasion by the tsetse fly, the best resistance against which was human habitation itself. Hence the colonial government's concern of restricting recruitment to roughly 10 per cent of the adult male population[179] and its obsession with ensuring adequate cultivation of food crops. The same concern was manifested at the level of law in the length of contracts allowed by labour legislation. Originally the maximum period of contract was six months but in 1925 it was extended to twelve months as a result of pressure from the employers.[180] After the completion of the contract period employers were obliged to return the labour to their districts of engagement.

The colonial policy with respect to various conflicting interests and concerns that we have just discussed was best summarized in a memorandum of the governor, Donald Cameron, sent to the Secretary of State. Cameron summed up his views as follows:

(a) As between the competing claims of peasant cultivation for export (where it is a practicable proposition) and labour for the plantations administrative officers should in the first instance remain neutral as far as possible. Propaganda work in connection with the former is in the first instance to be done by the agricultural department and not by the administrative staff.

(b) In localities which for any reason may not be entirely suitable for cultivating crops for export great caution is to be exercised in encouraging that form of cultivation.

(c) In localities in which the cultivation of crops for exports is not at present a practicable proposition administrative officers should, without giving any orders, encourage the people to go out to labour. As a general principle they should not endeavour to prevent them from taking their families with them if they so desire.

(d) Natives who have contracted a habit of working on the plantations in the vicinity of their homes should not be enticed away from that work to grow crops for export.

(e) In other areas which are suitable for the cultivation of crops for export by the peasantry administrative officers should exhort the natives to adopt some form of labour, informing them at the same time that they are free to labour on the plantations or to grow their own crops for export, as they may desire.

(f) The first duty of the agricultural department is to endeavour to prevent the famines which occur periodically in so many districts.

(g) If a native wishes to purchase seed for cultivating export crops it should be supplied to him if possible.[181]

These views were then embodied in a list of instructions to administrative officers[182] and became a policy which guided colonial officials until the Second World War. Although neat and clear on paper, this tightrope-walking was not always easy in practice. Depending on the state of social forces and various pressures, local colonial officials did indulge in excessive encouraging of cultivation of economic crops at the expense of the plantation sector and vice-versa. Nevertheless, on the whole — at least during 'periods of average activity' — the policy appeared to work. Its limits, which were the limits of the colonial system of semi-proletarian labour itself, were exposed during the periods of (to use Marx's words) 'production at high pressure, crisis and stagnation'. This is best seen in the depression of 1931–5 and the beginning of feverish mining activity in the middle of the 1930s.

The international depression of 1930 inevitably sent its shock waves to the dependent colonial economy of Tanganyika. Prices fell drastically: the sisal price plummeted from £32 per ton in 1929 to £11 per ton in 1932[183] while Chagga coffee fell from £70 per ton to £29 per ton between 1929 and 1931.[184] Wages were cut so much so that the 'first four years of depression approximately halved money wages'.[185] Thousands of workers were discharged. It is estimated that some 30–35,000 Africans were dismissed in 1930.[186] For the first time migrant workers came back without finding work.[187] There was a great deal of dissatisfaction and discontentment but in spite of this there were only two 'ugly incidents'. 'On one estate there was a riot and property was damaged. Eight ringleaders were tried and imprisoned. But generally the natives accepted their fate.'[188]

Those who were discharged went back to their land. The system of semi-proletarian labour had absorbed the shock of depression. As the Annual Labour Report of 1930 put it:

At first sight it may appear extra-ordinary that it should be possible for a large proportion of the workers of a country to be discharged within a very limited period, without causing widespread disaster and distress. The explanation lies in the resilience provided by the native connection with the land; if he can no longer earn wages or sell his crop, he can at any rate produce all that is essential to him. So the returned employee of a plantation brought back with him a disappointing amount of cloth and other luxuries, and resigned himself to cultivating his garden.[189]

Not only the discharged migrant but the colonial government itself fell back on the peasant economy. To maintain its export earnings and revenue the colonial state threw to the wind its carefully worked out Cameronian instructions and began a 'plant-more-economic-crops' campaign. It very well knew that unlike the capitalist enterprises whose costs of production could not be covered by the low depression prices, the peasant had no costs to cover except his own half-empty stomach. Therefore, regardless of price, 'pressure' and 'exhortation' would force him to grow more. 'The campaign was successful and undoubtedly assisted the country towards recovery. Exports of cotton, for example, rose from 3,670 tons in 1930 to 10,000 tons in 1935. Groundnuts and rice also showed marked increases.'[190]

But by 1935 the capitalist enterprise too had begun to recover and, more important, the new mining activity had begun with great force. Thus there was once again great need for labour. 'Shortage of labour' became a universal cry and the employers predictably blamed the government's 'grow-more-crops' campaign. To attract labour by increasing wages was out of the question for the colonial employer as 'the low labour wage prevailing has been frequently advertised as one of the chief inducements . . . in Tanganyika'.[191] His oligopsonistic power backed by the colonial state ensured his position as a price-maker in the labour market. Capital called upon its collective representative, the state, to oblige. It was as a result of this that Longland was appointed to investigate, following which a combined committee of officials and non-officials was appointed by the governor to advise the government on the question of supply of labour. The committee made its report in 1937 but before its recommendations could be implemented the world war intervened, ushering in a new phase in the development of labour.

Finally, the third contradiction of the semi-proletarian labour was rooted in the fact that the system of impermanent wage workers was possible only at a low level of productive forces, mainly in the primary economic sector. The very character of productive forces in, say, the manufacturing industry, would dictate a permanent, disciplined proletariat. The post-war period, among other things, began to witness the development of an import-substitution industry. This was also the beginning of the period of stabilization of labour and creation of a permanent labour force, discussed in detail in Chapter 4.

The phenomenon of semi-proletarian labour was no doubt a historical phase reflecting the character of the dominating finance capital and was made possible by the specific character of the low level of productive forces in the primary sector.

NOTES

1. Marx, K., *Pre-capitalist Economic Formations* (New York: International Publishers, 1965), p. 67.
2. Kjekshus, H., *Ecology Control and Economic Development in East African History: The Case of Tanganyika, 1850–1950* (London: Heinemann, 1977), pp. 32–3.
3. ibid., p. 32.
4. ibid., p. 82.
5. Iliffe, J., *A Modern History of Tanganyika* (Cambridge: Cambridge University Press, 1979), pp. 18–19.
6. Kjekshus, H., op. cit., p. 114.
7. ibid., pp. 115–16.
8. Lubetsky, R., 'Sectoral Development and Stratification in Tanganyika, 1890–1914', paper delivered at the 1972 East African Universities Social Science Conference (Dar es Salaam: mimeo, August 1973), p. 2.
9. Kjekshus, H., op. cit., p. 114.
10. Iliffe, J., *Modern History*, op. cit., p. 16.
11. ibid., pp. 44–5.
12. Lubetsky, R., op. cit., p. 3.
13. Quoted in ibid., p. 17.
14. Iliffe, J., 'Wage Labour and Urbanization', in Kaniki, M. H. Y. (ed.), *Tanzania Under Colonial Rule* (London: Longman, 1979), p. 280.
15. No. 13 of 1922.
16. Iliffe, J., 'Wage Labour', op. cit., p. 281.
17. 'Draft Report on Tanganyika Territory Covering the period from the conclusion of the Armistice to the end of 1920', CO 691/36/230.
18. Sayers, G. F. (ed.), *The Handbook of Tanganyika* (London: Macmillan, 1930), p. 75.
19. District Officer, Dar es Salaam, to Herr X, 29 April 1910, in Hartmann, F. F. and Wilmot, B. C., 'Translated extracts from the files of the German East Africa administration in connection with labour matters' (Dar es Salaam: Tanzania Ministry of Communications, Labour and Works, Labour Division, 1969), F20K in University of Dar es Salaam Library.
20. Article 5(3) of *British Mandate for East Africa* (in Laws of Tanganyika, 1928, Vol. 3, p. 1) provided that the Mandatory 'shall prohibit all forms of forced or compulsory labour, except for essential public works and services, and then only in return for adequate remuneration'.
21. ILO Convention on Forced Labour, No. 29, adopted at the 14th Session (Geneva), 1930. And see generally TNA 21097.
22. Governor Byatt to SS, 4 May 1921, CO 691/44/345–349.
23. No. 18 of 1926.
24. Section 11.
25. See note 22 above.
26. PC (Dodoma) to CS, 31 March 1928, TNA 10953.
27. Section 12(1).
28. The following estimates of the number of man-days worked through the so-called 'tribal turn-out' illustrate the point. In 1947, 1.4 million (for 13 districts); in 1948 1.7 million (for 15 districts) and in 1949 1.8 million (for 17 districts) man-days. (Total number of districts, 21.) Figures calculated from: Tanganyika, *A Preparatory Investigation of the Manpower Position, 1951* (Dar es Salaam: Government Printer, 1951), App. XV, p. 69.
29. DC, Singida, to PC, Central Province, 27 May 1948, TNA 10953/II.
30. PC, Central Province, to CS, 2 March 1951, TNA 10953/II.
31. PC, Central Province, to Member for Local Government, TNA 10953/II.
32. See s. 9 and s. 11 of the Hut Tax (No. 12 of 1922) and House Tax (No. 26 of 1922) Ordinances respectively.

33. Governor Byatt to SS, 3 October 1921, CO 691/47/6–10.
34. The Native Tax (Amendment) Ordinance (No. 25 of 1951) repealed s. 11 of the Native Tax Ordinance (No. 20 of 1934) which consolidated the earlier legislation on 'native tax'. Section 11 had continued to permit extraction of labour in lieu of tax.
35. TNA 21097/V.
36. ibid. See generally Shivji, I. G., 'Semi-Proletarian Labour and the Use of Penal Sanctions in the Labour Law of Colonial Tanganyika (1920–38)' in Sumner, C. (ed.) *Crime, Justice and Underdevelopment* (London: Heinemann, 1981), pp. 40–60.
37. Cf. TNA 21097/V.
38. Sections 8(i) and 11 of the Native Authorities Ordinance.
39. TNA 11625/I.
40. TNA 21097/V.
41. TNA A 23217.
42. Information in this paragraph is from CO 691/184/42374 and TNA 30178.
43. No.23 of 1940.
44. ARLD, 1944.
45. ARLD, 1946.
46. CO 691/187/42094 and CO 691/191/42374/Telegram Nos. 61 and 150.
47. Sandord of Tanganyika to the Colonial Office, CO 691/191/42374/2/Confidential.
48. ibid.
49. See below, Ch. 3, pp. 90–92.
50. PC, Central Province, to the Secretary of the Labour Board, 10 October 1952, TNA 10953/II.
51. Deputy Governor to SS, 31 July 1944, CO 691/191/42374/Despatch No. 116.
52. Iliffe, J. *Tanganyika under German Rule, 1905–1912* (Nairobi: East African Publishing House, 1969), p. 22.
53. Patel, L.R., 'East African Labour Regimes: Kenya and Tanganyika' (Dar es Salaam, mimeo, 1972), p. 13.
54. Lubetsky, R., op. cit., p. 9.
55. CO 691/100/29272/4–5.
56. Section 2.
57. Section 3(3)
58. Section 4.
59. Of course, the hut and poll tax did in its own right yield a very substantial amount of revenue, as much as 70–80 per cent of all taxation between 1927 and 1935. Patel, L. R., 'Labour and Law in East Africa' (Dar es Salaam: mimeo in my possession, n.d.), p. 17.
60. Iliffe, J., *Modern History*, op. cit., p. 306.
61. Gulliver, P. H., 'A Report on the Migration of African Workers to the South from the Southern Highlands Province, with special reference to the Nyakyusa of Rungwe District' (Dar es Salaam: Government Printer, 1955), pp. A10 ff.
62. Graham, J. D., 'Changing Patterns of Wage Labour in Tanzania: a history of the relations between African labour and European capitalism in Njombe District, 1931–1961' (PhD thesis, Northwestern University, 1968), p. 35.
63. Iliffe, J., *Modern History*, op. cit., p. 305.
64. TNA 11127 and TNA A25905.
65. Section 7(1).
66. Section 7(3). My emphasis.
67. Section 7(2).
68. CO 691/138/25157/39–42. See also note 34 above.
69. Annual Report of Tanganyika Territory 1938, CO 691/170/42003/7.
70. Patel, L. R., 'Labour and Law', op. cit., p. 18.
71. Section 11 (4) of the Native Tax Ordinance.
72. *R. v. Mathew bin Condala & Anor* (Tabora Criminal Sessions Case No. 124 of 1939), where accused No. 2, a tax clerk, was convicted of manslaughter for causing death of a peasant who was beaten on his instructions. The case is discussed in CO 691/176/42334/5–6.

73. Mrs E. A. Bakersmith of Arusha to SS, 30 June 1936, CO 691/151/42147/4/10–11.
74. Graham, J. D., op. cit., p. 34.
75. Freyhold, M., 'On Colonial Modes of Production', History Seminar Paper (University of Dar es Salaam: mimeo, August 1977), pp. 14ff.
76. Iliffe, J., *German Rule*, op. cit., pp. 67–9, 103ff., 134.
77. No. 32 of 1923 as amended from time to time.
78. Patel, L. R., 'Labour and Law', op. cit., p. 30.
79. The incident described herein is based on material in TNA 11803/I–III.
80. Term used to describe the poor peasants of Rwanda.
81. From the statement of one Muhangaza of Bugufi made before the investigating district officer. TNA 11803/I–III.
82. Quoted in Woddis, J., *Africa, the Roots of Revolt* (London: Lawrence & Wishart, 1960), pp. 69–70.
83. Speech by H. P. Amman made at the Annual General Meeting of the TSGA held on 25 April 1968. Reprinted in the *Kenya Sisal Board Bulletin* (No. 64, May 1968), p. 15.
84. Iliffe, J., *German Rule*, op cit., pp. 13–14.
85. Tambila, A., 'A History of the Tanga Sisal Labour Force, 1936–1964 (MA dissertation, University of Dar es Salaam, 1974), p. 45A.
86. See Table 1.2 above, p. 16.
87. Japhet, K., and Seaton, E., *The Meru Land Case* (Nairobi: East African Publishing House, 1967), App. 3.
88. Labour Report for Iringa Province, 1935, TNA A 23217.
89. Longland, F., 'Investigation in Labour in Goldmining Areas' (Draft Final Report, September 1935), p. 6, TNA 23047.
90. Gulliver, P. H., op. cit., App. 3.
91. For example, the Master and Native Servants (Written Contracts) Ordinance, No. 28 of 1942.
92. TNA 10218/I.
93. Iliffe, J., *Agricultural Change in Modern Tanganyika*, Historical Association of Tanzania, Paper No. 10 (Nairobi: East African Publishing House, 1971), p. 14.
94. Iliffe, J., *Modern History*, op. cit., p. 152.
95. TNA 11127/I.
96. This map is constructed from a similar map in Orde-Browne, G., *Report on Labour in the Tanganyika Territory* (London: HMSO, 1926), and based on information from: Tanganyika, 'A Preparatory Investigation', op. cit., App. III. I am grateful to Wilbert Kapinga and S. Bhandari for their assistance in drawing the map.
97. Gulliver, P. H., op. cit., p. A4.
98. Graham, J. D., op. cit., p. 89.
99. Iliffe, J., *Modern History*, op. cit., p. 160.
100. 'Report by Dr H. Fairbairn, Sleeping Sickness Officer, regarding recruiting of labour for Saragura', enclosed with the letter from Director of Medical Services to CS, 15 January 1936, in TNA 23047/I, folio 84.
101. TNA 215/511/V.
102. Iliffe, J., *Modern History*, op. cit., p. 305.
103. Central Province to CS, 31 August 1936, TNA 23202.
104. Annual Reports of NPLUB for 1947/48, 1948/49 and 1949/50 in TNA 37680.
105. Governor's minute of 18 July 1939 in TNA 10922/III.
106. Gulliver, P. H., op. cit., App. 3.
107. Rweyemamu, J., *Underdevelopment and Industrialization in Tanzania: A study of Perverse Capitalist Development* (Nairobi: Oxford University Press, 1973), Ch. IV.
108. See below, Ch. 4, pp. 109–11.
109. Rweyemamu, J., op. cit., pp. 112–13.
110. Quoted in ibid., p. 111.
111. Iliffe, J., *Modern History*, op. cit., p. 282.
112. See generally TNA 11803/I–III.

113. Longland, F., 'Report on Labour Matters in Sisal Areas', No. 1, Tanga (1936), App. 2, TNA 23544.
114. Annual Report of NPLUB, 1947/48, TNA 37680.
115. Sabot, R.H., *Economic Development and Urban Migration: Tanzania 1900–1971* (Oxford: Oxford University Press, 1979), p. 22.
116. Wilson, D. B., 'Report on a Medical Survey of Sisal Estates' (n.d.) (Official), EAF.
117. Iliffe, J., *German Rule*, op. cit., pp. 135–7.
118. Cf. Contract of Service between Bary Bondei Plantation Co. Ltd. and 99 native servants dated 7 March 1938 (in my possession).
119. Criminal Revision No. 213 of 1937 referred to in a letter from the Acting Governor to the Acting CS, 9 April 1938. CO 691/166/42191/5.
120. M & NSO, 1942, No. 24, 1st schedule.
121. Section 12 of M & NSO and later section 10 of M & NSO (Written Contracts) Ordinance, 1942.
122. Mitchell, P. E., *Notes on Labour in Tanganyika* (Dar es Salaam: Government Printer, 1933), p. 2.
123. See Table A.1, below, p. 244.
124. Longland, F., 'Labour in Goldmining Areas', Final Report, op. cit., p. 18.
125. TNA 11625/I.
126. Sabot, R. H., op. cit., pp. 18–19.
127. Wilson, D. B., op. cit., p. 3.
128. Sections 3 and 6 of M & NSO, 1926, No. 11 of 1926.
129. Tanganyika, *Report of the Committee Appointed to Consider and Advise on Questions Relating to the Supply and Welfare of Native Labour in the Tanganyika Territory* (Dar es Salaam: Government Printer, 1938), p. 19. (Hereafter cited as *Labour Committee Report*.)
130. Wilson, D. B., op. cit., p. 6.
131. Annual Report of NPLUB, 1947/48, op. cit.
132. Wilson, D. B., op. cit., p. 2.
133. For analyses of super-profits under imperialism see Lenin, V. I., *Imperialism, the Highest Stage of Capitalism* in *Collected Works*, Vol. 22 (Moscow: Progress Publishers, 1964); Stalin, J., *Economic Problems of Socialism in the USSR* (Peking: Foreign Languages Press, 1972), pp. 38–9. See also Khamis, L. *Imperialism Today* (Dar es Salaam: Tanzania Publishing House, 1983).
134. Sabot, R. H., op. cit., p. 37.
135. Orde-Browne, G., *Labour Conditions in East Africa* (London: HMS, 1946), p. 5.
136. ibid., p. 7.
137. Patel, L. R., *Labour Regime*, op. cit., pp. 60–1.
138. Longland, F., 'Labour Matters in Sisal Areas', No. 1, op. cit.
139. Quoted in Patel, L. R., *Labour Regime*, op. cit., p. 60.
140. W.D.R., 'The Nutrition of Sisal Labour' (Medical Laboratory, Dar es Salaam, August 1940), p. 4.
141. Marx, K., *Capital*, Vol. 1 (Moscow: Progress Publishers, n.d.), p. 668.
142. Cf. Gulliver, P. H., op. cit., Table B7, p. B15.
143. Mitchell, P. E., op. cit., p. 10.
144. TSGA, *Determination of Tasks and a Study into Improvement of Methods in the Production of Sisal* (International Land Development Consultants, Arnhem, The Netherlands, July 1966), p. 12.
145. Rigby-Jones, E., 'Sisal Production in East Africa', extracts in *Kenya Sisal Bulletin*, No. 63, February 1968, p. 16.
146. ibid.
147. Annual Report of NPLUB, 1949/50, op. cit.
148. Quoted in the Minute of Director of Mines, dated 12 September 1935, in TNA 23047/I.
149. Sabot, R. H., op. cit., pp. 24–5.
150. 'Supplement to East African Economic and Statistical Bulletin', No. 8, June 1949 (duplicated) in TNA 41/L1/8.

151. Sabot, R. H., op. cit., p. 4.
152. W.D.R., op. cit., p. 1.
153. *Labour Committee Report*, op. cit., para. 72, p. 27.
154. Master and Native Servants (Amendment) Ordinance, 1927, No. 9 of 1927.
155. From a comment by one Mr Lee on the draft ordinances submitted to the Colonial Office, CO 691/141/25259/6–7.
156. ibid.
157. TNA 11523/I, and Mitchell, P. E., op. cit., p. 15.
158. 'Memorandum on the Supply and Welfare of Native Labour, Iringa Province', pp. 4–5, TNA 23435/I.
159. TNA 23217.
160. Mitchell, P. E., op. cit., p. 15.
161. ibid., pp. 16–17.
162. TNA 10286/II.
163. Discussed in CO 691/103/29437/3–6.
164. Master and Native Servants (Amendment) Ordinance, 1931, No. 35 of 1931.
165. CO 691/89/18189/10 and CO 691/90/18318/56.
166. Mitchel, P. E., op. cit., p. 9.
167. Information in this paragraph is from Longland, F., 'Labour in Goldmining Areas', No. 1, op. cit., p. 3.
168. 'Medical Survey of Sisal Estates in Northern, Tanga and Eastern Provinces', done by Dr Mackey, January 1939, TNA 25931/I.
169. In CO 691/184/42374.
170. 'Campaign Against Malaria', *Tanganyika Standard*, 28 March 1936, quoted by Longland, F., 'Labour Matters in Sisal Areas', op. cit.
171. The Defence (Native Labour) (No. 2) Regulations, 1941 (GN No. 197/1941) provided that a 'native' under a contract of service in a prescribed occupation 'shall perform not less than thirty days' work during each complete period of forty-two days for which the contract is in existence' (Reg. 2-(1)). 'Prescribed occupations' included production of rubber and sisal, beans, maize, sugar, coffee and wheat, and production of diamonds.
172. Tanganyika: *Native Employees Census, 1947*, TNA 32679.
173. See the Annual Report of the PC, Tanga, in CO 691/187/42094.
174. TNA A 23217.
175. W.D.R., op. cit., p. 2.
176. Wilson, D. B., op. cit., p. 6.
177. Sabot, R. H., op. cit., pp. 31–2.
178. Marx, K., *Capital*, Vol. I, op. cit., p. 592.
179. See Longland, F., 'Labour in Goldmining Areas', No. 1, op. cit.
180. CO 691/77/409.
181. Enclosed with the governor's letter to SS, 14 July 1925; CO 691/78/152–3.
182. *Labour Committee Report*, op. cit., p. 14.
183. [Iliffe, J.] 'Supplementary Statistics and Documents' (mimeo, University of Dar es Salaam, n.d.), Table 6.
184. Iliffe, J., *Modern History*, op. cit., p. 279.
185. ibid., p. 352.
186. ARLD, 1930, p. 18.
187. Iliffe, J., *Modern History*, op. cit., p. 344.
188. ARLD, 1930, p. 20.
189. ibid., pp. 21–2.
190. D. M. Kennedy, CS, to the government, in a notice appointing the Labour Committee. General Notice No. 129 published on 29 January, 1936.
191. Minute of Director of Mines, dated 12 September 1935, TNA 23047/I, folio 14.

2

Conditions
of the Semi-Proletariat

Introduction

Lenin[1] and Kautsky[2] argued that the persistence of the small peasant under capitalism was possible because he reduced his requirements even below those of a wage-worker. Ultimately the peasant cedes to capital not only the surplus but even part of his necessary consumption.[3] In somewhat similar manner, in the case of colonial wage-labour the dominance of monopoly capital combined with the system of semi-proletarianization enabled capital to maximize its super-profits by consistently 'cutting into' the necessary consumption of the worker. Not only was an element of the reproduction of labour power thrown on to the peasant sector, as we have already seen, but the various elements of necessary consumption of even a 'bachelor' worker were reduced to the bare minimum.

In Marx's theory,[4] the value of labour power is the value of means of subsistence — food, clothing, housing and so on — necessary for the maintenance of the labourer. This value may be resolved into two elements. The first element is 'the means necessary for a labourer's substitutes, i.e., his children, in order that this race of peculiar commodity-owners may perpetuate its appearance in the market'.[5] The second element consists in the means of subsistence necessary to maintain the labourer in the normal state of being and health. What is necessary for the maintenance of this normal state includes a historical and moral element depending on the stage of development of a society and 'on the conditions under which, and consequently on the habits and degree of comfort in which, the class of free labourers has been formed'.[6] This theoretical analysis of the capitalist mode of production presupposes full proletarianization, that is, the existence of free labourers. Even then, in a concrete capitalist social formation, wages — the price-form of the value of labour power — do not automatically correspond to its value. It is the collective struggle of the working class that ensures that wages fluctuate fairly closely around the value of labour power.

In the colonial situation, the existence of the semi-proletariat consisting of bachelor workers meant that the first element mentioned above was borne by the peasant sector. As far as the second element was concerned, the very character of labour as semi-proletarian made it very difficult, if not impossible, for labour to organize collectively and bargain for terms and conditions to work. This meant that wages and other conditions of labour were determined almost unilaterally by capital.[7] The result was sub-human conditions and starvation wages for the working class. Hence the colonial worker did not exist in a normal state; he existed, to borrow Marx's phrase, in a 'crippled state'.

In this chapter we attempt to demonstrate and document the crippled state of the working class. If our chapter errs on the side of extensive description of the conditions of wage-labour as portrayed by contemporaries, it is partly because, as far as we know, the subject has not received detailed treatment before; also because it is a graphic testimony of the way in which imperialist capital mutilated the most important productive force of the colonized country, the producer himself.

The other issue that the chapter documents is the role of the colonial state and law in the supervision (or lack of it) of the conditions of work. In the fixing of wages and determination of other conditions, the state either pretended to leave it to the so-called market forces (which meant to employers since the necessary conditions of the operation of market forces did not exist) or legislated minimum conditions in such a general fashion that they were not enforceable — or if enforceable, there was no adequate or impartial personnel to do so. A great deal therefore depended on the whims and caprices of the administrators without much legislative and judicial check or balance.

In sum, monopoly capital had a freer hand, if not a field-day, in the colony where it reaped higher rates of profit than in metropolitan countries.[8]

The 'middle passage'

The journeys undertaken by the long-distance migrant labour travelling to the employment areas of the north-east were probably not as gruesome as those of the 'middle passage' that the slaves from the West Coast of Africa had to undergo, but they were bad enough to attract the label 'middle passage' from a well-known historian of Tanganyika.[9] Thousands of *manamba* travelled every year over hundreds of miles, sometimes packed like cattle in the wagons of a goods train, sometimes perched on tops of motor-lorries carrying export-crops, or — more often than not — simply on foot.

The principal labour routes are shown on the map (p. xvi) while the distances and the rest camps have been sketched in Figure 2.1. Labour from Songea, Tunduru and Mahenge travelled on foot to Kilosa via Iringa, resting at Chonde and Kidodi.[10] Others used small tracks and paths through the then Selous Game Reserve, entering Morogoro District at Kisaki: 'a considerable number of Wayao and Wangoni enter the Morogoro district by native paths converging on Dutumi and Mvuha, thereafter using the Kisaki–Mikese road northwards'.[11] Since there were no rest camps at Dutumi and Mvuha, they slept in 'derelict huts' and shopfronts. The immigrant labour from Mozambique, on the other hand, used the coastal route after surreptitiously crossing the Ruvuma and entered the plantation areas of Soga and Kidugallo via Maneromango.

From Njombe and other adjacent districts the migrants travelled on foot or in motor-lorries, a distance of over 300 miles, to Kilosa or to Dodoma; from thence spreading along the central railway or moving northwards to Korogwe and Tanga.[12] Probably the most gruesome journey was for the labour from Dodoma, Singida, Kondoa Irangi and Mkalama proceeding to Moshi and Arusha, braving harsh climate on the way. Although motor transport was available from Dodoma to Arusha, the majority of the labour preferred to travel on their own, on foot, rather than use recruiters' lorries and be bound to them by contract.[13] Ha labourers from Kigoma travelled by the central railway to Kilosa and from there spread to the employment areas of the east and north-east. 'Manamba

Figure 2.1 *Labour routes and camps (c. 1930)*

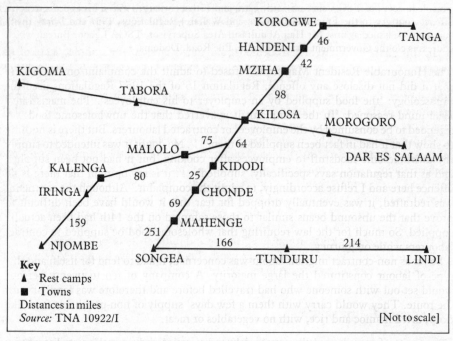

Key
▲ Rest camps
■ Towns
Distances in miles
Source: TNA 10922/I   [Not to scale]

had to choose whether to walk or to seek a recruiter to provide a ticket to the closed goods or cattle wagons in which the Ha travelled their hated 'middle passage' along the central railway.'[14] Warundi and Warwanda from the Belgian mandated territories entered the West Lake on foot and from there were often recruited to be taken by rail and road to the sisal areas of the Tanga and Eastern Provinces. Others worked a few days for the Haya rich peasants for food and walked over a hundred miles to the Sanza and other mines in the Western Province.[15]

The Tanganyikan labour working in the mines of Southern Rhodesia and South Africa also had to traverse long distances. Labourers from Songea or southern Iringa districts would have to embark at Mwaya, a port on Lake Nyasa, to travel to Kotakota, a distance of some 250 miles. From there the rest of the journey of some 540 miles to Salisbury would be on foot.[16]

These long journeys, mostly undertaken by male adults, involved much privation, starvation and death. Those recruited on formal contracts were supposed to be provided with food and shelter during the journey under the Master and Native Servants Ordinance, 1923 (ss. 24 and 25) and later under the relevant Employment Regulations. But the law was honoured more in the breach than the observance, for a number of interconnected reasons. First, there was not enough staff to inspect and apprehend the culprits; secondly, even if apprehended, labour officers were usually reluctant to prosecute an employer; and thirdly, even if prosecuted, more often than not an employer was acquitted on some or other technicality of law. The example of *R.v. Haji Abdulrasul*[17] is a case in point. One John Denni Sampson, a labour officer, lodged the following complaint with the Resident Magistrate, Dodoma:

On 14th February, 1957, I visited a kitchen and food store at Pile Road, Dodoma, used by TSGA Labour Bureau and took samples of cooked and uncooked beans which were heavily infested with weevils. Beans from the same source and in the same condition had been supplied to Jackson Makole [a cook] of TSGA staff on 11th, 12th, and 13th February, 1957. This appears to be an offence contrary to the Employment (Care and Welfare) Regulations, 1957 and I pray that a summons be issued against Mr Haji Abdulrasul Area Supervisor, TSGA Labour Bureau whose address is c/o the Government Transit Centre, Pile Road, Dodoma.

The Honourable Resident Magistrate refused to admit the complaint on the ground that it did not disclose any offence. Regulation 15 of the 1957 Regulations used the phraseology: 'the food supplied by an employer to his employees'. The magistrate's legal mind reasoned: 'In the complaint it is averred that the unwholesome food was intended to be consumed by the employees or contracted labourers. But there is nothing to show that it had in fact been supplied to them . . . No doubt it was intended to supply the unwholesome foodstuff to employees after cooking, but it had not been supplied and as that regulation says specifically 'supplied' . . . it is my opinion that there is no offence here and I refuse accordingly, to admit the complaint.' Although the complaint was redrafted, it was eventually dropped for fear that it would have been difficult to prove that the unsound beans similar to those sampled on the 14th had been actually supplied. So much for the law requiring that wholesome food be supplied to contract labourers while on journey.

So far as non-contract migrant labour was concerned, it had to fend for itself; and this type of labour constituted the large majority. A company of ten to twenty persons would set out with someone who had travelled before and therefore was familiar with the route. They would carry with them a few days' supply of non-perishable food like flour, dried manioc and rice, with no vegetables or meat.

The scarcity of utensils, and the extra weight to be carried, reduce cooking appliances to a minimum, so that even such food as is available, is badly and insufficiently cooked, while the daily march also militates against proper preparation of meals. In consequence, the labourer arrives at the place of employment after an exhausting journey on an inadequate and deficient diet; he is in fact quite unfit for any heavy work, and is ripe for scurvy and beri-beri.[18]

The government provided rest camps only on the main routes but no food except for an occasional dose of anti-scurvy lime to curb any epidemic.[19] Rest camps themselves were a mockery of human shelter. They were usually mud and wattle or grass structures costing less than £10 per camp. The staff of the labour camps consisted of an overseer to keep statistics, a sweeper and a dispenser. The grass structures that served as rest camps were literally the home of dead diseases, especially spirillum or tick fever. Parasitic ticks reside in the crevices of old huts, feed on mammals and are the carrier of spirochaete (spiral-shaped bacteria) which cause relapsing fever in man.[20] The District Officer of Mbeya was moved to say the following on these tick-infested grass huts:

The Medical Officer of Health, Chunya and myself wish strongly to urge the danger of any type of mud and wattle or grass structure. Such buildings on an established route become verminous in a few months and *are far more dangerous to the health of labourers than sleeping in the bush* [my emphasis]. Cases have been known of labourers setting such places on fire deliberately on account of vermin.[21]

Such were the structures which sheltered hundreds of thousands of workers on their journey to and from the employment centres. In 1935, the three camps of Korogwe, Mziha and Handeni accommodated some 21,264 persons of whom about 10 per cent were women and children. One-fifth of those who were accommodated were sick enough to be admitted to hospital.[22] Similar figures could be cited for other years and other camps — 1935 was certainly not exceptional. In the decade from 1953 to 1962, the government transit centres housed a colossal total of 1.8 million African workers travelling to and from the employment centres.[23] And not all could be accommodated in the government camps; others had to sleep under the open sky or be at the mercy of town landlords. Orde-Browne's description of the situation at Korogwe illustrates the point:

I stayed at Korogwe and was shocked at the scene around the railway station in the evening. Parties were arriving by train both from the Northern Province and from Tanga; others had come in from the surrounding country to take a train or lorry home on repatriation: and a number of men arrived by lorry shortly before midnight from the Southern railway on their way to various places of employment. The night was dark and wet, and hundreds of men were therefore wandering about looking for somewhere to sleep and some sort of food. The supervisor of the sisal growers' Bureau eventually sorted out his men, but they were only a small proportion of the whole. The remainder presumably eventually found some sort of shelter in the town, but this must have been of a very unsatisfactory type, while such a situation is readily exploited by the townspeople for overcharging for accommodation and food.[24]

In a similar vein the District Commissioner of Iringa lamented to his superior:

At present these unfortunates have nowhere to sleep, and therefore the banks of the Ruaha River, below the town have become a collection of dirty grass shelters housing these people. Railway buses arrive in the evening and they have nowhere they can go to; the Kitwiru camp is over an hour's walk from here, and in any case is of little use to natives who may have to leave in the early morning. Also, the congestion is now so great that natives are camping out in front of the railway station,where they eat, sleep, perform the usual functions of nature, to the great inconvenience of the people living in the vicinity.[25]

The miserable story of the 'middle passage' cannot be better illustrated than a tragic incident in 1928 which hit the files of colonial officials.[26] Sixty-two contracted labourers were recruited by Ali Yusuf and Embedodo Mshashi, a clerk and headman respectively of one Mr E. K. Biggs of Mwanza, a private recruiter. The workers had been recruited for the United Sisal Estates of Moshi. The party left Mwanza on foot on 8 April 1928 for Arusha, a distance of some 240 miles, via Mkalama and Mbulu. They were given 8 pounds of maize flour each, 1 blanket, 1 pair of *marekani* shorts and one white *marekani* shirt. Mr Biggs told his clerk that the party would get more *posho* at Mkalama for the journey from Mkalama to Arusha. On the way there was no shelter and no cooking facilities. They arrived at Mkalama after eight days of walking. By this time they had completely run out of food. At Mkalama they did not meet the European from the Estates who was supposed to give them more *posho*. Using some of his own money and borrowing some Shs. 60 from the District Commissioner, the clerk bought some food for the labourers, and took a lift to go ahead to Arusha to bring back food and a motor lorry. The party left Mkalama for Mbugwe on 18 April 1928. The clerk had given them some 84 cents each, said to be enough for three days' food, but it lasted them only two days. They took some five days to arrive at Mbugwe, where they slept for a night. 'At this time we had no food at all', narrated the headman. 'We were only drinking water day and night as our food, we arrived [sic] Arusha on 6 May 1928.' But it was not the full party that made it: three of them died on the way and one was to die later in the hospital at Arusha.

The post-mortem reports of the three dead bodies, by Dr G. R. C. Wilson, tell the full story of a month's journey of starvation and death. Let them speak:

1. The body of a wasted man said to be Gendurahezi identified by a relation Mguha bin Mhinrangi and the labour clerk Embe Dodo.
   There are no signs of injury. Subcutaneous fat is entirely absent. Ometal fat absent.
   Abdominal organs normal and show no signs of gross disease. L. Lung shows acute

bronchitis and a few pleuritic adhesions. R. Lung slight bronchitis and a few pleuritic adhesions.

Heart small but shows no signs of gross disease.

Cause of death. Long continued chest trouble (bronchitis and pleurisy) with exhaustion and exposure probably a degree of starvation.

2. The body of a youth about 14 years old identified by Kinyamlima bin Luguwira as Buliba bin Ngovu.

The body shows general wasting. No signs of injury.

Subcutaneous and intestinal fat is absent. Abdominal organs normal. Spleen slightly enlarged.

Uncooked matama and mealies were found in the intestines. Lungs showed old disease and not very marked engorgement. The intestines were full of worms both round and tape.

Heart normal.

In my opinion this youth died of starvation and exposure and had been unable to cook his food for some days.

3. The body of a well developed man about 26 years, showing no gross wasting identified . . . as Lukozi s/o Lungiri.

There is very little subcutaneous fat and no ometal fat at all. Abdominal fat is deficient.

There are old liver and colon adhesions. An enlarged spleen. Kidney normal.

The stomach showed a recent meal of meat and tripe (both raw) (the piece of meat 6″long and the tripe 12″long). There were also several smaller pieces of meat. Some previous food had been of raw matama.

Lungs showed massive adhesions on the left side and many on the right.

Lung [sic] showed slight inflammation. Heart — no gross disease.

The actual cause of death seems uncertain, probably starvation and exposure followed by a gross feed of raw material of meat and matama contributed to death.

That was a scientific opinion of a medical practitioner. In spite of that, the report of the Labour Commissioner, in its typical Orde-Brownian cynicism, concluded that 'the deaths resulted from a most unfortunate series of misfortunes', that the employer was good, so was the agent and although the amount of food was not generous, it was not really insufficient! 'The fact that the men were provided with an exceptionally good free issue of clothing (one shirt, one pair of shorts, one blanket and one length of cloth) is sufficient to absolve the recruiter from the charge of stinting necessities for his labourers.'

The opinion of the custodian of the 'care and welfare' legislation carried the day. The file was closed.

Wages and food

The colonial economy was based on extremely low wage rates bearing very little relation to the cost of maintaining labour power in a normal state. As has already been discussed, the wages provided only for the minimum requirements of an adult male. An estimate of monthly expenditure by a bachelor, just on food, for plantation labour near Tanga around 1935 amounted to Shs. 7.80. These workers were drawing Shs. 12–15 per thirty days' work. Assuming that the workers completed their thirty days' work in a period of, say, forty-five days their monthly wage would come to Shs. 8–10. It is clear that given the food expenditure of around Shs. 8 per month, a worker could hardly hope to clothe himself on this meagre wage. In fact, a family could definitely not even subsist on this amount. One investigator estimated that a family with three children of varying age would require about Shs. 26.83 for food.[27]

The second point to note is that wages varied fairly widely from district to district and over time. It is extremely difficult to relate the movement of real wages over the colonial period because a reliable price index is not available. However, a rough picture of the movement of money wages, say of the sisal cutters in the Tanga employment area, gives a reasonable guide. In the German period, wages appear to have been increasing towards the end of that rule before they fell again during the war. According to Iliffe's estimate the wage of unskilled contract labour in Tanga may have risen from about Shs. 12.50 to Shs. 20, about a 60 per cent rise per working month between 1881 and 1913.[28] In the 1920s wages rose and owing to relative stability of prices they regained the real value of the 1910s.[29] The depression spelled a real disaster so far as the wages were concerned. Orde-Browne estimated that in the Tanga employment area wages fell from Shs. 30 without food in 1930 to Shs. 10 in 1933, which wage was below that in the German times.[30] In fact the low depression-wages continued to rule during the 1930s and although money-wages rose somewhat in the 1940s, going beyond the Shs. 20 mark per month, high inflation probably kept the real wages lower than those of the 1920s. 'In west Usambara estate labour earned less in 1948 than in 1929 even in money terms — Shs. 18 as against Shs. 15–30 a month.'[31] Iliffe further estimates that the real wage of agriculture labour in 1951 was at the same level as in 1927.[32]

Wages in other sectors — infrastructure and mining — more or less followed similar trends. On government works involving road construction, the wage for unskilled workers in 1928 was Shs. 17–27 per month,[33] while in 1937 it was Shs. 9–21 per month.[34] In the mines the wages hardly ever exceeded Shs. 20 per month in the 1930s. In 1935, the gold-mine at Sekenke was paying Shs. 6–15 per month to its unskilled labour,[35] Kentan was paying an average of Shs. 10[36] while the mines in the Musoma area were paying Shs. 6–8 per month.[37]

Much of the semi-proletarian labour on the plantations, mines and infrastructural construction was paid by the *kipande* system, that is, for thirty working days and not by a calender month. Secondly, the working day was measured not by time but usually by task, that is to say the system was based on piece- rather than time-wages. This system allowed the employer to reduce his supervisory costs by making the worker his own supervisor. It also lent itself to numerous abuses by unscrupulous employers. For instance, it appears to have been a common practice among some employers not to enter a day on the *kipande* on the grounds that the work was not satisfactory or that the task was not complete and so on. For example, at the Kentan mines, whether or not a worker was going to get his day depended solely on a European supervisor. There a system of 'loafer-ticket' was in operation. Every worker was given a booklet of thirty counterfoils, each one of which was perforated into three parts. On completion of the day's work the outer portion would be torn off by a European supervisor and sent off to the time-office, signifying that the worker concerned was entitled to that day's pay. 'Every gang-boss or European in charge of the labour can, if he considers that a boy has not done a full day's work, refuse to send in his time-ticket - instead he sends in part of a 'loafer-ticket' — a coloured counterfoil of which several are included in each booklet. This does not enable the labourer to draw any pay for that day, but its second portion does enable him to draw posho.'[38] The inspector on a visit to this mine doubted the legality of the system and thought it unsatisfactory that an European supervisor should have power to deprive a worker of all pay for a day in consequence of a lapse in, say, the eighth or ninth hour of a shift.

Elsewhere the inspectors noticed the system of 'cutting days' – where, as a matter of discipline or punishment, an employer deducts a day's work or does not enter it on the labour cards.[39]

In the Lupa gold controlled area, the small alluvial diggers adopted another system of deception. There a worker got his ticket marked only if he produced a definite weight of gold per day. If not, no day was marked and in some cases even the day's ration would not be given. Thus the employer was in effect shifting capital's risk to labour.[40]

Finally, the most common offence committed by small employers, particularly from the minority nationalities as opposed to large foreign companies, was withholding wages. (See Table 1.6, p. 31). Greek, Italian and Indian sub-contractors involved in railway construction, small prospectors in gold-mining and small planters often failed to pay their employees. In 1930 a little under half the offences tried by labour officers against the employers involved withholding of wages.[41] Of the 38 criminal cases against railway sub-contractors, tried by the District Officer, Manyoni, between October 1930 and March 1931, some 18 involved withholding of wages. The culprits were 12 Italians, 3 Greeks, 2 Indians and 1 German.[42] Probably the worst offenders were the relatively poor alluvial diggers. In the Iringa Province, between 12 January 1936 and 15 March 1936, some 515 workers were denied wages amounting to over Shs. 12,000.[43]

Some small employers also indulged in the notorious 'truck system' whereby wages would be paid, either wholly or in part, in cloth or other goods.[44] This allowed the employer enormous gain because the wholesale prices of goods were far below retail prices and the employer charged the worker even higher than the retail prices. Strictly speaking, this practice was in breach of the Master and Native Servants Ordinance which required wages to be paid in the currency of the territory (s. 21). But that provision, unlike the later provision in the Emplopyment Ordinance (Cap. 366, s. 61). was toothless since non-compliance was not made an offence.

Next we turn to the question of food:

During the period of the service of any servant employed at such distance from his home as to render it impossible for him to return to his home at the conclusion of his daily work, the employer shall at his own expense cause such servant to be properly fed and to be supplied with sufficient and proper cooking utensils and means of cooking. Provided, however, that the obligation of an employer to cause his servant to be fed or to supply cooking utensils and means of cooking as aforesaid, as the case may be, shall not extend to any case when the servant is employed at a place where he can obtain for himself sufficient and proper food, or cooking utensils and means of cooking, if it has been agreed between the parties, at the time of entering into the contract of service, that the servant shall procure his food or cooking utensils and means of cooking at his own expense. (s. 25(i)).

That section of the Master and Native Servants Ordinance made it obligatory upon the employers to 'properly feed' their servants, but even if it could be enforced, it left numerous loopholes which the employers liberally exploited to their advantage.

The obligation applied only in the case of long-distance workers which meant that it excluded 'local labour' who could presumably return to their homes after work. Even in the case of long-distance migrant workers, in practice food ration was included only in the case of attested workers and they too could opt out of receiving rations. Thus the portion of labour force receiving rations was not very high.[45] In 1943 in the Tanga Province only about 17,000[46] out of some 56,000 workers[47] in the sisal industry were fed by employers, a figure that moreover was higher than elsewhere in the country. It was only in the 1940s, after the experience of, and the obligations imposed by, the war that a greater number of workers began to be fed by the employers. The 1947–8 Annual Report of the Labour Department gave the following data of the workers receiving rations:[48]

Province	Full rations (%)	Cash in lieu (%)	Neither (%)
Arusha	35	40	25
Southern Highlands (Mbeya & Iringa)	Most of the labour in this province is fed, with the exception of the Mbozi area where there is practically no fed labour		
Tanga & Pangani	Attested labour and contractor's labour only fed.		
Morogoro	72	12	16
Western Province	64	14	22
Dar es Salaam	All sisal estates issue rations or cash in lieu		
Lindi	22	11	67
Korogwe	30	50	20

Before the war the common practice among employers was to give a few cents per diem in lieu of rations rather than bother with storing food.[49] Such money given in lieu of rations was invariably insufficient to buy adequate food. The Tanga Provincial Commissioner's Annual Report for 1935 noted:

Rations: These have been very seldom issued, the usual practice has been to issue the full wages in cash, and advances have been made weekly to enable the labourer to purchase his own food. As the average labourer only draws from Sh. 1.50 to Shs. 2 per week and the cost of living (without any allowance for luxuries such as cigarettes, clothes, etc.) is approximately Shs. 6 to 8 per month, it is obvious that the food so purchased must be almost below the minimum required to keep the labourer fit.[50]

Where the employer did issue rations he preferred to buy in bulk so as to cheapen the cost. This meant that he tended to store the monotonous maize flour and beans without any variety and there was an almost complete absence of fresh vegetables and fruit. This is where the loop-hole in the law came in. The concept of 'properly fed' was left to the whims of unconcerned employers and labour officers. It appears that until the onset of the war[51] there was no definite scale of rations set down as being compulsory. The usual issue of ration consisted of 24–32 ounces of the notorious maize-meal or *posho* (coarse maize flour); 4–7 ounces of beans and a weekly issue of two or so ounces of salt.[52] With a little variation here and there, it was such a diet that was laid out in the contracts of service. In fact, legal opinion held that district officers had no right to refuse to attest a contract on the ground that the scale of rations provided therein did not amount to 'proper feeding'.[53] The question of 'proper feeding' was left to be investigated by labour inspectors at places of employment.

The food value of the typical 'maize–beans–salt' diet was grossly inadequate to keep a hard-working adult male in a normal state of health. It lacked in variety and its monotony made it unappetizing.

Several of the houses in the main compound were visited in order to learn what was made of the standard beans and maize. The best that was cooked was with added sprats, and coconut oil. The worst was cooked *all natural* [original emphasis], an unappetizing mixture of beans and maize only. It is not surprising if labour fed on this is inefficient.[54]

The diet lacked protein of animal origin and it certainly was short of important vitamins like A and C.[55] One investigator noted: 'There appears to be a belief among some of the smaller employers that, provided a native is given 2 lbs or so of maize or *muhugo* [cassava], meal [*posho*], all has been done which ought to be done. The labourer cooks this as best he may, or if firewood is not to hand mixes it with water and eats it raw.'[56] No wonder that any person existing on such a diet would be malnourished. Dr K. C. Charron, a medical adviser to the labour department, opined that the 'inability of the African labourer to perform a reasonably large task and the poor turn-out in most industries is attributed in no small measure to malnutrition'.[57]

There were numerous other problems connected with the issue of rations. A common practice often commented upon by labour officers was short-weighing. Maize-flour, for example, was given by measure rather than weight. The container often used was *kibaba*, weighing anything between 19 and 32 ounces depending on the way it was filled.[58] A medical officer reporting on the estates in Morogoro District noted: 'Careful weighing of rations on all Estates disclosed that many of them were giving under weight, in one case as much as 10½ ounces per man under weight.'[59]

Worse than short-weighing was the very widespread practice of issuing rations at the end of the day and linking the issue of certain items like meat to the completion of five or six days' continuous work. The result was that a worker had to labour on an empty stomach for the whole day and when he got his rations he was in no position to cook them well. 'The posho is given out at the end of the day's work i.e., when the men are tired, and very hungry. They are then faced with taking it off to their huts making a fire and cooking it. They are probably men who have been accustomed to have their food prepared for them by their bibis [wives], they are also tired out, and therefore it is almost certain that in many cases the food is not properly cooked, which certainly would be a contributing factor in their ultimate illness.'[60] The same observer noted that the majority of estates gave meat ration only once a week and that too on Saturdays to those who had done five days' work 'in spite of a meat ration being compulsory by contract and ignoring the fact that it is probably the man who is unable to work on account of weakness who is more in need of meat than his stronger brother'. The manager of Kingumi Estate, at the inquest of the death of one of his workers, testified:

The standard ration is flour and beans, 20 ounces flour and 8 ounces beans. I know the maximum ration of flour is 12 ounces but we cannot find meat (note by coroner: over 3000 h/c were offered on Mbulu Cattle Markets between 15th and 30th of this month alone). (Intd. M. A. F.) I give each labourer groundnuts 3 times a week, 4 ounces each issue. I give 3 fish per boy on Saturday if he has worked 6 days. If he has worked 5 days he gets none. I do not issue any meat. The Karanga (peanuts) issue on Mondays and Wednesdays are given to all, but the Saturday issue only for those who work six days. When a man does 5 or 6 days a week they get a ration for Sunday, but a boy who does 4 days does not, unless he was sick.[61]

In breach of their statutory obligation and contract, many employers indulged widely in the practice of not issuing rations to their absentee and/or sick workers, or issuing rations only if they came for them. A doctor on a medical survey to sisal estates observed:

Rightly or wrongly I had gathered the impression during my visits to estates that if a contract labourer does not complete his task, he gets no ration in respect of that day: and that rations are in any case conditional on his working. I suspect too that a contract labourer may elect not to tackle his task, but will perform a small job for his neighbour settled on the estate in return for a meal with the family: or he may simply stand off.[62]

It was the large-scale conscription of labour during the war which forced the colonial government to tighten up somewhat its inspection and insist on more definite scale of rations. The Master and Native Servants (Proper Feeding) Regulations of 1944 provided that:

the proper feeding of adult male servants to whom these regulations apply shall consist of foodstuffs yielding not less than 3,500 calories as an average gross daily issue which shall include all the following constituents in not less than quantities shown for each:

Fat	50 grammes
Protein	100 grammes of which at least 10 per cent shall be of animal origin
Carbohydrates	500 grammes

Salt	15 grammes
Iron	20 milligrams
Vitamin A	3000 international units
Vitamin B1	350 international units
Vitamin C	600 international units

Lack of constant inspection and enforcement of these regulations meant that breaches were not inconsiderable. The food issues on some sisal estates continued to fall short of these requirements, as some inspection reports show.[63] A typical inspection report, particularly on small-employer properties, would be like that of Mbagalla Estate in Uzaramo. On his inspection there in 1945, a labour officer found that the ration issued and its food value were as follows:

Item	Oz p. day	Cals.	Prot.	Fats	Vit. A	B1	C (IUS)
Cassava meal	24	1 920	10	—	—	—	—
Beans	3.3	284	23	2.0	—	72	—
Groundnuts	0.4	65	2	4.8	—	10	—
Sugar	1.0	116					
Salt	0.5						
		2 385	35	6.8	—	82	—
Deficiency		1 115	65	42.2	3 000	268	600

Mining concerns tended to be worse as far as supply of rations was concerned. The small alluvial diggers could not afford buying food in bulk and storing it and the supply of fresh vegetables and fruits was virtually out of the question. For example, the ration issued at Mrangi Mine, which was typical of the mining properties in the Musoma areas, was 1½–2 lb of maize meal daily; 3 ounces of salt weekly; 3 ounces of beans and 3 ounces of groundnuts weekly and game meat weekly - no vegetables, no fruits.[64] 'The alluvial digger has neither the time nor opportunity (nor perhaps inclination) to go searching for the correct foods, he buys just what he can get and just what is sufficient.'[65] Little wonder that the famous Lupa gold-fields were also notorious for their scurvy-infested labour force.

It hardly needs to be recalled that the rations issued were just to provide the minimum requirements of a single male adult. If a worker was accompanied by a wife and children he had to share his beggarly 24 ounces of 'mealie-maize' with the rest of the family which left all of them grossly undernourished. A doctor put the average requirement of a family of two adults and two children at 9,000 calories and went on to add:

Under present conditions the sisal cutter if he turns out to work every day receives 34.3 cents cash and 14.91 cents in food each day including Sundays. The estimated cost of the additional food he should obtain for himself and his family purchased *at the cheapest rate available to the employer* [original emphasis] is 37.38 cents. It is quite evident that if he spent the whole of his remaining money on food the family would still be malnourished unless the family can cultivate for themselves an appreciable quantity of additional food.[66]

The worry of a typical colonial employer was not so much that the whole family was malnourished as that '*his*' worker had to share the ration resulting in the worker's *inefficiency*. A comment by one Colonel Watkins, a representative of a private firm on a visit to Tanganyika, is a typical example of the way capitalist rationality was combined, and at the same time clashed, with colonial prejudice. Apparently recommending an increase in rations, Colonel Watkins noted in all seriousness:

Again the presence of a wife and family introduces complications, since it is the invariable custom of the African to share his rations and to try and scrape along with as little extra as possible. The result is that the increase in ration hardly benefits him unless his family is rationed also. It is no use telling him that he must supplement it out of his pay. He just does not do it.[!]

Almost more difficult is the custom of hospitality. Relatives out of work will inflict themselves for weeks on a man or his mess as a matter of right, and share his ration. Yet all these points affect the health of the man and his efficiency and in consequence, are of the greatest importance to the employer, who has to pay for medicine and repatriation.[67]

Indeed, that which affected the profits of a capitalist was of the *greatest* importance to him.

Housing

The law imposed an obligation upon the employer to house his servants 'properly' in the case of those who could not return to their homes at the conclusion of their daily work. The employer was also required to observe all 'reasonable' directions given by administrative, medical or labour officers with respect to sanitary arrangements (s. 24 of M & NSO). In spite of such provisions in the statute book the condition of workers' housing in the plantations, on government works and at the mines was deplorable even by the standard of colonial labour officers. One occasionally comes across moving reports of dilapidated housing picturesquely described in the inspection reports of the labour officers. In the 1920s and 1930s such reports are fewer and far between unless conditions reached scandalous proportions. In the 1940s such reports become more common and give a fair picture of the state of housing. During the war period and thereafter there were a number of factors which made the government tighten up inspection. First, there was the conscript labour provided to private employers by the government; the state of their feeding and housing had to be continually watched. Secondly, during the war, a number of 'enemy'-owned estates were taken over by the custodian of enemy property and leased out to other capitalists. Again there was stricter inspection of these properties. Finally, in the 1950s trade union pressure was significantly responsible for intensifying, to some extent, more regular inspection.

From the study of various inspection reports we can identify three types of housing or labour lines, as the housing on the plantations was called in the colonial literature. These were temporary, semi-permanent and permanent structures.

Temporary labour camps were essentially huts with mud floors or wattle and daub walls and roofs thatched with grass or palm-leaves (*makuti*). Often, even the walls would be of grass. These were meant to last a few months and would be burnt down as soon as they became infested with disease-carrying germs and insects. These structures were literally hovels of disease for they harboured in their crevices fleas, jigger fleas and the deadly spirillum-bearing ticks.[68]

The second type of housing was called semi-permanent. These were houses with mud or concrete floors, walls made of burnt-brick, concrete or kimberley bricks or occasionally concrete blocks, and with the usual thatched roofs of grass or palm-leaves. The permanent structures were those with concrete or cement floor, the latter being rare, and concrete walls and corrugated, galvanized iron sheets as roofs.

All these three types of structures were acceptable to inspectors provided they were in a reasonable state of repair and cleanliness. It was the mud-and-daub hut which dominated the labour lines during the 1920s and 1930s. Only in the 1940s did rather more permanent structures begin to be erected.[69] In a sample of sixty-seven estates that

Dr Mackay, a medical officer, visited in 1939 it was found that some 57 per cent had average housing (that is, wattle and daub huts); some 13 per cent had poor housing (that is, purely grass huts) and only 20 per cent had 'good' housing (that is, substantial brick or concrete-block).[70]

Lack of adequate floor space and general overcrowding, low walls and doors, either excessive or inadequate window-space and/or ventilation were the common observations made by labour inspectors on their visits. 'The accommodation on the Estate [Geiglitz Estate, belonging to Messrs Bird & Co.] I found was totally inadequate, the majority of the houses being mere hovels. I found that as many as seventeen were living in one small house and anything from two to four sleeping in one bed which was really big enough for one man.'[71] Dr K. C. Charron considered that each occupant should have a minimum of 40 square feet of floor space and that no living room should have less than 100 square feet. He prescribed further that the minimum height of the walls should be 7 feet and should be smoothly plastered inside; that the ratio of ventilation to floor-space should be 5 square feet of ventilation for every 100 square feet of floor space and that the floor should be raised at least 8 inches above ground floor. To avoid congestion single-roomed houses should not be less than 20 feet apart; two-roomed houses not less than 25 feet apart; and houses of more than two rooms should be at least 30 feet apart.[72] Yet these minimum requirements were honoured only in the breach as the inspection reports testify again and again. In the main camp of Tangoni Estate Ltd, a labour officer observed that there were no window shutters and no kitchens; cooking was being done in the dwellings while in the Duka camp there were only temporary structures which had no windows; floors were not raised; walls were only 6 feet high and doors had no shutters.[73] In the case of Paramba Sisal Estate rooms were overcrowded: one room had seven persons sleeping while another had six persons sleeping.[74] The mud and wattle housing of Karimi-Nderema Estate required repairs and plastering; floors of mud had to be raised; there were no kitchens and cooking was being done in the sleeping rooms. In another camp of the same estate, floor space per room was only 2 by 9½ feet.[75]

The state of the housing on government works was no better and in fact in some cases worse. On his visit to a government camp in Moshi Orde-Browne observed:

The camp consisted of a collection of little huts of most primitive design so small that they could only be entered by crawling, quite inadequate to keep out rain and unsuitable even for brief occupation: they were in a sodden condition even after three days without rain; long grass surrounded them except along the roadside, and empty tins, broken bottles and refuse were scattered about; the only sanitary arrangements consisted of a public latrine over a hundred yards away, while no attempt seems to have been made to appoint a sweeper, camp overseer or other staff.[76]

At a government dairy, workers were housed in three wooden buildings 'which were probably used as a store, kitchen store and vegetable preparation shed'. 'The first is a building some sixty to seventy feet long which is partitioned off into four rooms: the first contains a bull pen and feed, the second contains 11 men, the third four, and the fourth a man and wife.' The labour officer was moved to end his letter by saying: 'May I point out that one's work is not made the easier by a complete disregard of the law by government Department.'[77]

The housing conditions on the mining properties were once again the worst among the general bad state. The alluvial digger, usually a man of small means, had neither the ability nor the inclination to provide his labour with more than the roughest shelter to sleep in.[78] In his Labour Report of 1935, the Provincial Commissioner made the following observation on the Lupa gold-fields where some 20,000 workers were being employed.

On the Lupa gold-fields the housing conditions of the native labour employed in alluvial mining is far from satisfactory. For the most part the natives are accommodated in grass shelters, generally quite inadequate and there is an almost entire lack of sanitation from the nature of work in alluvial mining, where the individual digger does not remain long on a particular claim, accommodation for the labourer is of a very temporary nature; but there seems little if any reason why such shelters should not at least be weather-proof and of more substantial structure.[79]

The usual housing provided in almost all mining concerns was the typical grass hut, often old and overcrowded.[80] At the Aureole Mines in the Mwanza District, for example, there were 54 huts, 15 of which were conical-shaped temporary structures and the others circular 'rondavaals' with walls and roofs made of grass. They were about 12 feet in diameter with approximately four occupants in one hut. 'It was noted that for grass buildings the huts were too close together as in case of fire there was the great possibility of the whole camp being destroyed with probable loss of life.'[81] On some larger mining concerns an attempt was made to put up more permanent structures but these too fell short of proper human habitation. Commenting on the completion of a new camp of Kentan Gold Areas Ltd, at Geita, the Assistant District Officer noted:[82]

The huts are all circular, of galvanized iron, with squared timber rafters and straight grass thatching. Floors are intended to be of cement, but it will probably be some time before all huts are equipped with this. They have a galvanized iron door, no windows, and are being fitted with wooden benches, shaped to the wall of the hut, for sleeping purposes.

The clerks and askaris' huts are 12 feet in diameter, and the labourers' huts 10 feet. Within the block the huts are centred 30 feet apart — i.e. 20 feet in each direction from wall to wall, and a trifle less from eave to eave.

The District Officer noted that the huts would be too crowded for four men; that grass would harbour rats; the site was windy and there was a great risk of fire. Not least important, such galvanized iron structures would be very hot during day-time and very cold at night. No wonder the workers often refused to sleep in such 'improved types of houses' which would be like freezers at night and ovens during day-time. 'Employers are prone to argue that the African resents being made to live in improved types of houses and base their contention on the results of experiments. Investigation of these experiments usually shows that it has been found that the African labourer's reluctance is based on an objection to sleeping on cold concrete floors or in oven-like corrugated iron buildings.'[83]

Incidentally, the provision of wooden benches for beds must have been an improvement in those days for these camps hardly ever had beds provided. Dr Wilson considered lack of beds coupled with over-ventilation responsible for causing pneumonia in the 'underclothed African'.[84]

Apart from the state of housing as we have described, these camps hardly ever contained separate facilities for laundry, bathing and cooking.[85] While generally there was no shortage of drinking water, this would usually be from uncovered wells or nearby streams and rivers. Labour inspectors often warned employers against the dangers of contaminated water. 'The practice of drawing water from the airport drains which are liable to contamination must cease immediately. Also the drawing of water from burrow-pits (and other wells dug by camp occupants) is highly undesirable. All these excavations were in a filthy state and, apart from the danger of bad water mosquito breeding was rife.'[86] At Lusanda Sisal Estate, drinking water was being drawn from unproptected streams; at the homestead camp of Boma Plantations workers depended on rain from roofs for drinking water and during the dry season it was brought from wells in drums;[88] at Sisisegoma Estate water was collected individually from unprotected streams or direct from the river[89] and so on. And this, in spite of specific provision of law that an employer 'shall arrange for proper water supply for the use of . . . servant' (s. 25(2) of M & NSO).

Next we come to probably the most sordid aspect of the housing conditions of the semi-proletariat: this was the lack of adequate and clean sanitary facilities at the camp. In only 30 per cent of the estates visited by Dr Wilson around 1940 did there exist a reasonable standard of latrines, and in only 10 per cent of these could latrine accommodation be said to be satisfactory; it was invariably of the pit type.[90] In Dr Mackay's sample survey of sixty-seven estates carried out around the same time only one-fourth of the estates had 'good' latrines, that is, those with concrete slab or floor and roof, while two-thirds were 'poor'.[91] In one estate he found excreta everywhere because latrines were very far. Employers often complained that it was difficult to make 'primitive natives' use sanitary facilities[92] but the point is that many estates simply did not have latrines and those that had were so dirty and unhygienic that, not surprisingly, bush was preferable. The labour inspectors' comments on the state of sanitation bear out the filthy state in which the employers left their camps. Some typical comments may be cited. At Stirling Astaldi camps care of latrines was found defective, ten stances were unusable due to collapse, in another six flies were breeding and the rest were only fair.[93] The Tanganyika Engineering and Contracting Co.'s camps attracted the following comment on latrines: 'pit type, 20 stances: Poor — 16 stances on one side of the camp: Bed smelling and fly breeding evident: Direct sunlight not totally excluded: very poor camp in a filthy state'.[94] At Zenettiberg Estate 'latrines were full, poorly supervised and improperly constructed'.[95] The Tongoni Estates Ltd's main camp needed whitewashing and repairs. The inspector observed: 'No sign of their being frequently used and excreta tended to dry up due to insufficient pouring of water'.[96] On one estate around Dar es Salaam a labour officer commented:

There were very few latrines in the camp, and one I inspected had the floor raised 1 ft 9 in where the total height from ground level outside to the top of the wall was only 3 ft 6 in. The ridge was only 1 ft 3 in higher. From the stance to the ridge was only 3 ft.

There is no latrine at the factory. There was one of only one stance at a distance of about 150 yards, but even this was full, disused and decrepit.

There are no refuse pits and the camp is not swept regularly. The meat shop was very insanitary.[97]

The reader will be better able to gauge the nature and state of the camps and the sanitary facilities if we examine one not untypical case in some detail. The Burka Coffee Estate, which was the largest mixed farm in the Northern Province, was considered by the Labour Department as having good labour conditions.[98] In July 1950 a labour officer filed an elaborate inspection report on this estate describing the housing conditions as 'very unsatisfactory'.[99]

The camp, consisting of a total of some 124 semi-permanent and eleven permanent houses, was laid out on an area of some 150 acres. The permanent housing consisted of three buildings with brick and cement walls, corrugated iron roofing and compressed lime floors. The doors were adequate but there was too much ventilation and window space, leaving rooms completely exposed to wind, cold and dust. 'Windows are merely large open gaps in walls covering about one-third of wall area.' The labour officer described these permanent houses as being in 'incredibly poor condition'.

On the semi-permanent housing the labour officer's comment deserves quotation in full.

A most extra-ordinary method of housing labourers. *These labour lines cover 150 acres of ground* [original emphasis]. Built on a large village basis with each labourer having his own piece of land. There are four types of houses . . . built in streets between furrows. Each house has its own pit latrine. Houses of mud brick, thatch roofing, poor ventilation and in some cases no ventilation; earth floors and doors, very unsatisfactory being totally inadequate (20" wide 4' 10" high). Floors not raised adequately. Type 1 houses are of burnt brick walls plastered and white washed and burnt brick floors. Maintenance and supervision are most unsatisfactory. Houses and latrines in very poor condition: the latter are dirty due to lack of supervision and sweepers.

Drinking, bathing and laundry water was drawn from the furrows which ran through right in the middle of the camp. There was no means of refuse disposal; it was deposited near the camp and sometimes burnt.

There were two water-borne latrines with 22 stances and 51 pit latrines, all in a very unsatisfactory condition. The labour officer wrote:

LATRINES are quite curious being corrugated iron open construction — walls 4 feet high, no roof divided into cubicles. A dry furrow sloping to centre is used. This is washed down by sweepers with water in buckets and excreta washed away into a large tank, which is emptied periodically. At present, latrines are in a very dirty condition due to no supervision.

These, then, were the conditions in which were housed some 300 labourers of a well-known, reputedly 'good' employer.

The conditions of housing that we have described pertained to the labour housed by the employer. However, even some of the migrant labour preferred not to live in the labour lines so as to be free of the 'discipline' imposed by the employer on the labour compounds. There therefore developed 'sub-standard huts and shacks'[100] around the sisal estates without even minimum sanitary facilities. Often squatters built their huts on their own on the employers' land itself and these too tended to be the lowest standard of housing.[101]

Thus, overall, the condition of housing of the semi-proletariat was one of the worst and was one of the important factors responsible for the bad health of the workers.

Health

Deficient and insufficient diet together with the insanitary environmental and housing conditions described in the foregoing sections were two significant factors responsible for many diseases and deaths among the plantation, mining and other labourers. Through years of experience people in their rural environment had learnt to balance their diets by procuring necessary ingredients from wild fruits and vegetables. This balance was completely disturbed on the plantations and mines when the workers were put on the monotonous 'mealie–beans–salt diet'. The importance of deficient diet in causing some fatal diseases is probably best illustrated by the outbreak of scurvy that occurred in mid-1930s on the Lupa gold-fields.

Around 1935, some 18–20,000 workers were employed in alluvial and reef mining in the Iringa Province.[102] In the scramble for gold, the employers had neither the time nor probably the inclination to provide their workers with adequate food and housing. The housing usually consisted of temporary grass structures while the diet was the typical 28–32 ounces of maize flour, 4 ounces of beans and half an ounce of salt.[103] This diet lacked essential proteins and vitamins but in 'the breathless scramble for gold, master and man [sic!] have little time to provide for any but the barest necessities'.[104] The result was that a large number of workers fell prey to devouring diseases like scurvy and many respiratory infections. Nor did the state have adequate inspection and enforcement of its own pious legislation on medical care. For the whole Lupa gold area there was only one administrative officer who acted as a labour officer.[105] We shall discuss the enforcement of legal provisions on medical care later, but let us first look at scurvy.

Scurvy is caused by a deficiency of vitamin C of which an adult requires some 70 mg every day. According to one medical authority, scurvy is not very common in the tropics since fruits and fresh vegetables are abundant.[106] But here, in the very heart of the tropics, some scores of mining workers were dying because of scurvy. In his report of May 1935, a medical officer at Mbeya noted that in the four-and-a-half-month period from January to 18 May 1935 he had admitted some 119 cases of scurvy, of which seven died, a mortality rate of some 6 per cent.[107] Describing the symptoms, the same medical officer wrote:

The most common symptom was a painful hard swelling of the thigh and the calf of either both or one leg. In some cases the guiteal[?] region was affected and a swelling and pains were complained of in this area. The majority of the cases under observation had swollen and sometimes bleeding gums. This symptom was missing in a considerable number of cases where muscular pains were only complained of. A few cases had swollen joints, the knee being affected more often than the elbow. In some cases the arms, specially the upper arm showed the muscular infiltration[?] other symptoms being either present or missing. In almost every case an advanced anaemia could be observed and a very considerable loss of flesh . . . The chronic cases presented usually a very marked atrophy of the skin, hair and nails, contractions of the knees and very often profuse diarrhoea; which was difficult to control. Mentally practically all cases showed marked symptoms of apathy amounting frequently to debility and stupidity.

The usual treatment given to scurvy patients in the hospital was the juice of lemons and oranges and a diet of sweet potatoes and wild spinach, while in serious cases fresh meat was also provided. 'In the more serious cases an almost immediate improvement could be observed after the first few doses of lemon juice. The patient became mentally active and developed a tremendous appetite and very soon began to put on weight.'

So much for a disease which could be completely prevented by simply providing a proper diet — yet which managed to kill several dozens of mine workers every year.[108]

Elsewhere in the mining areas the pattern of diseases was similar to that found on the plantations: many of these diseases being directly or indirectly connected with nutrition, sanitation and general housing conditions. For example, overexposure and insufficient clothing were responsible for many of the infections of the respiratory system like bronchitis, and pneumonia. Table 2.1 shows data for the Geita mine belonging to Kentan Gold Areas Ltd, giving some idea of the pattern of diseases.

Pneumonia, bronchitis and cerebro-spinal meningitis are all connected with respiratory infection and in part due to inadequate protection against rapid changes of temperature and excessive dryness of weather. 'In . . . dry weather the mucous membranes of the nasopharyn tend to be dry, ceasing to act as an efficient barrier to infection. Conditions for transmission from carriers are favourable, and cases of meningitis occur.'[110]

Cerebro-spinal meningitis was a very common disease affecting very wide sections of the population and geographical areas with extremely high mortality rates.[111] The membranes of the brain become inflamed resulting in severe headaches and retraction of the head accompanied by high temperature.[112] Very often the disease proves fatal. It is undoubtedly connected with bad sanitary conditions and prevails in damp, sunless houses. Pneumonia, another killer disease, is also connected with improper housing. Dr Wilson thought that the provision of beds and proper- as opposed to 'over'- ventilation, could go a long way to prevent the occurrence of this disease.[113] But then out of some thirty-five estates visited by the doctor only two were providing beds.

Table 2.1 *Dispensary admissions for Geita mine, April 1935 – March 1936 (employing around 1 500 workers)*[109]

I. *Out-patient statistics*

	No.	%
Disease of respiratory systems	546	12.5
Disease of digestive systems	632	14.4
Surgical[a]	2 478	56.5
Malaria	348	7.9
Specific	80	1.8
Intestinal parasites	11	0.3
Miscellaneous	288	6.6
Total	4 383	100.0

II. *In-patient statistics*

	No.	%
Pneumonia	48	13.1
Surgical[a]	147	40.2
Malaria	62	16.9
Bronchitis	34	9.3
Cerebro-spinal meningitis (CSM)	28	7.7
Spirillum fever	3	0.8
Miscellaneous	44	12.0
Total	366	100.0

III. *Death statistics*

	No.	%
Pneumonia	10	23.2
Cerebro-spinal meningitis (CSM)	27	62.8
Other causes	6	14.0
Total	43	100.0

Source: Montague, F. A., 'Report on Visit of Inspection to Kentan Gold Areas Ltd, Saragura', May 1936, TNA 23435/I.
Note: [a] It is not clear from the report cited as to what is being referred to by this term.

Another very common cause of death on the plantations, as Table 2.2 shows, was ankylostomiasis or hookworm disease. The hookworms live as parasites in the intestines, sucking blood and thereby causing anaemia.[114] The larvae of these parasites develop in the human faeces very commonly spread in the vicinity of dwellings in the plantations. They reach the intestines by boring through the skin when the faeces are stepped on by the bare feet of the workers. Provision of latrines and simple sandals were the two main preventive measures suggested by Dr Wilson.[115] This disease, which affected thousands of workers rendering them apathetic, lethargic and feeble,[116] was thus directly connected with insanitary conditions in the camps. In the case of plantation labour the hookworm anaemia was made worse by lack of iron intake in their diet: so even light infection tended to cause anaemia.[117] Hookworm anaemia is also considered the cause of many heart failures.[118]

The other major killers listed in Table 2.2 — tuberculosis, malaria, dysentery, diarrhoea — are all known to be connected with insanitary conditions and inadequate diet. 'Tuberculosis has notoriously been associated with poverty, which means malnutrition, overcrowding and industrial stress.'[119] Dysentery and diarrhoea, on the other hand, are inevitable where the water supply is contaminated, flies proliferate and there

Table 2.2 *Deaths of plantation labourers from illness in Tanga Province, 1 Jan. 1933 –*
6 June 1936

Disease	No. of deaths	%
Ankylostomiasis	105	26.9
Pneumonia	75	19.2
Tuberculosis	32	8.2
Dysentery	23	5.9
Malaria	23	5.9
Diarrhoea	17	4.3
Heart failure	16	4.1
Heart disease	16	4.1
Liver cyrrhosis	13	3.3
Cerebral haemmorhage	13	3.3
Colitis	9	2.3
Typhoid	5	1.3
Debility	5	1.3
Lung abscess	4	1.0
Nephritis	3	0.8
Pleurisy	3	0.8
Drowning	3	0.8
Abscesses	3	0.8
Anaemia	3	0.8
Asthma	2	0.5
Cystotis	2	0.5
Meningitis	2	0.5
Syphilis	2	0.5
Yaws	2	0.5
Appendicitis	1	
Bilharzia	1	
Bronchitis	1	
Bee stings	1	
Blood poisoning	1	0.3
Hernia	1	
Hodelin disease	1	
Poisoning	1	
Snakebite	1	
Tetanus	1	
	391	100.0

Source: Same as Table 2.1 above.

is no adequate and proper disposal of human waste. The conditions on the labour lines, as we have already seen, were ideal for breeding these diseases. Warnings, like the one given to Tongoni Sisal Estate Ltd in 1945, were not uncommon: 'you will recollect that during the first half of 1945, there were six deaths among labour on your estate, which government is advised were all attributable to dysentery or typhoid and suggested that the standard of accommodation provided for labour on your estate left much to be desired'.[120] But then these warnings, few and far between as they were, did very little to improve the general conditions.

True, the care and welfare provisions of the Master and Native Servants Ordinance provided for supplying medical assistance to the sick workers but these were riddled with loop-holes, insufficient enforcement and numerous abuses. Let us examine some of these legal provisions.

Sections 8 and 9 of the Master and Native Servants Ordinance[121] provided that every servant whose contract was for more than sixty days' duration had to be medically examined by a government medical officer or a medical practitioner and unless he was certified to be physically fit to perform the work contemplated by the proposed contract, the contract would not be attested.[122] The medical officers were paid a fee of Sh. 1 for each person examined. In practice therefore there was a temptation on the part of the medical officers to make things easy for the recruiters resulting in very perfunctory medical examinations.[123] In many cases the examination was with a view to determine if the person concerned was *fit to travel* rather than fit to engage in the work proposed in the contract.[124] This resulted in cases of unfit persons passing medical control. For example, when a very high death rate (280 per 1,000 per annum)[125] among Tanganyika Africans constructing the Uasin Gishu railway in Kenya caused a scandal, it was revealed that a very high proportion of the recruits were probably not fit when recruited.[126] The rest no doubt could not withstand the deplorable conditions of food and housing at the place of employement. Even those certified fit were thoroughly exhausted by the rigours of the journey, and vulnerable to attacks by the time they arrived at the place of employment. Poor conditions at the plantation further worsened their conditions.

At the places of employment medical facilities were meagre. Under the law (s. 25(5) of M & NSO), the employer was supposed to provide 'proper medicines during illness and also if procurable with medical attendance during serious illness'. In practice, in a considerable number of cases, this meant minimal drugs hardly adequate even for first aid purposes; dilapidated dispensaries manned by unqualified dressers and a very small number of beds for in-patients. In Dr Mackay's medical survey conducted around 1939, it was found that while 61 of the 65 estates had dispensaries manned by dressers, only 35 had hospitals with beds while only 32 were visited by qualified doctors.[128] Dr. Mackay calculated that there were 324 hospital beds on 64 estates, giving 0.0073 bed per labourer on the basis of 696.5 mean daily average number. The state of drugs and dispensaries on some estates invited harsh comments from labour inspectors. The inspection report of 1927 on one of the principal estates in the Tanga Province belonging to Messrs Bird & Co. noted:

Medical arrangements. There is an iron shed which is used as a dispensary and sick ward for minor cases which is in charge of two native dressers. The stock of medicines appeared to be very limited and the state of the bottles etc., did not reflect much credit on the trained dressers. There was one case of pneumonia sitting on the cement floor with a blanket round him and when the European who was with me told the dresser to supply the man with another blanket the reply was that there were no more.[129]

Commenting on the dispensary at the Lusando Estate near Dar es Salaam which employed some 250 workers, a labour inspector observed:

Hospital Dispensary — condemned by me on 2.7.46. The room occupied is an unclean hovel with open door leading to a dirty store. Was locked when my inspection took place. There was no water, towel or soap in the dispensary. No dresser is employed on the grounds that the Manager or his Assistant are always available which is not the case when they are absent in Dar es Salaam or away in the Shamba [field]. A notice is being served upon the Manager regarding this state of affairs. In a corner of the dispensary room was a hen sitting on a clutch of seven eggs but who apparently was not disconcerted by our visit. The non-employment of a hospital assistant is regarded as a parsimonious measure in keeping with other matters prevailing in this estate.[130]

The medical facilities for workers involved in railway construction were no better, in many cases the dispensary being no more than a grass hut with a very few beds. The example of the Kidete camp hospital is illustrative. It catered for some 3,000 workers. The dispensary itself was a temporary structure and could house no more than twenty people. It was in the charge of an 'Indian compounder . . . assisted by an African Dresser and two labourers'.[131] There were no proper beds but improvised ones made from *matete* (reeds) and poles. This was the 'hospital' which was providing medical treatment to an average of some 400 out-patients every month.[132]

The medical facilities in the mining areas were worse than anywhere else. The medical facilities — or rather the lack of them — are well captured in the following report on the Lupa controlled area:

[A] small mud hut, with ten beds under the supervision of a native dispenser and which acts as a clearing station, is the only facility offered to the employer. The only other alternative is the hospital at Mbeya, 60 or more miles away across the mountains. Prospectors, struggling to make a bare living, are hardly likely to welcome the suggestion that they should detach two or three of their scanty labour force for several days at a time to escort a sick comrade to the hospital. As a natural result of this reluctancy a native labourer who becomes sick is often dismissed from the camp in which he is working either to make his way unassisted to his home, perhaps in Rhodesia or Tukuyu, or to recover as best as he can, or die . . . The majority of the diggers, again, because of their lack of means do not stock medical facilities, and also often entirely ignorant, would only run the risk of killing their patients, if they did.

The average number of natives at present being treated in the Chunya dispensary is about 40 in-patients per month, whilst about 600 visits a month are paid by out-patients. Owing to the dispensary hut only having 10 beds, in-patients are often obliged to sleep on the floor between the beds of their more fortunate comrades. About 20 patients are transferred monthly to Myeba. The death rate at the dispensary at Chunya, during the wet season, is about 10 per month. The principal sickness are scurvy, bronchitis about 40 to 50 cases each per month, pneumonia 2 to 3 cases, fever 30 to 50 cases, and diarrhoea 15 to 20 per month . . . The food supplied in the hospital, except in certain cases, is mealie meal and beans, whilst lemons are procured from the local tradesmen.[133]

The usual response of the labour officers when discovering such deplorable conditions on their inspection was to send notices to the employers. Prosecutions were rare unless the conditions caused many deaths and the incident became scandalous. However, when the cases did go to courts they faced the usual technical problems. The interpretation of the law in the majority of cases tended to be biased in favour of the employers. For instance, in the case of *R.* v. *H. Milde*[134] the judge went so far as to make a distinction between 'illness' and 'serious illness' and argued that according to section 25(5) of the Master and Native Servants Ordinance the employer's liability was simply to provide proper medicines during illness while he was obliged to provide *medical attendance* only during *serious illness* and not simply illness. In another case of *R.* v. *M. K. A. Uberle*,[135] which arose from the Morogoro tragedy to be discussed later, the employer's conviction for failure to provide medical attendance was upheld by the High Court but quashed by the Court of Appeal. In that case a worker was injured in his left eye on 1 November 1937 while working on the estate. He was not sent to hospital for medical attendance until twelve days later; as a result he lost the sight of his eye. The Court of Appeal argued that in order to prove the offence the prosecution ought to prove: '(a) that the servant was during the relevant period suffering from an illness which a person of the class of the employer ought to have realized was serious; (b) that medical attendance was procurable; (c) that the employer knowing that his servant was suffering from such illness did not provide medical attendance'.[136] In this case, their lordships argued, there was no evidence to show that at the time when the servant reported the injury it was serious. 'If it only appeared trivial it might well have been reasonable for the employer to consider that treatment by the dresser would suffice.'[137]

Secondly, they said, there was nothing in the evidence showing that medical attendance was in fact procurable. It is interesting to contrast this opinion with the observations of the judge of the High Court on these same points. The judge there had observed that the doctor in his evidence had testified that the iris was protruding through a wound in the eye and that, in the words of the doctor, it was a 'very severe eye condition through which I considered he would almost certainly lose the sight of his left eye'. The judge went on to comment: 'That does not seem to me at any rate to be a trivial illness or one that could not be called serious *at any* stage of its occurrence' (my emphasis).[138] On the question of the availability of medical assistance the judge had taken judicial notice of the fact that 'skilled medical aid was available a few miles away'.[139] In spite of these observations, the Justices of Appeal felt that the case had not been proved beyond reasonable doubt and so did the prosecution who did not support the conviction on appeal to the Court of Appeal.

Finally, to illustrate the various points that we have made so far we can do no better than recount the Morogoro tragedy.[140] This incident occurred in 1937 and became a big scandal. Between January and 8 November 1937 some 1,052 workers from the sisal estates of the Morogoro District, probably employing a total of around 5,000 long-distance workers, were admitted to the Morogoro hospital. Out of these 158 died, 86 of them from diarrhoea and others from such diseases as pneumonia, malaria, relapsing fever, hookworm, tuberculosis and cerebro-spinal meningitis. The Morogoro hospital itself, described by one commentator as 'a wretched building dating from German times, constructed of concrete and iron, and quite unsuitable for its purpose', was housing some three to four times its capacity during this period. Many of these workers had been recruited from Bukoba, Mwanza and Mbeya and were quite unfit even when they arrived on the estates. Even then they passed the medical examination at the point of recruitment, which prompted one colonial official to call it 'farcical' since it consisted in 'deciding whether the individual was fit to travel to work rather than actually fit to work'.

One of the estates involved in this tragedy was Tungi Estates Ltd managed by one Major Mullar, a German, who had been hitherto considered a good manager by the labour officers. In the six months from January to June 1937, some 480 workers had been recruited for Major Mullar's estate. According to the manager's report, at the end of June 1937 there were only about 80 per cent still working. Some 23 (or 5 per cent) had died; 30 (or 6 per cent) had been repatriated because of ill-health; 13 (or 3 per cent) were in hospital, and 26 (or 5 per cent) had deserted. The inspection report on the estate revealed that conditions, especially with regard to food, were deplorable. The ration consisted of 32 ounces of maize meal, 6 ounces of beans and 4 ounces of salt per week, 10 cents was given for meat on Saturday to those who worked for five days. The ration was not given in kind but by chit to be presented to the Indian shops. No rations were provided to the absentees. Many of the deaths were as a result of diarrhoea which the medical officer categorized as a nutritional disorder occurring in people who were used to the diet of bananas, milk and eggs and were now subjected to nothing but an exclusively starchy diet.

Furthermore, when the sick were repatriated by the estate not enough provision was made for their transport, nor were they given enough rations for the journey. The conditions on Tungi Estate were not exceptional but typical. A colonial official summarized the 'faults of the estates' as follows:

The faults of the estates were various. They can be called mostly sins of omission since the manager appears to have displayed a lack of interest in the welfare of the labourers which is exceptional. There was no examination of new recruits; there was, apparently, (contrary to the provisions of section 2 of the Master and Servants Ordinance) no record of service; labour cards were never correctly filled up; there was no system of roll call; there was a definite system by which no food was given if no work was done contrary to section 25 of the ordinance; there was a system by which labourers were given chits to be served on two Indian dukas [shop]. During [sick parade] the absence passed unnoticed; medical officers were never notified; and those who were hopelessly ill were repatriated, no arrangements were made for their return by the way they had come (against the provisions of section 27 of the Master and Servants Ordinance); nor, contrary to section 25(5) were MOs informed of the return. There were, in addition, numerous infringements with regard to the living conditions of the labourers; food measures were underweight; meat issues were spasmodic or conditional; flour meals were filthy; hours were too long; there was no provision for latrines; the siting of the lines was frequently as badly designed as the individual huts were built. There was considerable danger from machinery for children; and there was never any attempt at precautions against infectious diseases. All together, the picture presented . . . is dismal, and yet most of its gruest [sic] details spring directly from 'faulty management'.[141]

But it was not only the estates which were at fault. The colonial officials admitted in their correspondence that the inspection of the estates had been neglected over a long period of time.

This scandal gave rise to voluminous correspondence among the colonial officials, numerous meetings and some warnings *but no prosecutions*. In spite of the various contraventions and numerous deaths not a single manager was prosecuted for manslaughter or criminal negligence. The Attorney-General thought that there was enough evidence for such prosecutions, as was clear from the inquests, and yet the governor, the Provincial Commissioner and the police were against what they called 'primitive measures' like prosecution! The police even neglected to carry out proper investigations into these deaths with a view to pin criminal responsibility. The Attorney-General indignantly wrote in his long letter:

The failure of the police to undertake a thorough investigation into these deaths appears, from the above facts and from other facts which have been brought to my notice, to be due to pressure brought upon them or representations made to them by or through the provincial commissioner and district officer concerned that no prosecution should be undertaken against these employers.[142]

The governor took strong objections to these remarks and argued that not enough evidence was available. Only three prosecutions were instituted and those too for failure to provide medical attention. Convictions resulted in two cases, one of which was quashed on appeal.

Be that as it may. The incident does, however, illustrate an important point. In the colonial state, the judicial machinery acted very little, if at all, as an ultimate guardian of law and justice that it is made out to be in bourgeois democracies. It was the executive which played the dominant role. And the executive, as this incident demonstrates, acted in close concert with employers and capital as a whole.

Female and child labour

It is difficult to determine with any accuracy the extent of the employment of women and children in the colonial economy of the pre-Second World War period. The first enumerations of labour were not conducted until the late 1940s and early 1950s. However, from various reports it appears that although women and children did not constitute a very large proportion of the employed labour force, it was quite substantial, averaging 10–15 per cent of total wage-labour between 1947 and 1951.[143] Juvenile labour constituted almost three-fourths of this.

Much of this labour was concentrated in agriculture in such tasks as weeding and clearing, coffee picking and tea-harvesting, in the picking of pyrethrum flowers and kapok.[144] Child labour was also employed in sisal estates on the drying lines, in mining breaking ore and in ginneries feeding gins.[145] See also Appendix, Table A.2.

Within the cheap colonial labour force, women and juvenile labour constituted the cheapest. It was paid much less than male labour and filled an important gap especially during the shortage of labour. A few examples of wage rate will illustrate the extent of cheapness of female and juvenile labour. An inspection report on Mbagalla Estate in 1941 mentioned that women were being paid Shs. 7 for thirty tasks while male adults received Shs. 10 for the same.[146] In the Lusanda Sisal Estate the data for the same year show that women were being paid half of the wage rates of their male counterparts.[147] In 1933 the wage rates in the sisal estates of the Dar es Salaam district for unskilled children varied from Shs. 2.50 to Shs. 3.50 and rations, compared to unskilled adult workers' wages of Shs. 8-10 per month plus rations.[148] In mining, wages paid to juveniles were also low. In the Musoma mining areas in 1933, the average wage for unskilled adult labour was around Shs. 9 per month while juvenile labour was paid Shs. 4-5 per month and in one case as low as Shs. 2. Wages varied with age and capacity.[149] And in many instances the tasks done by juvenile labour were no less than adult male labour. For instance, in a number of mines juvenile labour was employed to break ore by hand 'to the consistency of fine ballast'[150] before it was fed to the mills. The standard task for the job was one standard cement drum full of broken ore per day. The District Officer reporting on this was moved to comment: 'the idea of a small child breaking up 120 lb of stone a day for 30 days for a remuneration of Shs. 2 seems uncommonly like sweated labour'.[151]

Figures for earlier periods are not available to enable us to draw comparisons between wage rates of male, female and juvenile labour on a country-wide basis. The data for 1951 in Table 2.3 we believe are probably representative of the general wage discrimination against female and juvenile labour. As the table shows, almost 100 and over 90 per cent of the juvenile and female labour respectively fell below the monthly wage of Shs. 39 compared to some 65 per cent of the adult male labour. The same story

Table 2.3 *Male, female and juvenile labour in regular employment, according to monthly wage rates, 1951*

Wage rate in Shs. per month	Adult males		Adult females		Juveniles	
	No.	%	No.	%	No.	%
0–19	59 598	18.4	9 314	55.2	26 934	92.6
20–39	149 078	46.0	6 336	37.6	2 032	7.0
40–49	46 240	14.3	508	3.0	86	0.3
50–59	20 082	6.2	249	1.5	41	0.1
60–69	13 019	4.1	171	1.0		
70–79	9 495	2.9	83	0.5		
80–89	9 608	3.0	148	0.9		
100–149	10 828	3.3	44	0.3		
150–199	3 320	1.0	6	0.0		
200 & above	2 932	0.9	—	—		
Total	324 200	100.0	16 859	100.0	29 093	100.0

Source: Annual Report of the Labour Department, 1951, Table IV.

is repeated in the case of higher wage brackets where hardly 1 per cent of the women workers earned more than Shs. 70 per month compared to some 10 per cent of their male counterparts. Not that the males earned particularly high wages either; but the point is that within the colonial system of extremely low wages, female and juvenile labour was the lowest on the wage scale. Employers therefore consistently fought for retaining this type of labour and, as we shall see, were extremely hostile to any legislation prohibiting and/or regulating juvenile and female labour.[152]

The local colonial policy-makers and administrators also consistently defended juvenile labour. Their main rationalization was that the work in which this labour was employed was light and not harmful; that in the absence of schools, youngsters were gainfully employed in this way and augmented the meagre earnings of their parents. In the latter two arguments the very 'evils' of the system created by the colonialists had become in turn a justification for perpetuating the 'evil' of child labour. The argument that child labour was employed only in light work was simply not true. Let us examine in some detail the conditions of work of juvenile labour to illustrate this point.

Coffee-picking and tea-harvesting, which involved back-breaking work for at least five hours, could certainly not be considered 'light' for a child of 8–10 years. Even tea-sorting which colonial officials considered light, involved sitting in cramped positions on hard desks, which medical opinion considered unhealthy for children.[153] Elsewhere children were employed in dangerous occupations and jobs involving hard manual work. Drying sisal fibre on the lines where juvenile labour was commonly employed exposed them to the risk of accidents as the drying lines tended to be close to locomotive tracks.[154] In the mines children were often employed as hammer boys to break up ore.[155] When a colonial official drew attention to this in the case of Aureole mines, where some forty children were employed to break stones, his colleague cynically minuted:

The use of watoto [children] . . . is common practice throughout the mining fields. They are normally the off-spring of the labourers and in the absence of schools nearby they are, I consider, better occupied in 'playing with stones' then in other forms of amusement peculiar to young Africans [sic!]. Seldom is the work arduous: usually the children are proud to receive a work-card and jubilant when paid.[156]

Elsewhere children were often employed to carry heavy loads without regard to their age and physique. On one of his inspections, an inspector found children carrying karais (metal vessels) filled·with stones weighing 25 lb. They were working on building the Arusha–Moshi road.[157] At the Kaoline Mine visited in 1946, an inspector found some eight children pushing iron wheelbarrows containing stone and wheeling dangerously parallel to a railway siding.[158] In another incident, on a visit to a TSGA labour camp in July 1945, a district officer found that children of approximately 12–14 years of age were employed in carrying bricks roughly weighing 35 lb. They were given an option of carrying either 50 or 100 mud bricks and paid correspondingly. After finishing this work, they were also allowed to carry fitos (poles) on the same day. When the district officer stopped this, the well-known employer and leader of the Sisal Growers' Association, Le Maitre, asked the children to continue in defiance. What did the colonial enforcement agencies do about this flagrant violation of their law? As usual, correspondence ensued back and forth and by the time they decided to take any action a long time had elapsed so the matter was closed![159]

Probably one of the most gruesome incidents that the author came across showing complete disregard for the life and limbs of child workers was a fatal accident that occurred in 1943 at Kingumi Estate in the district of Mbulu. This accident became subject of an inquest[160] and therefore we have more data on record than would otherwise be the case. It is therefore worth recapturing the incident in some detail.

The Kingumi Estate was owned by one Mrs Rydon. It had a system of recruiting its labour from the West Lake by sending its headman, who, besides his wages, got Shs. 2´ bonus for every person he brought. These workers were neither medically examined nor attested on contract. A number of Warundi children, most of them probably 14 years of age since they did not have pubic hair, had been recruited. The deceased was one of them. In his testimony, one of the youths testified that they had been promised some clothing ('. . . shorts and a *sharti ya mpira* [football jerseys] and a blanket . . . ') and it was this which induced them to sign on for nine *kipande* (labour cards). But when they arrived they were given no clothing. Their wages ranged from Shs. 6 to Shs. 12 per card. As for rations the youth testified:

We get flour, beans and karanga [peanuts] as rations. Also fish — if you do six days work in a week. If you do five days only you don't get any. Two dried fish are given. We used to be given Shs. 2 every 4 weeks to buy meat but now we do not get any. We also have permission to take pawpaws. This is a new order. Previously if you took a pawpaw you would get 6 strokes.[161]

The witness himself weighed only 84½ lb, his pubic hair had just started to grow and he was in a 'very poor condition with dull skin and a type of scabies affliction in the corners of his mouth and on his wrists and back of hands.'

On the fateful day of 10 March 1943, a group of seven such youths had been taken by a headman to carry planks. According to the Greek manager of the estate, the planks were 13 feet long, and 10 inches by 3 inches. Its weight, measured after the accident, was 187 lb. — more than twice the weight of the heaviest youth in the group which was supposed to carry it. Let the headman who accompanied the youths tell the story:

We picked one [plank] up, but I saw it was too heavy for all 7 youths to carry, so I had it put on one side. We lifted another and carried it. The 6 youths only carried it but deceased did not help. He was taller than the rest and it made it awkard if he helped. When we got near the river the others called out in Kirundi and I and deceased went to help till we crossed the river. I returned across the river to put my shoes on as I had taken them off to cross. The party with the plank were by that time out of my sight in the grass. There were 4 carrying the plank, 3 were behind still in my sight. I heard some one call to say 'a man is hurt'. This was in Kiswahili. I ran and saw a man lying down. I don't know his name but he was the youth who died. The plank (baulk) was lying on top of him. (Witness demonstrates with an onlooker and a bit of timber, showing that deceased was lying flat on his back with the plank lying slightly diagonally across his chest, the end of the plank reaching to and immediately above the face of deceased. (Intd. H. A. F.) The arms of deceased were bent up at the elbows as though he were trying to thrust the weight off him . . . He was not quite dead. He died just then and was buried that day.[162]

There is very little doubt as revealed by this inquest that the death was a result of gross negligence on the part of the estate manager and his headman. In spite of that, Mrs Rydon, the owner, was not prosecuted.[163]

The conditions of work of child labour which caused a stir even among colonial officials were to be found in the ginneries. The reports of the inspectors visiting ginneries revealed that a great deal of child labour was employed under very bad conditions in the ginneries. Children were employed mainly to feed the gins, which entailed sitting in cramped positions for eleven or twelve hours, the usual length of a shift. 'Working in a ginnery can never be looked upon as a pleasant form of occupation, but when there is no outlet for the dust and fluff, inseparable from the ginning of cotton, then it can only be considered as a mild form of purgatory.'[164]

This purgatory was dramatically described by one Dr Bell, a medical officer, in his article 'Visit to a Ginnery'.[165] The article, dated June 1939, was sent to the then 'Tanganyika Notes and Records' for publication but was blocked by the colonial secretariat.

In this particular ginnery, Dr Bell found that children of some 9–14 years of age were being employed. They all worked for eleven or twelve hours at Shs. 6 per thirty days' work. Their homes were very distant: some of them lived as far away as six miles which, according to the doctor, could have taken them as much as three hours to walk. 'Twelve miles each day for those undernourished little legs! The last ones to arrive at the ginnery are not given work, and must return empty handed to their parents, so that three hours must be allowed for the journey. Add it up and it comes to twelve hours work and six hours journeying to and fro.' During the night shift the children had to be kept awake by overseers, the *wanyapara*, who walked up and down the factory floor with sticks.

They were the employees of real importance. Other grown men did the porterage, but the sole job of these was to keep the children awake. They never touched them. The threat of force was enough, and scarcely enough for the older boys, who half opened their eyes with a grin, pushed the cotton along, and shut them again. They must have been worth a lot of money. At one time the overseer went out for a while. Immediately these two men relaxed their vigilance, nineteen of the little heads nodded onto their chests, nineteen gins were empty, oil was being wasted, profits reduced.

It was only when the conditions of child labour reached such scandalous proportion that the colonial officials began to think in terms of regulating it by legislation. The Cotton Ginneries (Age of Employment) Regulations of 1939[166]prohibited employment of any person in ginneries below the age of 14.[167] The only other legislation of any importance on child labour before 1940 was the Employment of Children on Machinery Regulations of 1927[168]which prohibited the employment of a child below the age of 16 years in cleaning 'any part of any machinery worked by water, steam or other mechanical power' (reg. 3). In 1931, the law was amended prohibiting children from working in the sisal brush rooms 'unless the machinery therein is protected in such manner as to prevent the approach of any unauthorized person within three feet of such machinery'.[169]

On female labour there was virtually no legislation except a short Ordinance passed in 1938 prohibiting employment of women in 'night work' in any 'industrial under-taking' (s. 3).[170] Thus for virtually twenty years of British colonial rule no important legislation on female and child labour existed on the statute book. The meagre legislation that existed in the form of Machinery Regulations was itself notorious for lack of enforcement. Labour officers often complained that children would run away when approached by labour officers. It was therefore difficult to identify and present the children concerned in courts for purposes of prosecution.[171]

Parents too had an ambivalent attitude towards child labour. They detested child labour (particularly female child labour) for fear of losing parental control. Yet to the extent that the earnings of the children contributed to the common pool and alleviated their deplorable economic conditions,[172]parents were prepared to 'collude' with the system. As one colonial report put it in characteristically patronizing style:

It has not been a very good year in this province owing to locusts and food shortage and one can understand the temptation, in many cases no doubt the necessity, for the children to become wage-earners at as early an age as is possible, so as to provide themselves with the food and clothing which their parents have not been able to give them. There seems too to be a growing tendency on the part of parents to shirk [sic!]their responsibility in this respect, and to tell their children that if they want food and clothes they must go and work for them.[173]

There was another factor underlying the colonial officials' reluctance to prohibit child labour. It was a common practice among migrant labour to be accompanied by their own or relatives' and friends' children. These children were often employed, thereby augmenting, to some extent, the rations provided by the employers. Far-sighted colonial officials realized that prohibition of child labour would have a two-fold effect. First, it might cause some problem with the supply of labour in that migrants might refuse to go without children. Secondly, and most importantly, if the adults were accompanied by children and yet these children were prohibited from being employed, it would reduce the rations available to the adults thereby further depressing the nutritional standard of the adult labour to the ultimate disadvantage of the employer.[174]

Apart from these considerations, the most important pressure perpetuating child labour came, of course, from the employers, particularly the Northern Province set-tlers. In this, they had consistent support of the local colonial policy-makers. The only local opposition to child labour came from missionaries, principally those involved in running schools.[175] The employment of children on coffee-picking and other jobs competed with attendance at schools and, if the attendance fell below 50 per cent, the schools forfeited grants from the government. This is where the missionaries came up against the planters. Even then, the missionaries tried to accommodate the planters' interests by synchronizing school vacations with peak harvesting seasons. But the planters' appetite for cheap child labour was insatiable. A letter from a supervisor of village schools under the Universities Mission to Central Africa, on his visit to Tongwe Parish in Tanga, is illustrative of the conflict between the missionaries and the employers on the issue:

The parents find that the children, both boys and girls, from the age about 8 or 9 are accepted for work and so they send the children to work and stay at home themselves [sic]. In some cases the Mzungu [European] goes to the school and more or less compels the children to go to work for him. Then they are written down for a thirty days contract, with wages according to their size beginning with Shs. 3.50 or Shs. 4.00 for the smaller ones.

I went to see Mr Tate (Junior) who is working the Ng'ambo shamba beyond Amani. I asked him if he would take on school children for a week only — he said that 30 days was the government regulation contract and he could not alter it. Is it really meant to apply to children of nine?

Then he said that when the coffee is ripe he proposes to take all the school children and that the work would take two months. In fact he was generally unsympathetic and seemed to think that education was a ridiculous fad of the mission and that the people only exist to do his work. Can he compel the children to go to work for him legally? Then when I go back to Tongwe I found a big drop in the attendance because the pepper is ripe at Lunguza and again the children who have gone are small. After a month or so at work they have no desire to come back to school and in many cases they are spoilt morally, and even physically.

The net result of all this is that in a school anywhere near a shamba the children, after the age of 9 or 10 when they can read 'Esopo' only come to school on odd days when they are too tired to work in the fields or for periods when there is little work to be done. Hence we have few suitable candidates for central schools.[176]

The author of this letter no doubt showed a clearer understanding of the role of mission schools in the longer-run interests of the colonial economy than the employers when he added: 'They [planters] seem to want karani [clerks] etc. who know English — they would not get them so long as they dam up the supply from the source.'

The pressure of the colonial employers in collaboration with the local bureaucracy kept legislation on child labour at bay for some eighteen years after the British govern-ment had become a party to the International Conventions fixing the minimum age for child labour.[177] When the legislation was finally adopted in 1940, the same interests ensured that it had no 'teeth' and was placed on the statute book simply to placate international opinion.

The story of the Employment of Women and Young Persons Ordinance, 1940,[178] needs to be told in some detail for it is a good illustration of the way in which the colonial legislative and bureaucratic machinery worked and ultimately protected the interests of capital.

In his dispatch of 21 December 1939 the Secretary of State pointed out that the relevant International Conventions fixing minimum age of employment for child labour had been adopted and accepted by HM government some eighteen years ago; that Tanganyika was the only colony thus far which had no legislation in this respect. Until 1940, the only legislation that existed were the 1927 Machinery Regulations prohibiting the employment of children near machinery; the Cotton Ginneries Regulations prescribing the minimum age for employment in the ginneries; and the 1938 Employment of Women Ordinance prohibiting night-work for women. The result of the pressure from the colonial office in London was the passing of the Employment of Women and Young Persons Ordinance, 1940. The Ordinance divided non-adults into three categories: children, juveniles and young persons. A 'young person' was defined as a person under the age of 18 years; a 'juvenile' meant a young person under the age of 16 years; and a 'child' was defined as a juvenile under the age of 14. The only restriction that applied in the case of young persons was employment as trimmers or stokers on ships (s. 13). Otherwise a young person could be employed on ships provided there was a medical certificate certifying that he was fit for the work (s. 4). Juveniles and women could not be employed in any industrial undertaking between the hours of 5 p.m. and 7 a.m. (s. 10). Juveniles could be employed even outside their districts of residence or within their districts in circumstances where they could not return home at the end of day's work, provided this was done with the approval of a labour officer and on a written contract the terms of which were also approved by such officer (s. 5). There were certain prescribed occupations — porter, fuel cutter, sisal cutter, trolley and rickshaw-boy — in which it was prohibited to employ a juvenile and in any other employment which would be injurious to his health, dangerous or immoral (s. 6). What would be injurious to health, dangerous or immoral was not defined in the law but was left for an administrative or labour officer to decide (s. 6(2)). The only other restriction on the employment of juvenile labour was that it could not be employed for more than eight hours a day nor for more than four consecutive hours. In the absence of a strong inspectorate, such a provision could hardly be enforced and was undoubtedly a 'toothless' provision on the statute book. Thus it can be seen that in the case of juvenile labour the law did not go much further than some meagre regulation and supervision.

The most controversial provisions related to the employment of child labour, that is, those under 14 years of age. Here employment of children in any industrial undertaking was completely prohibited (s. 9) while in any other work it was regulated by providing that 'a child shall be employed [on] a daily wage, and on a day to day basis, and only so long as the child returns each night to the place of residence of his parent of guardian' (s. 4). This left fairly open the employment of children in agriculture which in any case was the most important sector where child labour was engaged. As a matter of fact, even in the case of 'industrial undertaking' the governor was given powers to exempt any industrial undertaking from the provisions of the law (s. 3). No sooner was this law passed than the government received representations from the diamond and tea industries where children from the age of 8 to 14 were employed in sorting diamonds from gravel and sorting tea. As a result, diamond-sorting was exempted, the minimum age for this activity being fixed at 9 years.[179]

The exemption of diamond-sorting and the proposed exemption of tea-sorting contrary to medical opinion gave rise to another series of correspondence between the Secretary of State and the governor. The Secretary of State wrote that both diamond-sorting and tea-sorting fell within the definition of 'industrial undertaking' and children below the age of 14 should not be allowed to be employed in these industries. The colonial authorities had no alternative but to comply and the earlier order exempting diamond-sorting was revoked.[180] In the course of the correspondence, however, the Secretary of State also drew attention to his predecessor's circular of 29 September 1938 which prescribed the minimum age of employment of children in any undertaking at 12 years and exceptions were to be permitted only 'when the employment is with the child's own family — and involves light work of an agriculture or other character, which has been specifically approved by the competent government authority'.

The discussion that ensued among the colonial officials clearly shows that they were not at all in favour of prescribing a minimum age for they very well knew that it would have meant prohibition of child labour — under 12 years — in sectors where it was most important. The Labour Advisory Board, which was made up of officials and representatives of the employers, also made representations against prescribing a minimum age on the flimsy grounds that it was difficult to determine the age of an African child, that it would be difficult to enforce such provisions and in any case the employment of children in agriculture (for example) was not harmful to their health. The Secretary of State refused to accept these representations.

In the course of preparing an amending legislation to give effect to the Secretary of State's instructions, there developed an argument as to what the Secretary meant by 'when the employment is with the child's own family'. There were those who argued that this meant simply 'employed' just at home, in cattle-herding, domestic work and so on, while the other side interpreted this to mean 'employed' by someone else but with parents. The governor himself realized that the second interpretation would in fact circumvent the Secretary's order but did not mind it so long as the Attorney-General could produce authority for that view.[181]

Finally, when the amending Ordinance came to be tabled, it had undergone interesting changes that completely watered down the original intentions and instructions. The relevant section which was incorporated in law[182] read:

No child under the age of twelve years shall be employed except in company with its parents (or one of them), or in company with the child's guardian recognized as such by native custom, and on light work, of an agricultural or other character, which has been approved by a labour officer or an administrative officer.

Thus 'employed with the child's own family' in the original instructions of the Secretary of State came to be conveniently interpreted as meaning 'in company with its parents'. The term 'parents' was conveniently expanded to embrace the child's guardian recognized as such by native custom. Even the term 'guardian' was conveniently stretched to its limit in an administrative circular from the Chief Secretary to all administrative, medical and labour officers, informing them that 'the expression "guardian recognized as such by native custom" is intended to include any person to whose care children have been committed, even temporarily, by those who have authority over them . . .'[183]

The net result was that this amending Ordinance would leave the employment of children under 12 years in coffee, pyrethrum and tea estates virtually undisturbed. The Chief Secretary himself when presenting the amending legislation before the Legislative Council admitted that the amending Ordinance would involve no considerable change in the existing practice. Answering an unofficial member, a representative of the employers who described the law as a 'white-wash' and 'tongue-in-cheek' legislation, the Chief Secretary retorted that 'white-wash' might be valuable and continued:

We are all proud to belong to the British Colonial Empire. We are all hoping that after the war Tanganyika will be much more closely knit to the Empire than it was before. The Empire is exposed to a great deal of criticism not only from across the Atlantic and elsewhere, and I submit that by passing this little bit of legislation here we are adding a little tiny brick to the defensive wall which His Majesty's Government is trying to build round the Colonial Empire, a wall of defence against the tide of hostile and uninstructed criticism which does a great deal of harm .[184]

Probably, the London office too did not take the whole exercise more seriously than 'building a defensive wall round the Colonial Empire' for, in spite of the obvious watering down of the original instructions, the Secretary of State did not use his powers to disallow the Ordinance. It came into effect on 1 January 1944. But, as the Chief Secretary had earlier predicted with satisfaction, its effect in practice was negligible. Employment of child labour continued unabated. The Annual Labour Report on Tanga Province for 1949 made a veiled admission when it said: 'Although the law governing the employment of women and children has been in force for ten years it is surprising how many employers appear to be totally unaware of the provisions thereof.'[185]

How could employers be aware of the provisions of a law which was never meant to be seriously implemented?

We shall deal with female and child labour in domestic service in chapter 4.

Other conditions of work

In this section we briefly deal with an aspect of personal relationship between employers and employees — injuries and accidents at work and the provision of fringe benefits.

Flogging

The use of overt force in both the obtaining and retaining of labour that was an important characteristic of the early history of labour manifested itself on many occasions even at the level of personal relationship in the form of beating of workers. Virtually despotic master–servant relationships became even more oppressive by the intense racial prejudices of the employers and their agents who were always either Europeans or Indians. Insubordination or resistance on the part of individual workers would be interpreted by the employer as personal insult or abuse. In fact, under the Master and Native Servants Ordinance it was a criminal offence on the part of a servant to use 'any abusive or insulting language to his employer or to any person placed by his employer in authority over him . . .' (s. 40).

During the German period both official and unofficial flogging was widespread. 'Between 1901 and 1913 the government sentenced 64,652 Africans to corporal punishment, or an average of five a week at every district office in the country.'[186] No records were kept of unofficial flogging administered as 'parental correction' but there is no doubt it was widespread. In 1912–13 some 107 employers were convicted of assaulting their workers. This, however, is no measure of the extent of beating because 'natives were punished if they brought charges against their employers which they were unable to prove, and therefore usually suffered in silence'.[187]

This antiquated system of disciplining workers was justified in racial terms: after all, the African was very low on the racial scale and like a child required compulsion to educate him and make him work. The vocabulary reflected the racial theory. African child labour was referred to as '*totos*'* and African adult workers as 'boys'. This racial theory maintained that loyalty and obedience could be extracted from an African only by a master who was 'just but firm' and that an African 'is a born slave who needs his despot like an opium addict needs his pipe'.[188]

Corporal punishment was probably not as widespread during the British rule but a few cases that reached courts are an indication that there must have been many more which went unreported. In some 38 criminal cases, involving the railway workers, tried by the District Officer of Manyoni between October 1930 and March 1931, some 8 involved assaulting of workers by their employers. Among the 8 who were convicted, 3 were Italian, 2 German, 1 Greek, 1 Indian and 1 British.[189]

Incidents of beating were not confined to small employers. They often occurred in big enterprises as well where the middle level supervisors were virtually always non-Africans: not that African supervisors were free of these abuses. They too were often used as 'clubs' of despotic employers.[190]

Let us cite two incidents which became the subject of criminal cases to illustrate the oppressive character of the personal employer/employee relationship. In the cases of R. v. *Kirumba*[191] and R. v. *Hemedi*,[192] decided in 1938, the accused, both of them being African workers in a sisal estate, were charged with causing grievous bodily harm and assault, respectively. A white engineer, one Mr Locker, had ordered Kirumba to remove dirty sisal from the box, which the accused refused to do saying it was unfair and that that was not his job. Mr Locker was annoyed at this insubordination and hit Kirumba several times until the accused fell to the ground. The court found that Kirumba got up from the ground and held Mr Locker round his waist to protect himself. However, in his frightened and nervous state, Kirumba placed such pressure on Mr Locker's lower ribs that his eighth rib was fractured. The court found that the pressure was excessive and therefore the accused was guilty as charged, but a nominal sentence was considered adequate.

On hearing that his white engineer had been 'assaulted', the manager, one Mr Mauckle, became furious and rushed into the brush room, took hold of Kirumba's hand and started pulling him. In the process both of them fell down with Mr Mauckle holding tightly at Kirumba's throat. A number of workers, including Hemedi, the accused in the second case, tried to separate them. The court concluded that the accused had no intention to assault the manager. The learned magistrate added: 'Employees with such long service as all the defence witnesses and accused appear to have enjoyed with the Kigombe Sisal Estate would not resort to assaulting their own Manager, the one person they have to look up for justice, their employment, and in many cases their general welfare. I cannot believe such a thing to have been the purpose of accused or any of the others.' This paternalistic reasoning of the magistrate in this case resulted in the acquittal of the accused.

The decisions in these two cases upset the employer so much that he wrote letters to the Provincial Commissioner and even the Secretary of State. He forcefully argued that such decisions would have the effect of destroying all discipline in the labour force. 'We can assure you that labourers who have been on the estates for years, in their proper sense for justice, are very upset that their Manager, whom they look up to for order and discipline and general welfare has been assaulted by one of their member and cannot believe it to be true that the accuseds are returned to the estates unpunished. I would stress the fact that Mr Mauckle was not on the right, [sic], but that it was his legal duty to arrest and detain a native who had manhandled one of his European staff.' The author of the letter from Amboni Estates called upon the government to look into the

---

* The correct Kiswahili word for 'child' is *mtoto* and the plural *watoto*.

matter and 'provide some means of protection to responsible Europeans in carrying out their duties in maintaining proper order and discipline amongst the native labour force under their charge'.[193]

Wigglesworth, one of the London directors of the estates concerned, wrote a personal letter to the Secretary of State on the same matter.[194] In his reply the Secretary said he could not interfere with judicial proceedings but that he would send Wigglesworth's letter and the case reports to the governor.[195] One colonial officer in a minute reasoned that the sending of Wigglesworth's letter to the governor would bring the incident to the governor's attention and that the latter would keep it in mind.

The second case of *R. v. Mrs Fredeal Schimidz & Gustav Wreker*[196] decided in 1936 involved two whites who were charged with assaulting their 'houseboy', one Hamisi Suede. Mrs Schimidz owned a farm on which the assault took place. The statement of the victim gives the grisly facts of the case:

I work as a general houseboy. I get Shs. 8 a month and posho and was promised Shs. 10 when the Bwana came. I remember on the 8th of March at about 6.30 p.m. accused No. 1 came to the kitchen, and said she had lost a goat and that I must go and find it. I refused saying that my work was to cook. She said 'if you do not go and look for the goat I will see you in the morning'. There were four of us at the time in the kitchen, I was inside with both the accused and Husseni Bin Juma, a sweeper. Next morning at 10.00 a.m. I was called by accused No. 1 who was in her bedroom, and she, accused No. 2, Husseni and I went to the stores. The store was near to the house. Accused No. 1 fetched a box and then a rope and she gave the latter to accused No. 2. The ball of rope produced in the court is the rope used. She then got a large wooden native spoon, the one in court is it. Accused No. 1 then told me to sit on the box and I did so. The accused No. 2 held me tightly round the arms from behind (complainant showed the court how he was held). Accused No. 1 took the rope and tied it round my forehead raising the spoon as a lever to twist it. The first bit of rope broke and she then put it on again double. She said to me 'say where the goat is gone'. Husseni was standing near the burner and she told him to help hold me. He refused at first. Accused No. 1 slapped his face. Husseni then helped to hold me for a short time and I was struggling. Accused No. 1 then twisted the rope tight round my forehead using the spoon as a lever. I then fell down and lost consciousness and I bled a little from the nose. When I recovered I sat up on the ground. Accused No. 1 then said, 'where is the goat'. I replied that I had nothing to do with it as I was the cook. I said 'if I had done wrong send me to Dodoma'. She refused. She then said 'I will show you'. I was at this time sitting on the floor close to a block of wood on which a machine was fastened. Accused No. 2 then tied my wrists together and my feet and fastened me by the rope to the block of wood. Accused No. 1 stood by. Husseni helped to tie my hands. They then all three left the store and locked the door from outside. The store had corrugated iron sides. After a time I managed to release myself and I escaped from the store through a hole where the wood work was broken.

The magistrate found the whole affair to have been carried out in 'a particularly cold blooded manner'. He considered the offence very serious 'especially in Africa where the native looks to the European to protect him from savage acts of this sort'. For this *serious* offence, the Honourable Magistrate sentenced the accused to *nominal* imprisonment until the rising of the court and a fine of Shs. 500 each, Shs. 100 of which to be paid to the complainant as compensation. The honourable magistrate complimented himself for having sentenced a white woman to nominal imprisonment with the comment: I have purposely sentenced both accused to nominal imprisonment as I want definitely to be understood that crimes of this nature are not to be expiated by the payment of the mere fine'!

In its revisional jurisdiction the High Court opined that the nominal sentences of imprisonment 'were by no means commensurate with the carelessness and cruelty which characterized the acts of the respondents and the defiance of the law'. Nevertheless 'after hearing the respondents' expression of contrition and the medical evidence regarding the present state of health of the first respondent we have decided, while recording our probation of the conduct, to make no order enhancing the sentences'.

To be sure, the colonial judiciary's sense of retribution corresponded to racial scales. A white woman's contrition was enough to compensate the injured conscience of society since the victim was after all only a 'native'.

Accidents at work

If the humanity and dignity of the 'natives' did not count for much in the eyes of the 'whites', the life and limbs of the colonial labour had virtually no value to the profit-hungry employer. Safety regulations were conspicuous by their absence in the Master and Native Servants Ordinances. The Factories Ordinance was not passed until the early 1950s. The only legislation until then in the nature of protection from dangerous machinery was the Employment of Children on Machinery Regulations.

Thus in the decorticating factories of the sisal estates, in the cotton ginneries and in the mines, workers were constantly exposed to the danger of being mutilated by machines. If the accidents did not occur in thousands it was only because the large majority of the workers were using primitive tools and did not come into close contact with modern machinery. Nevertheless, hundreds of accidents occurred every year and the type of accidents reflected the technological nature of the production process of the time.

According to official data on accidents, between 1943 and 1948 there were an average of 495 accidents per year with 503 people injured out of which 59 died, 81 suffered major and 363 minor injuries. The annual average of accidents during the same period classified according to the causes of accidents was as follows:[197]

	No.	%
Machinery	120	24.2
Transport	175	35.4
Explosives fire	11	2.2
Poison, hot or corrosive substance	2	0.4
Electricity	2	0.4
Fall of persons	19	3.8
Fall of grounds, trees etc.	21	4.2
Animals	4	0.8
Miscellaneous	141	28.5
Total	495	100.0

In sisal estates the most common accidents involved trolleys pulled by locomotives and the brush machines.[198] The brush machines were obviously dangerous to human life and yet nothing was done to make them safe. The brush machine consisted of a revolving drum with a metal comb. The worker holding a bundle of sisal in one hand flicks it under the 'brush' and draws it out pulling it against the direction of the brush. What happened very often was that the worker's hand got pulled into the machine. This was especially so if the aperture was big.[199] The risk of accident could have been minimized by reducing the aperture but this would have reduced the speed of work.

Many of the accidents appeared to occur through sheer carelessness and lack of proper supervision on the part of the employer. For example, an inspector on his visit to Mbagalla sisal estate in 1942 found the opening of the brush machine to be 4 inches whereas it should not have been more than 2½ inches.[200] At Lusanda estate in the same year, an inspector found that the countershafts were dangerously exposed and needed protection while the feed gap for the raspadors was dangerously big.[201] In 1946, a fatal accident occurred at the Lusanda sisal factory through sheer lack of supervision on the part of the employer. A worker had been assigned to pile dry sisal in the engine room right near a revolving shaft. The sisal heap was some 8½ feet to the top and there was only a 3½-foot passage between the heap and the shaft. The shaft itself had a loose coupling which was being held in place by a packing of metal strips whose ends were dangerously jutting out. On the fateful day the worker slipped on the sisal heap and his clothing got caught by the metal strips. His body was picked by the revolving shaft and knocked against the floor and the nearby wall causing instant death. Even in such a case the employer was not prosecuted.[202] In fact, in the case of accidents there appeared to be general reluctance on the part of the authorities to hold the employers criminally liable for negligence and carelessness. Commenting on two fatal accidents on the Lupa gold-fields, in both of which the investigator had found the employer negligent in not providing adequate safeguards, a labour officer said: 'the position would appear to be that any employer may cause or help to cause the deaths of as many natives as he is willing to pay compensation'.[203]

The following testimony of an injured worker in a mining accident enquiry further underlines the callousness and utter disregard with which the employers treated the question of accidents.

I was working underground as a shovel boy. The accident happened eight days after Christmas at about eight o'clock in the morning at the bottom of the shaft where I was shovelling rock into the bucket . . . A rock fell on me and came from above the timbers while I was filling the bucket. There were two of us there at the time. I went to the capitao, KONDWE, and told him that I was injured. KONDWE said that he could not give me 'excuse duty', but if I so desired I might see the Chinaman and when I saw him he said that I was a lazy boy and would go and sleep. He gave me no medicine. I went to my camp and rested for four days, on the fifth day I commenced work again. I worked for seven days and the wound was very big. When I went to the European and told him that my wound was serious and that I wished to be taken to Chunya hospital he said that I could take my pay and go away. I told the European that my home was far away and that I would not go. The KAUNDA called me to get my pay first. I got Shs. 9 and secondly Shs. 2 for my seven days work. KAUNDA and the European chased me away. My friends ran away, but I did not run away. I went to the compound; next morning KAUNDA came and told me that European did not like such men in the camp. So I left the camp; the first day I slept in the bush, the second day I came to a second mine of which I do not know the name and there was chased again. I slept three days in the bush and then came to Ntumbi where I was taken to Chunya hospital. I was not warned about the dangers of my work. I got no medicine at all at the mine. I was given medicine at Ntumbi mine.[204]

When the injured worker was finally admitted to hospital, a period of some twenty days had elapsed; his wound had developed into a large ulcer and his bone had been virtually destroyed.

So much for the obligations of the employers to their injured workers. As for compensation for injury, section 29 of the Master and Native Servants Ordinance laid down the principles in a general way. The employer was liable to pay compensation to an injured worker for his personal injury if such injury was caused by: (a) any defect or want of repair in the ways, works or machinery of the employer which he knew or ought to have known; (b) 'the failure of the employer to take reasonable precautions for the safety of his servant'; and (c) the negligence of the employer or his agents. Thus, unlike the modern compensation law, this section did not embody strict liability. Further- more, although contributory negligence on the part of the employee was no bar to the recovery of compensation, such negligence could be taken into account in assessing the quantum of compensation. The maximum amount of compensation recoverable under the section was two years' wages. Therefore compensation even for fatal accidents tended to be a miserly Shs. 300–400.

Some data from varied years and places give an overall picture of a fairly high rate of fatal accidents, relatively small amounts of compensation awarded and a tendency on the part of investigating officers to find contributory negligence.[205] The figures for the Tanga Province for the year 1935 would suffice to illustrate the point. In that year there were 100 accidents caused as follows:[206]

Type of accident	No.
Trolley	35
Brush	10
Corona	12
Other machinery	17
Blasting	6
Other causes (e.g. burns, falls, drowning, motor, fights)	20
	100

Out of these there were 9 fatal accidents, in 6 of which the employers were held not responsible and therefore no compensation was awarded. The number of cases in which compensation was assessed and paid was 40, the total amount of compensation being around Shs. 2,500. Curiously enough the large number of trolley accidents was attributed by the report to 'direct disobedience of orders, carelessness and the native's love for joy riding[!] and should not be attributed to badly laid trolley lines or other defect in the plant'.

Fringe benefits

During the era of the Master and Native Servants Ordinances there was very little by way of fringe benefits provided in law. There were no paid holidays or rest days nor leave. Both the colonial legislation and practice followed the principle of what was called 'no work/no pay'.

Since the contracts were of fixed duration, there was no provision for advance notice of termination or payment in lieu of such notice. Other old-age benefits such as employers' provident funds were generally unknown.

Finally, the hours of work too were not fixed by law and incidences of long hours of work were quite common especially in the ginneries which frequently ran night shifts.[207]

Conclusion

In conclusion we may recapitulate the following broad theoretical propositions and observations which flow from our study of the conditions of the semi-proletariat.

It is significant that the most important conditions pertain to the realm of reproduction of labour power — wages, food, housing and health — rather than to the realm of the production process, as, for example, industrial accidents. This is not fortuitous but reflects the objective character of the productive forces during this period. The semi-proletariat was largely engaged in the primary sector, mainly plantation agriculture.

The technology was simple and the instruments of labour elementary. Given that the detailed division of labour was not highly developed, the labour process itself was much less complex. Hence it is not the conditions at the work-place that were important. Even the pattern of diseases afflicting the working class related to those arising from mal-nutrition and unhealthy state of housing rather than industrial diseases connected with the industrial process. Here, therefore, we see the reflection of the objective aspect of the productive forces.

But the subjective aspect of the productive forces was not less important. How was it possible for capital to impose and maintain such deplorable conditions without much resistance? The semi-proletarian character of labour was the most important factor in that it militated against collective resistance and collective organization of labour. Whereas capital was highly organized, as we shall see in the next chapter, labour was unorganized. In this respect therefore the deplorable conditions described in this chapter were a reflection of the relative strengths of capital and labour. This point will stand out in sharp relief when we examine the struggles of the proletariat in Chapters 6 and 7.

Another important feature that emerges from this chapter is with regard to the question of state and law. Our discussion reveals the predominant role of the bureau-cracy and the administration in the colonial state as opposed to that of the legislature and the judiciary. The colonial Legislative Council consisted of top colonial officials sitting together with the appointed 'representatives' of employers and business inter-ests in the colony. There was no separation between the judiciary and the executive at lower levels: district and labour officers also held magisterial powers as we have seen. At the higher levels too judges showed overt partiality to employers and openly reflected racial prejudices as the number of decisions cited in this chapter demonstrates. In sum, even the semblance of Montesquian principles of separation of powers and the indepen-dence of and impartiality of the judiciary that purport to inform bourgeois democracies did not exist in the colony. The marked characteristic of decision-making at the level of the colonial state was *bureaucratic–administrative* rather than *democratic–judicial*. The Morogoro tragedy and the history of the legislation on child labour clearly illustrate these arguments.

Our observation on the character of law dovetails with that on the character of the colonial state. Here, it is the instrumentalist aspect of law which is most characteristic. Even the 'care and welfare' regulations under the Master and Native Servants Ordi-nances were of this type rather than a culmination of any political struggles. Law was more a directive to administrative officers rather than an embodiment of justiciable rights of the subjects. Colonial subjects counted for little as (adult) *legal persons* (bearers of rights). They were, almost in the literal sense of the words, *manamba* (numbers), 'boys' and *bibis* (literally mistresses) or *totos* (children).

These observations will be explored further in the course of the rest of this work.

NOTES

1. Lenin, V. I., *The Development of Capitalism in Russia* (Moscow: Progress Publishers, 1967), p. 27.
2. Kautsky, K., 'The Agrarian Question' (University of Dar es Salaam, mimeo, n.d.), trans. J. Banaji.

3. Chen Po-ta, *A study of Land Rent in Pre-Liberation China*, (Peking: Foreign Languages Press, 1966). See also Shivji, I. G., 'The Exploitatin of Small Peasant', in *Human Futures*, No. 4, Vol. 4 (Delhi: PECCE).
4. Marx, K., *Capital*, Vol. I, op. cit., Ch. VI.
5. ibid., p. 164.
6. ibid.
7. See below, pp. 92–93.
8. This has been documented in Mandel, E., *Marxist Economic Theory* (London: Merlin Press, 1968), pp. 453–5. See also below, Ch. 3.
9. Iliffe, J., *Modern History*, op. cit., p. 308.
10. Mitchell, P. E., op. cit., p. 4.
11. PC, Eastern Province, to CS, 14 September 1939, TNA 10922/III. Subsequent information in this paragraph is from the same source.
12. Mitchell, P. E., op.cit., p. 4
13. Information from Northern Province, TNA 23202.
14. Iliffe, J., *Modern History*, op. cit., p. 308.
15. Longland, F., 'Labour in Goldmining Areas', No. 2, op. cit., para. 10.
16. Administrator to SS, 24 April 1920, CO 691/31/308–10.
17. Criminal Case No. 73 of 1957, District Court, Dodoma. Reported and discussed in MLH 808/11/1.
18. Orde-Browne, G., *Report on Labour 1926*, op. cit., p. 33.
19. TNA 10922/I. The remaining information in this paragraph is taken from this source.
20. See *Encyclopaedia Britannica*, Vol. 26 (11th edn), p. 937.
21. Quoted in the letter from PC, Mbeya, to CS, 21 July 1937, TNA 10922/II.
22. TNA A 23217.
23. Calculated from ARLD, 1953–62.
24. Orde-Browne, *Labour Conditions*, op. cit., p. 59, para. 204.
25. LC to CS, 7 August 1945, TNA 10922/III.
26. Information on this incident is from TNA 12289.
27. Baker, 'Report on Social and Economic Conditions in Tanga Province'. Extracts quoted in Longland, F., 'Labour Matters in Sisal Areas', No. 1, op. cit., App. 4.
28. Iliffe, J., *Modern History*, op. cit., p. 157.
29. ibid., p. 352.
30. Orde-Browne to Weaver, 14 June 1933, Orde-Browne Papers 3/4/123 RH.
31. Iliffe, J., *Modern History*, op. cit., p. 354.
32. Iliffe, J., *Agriculture Change*, op. cit., p. 29.
33. CO 691/95/29045.
34. CO 691/158/42191/3/5–8.
35. Longland, F., 'Investigation into Labour in Goldmining Areas', Interim Report No. 3 (Central Province), TNA 23047, App. 1.
36. Montague, F. A., 'Report on Visit of Inspection to Kentan Gold Areas, Ltd, Saragura', May 1936, TNA 23435/I.
37. Longland, F., 'Labour in Goldmining Areas', No. 1, op. cit., App. 1, and 'Summarized Report on Labour Conditions in the Musoma Mining Areas', TNA 23435/I.
38. Montague, F. A., op. cit.
39. Longland, F., 'Labour in Goldmining Areas', No. 1, op. cit., p. 7.
40. TNA 30336.
41. ARLD, 1930, App. III.
42. TNA 11523/I.
43. 'Memorandum on the Supply and Welfare of Native Labour, Iringa Province', p. 4, TNA 23435/I.
44. Orde-Browne, G., *Report on Labour 1926*, op. cit., p. 52, para. 90.
45. Longland, F., 'Labour Matters in Sisal Areas', No. 1 op. cit.
46. K. C. Charron to PC, Tanga, 23 February 1943, TNA 305/3/5/14.
47. Tambila, A., op. cit., p. 45A.

48. p. 14.
49. Orde-Browne, G., *Report on Labour 1926*, op. cit., pp. 66–7, paras. 139–42.
50. TNA A 23217.
51. The M & NSO (Written Contracts) Ordinance, 1942, for the first time imposed an obligation to supply a recruited worker with a prescribed scale of rations. See also M & NS (Proper Feeding) Regulations, 1944 (GN 325 of 1944).
52. See for instance the contract between Bary Bondei Plantation Co, Ltd and 99 'native servants', op. cit.
53. Acting Governor to Acting CS, 9 April 1938, CO 691/166/42191/5, p. 4.
54. W. D. R., op. cit.
55. ibid., p. 2.
56. Longland, F., 'Labour in Goldmining Areas', Final Report, op. cit., p. 22.
57. Charron, K. C., *The Welfare of the African Labourer in Tanganyika* (Dar es Salaam: Government Printer, 1944), p. 28.
58. 'Medical Survey of Sisal Estates', op cit.
59. Sanderson, I., 'Report on Estates and Estates Labour in the Morogoro District', 6 September 1937, TNA 19368/II.
60. ibid.
61. Inquest No. 3 of 1943 re: Luchamuhimba s/o Kilimana, p. 5, TNA 69/332/1.
62. 'Medical Survey of Sisal Estates', op. cit.
63. See, for instance, MLH 4/29/8 (Mbagalla Estate, July 1941); MLH 4/29/6 (Lusanda Sisal Estate, July 1941, August 1944 and April 1947 reports).
64. 'Summarized Report on Labour Conditions in Musoma Mining Areas', op. cit.
65. Memorandum in response to enquiry by C. Bottomley, 23 April 1936, TNA 23217.
66. W. D. R., op. cit., p. 4.
67. 'Report by Lieut. Colonel O. F. Watkins on Certain Plantations in Tanganyika', p. 6, CO 691/183/42191/16.
68. Charron, K. C., op. cit., pp. 5–8.
69. Annual Labour Report, 1949, for Tanga and Pangani Districts, TNA 4/962/9.
70. 'Medical Survey of Sisal Estates', op. cit.
71. Labour Officer's report of 18 May 1927 quoted in the Half Yearly Report of Tanga Province, 1927, TNA 11168/I.
72. Charron, K. C., op. cit., p. 5.
73. MLH 4/19/17/II, inspection report, 26 February 1955.
74. MLH 4/19/12/II, inspection report, 28 June 1956.
75. MLH 4/19/256, inspection report, 22 August 1956.
76. LC to CS, 2 May 1930, TNA 11127/I.
77. Merttens to LC, 27 May 1948, TNA 4/19/81.
78. 'Memorandum of Supply and Welfare, Iringa Province', op cit., p. 2.
79. TNA A 23217.
80. MLH 4/15/1, inspection report, 25 August 1941.
81. MLH 4/15/1, inspection report, 9 July 1939.
82. Montague, F. A., op. cit.
83. *Labour Committee Report*, op. cit., p. 31, para. 91.
84. Wilson, D. B., op. cit., p. 13.
85. For instance, Maramba Estate, inspection report, 25 October 1956, MLH 4/19/130; George Isias & Co., inspection report, 25 April 1955, MLH 4/19/121; Zannetiberg Sisal Estate, inspection report, 2 August 1955, MLH 4/19/52/I.
86. MLH 4/29/80, inspection report, 20 June 1952.
87. MLH 4/29/6, inspection report, 8 July 1941.
88. MLH 4/19/114, inspection report, 26 April 1956.
89. MLH 4/19/69, inspection reports, 27 April 1954 and 22 May 1956.
90. Wilson, D. B., op. cit., p. 11.
91. 'Medical Survey of Sisal Estates', op. cit.
92. Orde-Browne, G., *Report on labour, 1926*, op. cit., p. 65, para. 195.

93. MLH 4/29/139, inspection report, 25 March, 1953.
94. MLH 4/29/80, inspection report, 20 June 1952.
95. MLH 4/19/52/I, inspection report, 17 August 1945.
96. MLH 4/19/17/II, inspection report, 26 February 1955.
97. MLH 4/29/14, inspection report, 26 September 1945.
98. MLH 4/22/11, inspection report, 8 November 1944.
99. ibid., inspection report, 17 July 1950. Subsequent information and quotes on Burka are from this source.
100. *Minutes of the Provincial Commissioners' Conference, July 1952*, App. 'I'.
101. See, for example, MLH 4/19/22, inspection report ,9 August 1941.
102. 'Annual Labour Report, Iringa Province, 1935', TNA 23217.
103. TNA 29002.
104. TNA 23217.
105. 'Annual Report, Iringa Province, 1935', op. cit.
106. Manson, P., *Manson's Tropical Diseases* 17th edn. (London: English Language Book Society, 1972), p. 762.
107. 'Report from the Medical Officer, Mbeya, to the Director of Medicine and Sanitary Services', 18 May 1935, TNA 22938/I. The following quotes are from the same source.
108. TNA 23217.
109. Montague, F. A., op. cit.,
110. Manson, P., op. cit., p. 554.
111. See, for instance, the Annual Reports of the Provincial Commissioners of Western Lake, Eastern, Northern and Tanga Provinces for the year 1942, CO 691/187/42094.
112. *Encyclopaedia Britannica*, Vol. 15, (1962 edn.) pp. 249A–B.
113. Wilson, D. B., op. cit., p. 13.
114. Manson, P., op cit., p. 256.
115. Wilson, D. B., op cit.
116. Orde-Browne, *Report on Labour, 1926*, op. cit., p. 39.
117. Manson, P., op. cit., p. 250.
118. ibid., p. 259.
119. ibid., p. 448.
120. CS to Tongoni Sisal Estate, 15 September 1945, TNA 11168/II.
121. Cap. 51 of the 1928 Laws of Tanganyika.
122. See s. 6(1) of the M & NS (Written Contracts) Ordinance, 1942 (No. 28 of 1942).
123. TNA 13343/II.
124. Harold McMichel to SS, 24 January 1938, CO 691/167/42191/9/52.
125. Administrator to SS, 12 July 1922, CO 691/56/87.
126. Dr Maclean to Principal Medical Officer, 12 August 1922, CO 691/58/418–19.
127. Stiebel to CS, 14 July 1922, CO 691/56/217–220.
128. 'Medical Survey of Sisal Estates', op. cit., Schedule I.
129. Report on Geiglitz Estate, May 1927, TNA 11168/I.
130. MLH 4/29/6, inspection report, 2 May 1946.
131. Assistant District Officer to District Officer, Kilosa, 21 November 1930, p. 7, TNA 11523/I.
132. ibid., pp. 3–4.
133. 'Memorandum on Supply and Welfare, Iringa Province', op. cit., pp. 3–4.
134. I TLR (R) 215.
135. I TLR (R) 672.
136. p. 674.
137. ibid.
138. ibid., p. 214.
139. ibid., p. 215.
140. This incident has been reconstructed from voluminous correspondence on it in the Colonial Office records and records in the Tanzania National Archives. The materials consulted, and which form the source of all information and quotations, are:

a) CO 691/167/42191/9, folios 5, 11, 15, 24, 39–44, 52, 59–69, 72–6, 92–3, 100–1, and 225, (b) TNA 19368/II, TNA 11850/II.

141. From a summary by one H. R. Swansee, 9 February 1938, CO 691/167/42191/9/225.

142. Memorandum of the acting Attorney-General, 27 October 1937, CO 691/167/42191/9/39–44.

143. ARLD, 1948, Table 11, and ARLD, 1951, Tables E and C.

144. See, for instance, MLH/4/19/22, inspection reports, 5 April 1940 and 14 February 1944.

145. ARLD, 1928, 1929 and 1930.

146. MLH 4/29/8, inspection report, 10 July 1941.

147. MLH 4/29/6, inspection reports, 8 July 1941 and 11 December 1950.

148. Annual District Report, 1933, Dar es Salaam, TNA 54.

149. 'Summarized Report on Labour Conditions in Musoma Mining Areas', op. cit.

150. ibid. Longland, F., 'Labour in Goldmining Areas', No. 1, op. cit.

151. ibid. (Longland.)

152. Cf. *Tanganyika Standard*, 18 September 1943.

153. TNA 11850/II.

154. Minutes of the Departmental Conference, No. 5, 5–7 June 1957, MLH 808/23.

155. Cf. MLH 4/15/1 Aureole Mines, inspection report, 9 July 1939.

156. ibid.

157. Minute and photograph, 24 April 1939, TNA 11850/II.

158. MLH 4/29/22, inspection report, 9 July 1946.

159. TNA 11850/III.

160. Inquest No. 3 of 1943 re: Luchamuhimba s/o Kilimana, deceased. The information is taken from the Coroner's report and the deposition of witnesses, TNA 69/332/1.

161. Deposition of one Abdulah Hamisi, ibid., p. 3.

162. Deposition of Katoto Fundirumbi, ibid., pp. 1–2.

163. TNA 11850/III.

164. Bricks, P. W. 'Report on ginnery inspection, North Western Circle',1936, CO 691/158/42191/8/27–29.

165. TNA 25233/II.

166. GN No. 232 of 27 October 1939.

167. TNA 25233/I–II.

168. GN No. 46 of 1927.

169. GN No. 49 of 1931.

170. Employment of Women Ordinance, 1938, No. 14 of 1938.

171. TNA 25233/I–II.

172. TNA 11850/I.

173. ibid.

174. LC to CS, 12 May 1941, TNA 29619.

175. TNA 11850/II.

176. ibid.

177. ibid.

178. No. 5 of 1940. Subsequent information on the development of legislation is taken from TNA 11850/I–II.

179. Employment of Women and Young Persons (Diamond Sorting) Rules, 1940. GN Nos. 269 and 270 of 1940.

180. GN No. 111 of 1 April 1942.

181. Minute of 5 May 1943, TNA 11850/III.

182. Employment of Women and Young Persons (Amendment) Ordinance, 1943, No. 4 of 1943.

183. Circular No. 11850/66 from CS, 7 October 1943, TNA 11850/III.

184. *Tanganyika Standard*, 18 September 1943.

185. TNA 4/962/9.

186. Iliffe, J., *Modern History*, op cit., p. 150.

187. *Report on Tanganyika Territory covering the period from the conclusion of Armistice to the end of 1920*, CO 691/36/222.
188. Iliffe, J., *Modern History*, op. cit., p. 150.
189. 'Conditions of Labour Employed on Railway Construction', TNA 11523/I.
190. PC to CS, 26 February 1931, CO 691/116/30067.
191. Criminal Case No. 48 of 1938 in the First Class Subordinate Court of Tanga, CO 691/167/42191/10.
192. Criminal Case No. 49 of 1938 in the First Class Subordinate Court of Tanga, CO 691/167/42191/112.
193. Amboni Estates to PC, 3 February 1938, CO 691/167/42191/10/16.
194. Wigglesworth to SS, 18 March 1938, CO 691/167/42191/10/9.
195. SS to Wigglesworth, 31 March 1938, CO 691/167/42191/10.
196. Criminal Case No. 4 of 1936, First Class Subordinate Court, Morogoro, CO 691/151/42147/4/7–10, 24–25. The quotes and the subsequent information are from this source.
197. ARLD, 1948, App. I.
198. Summary of Accidents, Tanga Province, TNA A 23217.
199. Reverend Gibbons to CS, 13 October 1933, TNA 18679/III.
200. J. Dickson to Manager, 12 May 1942, MLH 4/29/8.
201. MLH 4/29/6, inspection report, 18 May 1942.
202. MLH 4/29/6.
203. J. Dickson to Chief Inspector of Labour, 5 January 1940, TNA 28285.
204. Statement made by Moses Saliboko, Mining Accident Enquiry No. 1 of 1941, MLH 4/13/7.
205. See, for instance, Annual Reports for Iringa, Eastern and Western Provinces, 1935, TNA A 23217. For an example of mining accidents see the minute of the Chief Inspector of Mines, 1 September 1939, giving figures for the Geita Gold Mining Co. Ltd, TNA 25950. See also Annual Report for Tanga Province, 1948–9, TNA 4/962/9.
206. Summary of Accidents, Tanga Province, 1935, TNA A 23217.
207. Annual Report by the Ginnery Inspector for the Eastern, Southern, Northern and Tanga Provinces, 1936, CO 691/158/42191/8/17.

3

Capital and
Semi-Proletarian Labour

In Chapters 1 and 2 we saw the development and the conditions of semi-proletarian labour. In this chapter we propose to deal with the ownership, character and organization of capital that employed this labour. During the five or so decades that semi-proletarian labour dominated the labour force of the country, it was distributed mainly in three important sectors: agriculture (plantations), mining and infrastructural construction (see Table 1.3, p. 20). Our discussion of capital therefore will also concentrate on the productive capital in these sectors.

In the final section in this chapter we will deal with the resistance and organization of semi-proletarian labour.

Ownership and character of capital

Tanganyika was one of the many countries that fell victim to imperialist invasion during the late nineteenth and early twentieth centuries. 'Imperialism is capitalism at that stage of development at which the dominance of monopolies and finance capital is established; in which the export of capital has acquired pronounced importance; in which the division of the world among the international trusts has begun; in which the division of all territories of the globe among the biggest capitalist powers has been completed.'[1] In this division of the globe Germany acquired what we today call Tanzania mainland. Just before the outbreak of the First (imperialist) World War, Germany possessed some 3 million square kilometres of colonies[2] and was the third most important capital-exporting country. In 1914, the long-term foreign investments of Germany amounted to some £1,376 million compared to France's £1,766 million and Britain's £4,004 million.[3]

Like all other imperialist countries Germany was interested in raw materials, markets and the super-profits that the colonies yielded. The colonies not only provided *cheap* raw materials, which played such an important role in warding off the crisis of falling rate of profit (Marx),[4] but also became a *secure* source of *strategic* raw materials. The latter was crucial to the survival of imperialist powers in their intense intra-imperialist rivalry. Thus, for example, although the German textile monopolies could obtain cheaper raw cotton from the United States, they wanted an independent and

84

secure source like Tanganyika which they themselves could control.[5] Hence their intense efforts to grow cotton, among other things, in the country.

It was Germany that built the estate sector and the basic infrastructure in the country. Before the first war, Tanganyika was Germany's second most important colony. In 1912, Tanganyika produced 20 per cent of all the goods imported by Germany from its colonies and bought some 16 per cent of the goods exported to them by Germany.[6] The amount of total capital invested in the country at any particular time is difficult to determine with accuracy. According to Iliffe, however, company and private capital in 1913 was estimated at £4,800,000, made up of £1,050,000 in railways, £2,400,000 in agriculture, £1,100,000 in trade, industry and mining, and £250,000 in banking.[7] Frankel estimated that the total foreign capital — that is, 'new money' subscribed from abroad — invested in Tanganyika and Zanzibar between 1870 and 1936 was £51.9 million.[8] This consisted of the public listed capital, £31.3 million;[9] the private listed capital, £15.8 million; and the non-listed capital, £4.7 million.[10]

The public listed capital comprised loans, grants in aid and grants. Out of £31.2 million of public listed capital invested in Tanganyika some £22.9 or 73 per cent consisted of loans.[11]

'Private listed capital' refers to net amounts of capital (both equity and loan) subscribed for non-government enterprises listed on the stock exchange or in the financial press. The non-listed capital comprised private capital not disclosed to the public and capital brought by the settlers and other immigrants. The latter by all accounts was very minimal, if any.[12]

Much of the public listed capital was invested in building the railways and other public works while the private listed and non-listed capital was mainly concentrated in the plantations and mining.[13]

The data we have cited refer only to foreign capital received during the period. We have no figures as to the amount of capital accumulated internally both by foreign firms and locally based capitalists. Undoubtedly the latter must have been substantial because the source of both the white settlers' and Asian capitalists' capital was almost exclusively internal accumulation.

It is also difficult to have accurate data as to the profits made by this capital and the amount repatriated. Rweyemamu estimates that as much as 30 per cent of the settlers' profits was repatriated in 1912.[14] These profits were part of the super-profits that capital extracted from Tanganyika's labour. When the prices of sisal were high in 1911, the profits were as high as 25 per cent.[15] During the Korean boom of the early 1950s the sisal companies reaped enormous profits. In a survey of ten companies, Guillebaud found that the profits were as much as 72 and 45 per cent of the average capital employed in the years 1951 and 1952 respectively.[16] Published figures can never tell us the true story about profits, though they do indicate that the rates of profits tended to be very high.

With this global overview of capital in the country we are now in a position to look more closely at different fractions of the capital invested in the three important sectors of the economy. We can distinguish four important fractions of capital in the colonial economy of Tanganyika: the foreign finance capital; locally based big capital; locally based medium and small capital and finally state capital.

At the theoretical level a number of propositions help us to distinguish and demarcate different fractions of capital. Let us refer to them briefly.

First, the foreign finance capital is historically tied up with the rise of imperialism. It formed part of the capital exported from imperialist countries which was its original source. It was owned and controlled, directly or indirectly, by large monopolies based in the metropolitan countries. Thus both in its origin and control it was foreign. The original source of local capital, on the other hand, was largely internal accumulation within the colony. It was owned and controlled by locally based capitalists. Its base therefore was essentially local.

Secondly, with local capital, different fractions — big, medium and small — are demarcated on the basis of their scale of operations. The other important point that distinguished the local big capital from the medium and small capital was that the local big capital had much closer and direct links and connections with foreign finance capital. In this respect, its compradorial character is direct and obvious. There are other differences among these fractions at the empirical level which will be explored in the course of our discussion in this chapter.

Thirdly, state capital refers to investments made by the state. They were raised primarily through loans. The development of state capital is connected with the development of state monopoly capitalism. With the rise of the financial oligarchy as the hegemonic fraction of the ruling bourgeoisie, the state organs become increasingly subordinated to this fraction. 'This process, this change in the form of state power — its progressive deployment in the interests of the monopoly bourgeoisie — is the content of the development of state monopoly capitalism in the imperialist countries.'[17]

Let us now turn to the empirical investigation of the different fractions of capital.

Finance capital

Finance capital, which arose as a consequence of the coalescence of monopoly banking and industrial capital, was the dominant fraction in the colonial economies. The big international monopolies based in the imperialist countries operated in the colonial economy either directly or more often through a web of subsidiary and associate companies.

During the German period the most important holding monopoly was the German East Africa Company (DOAG). Originally established as a chartered company to administer the areas in East Africa which fell within the German 'sphere of influence', it very soon gave this up to the German imperial state and continued to operate as an ordinary commercial undertaking.[18] It was founded in 1885 with a capital of 7,128,000 marks. Its capital was publicly subscribed and among its shareholders was Germany's leading industrialist Friedrich Krupp. DOAG's capital constituted almost half of the capital of eleven or so large German planting companies investing in Tanganyika around 1900.[19] In 1902 the DOAG developed a large rubber plantation at Lewa and was the first to experiment successfully with sisal.[20] Its interests were not confined to plantations, however. In fact the DOAG made its highest profits in trade, banking and shipping:

Following the principle of 'never standing aside', the DOAG came to control the German East African Bank; the Commercial Bank for East Africa (based in Tanga); the German East African Railway Company (which operated both railways); the German Tanganyika Company; the Central African Mining Company (exploiting Uvinza's salt); the Lindi Trading and Plantation Company and the East Africa Company, Rhenish-Handeni Plantation Company, and Ngomeni Plantation Company (plantations in the north-east); and the Usambara-Magazin (trade). The DOAG directly employed 120 Europeans and some 4,400 Africans and Asians. In 1910 and 1911 it paid 8 per cent dividends. It also held mortgages on much private land, often demanding 5–7 per cent interest per annum and a selling monopoly of the settler's crops at a commission ranging up to 2½ per cent.[21]

Besides the DOAG, there were a couple of other German big companies all operating in the plantation sector producing sisal, cotton, coffee, copra and rubber. By 1900 there were thirteen large German firms established in German East Africa: nine years later the figure was fifty-five. The smallest firm had a capital of 48,000 marks while the largest, a subsidiary of the DOAG running the central railway, had a capital of 21 million marks. Table 3.1 gives the investment of German firms in German East Africa between 1886 and 1909.

Table 3.1 *Investment of German Firms in German East Africa, 1886–1909*

	Capital in marks	No. of firms
Less than	100 000	1
	100 000–200 000	9
	201 000–500 000	13
	501 000–1 000 000	11
	1 000 000–2 000 000	11
Over	2 000 000	2
	Private	5
	Others	3
	Total	55

Sourke: Mascarenhas, A. C., 'Resistance and Change in the Sisal Plantation System of Tanzania' (PhD thesis, University of California, LA, 1970) p. 67.

A few British companies had also invested in German East Africa especially in the rubber plantations.[22] British investment in German East Africa was estimated at £1.5 million in 1913.[23]

Just before the war, in Tanganyika there were some 270 commercial and industrial undertakings, 8 cotton plantations, 60 coffee plantations and about 440 plantations and farms for mixed agricultural products. Although there were also some six mining companies, they had not attained any success thus far.[24]

As part of its war booty, the British imperialist state expropriated all the former German property and disposed of them by public auctions. Later when the Germans were allowed to return they reacquired some of the properties. The DOAG itself survived through its successor, the Usagara Company, which was formed in co-operation with certain Greek capitalists.[25] However, many of the large ex-German estates were bought by big British monopolies which henceforth became dominant. Among the giants that owned and operated the sisal plantations were the famous Wigglesworth and Company, London's leading sisal brokers; Bird and Company, and Ralli Brothers.[26] On the eve of the Second World War, the DOAG's Usagara Company produced some 10,459 tonnes of sisal while Amboni Estates Ltd, jointly financed by Swiss capital and Wigglesworth, produced some 9,643 tonnes.[27] Around 1938, the six large plantation companies in Tanganyika owned by British finance capital represented a share and loan capital of some £12,900,000.[28] In 1937 these six concerns made a total profit of £1,296,000.[29]

The domination of finance capital is even more blatant when we come to mining. Mining in Tanganyika became significant during the German period when only one gold-mine, Sekenke, had reached the production stage. In the 1920s prospecting resumed and gold was found in Mwanza, Musoma and Lupa Districts. The scramble for gold began in earnest in the 1930s with the depreciation of the pound sterling in relation to gold. Considerable investments were made in reef mining which in 1938 produced some 70 per cent of the total production of some 82,000 ounces of gold.[30]

Reef mining was the exclusive preserve of the British and South African-based mining monopolies which also operated in other East African countries. In 1938, the six large mining concerns in Tanganyika, directly or indirectly owned by British finance capital and the Oppenheimer octopus, represented a share and loan capital of £93,136,000. These were: East African Gold-fields, Kentan Gold Areas, Tanganyika Central Gold Mines, Tanganyika Concessions, Tanganyika Diamond and Gold Development and Tanganyika Minerals. The Kentan Gold Areas and Tanganyika Concessions with their share and loan capital of £12,500,000 and £68,180,000 respectively were the largest.[31]

The Tanganyika Concessions was registered in London at the end of January 1899. It is a giant conglomerate whose interests proliferate all over Africa, especially in the south.[32] The following extract from *The Economist* of December 1938 shows interconnections among various mining monopolies at the time:

Tanganyika Concessions and Kentan Gold interests are represented by the developing mines owned by Geita Gold Mining Company and certain concessions . . . held by Saragura Development Company, Ltd. Tanganyika Concessions' interest in the mines is indirect, firstly through its holding of 444,345 10s. Kentan shares (out of 2,500,000 shares); secondly through its 50 per cent interest in Geita Gold Mining £421,000 8½ per cent debentures (of which Zambesia Exploring Company holds the other half); and, thirdly, through the 451,175 Kentan shares held by Rhodesia-Katanga Company, in which 'Tanks' hold 435,729 out of 1,281,414 shares. Kentan holds 1,468,912 out of 1,625,000 5s. shares in Saragura, which in turn holds 200,000 out of Geita Gold's 780,002 10s. shares, of which Kentan holds the rest.[33]

'Tanks' refers to Tanganyika Diamond and Gold Development Company, one of the six largest mining concerns mentioned before. It was the subsidiary of the Anglo American octopus based in South Africa and was involved in prospecting for diamonds before it withdrew towards the end of 1930s.[34]

Tanganyika Concessions through the Kentan Gold Areas Limited had interest in at least the following mining companies operating in Tanganyika: 'Eldoret Mining Syndicate Limited; Uruwira Gold-fields Limited; East African Concession Limited; Saragura Development Company; Geita Gold Mines Limited'.[35]

Thus, gold-mining which was in 1938 second to sisal in terms of workers employed (around 28,000) and its contribution to exports,[36] was under almost the complete sway of finance capital. Until the end of the 1930s 'Tanks' had not found much luck with diamond prospecting and withdrew, while salt, tin and mica were mined on a small scale, production of which in 1938 was valued at £54,000, £50,460 and £12,383 respectively.[37]

Local big capital

Local big capital belonged almost exclusively to the immigrant nationalities, these being Asians, Germans, British, Greeks and other Europeans. These immigrants did not come out as big capitalists to the colonies. Their capital was predominantly accumulated from and within the colony.

In German East Africa the German nationality was predominant numerically as well as the most important element in the plantation economy. In 1913, some 4,000 out of a total of 5,000 Europeans were Germans.[38] Those involved in the plantations usually owned medium and small sized estates, the big ones being controlled by the foreign companies.[39]

The big Asian capitalists on the other hand had their capital concentrated in commerce.[40] It was not until after the war that the Asian capitalists for the first time entered the plantation economy in any significant way.[41] This they did by buying up ex-enemy property sold through public auctions. Uncertainty over the mandate status of the territory made white settlers reluctant to buy many properties. Secondly, owing to the depression the prices too were low. These factors combined to make it possible for the Asians — who were the only ones with ready money — to buy many properties including plantations.[42] According to one estimate, Indians bought some thirty-six plantations in the auctions between May 1921 and May 1922.[43] With its twelve plantations, Karimjee Jivanjee and Company was the biggest buyer. From then onwards the name of Karimjee was among the few prominent local big capitalists. In 1940 Karimjee Jivanjee was the largest sisal producer (10,966 tonnes)[44] and by the end of the 1950s it had a total of 7 sisal estates, 2 tea estates and 6 farms.[45] Another major local capitalist was also an Asian firm, Taibali Essaji Sachak and Company, who like Karimjee made their initial accumulation in commerce.[46]

Among the white settlers the big names were Major William Lead and George Arnautoglu. Besides his own sisal empire, Arnautoglu was a director of the Usagara Company, the successor of DOAG. 'By the 1950s Arnautoglu was among Tanganyika's wealthiest men.'[47]

In spite of the overall dominance of finance capital, there is no doubt that local big capital played a prominent role in the plantation economy, including its most important crop, sisal. This was not so in mining which was almost an exclusive preserve of finance capital. Williamson Diamond Ltd was probably the only exception, if it could be called an exception.

After the Tanganyika Diamonds and Gold Development Company had withdrawn in 1938, its geologist, Dr J. T. Williamson, continued prospecting. Eventually in 1940 he struck the Mwadui mine which was to become the most lucrative in the 1950s. Borrowing initial capital from Indian merchants, and helped on by the war boom, Williamson's Mwadui mine finally became profitable after some five years of enormous problems. However, it did not remain independent for very long. After Williamson's death in 1958, half of the shares of Williamson Ltd were bought off by the De Beers Empire, thus bringing it under the firm control of finance capital.[48]

Local medium and small capital

Local medium and small capital existed in all the important sectors of the economy, including the most important ones of agriculture, mining and construction. Like the big capitalists, the most significant of the small and medium capitalists belonged to the immigrant nationalities.

A fairly large number of medium and small sized sisal estates were owned by Germans, Greeks and Asians. 'In April, 1934 Germans owned 40 sisal estates, Greeks 29, Britons 24 and Asians 22.'[49] By 1948, the Asian and Greek nationalities produced a little under half of sisal production while the British and Swiss (mostly large firms) produced the rest.[50] Of course, it was the big Asian and Greek capitalists and the large foreign firms which were the largest producers among these. Around 1946, seventy-six small sisal estates (that is, those producing less than 1,000 tons per annum), or some 60 per cent of the total number, produced only 29 per cent of the total output.[51] In 1964 two-thirds of the sisal estates, producing below 1,000 tons per annum, produced only one-third of the total output. The average output of these small estates was 640 tons per annum compared to 2,460 tons of the large estates.[52]

Apart from sisal, medium and small capital belonging to the European settlers was heavily concentrated in the coffee and mixed agricultural farms of the Northern

Province. In 1948 there were some 336 estates in this province, employing a total labour force of 29,500. These estates covered a cultivated area of almost 100,000 acres, the most important crops being coffee, papain, wheat, maize, beans and seed beans.[53]

As for construction, the most prominent nationality at this time was the Greeks. The Greek sub-contractors played an especially important role in railway and road construction. They in turn often used the money from their sub-contracting work to invest in their sisal estates. Much of the labour on railway construction was employed by the sub-contractors rather than by the main construction companies.[54] Some of these sub-contractors later formed their own construction companies like G. Iasis and Althaneous who founded the famous Tanganyika Engineering and Contracting Company (TECCO).[55]

Another area where small capital was involved was mining. In the gold rush of the 1930s many men of small means from different nationalities tried to make a fortune in alluvial mining. The Lupa gold areas, where alluvial mining accounted for almost 66 per cent of the total output, attracted many diggers, 'mostly Europeans — employees who had lost their posts and farmers who found it impossible to make a living by the sale of their crops but also a considerable number of Asians and Africans.''.[56] At the end of 1941, out of some 256 diggers in the Lupa controlled area, 50 were Africans, 56 Greeks, 47 British and 39 Indians.[57]

State capital

Throughout the history of capitalism the state has played an important role in economic life. Nevertheless, in the era of competitive capitalism, to a certain extent, it could remain neutral *vis à vis* the multitude of bourgeois fractions. Not so in the monopoly imperialist stage. With the ascendance of finance capital, the financial obligarchy became a hegemonic fraction of the ruling class.[58] Under the circumstances, the role of the state has become much more consistent and deliberate in the interest of monopoly oourgeoisie.

The trusts and combines not only fought with each other economically but also called upon the assistance of their home states against their rivals. For these monopolies who operated outside their 'homes' in search of raw materials, markets and super-profits, nothing could be better than colonialism 'for in the colonial market it is easier to employ monopoly methods . . . to eliminate competition, to ensure supplies, to secure the necessary connections, etc.'[59]

Imperialist states in the colonies not only protected their finance capital militarily and politically — bearing the administrative expenses and so on — but even provided the necessary infrastructure to enable exploitation of natural resources. The costs of this infrastructure were thus *socialized* and were mainly borne by the colonial subjects themselves without touching the super-profits of finance capital.

In Tanganyika it was the German imperialist state (and later the British) which was responsible for building the road and railway network. It was simply not profitable for private enterprise to invest in the construction of railways in spite of such attractions as the grant of land ownership and mineral concessions.[60] For example, the German East Africa Company was given the contract to build the Tanga railway together with a grant of land, 3 kilometres wide on either side of the railway. In spite of the fact that the railway company was backed by imperial finance and even received subventions from the state, it failed to run it and the railway was finally taken over by the state in 1899.[61]

The Central Line from Dar es Salaam to Morogoro was built by the Ost-Afrikanische Eisenbahn Gesellschaft. Besides being given free grants of land, prospecting and mining rights, the Reich guaranteed the payment of 3 per cent interest on the company's capital.[62] The railway reached Morogoro in 1907 after three years. At the same time further plans were announced to extend it to Tabora. The company was given the contract together with a loan of 80 million marks from the colonial government.

The Reich guaranteed four per cent interest on the loan. As security the Dar es Salaam–Morogoro section of the railway was mortgaged to the colonial government. As each section of the extension was completed it was also mortgaged, and 95 per cent of the company's original share capital was purchased by the colonial government. In consequence the Mittelland Bahn virtually became a state railway operated by the Ost Afrikanische Eisenbahn Gesellschaft as a public utility company.[63]

All in all, the Central Line cost 111 million marks, involving an interest burden of 4.4 million marks a year. The company made very little contribution towards the payment of interest, which had to be borne by the colonial government[64] — meaning, of course, by the colonized masses. By 1914, debt servicing claimed 32 per cent of the revenue derived from the colony's own resources.[65]

At the end of their rule, the Germans left Tanganyika with 990 miles of railway and a public debt of £8,800,000 with annual debt charges of some £317,500.[66] But the British imperial state took over the mandate free of previous debts while inheriting all the assets, including the railways.[67]

For reconstruction after the war the British exchequer provided loans and grants. Later many so-called development works were financed by loans raised with imperial guarantee on the principal and interest. These loans were raised at a very high rate of interest ranging from 4 to 5 per cent.[68] By 1938, public debt amounted to £8,757,879 or £1 13s 9d per head of the population. The debt charge was £436,477 or approximately 20 per cent of both ordinary expenditure and ordinary revenue. The debt was made up of three groups of loans from different sources: £3,135,446 was from the imperial funds; three loans were issued to the public with the Imperial Guarantee, two of £2,070,000 and £3,000,000 being under the Palestine and East African Loans Act of 1926 and one of £500,000 being under the Tanganyika and British Honduras Loans Act of 1932; loans granted from the Colonial Development Fund amounted to £56,654 while a small loan of £10,194 was advanced to the British Air Ministry, this being Tanganyika's share in the estimated capital expenditure on the Empire Air Mail Scheme.[69]

Much of the public debt had been incurred for building the railways which were not particularly profitable. It was not until 1938 that there was a surplus over expenditure in the working of the railway.[70] Between 1926 and 1948 the working profit of the railways and ports amounted to £7,990,300 while the loan charges amounted to £6,115,700. That is to say, some 77 per cent of the working profit was absorbed by loan charges.[71]

The net result of the state capital building the infrastructure was that costs were socialized, the heavy burden of debt charges being borne by colonial producers. At the same time finance capital was provided with the necessary infrastructure without which the exploitation of the colony's resources would have been impossible. Brett has argued that in fact the programme of railway building initiated by the British in the 1920s was, in addition, a great boost to the metropolitan heavy industries and provided a relief to the unemployment problem.[72] As Baldwin, opening the Conservatives' campaign for the 1929 election, put it:

If you sum up what our ideal is — to find permanent employment — you may sum it up in this way, I think: that it is the modernization of industry at home and the multiplication of markets overseas. And that has caused us to look once more at the development of our colonies . . .

Overseas, and particularly in Africa, we have territories of vast potentiality, and we want to help them to develop. We have done something; we have done something through the Palestine and East African Loans; and it is our policy, and it has been to see that further capital is forthcoming in the most convenient form as the need arises from time to time for colonies which obviously cannot finance their own development . . . The interest charges which fall on a colony while works are under construction, or while they are still unfruitful, are often too heavy for the colony in its present state to bear. That militates against early development, and so we shall provide out of Imperial funds for such sums as are required — within a maximum to be attuned to our needs, but it will be substantial in the way of giving the help of which I have spoken — to pay the interest in initial years of unfruitful schemes which otherwise must be postponed, and in any other way to assist them to mature. We propose to establish an independent commission to watch over this matter and to advise the government on the most profitable use of these new resources for the development of our colonial territories.[73]

Thus the laying of infrastructure in the colonies was very much part of finance capital's thirst for super-profits.

Organization of and conflict within capital

The organization of capital until the late 1940s was influenced by three main factors: the need to put pressure on the colonial government; minimization of competition and conflict among different fractions of capital; and the fact of labour being highly unorganized. All these three factors heavily impinged on the character of capital's organizations.

In the realm of labour, the need to put pressure on the colonial state and minimize inter-capital contradictions manifested themselves most significantly through the problem of shortage of labour. Except for a few short periods, for example during the depression, employers faced this problem almost throughout the colonial period. As we have already seen in Chapter 1, this problem was a reflection of the system of semi-proletarian labour. Under the circumstances *political* means was the only way open to capital to ensure a constant and adequate supply of labour. Thus their organizations were invariably *semi*-political pressure groups which sought through various means — including representations on various governmental boards and committees — to influence the short-term policies of the government.

The question of supply of labour also loomed large in the relation among various fractions of capital giving rise to secondary contradictions among them. To be sure, this was not the only bone of contention. Another area which was a fertile ground of contradictions was the question of pricing and marketing of the products. As we shall see in a moment, in both these cases capital adopted the method of forming strong *monopoly* organizations to resolve these issues.

The third factor, the unorganized character of labour, influenced the nature and machinery of the organizations of capital in a negative way. While the first two factors determined what these organizations would be like, the third one influenced what they would not be. Thus, capital was *not* organized as a collective *employers'* organization facing collective labour. These were not employers' *trade unions* organized to negotiate and bargain with labour, for wages and conditions of work were almost *unilaterally* determined by capital itself. And these organizations also ensured standardization of terms and conditions of employment so as to avoid competition within capital. Labour had virtually no influence on this question and the state deliberately kept out of it under the ideology of leaving these questions to be determined by 'market forces'. In short, until the 1950s when for the first time the capitalists' organizations had to sit face to face with the trade unions, employers' organizations were not bodies for collective negotiations and bargaining. It was not until 1963 that, under pressure from the government and the trade unions,[74] the TSGA altered its articles of association giving its executive committee powers 'to negotiate on behalf of the Association wages and conditions of employment with the recognised Trade Union or any other body as representing the employees of the sisal industry'.[75]

We shall now illustrate the propositions made above by looking at the most important organizations of the capitalists during this period.

As might be expected, the most important organizations of the capitalists were those which brought together the planters. Right from the German period the settlers involved in the plantation sector had organized themselves in a number of planters'associations, for example, the Tanga Planters' Union (formed in 1898) and West Usambara Planters' Union (formed in 1903), while a number of such organizations probably also existed in Morogoro, Lindi and Dar es Salaam.[76] These were all settlers' organizations heavily involved in local politics.

As distinct from the settlers' organizations, around 1905 was formed the League of German East African Plantations representing larger non-resident plantation owners. Twice, in 1905 and 1908, the league attempted to form a central recruiting agency with the support of the government.[77] Both times it failed partly because of the hostility of the settlers' organizations which feared for their independence. Nevertheless, the question was one of the dominant issues discussed in the meetings of the league.[78]

In its meeting of 20 June 1908 held in the offices of the German East Africa Company, the league decided unanimously against feeding regulations which the governor was trying to impose but fully supported the standardization of wages and conditions of contract for estate and railway work. Members of the league also 'pledged themselves by signature not to induce European employees to leave the service of any other member and not to engage African deserters from the employment of any other member . . .'. The question of 'decoying' labour (as it was to be called later in the British legislation) from fellow employers was in fact a recurring theme in the meetings of the league and every time the meetings passed resolutions calling upon its members to refrain from indulging in such a practice.[79]

Both the local German settlers and the companies put up resistance to certain provisions of Rechenberg's 1909 labour legislation. For example, the settlers opposed the fact that they could be subject to the jurisdiction of administrative officers. They wanted the labour commissioner and other labour officers to help them ensure a steady supply of labour and not act as factory inspectors. In fact, they won on the point of jurisdiction, for whereas the commissioner was empowered to punish an employee he could prosecute European employers only before courts.

The trend towards monopoly organizatiions which had begun to work out hesitatingly during the German period gathered momentum under the British. The most powerful of these organizations was the Tanganyika Sisal Growers' Association (TSGA). In December 1923, a former British army officer and one of the big sisal planters, Major William Lead, together with other leading growers in Tanga, formed a Planters' Association.[80] In 1924 it changed its name to Tanganyika Planters' Association although it still continued to represent the interests of Tanga sisal growers.[81] After the depression the association was reconstituted as a corporate body and adopted the name of Tanganyika Sisal Growers' Association. By 1936 it had been joined by the Planters' Association on the central line, which became the Central Line branch, and the Lindi Planters' Association which became the Southern Province Branch, while another branch was formed in the Northern Province.[82] Thus the TSGA became a truly territorial organization encompassing virtually all the big, medium and small sisal growers in the country.

Among the most important objectives of the association, as summarized by Mascarenhas, were:

1. To promote, protect and further the interests of the sisal industry in Tanganyika Territory.
2. To promote, support and oppose any legislation or other measures affecting the sisal industry.
3. To improve the methods of production and preparation of sisal fibre.
4. To make representations to government.[83]

The association aggressively translated these objectives into practice, particularly in making representations to the government. It sought to establish relations with the government at the highest level, bypassing local administrators.[84] Its president, Major William Lead, who led the association until his death in 1942,[85] was the leader of the unofficial side of the Legislative Council; he served on many important committees (including the famous one of 1937 appointed to look into the question of supply of labour) and during the Second World War became the sisal controller[86] and the Director of Manpower.[87] On the Labour Advisory Board established in 1938 'to consider and advise on all matters referred to it by Government concerning the supply, welfare and employment of manpower for all activities' the sisal industry was strongly represented by Major William Lead and Karimjee's executive, A. A. Adamjee.[88]

When the Tanganyika Sisal Board was formed in 1934 as a statutory body to oversee the sisal industry, the TSGA was represented by nine unofficial members.[89] The board was reconstituted under the Sisal Industry Ordinance, 1945.[90] The chairman of the association and nine other members appointed by the TSGA became members of the board (s. 3).

Capitalist farmers involved in growing other crops besides sisal were also organized in a number of growers' associations, some of them regionally based while others were territorial. Although not as powerful and influential as the TSGA, these associations too were represented in the government and sought to influence it in various ways. The most crucial question on which these organizations often made representations to the government concerned the shortage of labour. Particularly on two issues — encouraging the growing of economic crops by African peasants and closing of certain areas to recruitment because of sleeping sickness — they came into conflict with the government. This was especially so during the depression years and after the government had instituted its 'plant-more-crops' campaign to ensure a supply of raw materials and food for export as well as its own revenue. The TSGA bitterly criticized the government for encouraging, for example, the planting of cotton in the Tanga area by supplying seed cheaply and generally publicizing the growing of cotton.[91] The colonial administration usually went quite far in reassuring the planters of its neutrality in this matter. Replying to a complaint of the TSGA's Central Line Branch the Chief Secretary said:

In the opinion of Government there is a sufficiency of local labour available in those areas both for the cultivation of sisal and for the production of economic crops including cotton which is an old established crop on the Central Railway. The policy of allowing natives the free choice of work will continue but no steps will, of course, be taken to induce those who have contracted the habit of working on plantations to abandon that habit in order to produce crops for sale or export.[92]

The Northern Province planters often complained that their traditional sources of supply of labour such as Singida, Dodoma and Kondoa were interfered with by the officials calling out people for 'communal' works like tsetse bush clearing projects.[93] The administration frequently obliged by instructing its officials to time the 'tribal turn-outs' in such a way that they did not coincide with the peak labour periods in the Northern Province.[94] In one of his letters the Director of Agriculture went so far as to suggest that the employers should make known the number of men they wanted 'to time their tax drives to coincide with the months when labour is most required . . .'[95]

The war brought the state and capital even closer. Allied powers needed sisal and food products of the colony most urgently and therefore the colonial government went all out to ensure adequate labour to the employers. Thousands of Africans were conscripted and made available to capital.[96] The benefits of central organization which this involved no doubt made an important impression on both the government and the employers. Thus in 1944 the TSGA founded its own central recruiting agency, the Sisal Labour Bureau or SILABU.[97] With the formation of this powerful central recruiting agency, the labour problems of the sisal industry were eased to a great extent. From its inception in August 1944 to its closure in March 1965, the Labour Bureau had recruited some 463,500 adult males and repatriated about 442,000 persons, in the process making a net expenditure of some £2,639,400.[98]

Much more fragmented than the sisal growers, the planters in the Northern Province could not on their own form a similar recruiting agency. The end of conscription therefore posed a dilemma which only state assistance could solve. Initially SILABU recruited for the Northern Province planters and later a Northern Province Labour Allocation Board was formed under the chairmanship of the Northern Province Provincial Commissioner.[99] The board continued to function without any statutory standing until 1947 when the Labour Utilization Ordinance, 1947,[100] was passed. Under this Ordinance the former Allocation Board became the Northern Province Utilization Board.[101] The boards established under the Ordinance by the governor-in-council were to exercise such functions as prescribed 'and shall be deemed to be an organization of employers established for the purpose of recruiting labour for such employers . . . ' (s. 2(2)). The board consisted of employers' representatives appointed by the employers' associations and departmental representatives from the government departments and nominees of the governor (s. 2(3)). In short, although statutorily organized, these boards were to be central recruiting agencies for the medium and small employers.

The organizations of capitalists played a crucial role in minimizing competition among them, particularly in the fixing of wages and terms and conditions of employment. Employers followed the policy of fixing the standard maximum wage which they did unilaterally since labour was not organized enough to react.[102] As the Northern Province Provincial Commissioner put it in his half-yearly report of 1927: 'owing to the pernicious fallacy of a standard maximum wage, the effects of competition have been for wages to react very slightly, but for the labour demanded in return for a given wage to shrink rapidly'.[103] During and after the depression of 1930, the TSGA, for example, reduced wages drastically by nearly 50 per cent,[104] and maintained control over wages and conditions for nearly thirty years.[105]

Whereas the employers fixed wages without regard to 'market forces', having reduced competition among themselves by their monopoly organizations, the government followed these wages under the guise that they were the ruling wages in the market. In fact, the government scrupulously avoided increasing wages to attract labour for fear that private employers would be up in arms.[106] The net result was, as Sabot puts it, that 'the market for labour was not free and that the small number of large estate owners and the government took advantage of their oligopsonistic position to administer wages at a level below that which would equilibrate the market'.[107]

Although capital was pretty successful in minimizing competition so far as wage-determination was concerned, this did not mean that it had succeeded in eliminating competition completely. Hundred per cent monopoly is simply not possible in the economic life of capitalism, even in the colonies. Thus competition and conflicts among capitalists took different forms. One of these was 'crimping' or stealing of labour, and another was encroaching on others' sources of labour. The Northern Province planters often complained to the government that the stronger TSGA was recruiting in their traditional 'reservoir' of Singida and Kondoa Irangi. The government's response in such cases tended to be ambiguous. In one case, for example, some officials felt that there ought not be any restriction on 'legitimate competition' and 'free flow of labour'; in other words they were favouring the big and stronger capital. Others who wanted to protect small capital argued that there was a very thin line between legitimate competition and crimping and that one industry ought not to recruit at the very door of another. In the final analysis the powerful TSGA often got away with these incursions.[108]

The TSGA itself was controlled and dominated by big local and foreign finance capital.[109] This was resented by the medium and small growers. For instance, in one of TSGA's annual general meetings, one P. M. Joshi vigorously argued that small growers should have special representation on the association's executive committee and the Sisal Board. Furthermore, since the voting was based on production big growers could always outvote smaller ones, he complained. He further implied that big growers were able to get government help and assistance while smaller ones were ignored. These protests of Mr Joshi were conveniently passed over and disregarded.[110]

There was, however, much truth in what Joshi said. For instance, section 12 of the Sisal Industry Ordinance empowered the governor-in-council to make rules (after obtaining advice from the Sisal Board) for, among other things, controlling the cultivation, treatment, keeping storage, marketing and export of sisal. The proviso to this section gave decisive power in this respect to big capital. It provided that 'no rule shall be made under this paragraph unless a resolution recommending the same shall have been passed by the Association and the members voting in favour of such resolution shall have produced during the period of twelve months ending on the 31st December immediately preceding the date of such resolution not less than two-thirds of the total quantity of sisal produced in the territory during such period . . . ' Around 1946, this meant that a little more than one-third of the estates which produced more than two-thirds of the output held a decisive voice in this matter.

On the question of supply of labour, too, small growers had grievances. One small Greek planter whose estate was being threatened with closure because of lack of supply of labour complained:

It appears that the more influential members of the Association are having all the labour at the cost of other small planters. The labour which are given to small planters are of much inferior quality to the influential planters . . . The doctors and other officers in sisal are very strict with the small planters while they tolerate a lot of things from the big ones.[111]

Similar divisions existed among the Northern Province planters as well. Conflict between small and big planters there came to a head on the question of forming the Labour Allocation Board. The majority of small employers — mostly Greeks growing papain — opposed the formation of a statutory board which they feared would be controlled by the government and the big growers. They preferred recruiting to be left to private recruiters and the employers themselves. At a general meeting of the employers called to discuss the proposals to form a statutory board, the Greeks voted *en masse* against the proposals. In spite of the majority vote against it F. Anderson, owner of Rasha Rasha coffee estate, member of the Legislative Council and one-time chairman of the Export Seed Growers' Association, petitioned the government to pass the Bill because those who opposed it 'consisted almost entirely of members of one community only most of whom are engaged in the production of paw-paw, together with a number of small stock farmers who are not employers of contract labour'.[112]

Contradictions also existed between and among the industries on the question of prices and marketing. For example, Anderson, as chairman of the Export Seed Growers' Association, felt that the food producers were being paid low prices thus subsidizing the export industry.[113] He complained that the big Dutch-owned Tanganyika Planting Company was able to pay higher wages because it got higher prices than the Northern Province planters: this meant that their labour deserted to join the Planting Company.

Within the TSGA also there existed a conflict so far as marketing was concerned. For a long time the marketing of sisal was carried out by a dozen or so London-based finance houses, which financed a number of sisal estates and acted as their agents and brokers. These houses advanced finances to the estates at an interest and got commission on the sisal sold through them.[114]

After the war, the representatives of local big capital and the finance capital invested in sisal got together to form their own selling organization, the Tanganyika Sisal Marketing Association (TASMA).[115] The move was against the London-based agency and finance houses. Previously, some 22.5 per cent of TSGA members (producing 41.5 per cent of tonnage) had managed to defeat the proposals for co-operative marketing.[116] Thus the formation of TASMA involving some 70 per cent of the growers (producing some 53 per cent of the territory's production)[117] represented an alliance between local big capital, the foreign finance capital invested locally* and the small growers against the foreign finance and merchant capital with no *invested* capital in the country.

In spite of the numerous contradictions among the various fractions of capital, it is clear that capital was generally united against labour. From our foregoing discussion, we can also safely conclude that the hegemonic fraction in the organization of the capitalists was constituted by the local big capital and foreign finance capital with close collaboration between them. Big capital, both local and foreign, was also closely allied with the colonial state.

The resistance of semi-proletarian labour

Although the laws of the capitalist mode of production and the long-term interests of capital dictate that labour power be paid according to its value and be provided with normal conditions of work so that labour may reproduce itself in a normal state, this does not come about automatically. The passion and greed of individual capital to

---

* Abdullah Karimjee and Eldred Hitchcock (shareholder and representative of Bird & Co.) were the leading personalities behind the formation of TASMA.

extract maximum surplus-labour often leads it in practice to overstep these bounds.* It is the competition among capitals and specially the collective resistance and struggle of the working class which limit capital in its otherwise unrestrained hunger for surplus-labour. Thus the various laws and regulations — for example, those limiting working hours, fixing minimum wages or regulating conditions of work in factories — are a result and a reflection of *class struggle* between capital and labour. The fact that colonial capital was able to perpetrate starvation wages and deplorable conditions of work, as we saw in Chapter 2, was not only because of its near-monopoly organisation but also because of lack of *collective* resistance of labour. The latter in turn reflected labour's semi-proletarian character, impermanence and instability.

The semi-proletarian labour had not severed its links with the means of production; it was not entirely dependent on wages. With one foot still in the peasantry, it carried over the individualism of a small producer to places of employment. Such a labour therefore did not provide a material and social basis for the development of a collective conscious-ness, resistance and organization: this being one of the reasons why the colonial employer and state preferred it to completely proletarianized labour.[118] Thus, for instance, the colonial employer could discharge 30–35,000 workers during the depression, impose a wage cut of as much as 20 per cent and later even reduce the scale of rations[119] without much more than 'one or two ugly incidents'.[120] The 1930 ARLD summarized the situation succinctly.

At first sight it may appear extraordinary that it should be possible for a large proportion of the workers of a country to be discharged within a very limited period, without causing widespread disaster and distress. The explanation lies in the resilience provided by the native connection with the land; if he can no longer earn wages or sell his crop, he can at any rate produce all that is essential to him.[121]

The report went on to quote approvingly a South African report which said: 'The reserve [i.e. land] . . . meets the same needs in the life of the native as the strong trade union meets in the life of the European wage-earner and it meets it in a way which is consonant with his traditions and is, in a way, automatic.'[122] This, in a nutshell, summarized an important difference between a proletarian and a semi-proletarian. Whereas, during the depression, the European proletarian became radicalized and even moved to *communist* organization, his semi-proletarian brethren in Tanganyika returned to the land!

If there was minimal *collective* resistance on the part of the semi-proletariat, it is not to say that he was resigned to his fate. The resistance to a bad employer, deplorable conditions of work and general state of oppression took *individualized* forms among the semi-proletarians. Prominent among these were desertion and absenteeism. As we have already seen, there was a high incidence of both of these.[123]

Desertion or contract-breaking was one of the biggest headaches of the employers and the state who complained endlessly that the 'native' did not honour the sacred contract which bound him to his master. 'The outstanding source of trouble is the impunity with which the native can break the agreement, and desert to return home to seek work elsewhere.'[124] 'From the evidence placed before the committee it is incontestable that the labourer in this Territory has still little or no conception of the

---

* '[In] its blind unrestrainable passion, its were-wolf hunger for surplus-labour, capital oversteps not only the moral, but even the merely physical maximum bounds of the working-day. It usurps the time for growth, development, and healthy maintenance of the body. It steals the time required for the consumption of fresh air and sunlight.' (Marx, *Capital*, Vol. I, p. 252.)

sanctity of an agreement.'[125] '[They] agree to a contract, as being an arrangement which seems to suit them and which they will respect as long as they find no reason to do otherwise; should they dislike the conditions of employment, or should they see a more attractive opportunity elsewhere, they consider themselves free to desert.'[126] Although the state made desertion a penal offence and gave considerable assistance to the employer in tracing deserters, not many deserters could be apprehended. Employers therefore unanimously pressurized the colonial state to introduce a kind of registration system: a system of pass laws on the lines of the then Northern Rhodesia. In an address presented to the Acting Governor in August 1933, the Mufindi Tea Planters' Association implored:

We press for the Registration of natives in the manner already adopted in Kenya. This has previously been asked for, but government, owing to the expense involved has not yet been able to see its way to do it . . . I would point out to your excellency that at present if we break a contract we are quite rightly fined fairly heavily, whereas if a labourer does so he is practically never punished. So registration would benefit the settler in stopping sudden desertions, and it would place on the native a responsibility which he would find difficult to evade.[127]

And the Arusha Coffee Planters Association argued:

Our experience is that once a native under contract deserts, he is seldom, if ever traced and this fact undoubtedly encourages his friends to follow his example. The desertion of contract labour represents a considerable financial loss to the employer and we feel certain that this would be to a great extent prevented, were registration introduced.[128]

The Sisal Growers' Association diplomatically added its voice:

This Association is strongly in favour of some form of registration and would like to know the governor's point of view on this matter, whether he is in favour of registration being introduced and if so when the introduction is likely to occur.[129]

It was such pressure that made the colonial government pass the Identification Ordinance in 1935.[130] However, this was a watered-down version of what the employers wanted and they were not interested in it. The government too realized that its strict enforcement would involve finger-printing of the African population, issuing of identification cards, restriction of movement, and so on. Besides the expense and practical difficulties involved, it would inevitably invite a great deal of harsh criticism from abroad as being essentially a *racial* legislation. In view of all these considerations, the Ordinance was never enforced.[131]

In spite of some 'financial loss' to an individual employer, desertion as a form of resistance was no more than an irritation to the capitalist class as a whole and the colonial state. What they feared most was any form of *collective* resistance. The colonial employer and the state were extremely sensitive and reacted violently to any signs of collective opposition. The latter, however, was not highly developed in the semi-proletariat — both in terms of its magnitude and organization.

Occasional collective resistance took the form of unorganized, spontaneous riots or 'downing of tools'. These do not appear to have been planned in advance nor did they have any coherent set of demands. Let us cite one or two incidents to illustrate this form of resistance.

On 5 August 1959 at 10.30 a.m., 3–400 workers, mostly sugar-cane cutters, of the Tanganyika Planting Company suddenly downed tools, moved towards the factory and assaulted two Greek supervisors placed over them. One of the Greeks took refuge in a nearby hotel. The crowd surrounded the hotel and threw stones on the roof. 'At this juncture, a young German employee, Fritz Hartmann, proceeded to the hotel, quietened the mob and was instrumental in preventing further damage to property or person.' Meanwhile news was sent to the District Office. An Assistant District Officer, Mr Rowe, followed by the Chief Inspector of Police, Mr Olliver, and nine policemen, arrived on the estate.

Mr Rowe, on arrival, found that all labour had returned to their camps. After some delay, he was able to interrogate the headman of some 200 labourers, but little could be got out of them as to the cause of this disturbance. Chief Inspector Olliver arrested two of the labourers who were alleged to have assaulted the Greeks. Finding the situation no longer serious Mr Rowe and the Police returned to Headquarters. A detective was sent later to see whether he could get any information which might throw light on the cause of disturbance. The detective returned on the 22nd . . . and reported that he could elicit no information which might help us.

Since there were no further outbreaks, and the labour had resumed their normal duties, both the employer and the labour officer were anxious not to disturb it. Nevertheless, the labour officer continued his independent investigations and after interrogating several eye-witnesses arrived at the conclusion that the causes of the 'downing of tools' were:

(a) the measures adopted in seeing that the sugar-cane was properly stacked by labourers completing their tasks. Orders that morning were apparently given (rightly or wrongly), that the sugar-cane was to be pressed down after stacking so that a fair and full metre could be demanded as the day's task (b) rumours also apparently spread that the metre itself was to be increased and (c) I am inclined to believe that the two assaulted Greek supervisors were not always as tactful and considerate as they should be. Evidence adduced before me tends to show that the labourers were subjected to abuse and minor assaults.[132]

The workers had very legitimate grievances. Even so they were persuaded by the young German to return to their jobs and *complete the tasks*. Although we have no independent source of information except the labour officer's report, we can surmise that the incident was a result of spontaneous rage; the collective action itself appears to have been born of this rage rather than a result of any preconceived plan. This would also explain the fact that the workers did not stick out for longer than a few hours. Some 'nice words' were enough to send them back to work since they did not have specific demands, organization or leadership — however elementary — to sustain them.

Nonetheless, the state took a very serious view of even this elementary form of collective resistance. The Chief Inspector of Labour was disturbed by the fact that the labour officer decided to leave the matter alone. As he put it: 'the fact that a disorderly mob of 3/400 natives made a concerted attack on two Europeans discloses a most serious state of affairs. It does not really matter whether the supervisors were of an indifferent type or not, and does not really explain the occurrence . . . The arrest of only two of the mob seems to me a totally inadequate settlement of the affair and a direct encouragement to a repetition of the disturbance.'[133]

Officials went to great lengths to find out if there were any 'subversive elements' at work besides imposing harsh penal measures on the leaders. For example, around October 1935 there were several incidences of 'downing of tools' in the coffee estates of Arusha. In a number of these cases, the workers involved came from Songea and their usual complaint was that the tasks were too big. In a typical case, a gang of 20–25 people would walk off their work and lay complaint with the 'Boma' (District Office), only to find that there penalties of 'imprisonment with hard labour' awaited them for breaking contracts.[134]

In its investigations, the officials went as far as investigating the family histories of the 'leaders', as in the case of one Nandela Makita whose gang had walked off their work at Loliondo Estate. 'As a personal view', opined the District Officer from Songea who had been asked to investigate any 'subversive influence' at his end, 'I am suspicious of the presence of Nandela Makita and I would not be surprised if he was the cause of the trouble. The Makita family are born intriguers and trouble makers and Nandela has been in trouble before and is quite capable of avoiding trouble himself.'[135]

Towards the end of 1930s, some strikes did begin to take place among the plantation workers.[136] But in the absence of organization, they appear to have been localized incidents confined to small groups of workers from particular ethnic groups, on particular estates, very short-lived and easily intimidated and overwhelmed by police presence.[137] The incident at Lanzori Estate which occurred in September 1939 is a case in point. Some 150 Wabemba cutters marched to the manager's office with *pangas* (knives) and sticks demanding: (a) increase in wages, (b) reintroduction of the bonus and (c) reduced task. The Assistant District Officer appeared on the scene with the police and read out the contract to the workers. Immediately the first two demands were withdrawn while the workers insisted that the task was too big. The next day the District Officer himself timed the tasks and informed the workers that they could be completed in 4–5 hours. Later, when the workers refused to disperse, two or three policemen were called in and all the workers moved off. Meanwhile, the work resumed although official investigations continued, presumably to apprehend the 'culprits', that is, leaders.[138] To cite one more typical incident, the District Officer, Morogoro, received a telephone message from the manager of Kidugalo Sisal Estate that some '600 natives were rioting on that estate'. He immediately dispatched his assistant with a police officer and '18 native police ranks'. 'This morning the District Officer reported [to the Provincial Commissioner] that the Assistant District Officer and Party had returned at 3.00 a.m. Thirty arrests had been made and that one native had been sent to hospital as a result of injuries received in the riot.'[139]

So much then for collective action on the part of semi-proletarian labour and the response of the colonial state. As for collective *organization*, once again the impermanent character of this labour militated against its formation. As we shall see in subsequent chapters, it was essentially among the proletariat (motor-drivers and dock-workers) that the first pre-trade-union organizations were born.

In the organizational field as well, it was the colonial employer who commanded the initiative. So as to have easy communication with his labour and maintain a degree of discipline, the employer divided his labour residentially in line with ethnical divisions headed by headmen or 'tribal representatives'.[140] The furthest that this type of organization went was to take care of some welfare measures. It was this type of organization which the colonial state enthusiastically supported and encouraged. The 1927 ARLD, while deprecating trade unions, enthusiastically welcomed welfare societies:

A most interesting and far more desirable [i.e. preferable to trade unions] movement occurred on one plantation, where the employees spontaneously formed a welfare society and set up an organization for mutual help. Beginning with certain tribes, it was at first restricted to those; but the rest speedily followed suit and set up their own tribal society. The funds are collected by a monthly subscription from every member and are banked with the Manager, careful accounts being kept and posted on the estate notice board; officers are elected by the members and form a committee of management. The funds are devoted to providing burial ceremonies for members who may happen to die; furnishing help to sick, injured, or unfortunate, beyond that given by the estate; assisting widows or orphans; and generally in benefiting the members in a most useful way.[141]

The total membership of all the societies on this particular plantation was 644 men and 147 women, with a total cash balance of Shs. 3,222. After careful examination of the organization the labour officer noted with satisfaction that 'there is no doubt that it is genuine and not 'inspired' by any outsider'![142]

It is not clear how widespread these organizations were, although it seems that they were no more than the 'tribal associations' that Iliffe speaks of.[143] They cut across class lines and their main concern was to assist in such things as funerals, sickness and accommodation of the people from the same ethnic groups. They were certainly not even an elementary form of 'friendly societies' which acted as a precursor to 'trade unions', like the one which developed among the dockworkers.[144] It appears therefore that collective resistance, consciousness and organization were not the characteristic of semi-proletarian labour. These are rather to be found in the more permanent labour force, the examination of which forms the subject matter of our subsequent chapters.

NOTES

1. Lenin, V. I., *Imperialism, the Highest Stage of Capitalism*, op. cit., pp. 266–7.
2. ibid., p. 258.
3. Frankel, S. H., *Capital Investment in Africa* (London: Oxford University Press, 1938), p. 18.
4. Marx, K., *Capital*, Vol. III, op. cit., pp. 237–9.
5. Rweyemamu, U., *Underdevelopment*, op. cit., pp. 15–16.
6. Seidman, A., *Comparative Development Strategies in East Africa* (Nairobi: East African Publishing House, 1972) p. 18.
7. Iliffe, J., *Modern History*, op. cit., p. 147.
8. Frankel, S. H., op. cit., Table 28.
9. Up to the end of 1935 only.
10. Estimated by Frankel as 10 per cent of the total listed capital. The total listed capital includes £33.6 million invested in German East Africa.
11. Frankel, S. H., op cit., p. 171.
12. ibid., p. 155. Leubuscher, C., *Tanganyika Territory; a Study of Economic Policy Under Mandate* (London: Oxford University Press, 1944), p. 167.
13. Leubuscher, C., op. cit., p. 8. Frankel, S. H., op. cit., p. 164.
14. Rweyemamu, J., *Underdevelopment*, op. cit., p. 20.
15. Seidman, A., *Comparative Development*, op. cit., p. 18.
16. Guillebaud, C. W., *An Economic Survey of the Sisal Industry of Tanganyika* (Welwyn: James Nisbet, 1966), 3rd edn, p. 63. Lawrence, P. R., 'Plantation Sisal: the Inherited Mode of Production', in Cliffe, L., *et al.* (eds), *Rural Cooperation in Tanzania* (Dar es Salaam: Tanzania Publishing House, 1975), p. 106, Table 1.
17. Khamis, L., *Imperialism Today*, op. cit., p. 21.
18. Frankel, S. H., op. cit., p. 22. Iliffe, J., *Modern History*, op. cit., p. 91. Hill, M. F., *Permanent Way: the Story of the Tanganyika Railways*, Vol. I (Nairobi: East African Railways and Harbours, 1957), pp. 40ff.
19. Annual Reports, 1900–10, Annex AXII. Typescript of translations in possession of Professor A. Sherriff, University of Dar es Salaam.
20. Iliffe, J., *Modern History*, op. cit., pp. 16, 147.
21. ibid., p. 148.
22. Ibid. p. 146. Iliffe, J., *German Rule*, op. cit., p. 101. Lewa Rubber Estates to Secretary to Administration, 10 May 1919, CO 691/23/Part I/14139–143.

23. Hill, M. F., op. cit., p. 109.
24. Frankel, S. H., op. cit., p. 164.
25. Depelchin, J. and LeMelle, S. J., 'Some Aspects of Capital Accumulation in Tanganyika, 1920–1940' (paper presented to History Seminar, University of Dar es Salaam, mimeo, 1979), p. 9. Iliffe, J., *Modern History*, op. cit., p. 264.
26. Depelchin, J. and LeMelle, S. J., op. cit., p. 22. Iliffe, J., *Modern History*, op. cit., p. 261. Hartnoll, A. V., 'Notes Regarding the Tanga Province', 7 August 1946, CO 691/187/42094/1.
27. Iliffe, J., *Modern History*, op. cit., p. 304.
28. 'Investment in the Mandates', *Economist*, 24 December 1938, p. 662. Leubuscher, C., op. cit., p. 166.
29. 'Investment in the Mandates', op. cit., p. 662.
30. Leubuscher, C., op. cit., Ch. VI. See also Depelchin and LeMelle, op. cit.
31. 'Investment in the Mandates' op. cit., p. 662.
32. Nkrumah, K., *Neo-Colonialism: the Last Stage of Imperialism* (London: Heinemann Educational Books, 1968), pp. 164–5.
33. 'Investment in the Mandates', op. cit., p. 662.
34. Ofunguo, A. C., 'History of Labour on the Mwadui Diamond Mine: 1940–1975' (MA dissertation, University of Dar es Salaam, 1977), p. 7. See also Nkrumah, K., op. cit., Ch. 10.
35. Depelchin, J. and LeMelle, S. J., 'Research materials on companies registered in Tanganyika'. I am grateful to the authors for letting me make use of their research material on companies registered in Tanganyika during the early colonial period.
36. Leubuscher, C., op. cit., p. 57.
37. ibid., p. 56.
38. ibid., p. 24.
39. Mascarenhas, A. C., 'Resistance and Change in the Sisal Plantation System of Tanzania' (PhD thesis, University of California, LA, 1970), p. 84.
40. See generally Walji, S. R., 'Ismailis on Mainland Tanzania, 1850–1948' (MA dissertation, University of Wisconsin, 1969). Honey, M., 'A History of Indian Merchant Capital and Class Formation in Tanganyika, *c.* 1840–1940" (PhD thesis, University of Dar es Salaam, 1982). I am grateful to Martha Honey for letting me make use of her thesis while still in draft. I have drawn significantly from her work as far as empirical information is concerned. Unless otherwise indicated, subsequent citations refer to the final version of her thesis.
41. Walji, S. R., op. cit., p. 154.
42. ibid.
43. Honey, M., op. cit., Table XXI, pp. 468–9.
44. Iliffe, J., *Modern History*, op. cit., p. 304.
45. Honey, M., op. cit., p. 9 of the draft thesis.
46. Iliffe, J., *Modern History*, op. cit., p. 304.
47. ibid., pp. 264, 304.
48. Ofunguo, A. C., op. cit., Ch. 1.
49. Iliffe, J., *Modern History*, op. cit., p. 304.
50. Honey, M., op. cit., Table XXIII, p. 475.
51. Minutes of the Annual General Meeting, TSGA, 29 March 1946, TNA 4/25/6/IV.
52. Guillebaud, C. W., op. cit., p. 133.
53. Annual Report, 1948/49, NPLUB, op. cit.
54. 'Conditions of Labour on Railway Construction', op cit.
55. Interview, Hamisi Mandaro, 31 July 1975. Mr Mandaro joined TECCO in 1948. Before that he had worked as a domestic servant of one of the partners of TECCO. At the time of the interview he was a foreman in the Mwananchi Engineering and Construction Company (MECCO), the successor of TECCO.
56. Leubuscher, C., op. cit., p. 55.
57. TNA 30336.

58. See, for instance, Baran, P. A., *The Political Economy of Growth* (New York: Monthly Review Press, 1968), pp. 92ff.
59. Lenin, V. I., *Imperialism*, op. cit., p. 262.
60. Frankel, S. H., op. cit., p. 375.
61. Hill, M. F., op. cit., pp. 62–5.
62. ibid., p. 85.
63. ibid., p. 93.
64. ibid., p. 96.
65. Leubuscher, C., op. cit., p. 154.
66. ibid., p. 159.
67. ibid., pp. 14–15.
68. Frankel, S. H., op. cit., p. 171.
69. Leubuscher, C., op. cit., pp. 158–9.
70. Frankel, S. H., op. cit., p. 393.
71. Calculated from Hill, M. F., op. cit., p. 280, App. A.
72. Brett, E. A., *Colonialism and Underdevelopment in East Africa: The Politics of Economic Change, 1919–39* (London: Heinemann Educational Books, 1973). pp. 124ff.
73. Quoted ibid., p. 132.
74. See below, Ch. 6.
75. Mascarenhas, A. C., op. cit., p. 212.
76. Iliffe, J., *German Rule*, op. cit., pp. 84–5.
77. ibid., pp. 67, 69, 84, 107.
78. See File Vol. I, No. VIII, I, 50, in Hartman, F. F. and Willmot, B. C., op. cit.
79. ibid.
80. Speech by H.P. Amman, op. cit., p. 15.
81. Mascarenhas, A. C., op cit., p. 104.
82. Speech by H. P. Amman, op. cit. p. 15.
83. Mascarenhas, A. C., op. cit., p. 107.
84. ibid, p. 109.
85. Speech by H. P. Amman, op. cit.
86. Iliffe, J., *Modern History*, op. cit., pp. 304, 374.
87. Mascarenhas, A.C., op. cit., p. 181.
88. GN No. 441 of 6 May 1938.
89. Mascarenhas, A. C., op. cit., p. 111.
90. No. 15 of 1945.
91. Senior Agriculture Officer, North Eastern Circle, to Director of Agriculture, 4 June 1932, TNA 11168/I.
92. CS to TSGA, 15 February 1937, TNA 24693/I.
93. Minutes of the 13th meeting of the Labour Advisory Board, 19 August 1952, TNA 10953/II.
94. A. Sillery to PC, Central Province, 27 July 1937. PC to A. Sillery, 30 August 1937. Tanganyika Coffee Growers' Association to CS, 21 September 1937, all in TNA 11127/I.
95. Director of Agriculture to [?], 31 December 1938, TNA 11127/I.
96. See above, Ch. 1.
97. Iliffe, J., *Modern History*, op. cit., p. 345.
98. Speech by H. P. Amman, op. cit.
99. TNA 11127/I.
100. No. 2 of 1947.
101. GN No. 62 of 1947.
102. 'Half-yearly report of PC, Northern Province', 1927, TNA 11127/I.
103. ibid.
104. Longland, F., 'Labour Matters in Sisal Areas', No. l, op. cit. TNA 23544.
105. Iliffe, J., *Modern History*, op. cit., p. 345. Mascarenhas, A. C., op. cit., p. 108.
106. Tanganyika Engineering Supply Co. to CS enclosing a report by the construction superintendent of Balfour Beatty & Co., 21 January 1935, TNA 11168/I.

107. Sabot, R. H., op. cit., p. 37.
108. PC, Northern Province, to CS, 6 August 1937, and minutes thereon, TNA 11127/I.
109. Honey, M., op. cit. p. 474.
110. TNA 4/25/6/IV.
111. Quoted in Honey, M. draft thesis made available to this writer by the author.
112. TNA 69/316/24/II.
113. Anderson to a friend in the Secretariat, 19 May 1946, TNA 11127/I.
114. Guillebaud, C. W., op. cit., p. 103. Iliffe, J. *Agricultural Change*, op. cit., p. 29.
115. Hitchcock, E., 'The Sisal Industry of East Africa', *TNR*, No. 52, March 1959, p. 9.
116. Iliffe, J., *Modern History*, op. cit., p. 345.
117. Hitchcock, E., op. cit., p. 9.
118. See, for example, Mitchell, P. E., op. cit., p. 10.
119. K. C. Charron to PC, Tanga, 23 February 1943, TNA 305/3/5/14.
120. ARLD, 1930, pp. 18–22.
121. ibid., pp. 21–2.
122. ibid.
123. See above, Ch. 2.
124. Orde-Browne, G., *Labour Report 1926*, op. cit., p. 46.
125. *Labour Committee Report*, op. cit., p. 18.
126. Orde-Browne, G., *Labour Report 1926*, op. cit., p. 46, para. 72.
127. Address to the Acting Governor, August 1933, TNA A 25905.
128. Memorandum to Acting Governor, 3 October 1937, TNA A 25905.
129. Memorandum to Governor, August 1938, TNA A 25905.
130. No. 13 of 1935.
131. See generally, TNA A 25905 and *Labour Committee Report*, op. cit., App. II.
132. 'Report to the District Officer', Moshi, 15 August 1939, TNA A 27336.
133. Howman to the Labour Officer, Arusha, 7 September 1939, TNA A 27336.
134. TNA 11127.
135. PC, Southern Province, to [?], 10 December 1935, TNA 11127.
136. 'Quarterly Labour Report of the Labour Officer', Tanga Province, 30 June 1937, TNA 11168/I.
137. See, for instance, Dillon to LC, n.d., reporting on a minor strike at Lusando Estate, 27[?]1946, MLH 4/29/6.
138. Assistant District Officer to Chief Labour Inspector, 12 September 1939, TNA 25956.
139. PC, Dar es Salaam, to CS, 25 August 1939, TNA 27284.
140. I owe this point to G. Hadjivyanis.
141. pp. 44–5.
142. ibid.
143. Iliffe, J., *Modern History*, op. cit., p. 389.
144. See below, Ch. 5.

4

The Development and Conditions of Permanent Wage-Labour

The development of permanent wage-labour

An overview

The development of the proletariat in England and Europe was an integral part of the process of transformation of feudal agriculture into industrial capitalism. In England this process was long drawn out, the most important element of which was the Agrarian Revolution. The enclosure movement of the sixteenth and eighteenth centuries instituted large-scale capitalist production on land, at the same time dispossessing the peasantry. The dispossessed peasantry constituted the most important source of the later proletariat.[1]

The second source of the proletariat was the guild-craftsmen of the medieval towns. Over a period of time the craftsmen lost their independence and became wage-labourers of the rich merchants now turned manufacturers.[2] These craftsmen were joined by their rural brethren whose 'domestic industry' had been ruined by a combination of the Agrarian Revolution and the development of mass production.

The third source of the proletariat, which Engels emphasizes, was 'the declassed, almost pariah-like, elements wholly outside the feudal structure, who were inevitably bound to come into existence whenever a town was formed; who constituted the lowest stratum of the population of every medieval town and, having no rights, were detached from the *Markgenossenschaft*, from feudal dependence and from the craft guild'.[3] These were the famous vagabonds, beggars and thieves of that time.

These three sources then constituted, in Engels's apt phrase, the *pre-proletariat*.[4] All these three categories had one thing in common; they were people ' "freed" completely from any connection with the soil, men without ties of place or property'.[5] And they formed the reserve army from which the Industrial Revolution drew its mass of wage-earners. The mass of 'free' labourers was a necessary condition without which the Industrial Revolution would not have been possible.

This in a nutshell was the origin of the proletariat in the industralized countries of Western Europe and England. The origins of the proletariat (and the wage-earning class generally) in Tanganyika, however, took a different turn altogether. What was decisive in the latter case was the dominance of imperialism.

The class of wage-labourers in Tanganyika developed within the political economy of colonialism. In its quest for raw materials, imperialism partially destroyed the self-sufficiency and the domestic industry of the pre-colonial peasant and turned him into a pure agriculturist. Yet this did not constitute a fundamental transformation of agriculture for agriculture essentially continued as a patriarchal, small-scale mode of production now integrated in the imperialist division of labour. Small enclaves of capitalist large-scale agriculture — the plantations — also reflected only a partial change. For some six decades the labour-force in the plantations (and mines), as we have already seen, was predominantly semi-proletarian, retaining its links with both 'its place and property' (land). It was in the interstices of this predominantly migrant labour force that small nuclei of the nascent proletariat began to develop. These were mainly concentrated in the factories processing primary products (sisal decortication, cotton ginning and so on), building, construction, maintenance and repairs and communication. This was the first source from which the proletariat was formed.

The second source was the small manufacturing sector. Between the two world wars there was hardly any manufacturing sector worth speaking of. It was only after the Second World War that import-substitution industrialization began, gathering momentum after independence.

The third source was constituted by the work-force in the agriculture and mining sectors. The beginning of import-substitution industrialization in turn had an impact on the primary sector which set in motion a gradual stabilization of the migrant worker, giving rise to the agriculture and mining proletariat.

The fourth and final source in the formation of permanent wage-labour was the service worker in the state and private administration. Among service workers, the domestic servant was an important component.

Thus the modern proletariat in Tanzania did not develop as a result of an agrarian and industrial revolution but as essentially a by-product of the integration of a pre-capitalist, patriarchal economy into a world capitalist market dominated by finance capital. Such an origin of the proletariat has left its imprint both on the size and the character of the proletariat.

With this overview we now turn to consider in detail the development of different sections of the permanent wage-earning class.

The industrial proletariat

As we have already seen, the backbone of the colonial economy was the primary sector, chiefly agriculture and mining. The other important sector, in terms of employment, was infrastructure (building, construction and transport) which was geared to serve the primary sector. The labour force in these sectors until the late 1950s was predominantly migrant, that is, semi-proletarian. It was within this semi-proletarian labour force that small nuclei of an 'industrial proletariat' had begun to be formed.

Agriculture, mining, construction and transport inevitably required some skilled labour, however small the number. For instance, sisal decorticating factories and cotton ginneries needed mechanics and fitters and other skilled artisans. Owing to a fairly substantial transport system that sisal estates had to maintain to ferry bulky sisal leaves and fibre, engineering and maintenance workshops were an indispensable part of the estates' apparatus. This too required drivers, mechanics and so on.

Another group of craftsmen that was an inevitable feature of the plantation labour force were those involved in building and construction of 'labour lines' and other housing on the estates: carpenters, masons, joiners, surveyors and so on. True, in the

Table 4.1　*Distribution of employment of all adult African males by skills and industries, 1949 and 1956 (%)*

Industrial classification	White-collar service workers		Craftsmen		Other skilled workers		Unskilled workers		Total	
	1949	1956	1949	1956	1949	1956	1949	1956	1949	1956
Agriculture	16_3	28_7	26_7	32_6	19_5	25_6	46_{85}	59_{81}	39_{100}	49_{100}
Mining & quarrying	3_4	3_9	7_{11}	4_8	8_{13}	5_{14}	6_{72}	4_{69}	6_{100}	4_{100}
Manufacturing	3_3	3_9	7_{10}	9_{17}	7_{10}	6_{13}	7_{77}	4_{62}	7_{100}	5_{100}
Transport	6_6	6_{10}	7_{11}	9_{10}	6_8	18_{27}	8_{76}	6_{53}	8_{100}	7_{100}
Building & construction	5_4	1_5	23_{25}	13_{28}	6_6	2_5	9_{66}	3_{63}	10_{100}	4_{100}
Government employment	34_{16}	41_{33}	15_{10}	23_8	33_{21}	37_{17}	12_{54}	19_{54}	16_{100}	24_{100}
Commercial & professional	21_{23}	7_{33}	7_{11}	4_{12}	9_{14}	3_{12}	5_{52}	2_{43}	7_{100}	2_{100}
Educational	7_{22}	9_{40}	4_{21}	4_{12}	5_{25}	2_8	1_{32}	2_{40}	2_{100}	3_{100}
Miscellaneous	5_9	2_{16}	4_9	2_{11}	8_{16}	2_{17}	5_{66}	1_{56}	5_{100}	1_{100}
Total	100_8	100_{13}	100_{11}	100_8	100_{10}	100_{11}	100_{71}	100_{68}	100_{100}	100_{100}

	Total no of workers	
	299,113	335,637

Notes:　Figures in the left-hand side of each column, when read vertically, give the sectoral distribution of each category while figures on the right-hand side of each column, when read horizontally, give the proportion of each category of workers in the particular sector. (Percentages may not add up to exactly 100 due to rounding.)

Source:　Calculated from Tables A.3 and A.4, below, pp. 246 and 247.

early period of colonialism many of these occupations were largely filled by non-Africans, in particular Asian craftsmen. But very soon the government as well as private employers realized that Asian craftsmen were far more expensive and that there was no alternative but to train African artisans.

As early as 1922, Governor Byatt had proposed training African skilled personnel (both clerical and craftsmen) to man government departments. The governor's rationale was, as he put it:

This government depends at present almost entirely upon artisans and clerical personnel recruited in India, and it is impossible to regard this dependence as satisfactory. Experience has shown the arrangement to be both disappointing and very costly, and that high wages must be paid for no correspondingly high efficiency, and too frequently expense is incurred in returning to India men who are either incompetent or dishonest. It is . . . my hope to train up an African personnel which will relieve the territory of its dependence upon Asiatics, partly because I believe that it is wise to give the native a due share in the administration and the prosperity of his own country, but chiefly because the employment of subordinates who are content with a far smaller wage, who are inured to the climate, and who do not require long period of leave with an expensive oversea journey, will affect a very large economy in the expenditure of the country.[6]

By 1926 the governor had instituted the non-clerical part of the African Civil Service providing grades and salary scales of, mainly, artisans and craftsmen.[7]

Although we do not have any direct evidence, observations in colonial reports[8] and by other researchers[9] indicate that among those who settled down permanently on the estates were skilled workers (clerks, headmen, dressers) and craftsmen and artisans (carpenters, mechanics, drivers, masons and so on). They were provided with more permanent housing and were generally treated better than the migrants. We can then treat the craftsmen and artisans in this group as the nuclei of an 'industrial proletariat'.

There are no complete data to give us the proportion of the permanent labour in the labour force. However, analysis of the 1949 employment figures from Annual Reports of the Labour Department shows that the permanent skilled labour force, both white-collar and craftsmen, constituted probably 25–30 per cent of the total labour force (see Table A.5, p. 248).

Table 4.1 also throws some light on the approximate distribution of skilled manpower by industries. The greatest (almost two-thirds) concentration of craftsmen in 1949 was to be found in agriculture, building and construction and government employment although it was only in building and construction that they formed a substantial proportion (about one-fourth) of the total African adult male labour force in that sector. The pride of place occupied by craftsmen in building and construction industry is further illustrated in Table 4.2 which gives data for the labour force of an important construction company. There it constituted one-fifth of the total and three-fourths of the skilled labour force.

Apart from building and construction there were craftsmen and other skilled workers in the transport industry, particularly in the railway workshops and docks. Their work involved primarily the maintenance and repair of transport equipment.

The second source in the formation of the industrial proletariat was the manufacturing sector, which occupied a minuscule place in the colonial economy. Tanganyika's economy was a textbook case of a typical colonial economy producing primary products for export and importing manufactured goods for the small home market.

The period between the two wars has been dubbed the period of non-industrialization.[10] Martha Honey cites three factors which were responsible for discouraging any substantial manufacturing activity during this period.

Table 4.2 *Stirling Astaldi (EA) Ltd: distribution of the labour force by occupation on Dar es Salaam–Morogoro road as at 31 December 1951 (Africans only)*[a]

Occupation	No.	%
Clerks	44	2.4
Dressers	8	0.4
Headmen	22	1.2
Cooks & domestics	50	2.7
Total white-collar service workers	124	6.7
Mechanics	42	2.3
Drivers & tractors operatives	113	6.1
Carpenters & masons	184	10.0
Others (semi-skilled)	29	1.6
Total craftsmen	368	20.0
Unskilled	1,360	73.4
Grand total	1,852	100.0

Note: [a] There were only 10 Asian skilled workers, 8 craftsmen and 2 white-collar.
Source: Annual District Report, TNA 57/1/3/II.

First, there was the opposition from metropolitan industrial interests. They were interested in maintaining Tanganyika as the protected market of their manufactured goods and a source of cheap raw materials on the one hand, and discouraging any competition from colonial imports of manufactured goods into their UK market on the other. The example of the Tanganyika Cordage Company of Tanga illustrates the point. Some British manufacturers had established three binder twine factories in the early 1930s with a view to export duty-free sisal twine to Britain and other Commonwealth countries under the Imperial Preference System. In 1934 the British Rope, Twine and Net Makers' Federation made strong representations to the British government on the grounds that 'their home market in the United Kingdom was being menaced by the sale here by the Tanganyika Cordage Company of binder twine produced by low-paid African labour in Tanganyika'.[11] (Moreover, British rope manufacturers imported their sisal from the same source.) The British government obliged by imposing a 100 per cent duty on binder twine (but no duty on raw sisal) imported into Britain, thus making it impossible for the Tanganyika company to compete. The factory had to close down in 1938.

Secondly, the colonial government itself opposed the industrialization of the territory, partly because in the final analysis it represented the interests of the metropolitan bourgeoisie, but partly because it had local interest in maintaining its revenue. A substantial portion (nearly 40 per cent in 1930) of its revenue came from customs duties on imports. It is not surprising therefore that this was one of the concerns expressed by colonial officials when opposing the construction of a proposed textile mill by some Bombay industrialists. One of them noted: 'I think it should be realized before it is too late that the fiscal framework of the administration is based largely on indirect revenue and that any considerable development of local manufacturing activities *supplying only local demands* would undermine the whole structure . . .'[12]

The third factor responsible for Tanganyika's virtual non-industrialization was its unfavoured status within the regional framework. It was Kenya and foreign investors who were favoured by the British government. Rweyemamu explains it as follows:

The British settlers in Kenya were a well-established pressure group in London while Tanzania's settlers were of mixed nationalities, without a cohesive force. Moreover, Tanzania was merely a conquered territory with less value to Britain during this period since her economy had been partly moulded to suit the needs of the German market. Thus, partly because of the uncertainty of the status of the country (especially after Hitler came to power and threatened to reconquer Germany's lost colonies), the administration's pessimism about the viability of investment opportunities and the centripetal pressures converging on Kenya to which the common market arrangements gave full play, industries tended to be established in Kenya. The adoption of a common external tariff with the other East African territories (a tariff structure which was conceived in the interests of Kenyan industrialists) and the elimination of all trade barriers among the partner states, not only deprived Tanzania of a significant amount of customs revenue but by protecting Kenya's industries, forestalled for a considerable period their establishment in Tanzania.[13]

Thus, for example, at the 1935 Governor's Conference, while Tanganyika's and Uganda's governors argued against industrialization, Kenya's acting governor proposed to encourage it actively. In fact, unlike Tanganyika, Kenya protected its infant manufacturers by imposing high import duties. The net result was that Kenya was relatively more industrialized, supplying not only its own but also Tanganyika's and Uganda's markets.

The result of these interrelated factors was stagnation so far as Tanganyika's industrial development was concerned.

In the inter-war period therefore the little manufacturing that took place was at the level of small-scale manufactories and craft workshops. Besides sisal decorticating factories and cotton ginning machines carrying out essentially first stages of processing of primary raw materials, most of the industrial establishments were in food, beverage and woodworks catering for the small internal market for luxury consumer goods and the processing of a few staple grains. This can be seen in Table A.6. To take just one example: in 1939, out of a total of 538 industrial establishments, 246 or 46 per cent were in the food and beverages sector and 154 or almost 30 per cent in the textile sector (these being 34 cotton ginneries and 120 sisal decorticating factories). These together constituted three-fourths of the total number of establishments employing over 95 per cent of the labour force. In fact, ice and soda factories, rice, flour and oil crushing mills and bakeries together constituted over 75 per cent of all establishments in the food and beverages sector.

Most of these establishments were essentially small-scale, with very little capital and utilizing substantially family labour. Most of them were owned by Asians and a few by Europeans of diverse nationalities.[14] In the absence of any employment censuses, it is difficult to have precise figures of the workers employed in these establishments. However, relying on the figure of the Blue Books we estimate that just before the war their number was probably around 15,000 in 1939, increasing to around 35,000 in 1945.

Given the character of the manufacturing industry, this small labour force was highly scattered rather than concentrated. For instance, in 1945 the average number of workers employed per establishment in food and beverages was twenty while in wood and furniture it was about thirty.

Industrialization in a significant way began towards the late 1940s, continued steadily through the 1950s and gained a considerable momentum after independence. Table 4.3 gives a historical review of manufacturing establishments employing ten or more persons. As the table shows, only 18 per cent of the 569 establishments that existed in 1965 began before 1946, some 34 per cent between 1946 and 1956, with 48 per cent after 1957. Towards the end of the 1950s there was some slackening followed by an upsurge in the post-independence period.

The spurt of industrial development after the war is explained to some extent by Britain's need to earn dollars and shortages of certain materials created by the Korean War. Thus Tanganyika Packers was established jointly by the colonial government and Liebig's Extract of Meat in 1949 to relieve Britain's shortage of meat and dollars. This was followed by the Metal Box Company to supply cans and 'a number of demand-based industries such as Tanzania Bottlers' Company, Sapa Chemicals Ltd, East African Vegetable Industries, Robbialac Paints, Express Dairy and Tanzania Millers'.[15]

Table 4.3 *Historical review of manufacturing industries by industrial activity* (establishments employing 10 persons or more)

CODE ISIC	Industrial activity	No. of establish-ments 1965	Pre-1946	1946–56	1957–60	1961–65
				Year of commencement of production		
20	Food manufacture	125	15	47	24	39
21	Beverage industries	11	4	3	–	4
22	Tobacco manufacture	3	1	1	1	–
23	Manufacture of textiles[a]	158	50	46	20	42
24	Footwear & clothing	10	–	2	1	7
25	Wood except furniture	73	10	25	8	30
26	Furniture and fixtures	17	1	10	3	3
27–28	Paper, printing & publishing	22	–	11	2	9
29	Leather products	8	4	3	–	1
30	Rubber products	5	–	–	2	3
31	Chemicals and products	18	–	9	2	7
33	Non-metallic mineral products	9	1	4	1	3
34–35	Metals and products	19	1	4	1	13
36–37	Repair of machinery	12	1	3	3	5
38	Assembly & repair of transport equipment	73	11	24	19	19
39	Miscellaneous manufacture	6	2	–	–	4
	Total	569	101	192	87	189
	%	100	18	34	15	33

Note: [a] Includes sisal decortication (110 establishments) and cotton ginning and cleaning (30 establishments).
Source: UR of Tanzania *Survey of Industries* (Dar es Salaam: Central Statistical Bureau, 1972), Table 5.

The next significant upsurge in industrialization was during the post-independence period, mainly the establishment of import-substitution industries.[16] The kind of monopoly that British imperialism exercised in colonial Tanganyika was no longer possible. In fact, the new state sought to break *this* monopoly and *multilateralize* its relations with imperialism. In practical terms it took a number of policy measures such as guaranteeing protection of foreign investments,[17] tariff protection and tax incentives to attract foreign capital. At the same time the new bourgeoisie set to correct the past imbalance so far as its relations with Kenya were concerned. Hence the Kampala

Agreement under which Tanzania was allocated certain industries. On the side of foreign capital, on the other hand, inter-imperialist rivalries and competition among the various multinationals now came to full play in the battlefield of Tanzania's economy. The traditional multinationals for which Tanzania was either a reserved market or a source of raw materials were quick to realize the danger of losing these to their rivals. They began to move closer to the supply source and markets establishing processing and assembly plants. Thus, for instance, British Ropes Ltd, which controlled 80 per cent of the British Sisal twine market and previously bought 35 per cent of Tanzania's sisal, established Craven and Speeding to forestall a local manufacturer.[18] Other local and foreign investors quickly moved in as well to ensure their place in the same sector.

Phillips of Netherlands which had begun to lose its Tanzanian and East African market to its rival, Matsushita Electric Co. of Japan, established a radio assembly plant. Assisted by a 50 per cent tariff protection, it managed to break down the Japanese competition. However, Matsushita retaliated by establishing a battery plant to be followed after a few years by a radio assembly plant.

Other multinationals which had no foothold whatsoever in the Tanzanian market tried to create one. Thus the Italian government firm, ENI, built an oil refinery (TIPER) in order to break the monopolistic position of the British and American companies.

Another sector in which there was rapid development was textile. Both the local merchants, formerly involved in wholesale textile business, and foreign capital built several textile mills either alone or in partnership.

The Kenyan and Ugandan entrepreneurs too moved into Tanganyika lest their former market be usurped. The Madhvani group (Uganda based) invested in breweries, sugar, glass, soap and milling while the Chandaria family (based in Kenya) established the first aluminium plant.[19]

The industrialization just outlined closely followed the pattern of neo-colonial industrialization observed in many Third World countries. The industries established were essentially oriented to the production of consumer goods or in some cases intermediate inputs. Based on the techniques and machinery developed in the industrialized countries they were inevitably highly capital-intensive.[20]

Starting from a very small base, the manufacturing sector during the 1950s and early 1960s registered a very high growth rate of an average of some 15 per cent per annum.[21] Wage-employment in this sector also grew steadily although at a much slower rate. The place of the manufacturing sector in the overall economy, however, continued to be small.[22]

It is difficult to establish with any accuracy the exact size of the proletariat in the manufacturing or the industrial sector generally. Various figures for wage-employment, besides numerous other inaccuracies, do not distinguish between managerial and clerical staff on the one hand and actually productive labour on the other. The nearest we can come is the enumeration of *factory labour* as a whole published by the Labour Department under the Factories Ordinance.

In Table A.7 we have tried to analyse the data for a number of factories and employment for four selected years. These figures can be only an approximate guide. They undoubtedly include factories that were registered but no longer operative since an owner of a factory is not required by law to deregister it once it ceases operations. The figures for numbers employed too, most probably, include managerial and clerical staff.

With these qualifications in mind, we can make the following observations. Factory labour had grown from some 52,000 in 1952 to some 90,000 in 1966, a rise of over 70 per cent. Consumer goods sectors like food manufacture, textile and woodworking continued to dominate the industrial scene. Until about 1960, 'textile' simply meant numerous sisal decorticating factories and cotton ginning machines since there were hardly any textile mills as such. All these sectors — especially food manufacture and woodworking — were also characterized by essentially a large number of small establishments including both powered and non-powered factories. This meant a considerably scattered proletariat. As a matter of fact, only in the late 1960s a few establishments with large concentrations of the proletariat began. However, even by the middle of the 1960s the picture had already begun to change somewhat. In 1965, for example, over half (about 54 per cent) of regular employees in the manufacturing sector were in establishments employing fewer than 100 employees, 33 per cent in establishments employing between 100 and 500 employees and about 13 per cent in those employing more than 500 employees.[23] Thus medium and large-size establishments had begun to gain some ground.

So much then for the *size* of the proletariat in the manufacturing sector. Let us briefly review its *quality*, so far as industrial training was concerned.

Industrial training during colonial times was meagre; even then some training of craftsmen and artisans was unavoidable both for the government and private sector. In colonial Tanganyika, it was provided mainly by three agencies; government schools, missionary schools and private and government workshops.[24]

During the German administration, besides workshops for carpentry, tailoring, masonry and so on run by various missions, there were several large schools at Tanga, Dar es Salaam and Tukuyu, teaching printing, carpentry, turning and blacksmithing. The First World War reduced these activities considerably but they began to pick up again on a small scale in the late 1920s.

Whereas at the missions the trades taught were essentially those of immediate use to the missions themselves (carpentry, masonry and tailoring), the government schools also taught mechanics, blacksmiths, printers and bookbinders for railway and PWD (Public Works Department) workshops.

All told, however, formal industrial training was meagre by any standards and generally rudimentary, reflecting the very low level of industrial development itself. Actually, much of the 'training' was confined to skills picked up on the job and this satisfied the needs of the industry then.

The scale of formal industrial training can be gauged from the following figures. At the end of 1938 there were altogether 307 carpentry, 80 tailoring, 18 masonry, 15 metalworks, 23 printing and 9 rural-industries students enrolled in government and private schools. And there were altogether only eight industrial instructors in the whole of Tanzania, 'one for each of the towns of Dar es Salaam, Tanga, Mpwapwa, Mwanza, Moshi, and Malangali for carpentry and masonry together and two for metal-working and printing in Dar es Salaam'.[25]

It was only in the early 1950s that the government made its first moves to centralize industrial training and detach it from ordinary schools. In 1951 the first industrial school at Ifunda was begun. Half of its first students were ex-soldiers and half ex-standard VIII. Around 1954 another training school was started in Moshi. These were then the two main industrial schools which after independence were converted to secondary schools specializing in technical subjects.

Apprenticeship was practically non-existent. After much dilly-dallying in the 1950s, it was only in 1960 that the new Apprenticeship law (Chapter 81) was introduced. However, in practice no formal schemes for apprenticeships in the private industry existed.

There was no organized apprentice training in the strict sense in which an apprentice would learn a trade from every aspect and in every level. What was (and still is) taught was a series of manual skills necessary to execute a specific type of job (e.g. sewing the sole of a shoe, cutting legs for a bed, etc.) — the more sophisticated work being done by the owner himself or by a hired expatriate. The deficiency of this custom was, of course, that the average Tanzanian boy hardly ever was able to acquire an allround knowledge of the trade he learned — he was stuck at an inferior level, i.e. more or less at the level of an auxiliary worker.[26]

The only exceptions to this pattern were the craftsmen of the Asian nationality who learnt their trades through their family ties and continued to dominate craftsmanship generally.

Our brief discussion of industrial training and its impact on the formation of an industrial proletariat may be summarized as follows.

Indigenous craftsmanship, including such specializations as blacksmithing which had already developed in some parts of the country, was irretrievably destroyed by colonialism. Thus there is very little, if any, continuity between today's craftsmanship and that of the pre-colonial period.

During the period of non-industrialization (between the two wars) the level and character of productive forces itself could not be a base for any considerable skills and craftsmanship. The large majority of hired labour was essentially semi-proletarian, unskilled. The small-scale industry and some modern craftsmanship and skills (mechanics, engineering and so on) were heavily concentrated in the hands of the workers of a minority nationality. Whatever skills were imparted to the African workers were essentially rudimentary, mostly picked up on the job, with a very small section going through formal training in a few government and mission trade schools. Thus this 'opportunity' of creating some base of indigenous skilled proletariat and artisan class too was circumvented.

The import-substitution industrialization which began after the last war did not encourage significant development of a skilled proletariat either. It was characterized by a double bias, bias in favour of capital-intensive technique and consumer goods production. In these industries there was a small group of managerial-type engineers and technicians, more often than not expatriates, a very small cadre of skilled and semi-skilled proletariat and a relatively large section of unskilled operatives.[27]

Thus colonial and neo-colonial industrialization had a two-fold negative impact on the development of the proletariat. Although it created a proletariat, the proletariat so created was small in size with a large proportion of unskilled workers.

The agrarian and mining proletariat

The predominantly semi-proletarian character of wage-labour in agriculture and mining was, as we have shown, based on two factors. The first was the low level of productive forces that characterized the primary sector. The productivity was extremely low and the mass of the labour was unskilled requiring virtually no training. The second factor was cheap labour: the colonial low-wage economy, as it has been called, was the *raison d'être* of the system of migrant labour. These two factors reinforced each other as they also reflected the general political economy of colonialism.

It is true that even during the heyday of the migrant system there were some lone voices which deplored the wastage of manpower, inefficiency, high turnover and low productivity that the system of virtual non-mechanization involved. Writing in 1927, one highly placed official minuted: 'In Dar es Salaam itself grass is still cut by rows of men armed with hoop iron, earth is carried by files of men with a lb or two of earth on their heads, the roads are tickled by gentlemen armed with a brush which appears to be composed of bamboo splints . . . Apparently the labourer here likes to earn his living by using his head. Machinery will probably be more expensive than labour. However there is a wide field open for investigation in which I think some members of the public and businessmen might help considerably.'[28]

The question of mechanization was raised once again when acute shortage of labour developed in the middle of the 1930s. The Director of Agriculture strongly argued that the productivity of labour on the estates was extremely low and that the real solution was that men must be backed by machines. The solution was not 'a greater and greater labour force but a gradual change towards a more specialized force using the instruments of today'. Yet he could not say these things in public for the forces backing cheap labour were simply too strong. 'In practice, however . . .', as he put it, 'we have to assist this industry [in obtaining labour] as far as possible in its labour requirements . . .'[29]

Suggestions for mechanization and therefore training and stabilizing of the labour force were decried as 'detribalization' which conjured up pictures of evil that this would give rise to. However, once the objective situation and balance of forces began to change after the Second World War, the detested 'detribalization' assumed the respectability of 'stabilization' of the labour force.

In the early 1950s there developed an acute shortage of labour. With rapid development of cash crop production (for example, cotton in Sukumaland), less and less labour offered itself for wage-employment.[30] It was as a result of this that a Committee on Manpower was appointed in 1951. A preparatory investigation carried out for the committee indicated that labour was characterized by low productivity and gross inefficiency and this was due to 'high rate of turnover, desertion, absenteeism, [and] long and costly journeys . . .'. 'The absence of a stable labour force is one of the root causes of inefficiency.'[31] It emphasized that the widely held notion that African labour was cheap and 'that another African on the job is an insignificant matter' was being fast eroded as labour would become more expensive and scarce. The solution therefore was to raise output by training.and reorganization which would be possible only by stabilizing the labour force.

This open advocacy for stabilization was manifested further by M.J.B. Molahan's report on *Detribalization* published in 1957. As he put it:

I have indicated earlier in this report that reduction in the number of Africans coming forward for employment in agriculture has become more apparent during the past few years and this trend is likely to continue. Government has always favoured a policy of stabilization of labour in the economic interests of the territory and in the post war years has given active encouragement to such a policy, although for various reasons to which it is unnecessary to refer here the measures it has introduced have not in practice been so successful as one had hoped in inducing Africans to uproot themselves and settle down into a new life where they could obtain their livelihood mainly by paid employment. On the other side it is correct to say that some causes of the failure of this policy are attributable to industry itself, which has sometimes failed to provide conditions which will attract and retain labour. Many employers are still only too prone to take the easiest course and to continue to rely on migrant labour for their needs, with the result that they suffer a continual turnover, skills and output are not increased and wage rates remain depressed and unattractive.[32]

While the government 'favoured' and 'encouraged' stabilization, it was not prepared to do one thing that would have succeeded, that is, to raise wages and enforce improved conditions of work. It is only when labour itself took up the struggle that both the employer and the government were forced to respond.

Collective and organized struggle on the part of labour was made possible by the development of a small, urban-based permanent labour force. The 1940s had seen a big development in the urban labour force mainly involved in transport and building industries and later in the incipient manufacturing sector. The technology, and so on, in these sectors were relatively higher and of necessity required a more skilled and therefore stable labour force. It was this urban, permanent labour force, in turn, which provided for the first time the basis for collective action on the part of labour.

Thus the long-drawn-out struggle of the dockworkers (see below, Chapter 5) for the first time began to challenge the absolute power of the employers to decide unilaterally the terms and conditions of employment. In the late 1940s and early 1950s labour began to organize, bargain collectively and successfully demand higher wages. 'African labour is becoming increasingly aware that collective action on their part is a strong bargaining instrument, and there have been some instances where, by such collective action they have successfully demanded a wage increase or drawn attention to their grievances.'[33] This was the most important single factor which began to break the colonial vicious circle of 'low wages–high turnover–unstable labour force'. Although the original struggles and collective actions were initiated by the urban labour force, they inevitably had an impact on the agricultural wage labour as well.

As would be expected, the greatest resistance to higher wages and stable labour force was put up by the agricultural employers and especially by the better organized sisal employers. Nevertheless, towards the end of 1950s the tendency towards stabilization was unmistakable. The number of workers passing through government transit centres fell from 177,795 in 1959 to 76,771 in 1961, while the number of workers recruited for the same years fell from 22,498 to 3,967.[34] The average monthly cash earning of an African male adult in agriculture had increased from Shs. 36 in 1958 to Shs. 132 in 1965, a rise of some 300 per cent.[35]

In the sisal industry, the most decisive break came with the 1960 collective agreement between the employers and the trade unions under the Central Joint Council. Under this, wages increased by some 100 per cent, and in the next few years there were further increases. 'The average earnings, including overtime, of field and factory labour over the month of January, 1959 were Shs. 2.3 per working day. The corresponding earnings in January, 1964 were Shs. 5.2 — an increase of approximately 130 per cent.'[36] These increases forced the employers to stabilize and reorganize their workforce and introduce some mechanization. The overall result of stabilization is shown in Table 4.4.

The rise in wages and the movement from bachelor to family wages came about as a result of intense trade union struggles (see below, Chapter 6) waged during the late 1950s and early 1960s. This in turn led to the stabilization of the labour force. The stabilization of labour was crucial also for the neo-colonial industrialization policy adopted by the new regime after independence. Both the Chesworth Report which fixed the territorial minimum wages and the *Report of the Non-Plantation Agricultural Workers Minimum Wages Board* deplored the system of migrant labour and argued for a 'living wage'. The board argued that the country required stable workers so that 'they can learn their work, improve their efficiency and increase their output'.[37] The board emphasized that a stable labour force would benefit the employers because it would achieve higher productivity on the basis of a smaller permanent labour force.

Besides fixing statutory minimum wages, the government also amended the Employment Ordinance[38] converting the former *kipande* system to monthly contracts. A divisional circular explained the amendment and the motive behind it as follows:

Section 7 [of No. 82 of 1962] gives effect to Government's decision that the ticket contract system, which is extremely wasteful in manpower, should be discouraged. Government's view on this point is that a poor country such as Tanganyika can no longer afford to recognize a system which encourages absenteeism. The new Section 33 provides, therefore, that if a contract is made which, like the old ticket system, provides for the worker to perform a stated number of days' work during a greater number of days and for the worker only to be paid in respect of the days on which he had worked, then that contract is deemed in law to be a monthly contract at a monthly wage equal to the daily rate multiplied by twenty-six . . . The new provision also means that the employer is required to provide work on each working day (Section 16 of the principal ordinance), and the worker is also required to turn out for work on the normal six working days: he is then entitled, of course, to a weekly rest day . . . At the same time, this change will mean that any such worker who is absent from work without the permission of the employer or without a reasonable excuse will be liable to summary dismissal under the provisions of Section 37(e) of the principal Ordinance.[39]

Table 4.4 *Employment, productivity and long-distance migrants in the sisal industry, 1954–65*

Year	Tons of plantation sisal	Total labour force employed	Output per man-year	Index of productivity	Male migrants through SILABU
1954	178 250	137 589	1.30	100 00	30 100
1955	176 499	129 843	1.36	104 60	24 900
1956	184 700	127 400	1.45	111 50	25 200
1957	184 400	125 600	1.47	113 00	25 900
1958	196 200	125 000	1.57	120 80	32 600
1959	202 100	133 200	1.52	116 90	24 320
1960	195 400	121 900	1.60	123 10	8 900
1961	186 100	109 800	1.69	130 00	3 200
1962	208 400	109 700	1.52	116 90	6 800
1963	212 400	88 000	2.41	165 40	3 700
1964	222 600	83 000	2.68	206 20	3 500
1965	210 572	63 066	3.34	256 90	100

Source: Calculated from Guillebaud, C. W., *An Economic Survey of the Sisal Industry of Tanganyika* (Welwyn: James Nisbet, 1966), p. 135; Patel, L. R. 'East African Labour Regimes: Kenya and Tanganyika' (mimeo: University of Dar es Salaam), p. 312; Lawrence, P. R., 'Plantation Sisal: The Inherited Mode of Production', in Cliffe, L., *et al.* (eds), *Rural Cooperation in Tanzania* (Dar es Salaam: Tanzania Publishing House, 1975), p. 114.

The amendment had a dramatic effect. Regularity and attendance improved substantially. One sample survey of some sixty-five sisal estates showed that the proportion of labour force turning out each working day in 1963 was 92.5 per cent on average, compared to the corresponding figure of around 70 per cent for earlier years.[40]

It is interesting to note that the change in wages and conditions of work managed to stabilize and regularize the work-force, thus giving the lie to all previous colonial rationalizations which had argued that an African was prone to laziness and leisure and did not react to economic incentives. As Sabot puts it: 'The high level of instability of both the sisal and the urban labour force during the colonial period was a rational response to working conditions, rather than a specifically African behaviour pattern. Changes in working conditions, independent of increased mechanization, have resulted in increases in stability and productivity.'[41]

Various developments that we have noted had another important effect on the structure of wage-labour. Whereas during the colonial times agricultural labour dominated the labour scene, in the post-colonial period the organic composition of wage-labour had shifted decisively in favour of non-agricultural development, the fastest growing sectors being manufacturing and government. The ratio between non-agriculture and agricultural employment had increased from 47 in 1952 to 53 in 1964.[42] At the same time the urban-based employment had increased over rural employment. Thus wage-employment in Dar es Salaam had increased from 9 per cent of total wage employment in 1961 to 13 per cent in 1964, which constituted some 25 per cent of the total non-agricultural employment.[43]

The service workers

Permanent wage-labour, as far as administration and services were concerned, may be divided into two main categories: white-collar workers and domestic servants.

Among white-collars, two groups are distinguishable, the supervisory staff — headmen, foremen and so on — and the clerical staff. Both these groups were indispensable in the private as well as the government sector. The task-oriented organization of the labour process in sisal plantations, for instance, necessitated a considerable supervisory staff commonly called headmen or *wanyapara*. Their function was to oversee the quality and quantity of the product — for example, that the sisal leaves cut were of appropriate length and that a bundle contained the required number of leaves. In 1956, the headmen were the biggest single group, about 70 per cent, of the white-collars employed in agriculture.[44]

The second, the clerical staff, constituted a significant portion of the white-collars, particularly in the government sector. In 1956, they were about one-third of the total white-collar employees in the government. Their development was tied up with the development of formal education. The Germans had geared their school system to provide clerks and other officers for the lower rungs of the colonial state administration.[45] By 1902 there were some 4,000 pupils attending government schools.[46] After the First World War government schools were disbanded and mission schools closed.[47]

The British dragged their feet somewhat in the formation and training of African administrative cadres. As early as 1922, Governor Byatt had proposed instituting an African Civil Service to replace clerical personnel recruited from India. He had also argued for a more liberal education policy to enable the training of a civil service.[48] But his proposals did not receive a favourable response in the colonial office and his successor, Scott, instituted an African Clerical Service only in 1925.[49]

The school system during the British period was racially segregated. The most important component, as far as African education was concerned, was the mission schools. Besides providing catechists and other church workers, the mission schools also supplied a steady stream of clericals. The government concentrated on elementary education and only towards the end of the 1930s were some beginnings made in secondary education. By 1945, there were 1,000 primary schools, 18 secondary schools and 24 teacher training centres for Africans in the whole territory. Enrolment of African students in secondary schools was only 1,000. The total number of African students in schools was only 2 per cent of the African population compared to 10 per cent in the case of Europeans and 30 per cent in the case of Asians.[50]

These, then, were the origins of white-collar workers who were to play a leading role in the trade union movement of the 1950s.

Domestic service constituted the second important source of service workers. No accurate data exist on the number of domestic servants. The Labour Department's estimates for the years 1948–50 range between 30,000 and 40,000.[51] Domestic servants were employed mainly in European and Asian households. One estimate in 1948 allowed three domestic servants per male and one per female of the European population[52] while a letter written in 1947 by the Domestic Servants' Association, Mwanza, asserted that it was customary for a European to keep at least five or six servants.[53]

Generally, domestic servants worked under deplorable conditions with long hours, paltry wages and 'left-overs from the master's table' as their food.[54] There was also a high incidence of the employment of child and female labour in domestic service. They fared even worse than their adult male counterparts. An investigation[55] in 1941 estimated that some 830 children were employed in domestic service in Tanga, Tabora, Arusha, Morogoro and Mbeya. In Dar es Salaam, in 1939, more than 1,000 children were employed in that sector. Their wages ranged from a minimum of Shs. 1.50 to a maximum of Shs. 15 per month 'with such food as they could obtain from their master's table'.[56]

Urbanized, permanent and subjected to humiliating conditions, domestic servants, too, were to play a significant role in the trade union struggles of the 1950s.

From servant to employee: the legal development

The background

The Master and Native Servants Ordinance was geared to regulate semi-proletarian labour. The small, permanent wage-labour — particularly of the white-collar type — was thus excluded from its purview. For example, the amending Ordinance of 1927[57] deleted clerks, members of the African Civil Service and railway servants from the definition of 'servant' because it was felt that the provisions of this Ordinance 'are not suitable to such employees'.[58] In the late 1930s, owing to the pressure from the Secretary of State, attempts were made to draft a new labour legislation. By this time there had been a considerable development of the permanent labour force and the Manual Workers (Employment) Bill, as it was called, did attempt to make a distinction between permanent and impermanent labour.[59] However, the war intervened and the proposed Bill never became law.

'The accelerated development of industry during the war and during the immediate post-war years and the increase in the numbers of persons in wage-earning employment rendered the need for the revision of the law relating to master and servant apparent to many people', said the Labour Commissioner when introducing the Employment Bill to the Legislative Council.[60] The drafting of the Employment Ordinance,[61] begun in 1949, took three years. Another three years were spent in circulating the draft and getting comments from interested parties, in particular employers' organizations. The Bill was finally passed in 1955 and was brought into force on 1 February 1957.[62]

The Employment Ordinance was a kind of umbrella legislation designed to regulate relations between employers and employees by setting up minimum standards. Although, as we have seen, the trend for the stabilization of the labour force had already set in, it was not until after independence that the system of a migratory labour force came to a complete end. Hence the Employment Ordinance, as passed in 1955, still had comprehensive provisions to deal with semi-proletarian labour.

Unlike the Master and Native Servants Ordinance, the Employment Ordinance was non-racial in its application. However, formerly the governor, and after independence the minister concerned with labour matters, were given wide powers to exempt 'any public authority or class of public authorities or any person or class of persons from the operation of this Ordinance or any provision thereof or of any regulation or order made thereunder' (s. 1(3)).[63] Under this section, among those exempted from some of the important parts of the Ordinance were employees earning more than Shs. 8,400 per annum.* A careful reading of the relevant Orders[64] reveals that the said exemption applied to the employees mentioned *qua* employees. But employers in their capacity as employers were not exempted in respect of their *obligations* under the Ordinance even with regard to employees earning more than the stated amount.

The provisions of the Employment Ordinance may be grouped together in three categories.† First, there were provisions specifically designed to cover long-distance migrant labour (contract labour) and irregular local labour. Save for greater systematization and verbal changes, these provisions were substantially the same as those of the Master and Native Servants Ordinance. The second group of provisions attempted to restrict, and in some cases eliminate, the semi-bondage features of wage-labour which were recognized and reflected in the previous legislation. The third group of provisions attempted to come to grips with the development of a permanent labour force.

Regulation of contract labour

Part V of the Ordinance on 'written contracts' was in substance a reproduction of the Master and Native Servants (Written Contracts) Ordinance 1942. Section 42 provided that where a contract of service: (i) is made for a period exceeding six months or (ii) stipulated conditions of employment which differed from those customary in the district of employment or (iii) is a foreign contract or (iv) was made between a recruiter and an employee who was recruited,[65] such a contract had to be in writing. Thus this part covered long-distance migrant workers who came on contracts. The provisions that followed then went on to provide the form and content of such contracts (s. 44): the necessity for attestation (s. 45), and medical examination (s. 47); the obligation of the employer to repatriate (s. 53) and to provide transport (s. 55), and so on.

Part VIII of the Ordinance stipulated the usual 'care and welfare' provisions on housing, feeding and medical care of the recruited employees which once again were not substantially different from similar provisions in the previous legislation.

Part IX dealt with recruitment. Although recruitment in practice came to an end around 1965, these provisions continued to be on the statute book until 1969 when they were repealed and recruitment (whether by an employer or by a professional recruiter) was made illegal.[66]

It is interesting to note that the parts dealing with written contracts, care and welfare and recruitment applied only to African employees in spite of the fact that the Ordinance as a whole was non-racial. This only corroborates our view that these provisions were a continuation of the past, regulating semi-proletarian labour.

In addition, the Employment Ordinance gave legal validity to the system of 'ticket contracts'. Section 33 of the Ordinance stipulated that it 'shall be competent for any person to enter into contract of service to work for an employer for thirty days (in succession or otherwise at the election of the employer) which shall be known as a ticket

---

* Originally the figure was Shs. 16,800 per annum. This was changed to Shs. 8,400 in 1958 (see note 64, p. 151).
† There was also a set of provisions under Part VII which dealt with female and child labour. This was a consolidation of the previous law and in some cases more elaborate restrictions on the employment of child labour were imposed. These provisions will be conveniently dealt with in the next section, 'Conditions'.

contract . . .' After independence, the system of 'ticket contract' was abolished and all such contracts were converted into monthly contracts.[67] This was in line with the policy of stabilization of the labour force and an attempt to reduce irregularity and absenteeism.

Restriction of semi-bondage features

Among the provisions trying to restrict and abolish what might be called the semi-bondage features of wage-labour were anti-truck sections, and provisions on transfer of business, penal sanctions and forced labour.

Part VI of the Ordinance dealt with the 'protection of wages'. Wages were to be paid in currency in legal tender and at or near the place of work (s. 61). It was prohibited to pay wages due to an employee 'in any shop, store, canteen, hotel or other similar establishment nor depute the owner or manager of, or any person employed in, any shop, store, canteen, hotel or other establishment to pay wages due by him to his employee' (s. 66(1)).[68] Furthermore, any contract of service imposing conditions as to the place, manner or the person with whom wages paid to an employee were to be expended was illegal, null and void and an employer contravening this provision was liable to criminal prosecution (s. 62).

These provisions were directed against abuses which in Britain were described as the 'truck' and 'Tommy Shop' systems. ' "Truck" describes any system whereby the worker is paid in something other than coin of the realm (e.g. in kind)', and 'Tommy Shop' was the 'name given to a shop generally run by the employer or his relatives where the vouchers or credits given in lieu of wages could be exchanged for goods, often of inferior quality . . . the opportunities for abuse in the hands of unscrupulous employers or their managers make the whole system stink'.[69]

In Britain these systems were done away with by a series of statutes, the most important of which was the Truck Act, 1831. The Master and Servants Ordinance of Tanganyika did not contain comprehensive provisions against similar abuses.

The Employment Ordinance also restricted deductions from employees' wages by their employers. The deductions that were allowed were those sanctioned by the Labour Commissioner in the case of foreign contracts of service under section 46: deduction for tax or rate imposed by law (s. 64(1)(i)); deduction for pension or provident fund scheme; deduction for the rental if the housing was provided by the employer; and deduction for 'loss or damage caused by the default or neglect of such employee to any tools, materials or other property of an employer, up to such maximum amounts, and in accordance with such terms and conditions as may be prescribed' (s. 64(1)(b)). The relevant regulations prescribed fairly restrictive preconditions to be satisfied by an employer before he could deduct an employee's wages for loss of property and then too the maximum amount deductible was only one day's pay.[70] In the former legislation there was a provision enabling an employer to deduct a sum not exceeding in any one month a quarter of a servant's wages by way of a fine if the employer was satisfied that the servant had committed any of the following offences:

(a) fouling any water supply at the place of employment;
(b) depositing any matter likely to become dangerous to health except at a place set apart by the employer for the purpose;
(c) failing without reasonable excuse to attend at a hospital or dressing station when directed to do so by the employer of his agent. (s. 12 of the M & NSO)

This provision was not reproduced in the Employment Ordinance although, as we shall see below (p. 127), the system of fining by employers was brought back in a later legislation in a different form for a different purpose.

Section 64(2) allowed the employer to deduct by instalments a loan advanced to an employee. Such loan, however, had to be in cash or cheque and had to be accompanied by a memorandum (impliedly in writing) signed by both the parties and providing for the repayment of the loan by one or more instalments.

Finally, it was specifically and explicitly prohibited to make 'any deduction by way of discount, interest or any similar charge on account of any advance of wages made to any employee in anticipation of the regular period of payment of such wages' (s. 69). This provision is interesting in that it recognized, contrary to the ideological explanations of bourgeois economists, that the so-called advance of wages is not an advance or a credit at all from an employer to an employee. The truth is that, as Marx explained, it is the worker who makes an advance or gives credit of the use of his labour power to the capitalist and only *after* its use that he is paid.*

Another interesting section that may be mentioned provided that: 'No person shall give or promise to any other person any advance of wages or any valuable consideration upon a condition, expressed or implied, that such other person or any dependant of his shall enter upon any employment' (s. 68(1)). Clearly this provision was a recognition of the fact that under a capitalist mode of production, the wage-worker is supposed to be 'free': 'free' to choose his employer and move from one employer to another (mobility of labour); that unlike a slave or a serf he is not bound to any one employer and therefore cannot sell off his labour power in advance or put it on mortgage as was done in the famous English case of *Horwood* v. *Millar's Timber and Trading Co. Ltd.*[71] In that case Bunyan, an employee, had contracted with Horwood, a money-lender, for a loan in consideration of which he had bound himself, among other things, to continue to work for Millar's Timber deligently; not to do anything for which he could be dismissed from his job; not to take up any other job without the written permission of the lender. In addition he assigned all his remuneration, present and future, from his job to the lender. The court refused to enforce this contract on grounds of public policy. The Master of Rolls likened the contract to that of a villein in medieval times and went so far as to say that it 'savoured of slavery'.

Related to the question of 'freedom' and mobility of labour was the provision on transfer of business. Under section 18 of the Ordinance an employee was not bound to follow his employer if the latter 'removes his residence or place of trade or business to a distance more than four miles from the place in which such employee theretofore performed his service . . .'.

We saw in the earlier chapters that the use of penal sanctions to regulate contractual relation between master and servant was a prominent feature of the master and servants legislation. The offences dealing with desertion† and abusive language against employer were done away with in the Employment Ordinance. Criminal sanctions in the Ordinance were confined to breaches of 'care and welfare' type of obligations on the part of employers; breaches of anti-truck provisions; 'decoying' of labour from fellow employers (s. 151), and failure to pay wages (s. 149(a)). As regards employees, the offences that remained were those where the employee left the service of his employer

---

* 'In every country in which the capitalist mode of production reigns, it is the custom not to pay for labour power before it has been exercised for the period fixed by the contract, as for example, the end of each week. In all cases, therefore, the use-value of the labour power is advanced to the capitalist: the labourer allows the buyer to consume it before he receives payment of the price; he everywhere gives credit to the capitalist.' (Marx, *Capital*, Vol. I., p. 170.)

† This was really giving effect to the ILO Convention on Penal Sanction (Indigenous Workers) Convention, 1939, No. 65.[72]

when he owed money to his employer and with intent to defraud (s. 150) or for giving false information with a view to obtain employment (s. 152). Thus convictions of employees under labour legislation fell considerably after the passing of the Ordinance. From an average of 168 persons convicted annually between 1954 and 1956, the number fell to an average of only nineteen persons per year between 1957 and 1959.*[73]

Besides penal sanctions, the use of forced labour too was a common feature previously, as we have already seen. Before the Employment Ordinance, forced labour was regulated mostly by administrative directives.[74] Part X of the Ordinance for the first time tried to give statutory effect to the International Convention on Forced Labour (1930), to which Britain had always been a party.

Forced labour was defined as that work or service which was exacted under the menance of any penalty and for which the person concerned had not offered himself voluntarily (s. 121). Certain types of services were, however, excluded from this definition. These were: (a) compulsory military service, (b) services exacted from convicted persons, (c) services exacted in case of emergency such as war, famine, fire and epidemics, and (d) minor communal services. Probably the most important† exemption in practice was the last one. 'Minor communal services' was interpreted in colonial parlance to include 'tribal turn outs'[76] and was one of the main forms of forced labour under colonialism. Under the so-called tribal turn outs, as we saw, thousands of persons were compelled to put in tens of thousands of man-days constructing roads and buildings, maintaining sanitation, water supplies and clearing bush and so on. This form of forced labour remained virtually untouched by Part X. The hitch came when the ILO passed its new Convention No. 105 on forced labour in 1957.

Convention No. 105 was directed mainly against the countries of the Soviet bloc and therefore the capitalist countries, including Britain, enthusiastically supported it for political reasons. Article 1 of that convention required the members to suppress and not to make use of any form of forced or compulsory labour:

(a) as a means of political coercion or education or as a punishment for holding or expressing political view or views ideologically opposed to the established political social or economic system;
(b) as a method of mobilizing and using labour for purposes of economic development;
(c) as a means of labour discipline;
(d) as a punishment for having participated in strikes;
(e) as a means of racial, social, national or religious discrimination.[77]

Paragraph (b) meant that the so-called 'minor communal services' could not be exacted for purposes of 'economic development'. The colonial government in fact advised the Secretary of State that the convention be applied to Tanganyika subject to modification of Article 1(b). The Secretary declined because it would have opened up Her Majesty's government to criticism in the international forums. The result was that section 121(d)

---

* The corresponding figures for the number of employers convicted for the same period are: average of 76 persons convicted annually between 1954 and 1956, while during 1957–9 the annual average rose to 100 persons. The rise is partly explained by the fact that there were now many more offences under such legislation as Factories Ordinance, Workmen's Compensation and especially Minimum Wage Orders, for which employers were liable.

† 'The most important of these exceptions is "minor communal services", i.e. the tribal turn-out, which is widely used in some provinces as a means of obtaining labour without payment for public works of local importance.' This extract from the memorandum of the Minister of Education and Labour to the Provincial Commissioners' Conference held in July 1959 bears out the importance of this form of forced labour.[75]

of the Ordinance was amended in 1960[78] exempting only those minor communal services which were 'not . . . for the purpose of economic development''. The colonial officials were thus left only to limit its impact on tribal turn outs by interpreting the phrase 'economic development' very strictly. 'This phrase is not altogether clear, but if it is to be interpreted strictly, as it is understood that it would be, it would cover only works which are of economic significance as distinct from works carried out for sanitary or health purposes; furthermore it would cover only development works, so that work on, say, road maintenance would not be covered, whereas work on a new road would be.' 'The conclusion has been reached in the colonial office that a distinction may properly be drawn between forced labour which is essential for the maintenance of the material fabric of the community and forced labour for economic development properly so-called.'[79]

But the colonial officials did not have to juggle around these restrictions for long, for one year later the country became independent and the new state had its own particular preoccupations. One of the most prominent among these was to enhance the growing of cash crops for export so as to earn necessary foreign exchange to pay for manufactured consumer and intermediate goods. It put a great deal of emphasis on 'mobilizing' the peasantry for cultivation. This mobilization included coercion through agricultural laws requiring peasants to cultivate certain minimum acreage.[80] This was reflected in an amendment in 1962[81] which added a new exemption to the definition of 'forced labour'. This was: 'any work to be performed by a person allotted or occupying land in accordance with customary law . . . in order to comply with any lawful requirement of a local authority as to the cultivation of such land : . . .'

Finally, it must be noted that the power of the governor, and later the president, to implement or to consent to the imposition of forced labour under certain circumstances was retained under section 125 of the Ordinance. And under section 126 this power could be delegated to any provincial commissioner.

Regulation of 'free' labour

The third set of provisions of the Employment Ordinance attempted to regulate the permanent labour force under typically capitalist conditions.

The Ordinance made a distinction between oral and written contracts. 'Written contracts' dealt with mainly long-distance migrant labour and foreign contracts of service. 'Oral contracts' referred to all contracts of service other than written contracts (s. 2). Broadly, therefore, 'oral contracts' dealt with the permanent labour force.

The most important provisions dealing with oral contracts were to be found in Part IV of the Ordinance. Lack of much legal, contractual tradition meant that the statute had to provide for such elementary rules of contract as the time of its commencement, period of contract, termination and ways of terminating it. The central concept of these provisions was 'contract period' which was defined as 'the period of time or number of days or hours to be worked for which expressly or by implication a contract of service is made'' (s. 2). The original section 29 in the 1957 Ordinance appeared to have assumed that the parties explicitly specify 'contract period' when entering into contracts of employment and therefore provided for termination of daily, weekly and monthly contracts without specifying any test for determining types of contract. In the absence of an explicit agreement, the law stipulated that all oral contracts were deemed to be 'monthly contracts' (s. 31). In practice these provisions no doubt proved to be unrealistic for the parties hardly ever negotiated and agreed upon 'contract period' and the 'deeming' provision was probably unacceptable to the employers. The amending

Act of 1960[82] repealed and replaced section 29. For the first time it introduced the presumption that in the absence of any agreement, an oral contract was deemed to be a contract for the period by reference to which wages were calculated. However elementary the level of negotiations between the parties may be, since there must always be some agreement on the question of wages this was the most practical way of specifying the contract period. In day-to-day practice the presumption as to contract period played an important role because it defined the type of contract (for example, daily, weekly, fortnightly and monthly) on which depended a number of rights of the workers and especially the right to be given notice of termination.

Although the Ordinance as a whole recognized the increasing development of a permanent labour force, the pressure of the colonial employers meant that it did not readily provide for such rights as notice of termination and holidays with pay. In the 1957 version a contract of service could be terminated at the end of the contract period without notice. The 1960 Amendment provided for notice of twenty-four hours for contracts whose period did not exceed one week and seven days' notice for contracts exceeding one week (s. 31). The duration of notice was increased to thirty days in the latter case by the amendment of 1962.[83] Unless notice of termination had been given or a contract was terminated otherwise for any lawful cause, the parties were conclusively presumed to have entered into a new contract of service at the end of the contract period (s. 30).

Section 40 of the 1957 Ordinance provided for annual holidays with pay but the employers insisted that such holidays should be earned.[84] An employee was entitled to annual holidays at the rate of one day in respect of two months' service *provided* he 'shall have worked for not less than two hundred and eighty-eight days within the preceding twelve months for the employer' (s. 40(1)). The weekly rest day with pay was introduced only in 1962.

Before we leave the discussion of the Employment Ordinance we should briefly examine the provisions on the dispute-settlement procedures. The Ordinance of course did not deal with collective disputes; rather it attempted to provide for ordinary breaches of contract on the part of employers and employees. Under Part II of the Ordinance the Labour Commissioner and labour officers under him were given fairly wide powers of inspection and investigation to enforce and administer mainly the care and welfare provisions of the Ordinance. The commissioner was empowered to 'institute proceedings in respect of any contravention of any of the provisions of this Ordinance or any regulations made hereunder and may prosecute and appear in his own name in respect of such proceedings' (s. 8).

Part XI of the Ordinance, on the other hand, attempted to come to grips with what may be called contractual disagreements between employers and employees. Section 130 provided:

Whenever an employer or employee shall neglect or refuse to fulfil the terms of any contract of service, or whenever any question, difference or dispute shall arise as to the rights or liabilities of either party to a contract of service, or touching any misconduct neglect or ill-treatment of or by such party, the party aggrieved may report the matter to a labour officer who shall thereupon take such steps as may seen to him to be expedient to effect a settlement between the parties.

In case a labour officer failed to effect a settlement he was empowered, at the request of either party, to make a report to a magistrate setting out the facts of the case (s. 132). Every district magistrate had jurisdiction to hear such cases and where he found that the facts were such that they might found a civil suit, he could issue such process as was necessary to summon the parties and witnesses before him. Although in such a case the magistrate was required to follow the provisions of the Civil Procedure Code, 'the magistrate shall hear and determine such proceedings according to substantial justice without undue regard to technicalities of procedure' (s. 134(3)).

The aim behind these provisions was undoubtedly to simplify and expedite the settlement of contractual labour disputes so as to minimize loss of production time. Labour officers were expected to play a major role and the judiciary was brought in only as a last resort.

Disciplining of labour

Our foregoing discussion has shown that when the Employment Ordinance was first passed in 1957 it reflected the transitional character of the labour force. Although it provided a kind of umbrella legislation for regulating the increasingly permanent labour force, it still contained provisions for the semi-permanent labour force. The Amendments that followed, and in particular the Amendment of 1962, were in line with the policy of the new state to abolish the migrant system of labour and instead have a permanent — even if small — labour force.[85] However, the Ordinance, to the extent that it provided for regulating the contractual relations of permanent wage-labour, took care of only one aspect of the new developments. The wage-labour that was developing in the wake of post-independence, import-substitution industrialization was not only *permanent* but also *industrial*. This gave rise to a new set of problems which were not confronted to the same extent in the case of semi-proletarian, or even proletarian, plantation and mining labour. The most important of these problems was the problem of industrial discipline.

The working class in the developed countries has had a long history and tradition of rhythmic and time-regulated industrial discipline reflecting the autochthonous industrialization of those countries. In Tanzania, the five or so decades of proletarianization were not only distinguished by its semi-proletarian character but, as we have seen, were also marked by its concentration in the plantation sector. In its organization of labour and labour process, this sector tried to imitate the rhythm of peasant production. Thus, to cite only one example, it was the piece-rates and piece-wages that dominated the method of payment of wages rather than time-wages. This tradition was ill-suited to the vigorous demands of the industrial labour process. What had not been done by history and tradition, the new state attempted to do by passing a fairly comprehensive legislation in 1964, deceptively called the Security of Employment Act (SEA).[86]

The centrepiece of the Act was Part III which provided for and laid down the procedure for imposing disciplinary penalties on employees. The Disciplinary Code in the Second Schedule, not unlike a penal code, set down a list of nineteen offences. For each offence a corresponding punishment or penalty was prescribed. Penalties were graded according to their severity. For example, for committing the offence of being 'late for work', the penalty for the first breach was written warning; for the second breach reprimand; for the third breach severe reprimand; for the fourth 'fine'; and for the fifth breach 'summary dismissal'.

The offences ranged from those relating to attendance at work, through indiscipline and insubordination, to those connected with safety of persons and property. Out of the total of nineteen offences, thirteen — or a little under 70 per cent — attracted the penalty of 'summary dismissal' on the very first breach. This meant that only in the case of six minor offences did the elaborate gradation of penalties apply.

Having set down the Disciplinary Code, the Act also provided for its administration. It can readily be seen that such a rigorous discipline could not be imposed without resistance from workers. To forestall such resistance and assist the employer in the administration of the code, the Act set up two important organs, workers' committees and conciliation boards.

Every enterprise employing ten or more union members was required to set up a workers' committee (s. 5), composed of employees as defined in the Act, that is, those earning less than Shs. 8,400 per annum.* The functions of the workers' committees were purely advisory and consultative (s. 6). They did not have any executive powers. The most important function of the committee was 'to consult with the employer on matters relating to the maintenance of discipline and the application of the Disciplinary Code' (s. 6(1)(a)). Before an employer imposed a disciplinary penalty on an employee he was required to inform and consult the workers' committee. However, he was not bound by the opinion of the workers' committee.

In cases of 'summary dismissal' and deduction of wages as fines, an employee who was aggrieved by the decision of his employer had a right of making a reference to the conciliation board. Conciliation boards, established by the minister, acted as a kind of appellate organ. They were composed of a labour officer, who acted as the chairman, a representative from the trade union and a representative from the employers' organization. The next rung in this appellate structure was the Minister of Labour, who did not hold any hearing but who could receive memoranda from both the parties. The board's decision, unless appealed from, was 'final and conclusive' and could not be challenged in any court of law. So was the case with the minister's decision on appeal. As a matter of fact, the courts' jurisidiction in any matter regarding summary dismissal was ousted under section 28. 'Summary dismissal' was not defined in the Act, but judicially defined as 'dismissal without notice' in the leading case of *Kitundu Sisal Estate* v. *Shingo and Others*.[87] The result was that all important matters under the Act fell under the jurisdiction of labour officers, conciliation boards and the minister. The courts have shown general reluctance to touch any case involving 'summary dismissal' even if such a matter was not connected with discipline.[88] In sum, the administration of this important piece of legislation was placed squarely in the hands of the executive arm of the state, away from judicial enquiry and public glare.

Conditions

The colonial, low wage economy had as much impact on the conditions of life and work of the permanent urban wage-labour as in the case of semi-proletarian labour. In this section we will deal with three broad areas: wages, housing and conditions at the work-place with particular emphasis on industrial safety. In our discussion we propose to investigate the extent to which the state intervened through the instrument of law in regulating the conditions of work of the permanent, mainly urban, wage-labour and where possible to ascertain the objective reasons and impact of such intervention.

---

* Under section 4 of the Act, those exempted from Parts III, IV, V or VI of the EO were not considered employees for the purposes of the SEA. Since employees earning more than Shs. 8,400 per annum were exempted from the operation of these parts of the EO, they were not covered by the SEA either.

Wages

Until about the beginning of the 1940s, the determination of wages was left theoretically to the forces of supply and demand. In practice this meant wages were determined almost unilaterally by the employers. First, employers were much better oganized than workers. In the absence of organization on the part of workers, their bargaining strength was virtually non-existent. Secondly, workers in strategically important sectors like transport and construction, who would have otherwise been in an ideal position or organize and bargain collectively, were weakened by their largely casual nature. Thus, for instance, a large majority of dockworkers were employed casually, that is to say from day to day.[89] In 1951, there were over 20,000 casual workers in building and construction and nearly 5,000 in transport and communications.[90]

In spite of the struggles of the 1940s and 1950s,[91] resulting in considerable increase in wages, these were still not adequate to provide a decent living. Table 4.5 summarizes the cost of living estimates for various years worked out by different investigators.

The estimates are not comparable since they include different items in the budgets. But they are unanimous in one basic assumption. Each one of these cost of living estimates, according to the authors, computes only the bare minimum necessities for survival. And each one of the investigators inevitably wonders how workers survived on the prevailing wage rates for unskilled labour. The following comment by a colonial official on the 'Report of Enquiry into wages and cost of living of low grade African Government Employees in Dar es Salaam' carried out some time in 1942 is typical:

As was, of course, fully expected, this report has produced the usual result of such enquiries. It adduces substantial evidence to show that a considerable number of the more lowly paid Africans in the town — both Government Employees and, still more so, those not in Government services, are somehow or other accomplishing the seemingly impossible. They are living and supporting their families, and have been doing so for a long time now, on an income considerably below what is regarded as the bare 'minimum living wage'.[92]

The truth is that on these 'starvation [wage] scales' (to use the phrase of another colonial official),[93] they neither lived nor supported their families. They and their families merely existed in squalid living conditions subsisting on nutritionally deficient and monotonous diets of starchy foods. The following is a comparison between recommended rations in the Government Notice No. 325 of 1944 (Proper Feeding Regulations) and daily rations contained in a family budget survey of Dar es Salaam workers conducted in 1950.[94]

	Recommended scale	'Family budget'	Deficiency
Calories	3 500	1 545.00	1955
Total protein	100 gm	50.91 gm	49.09 gm
Animal protein	10 gm	12.40 gm	
Fat	50 gm	11.95 gm	38.05 gm
Carbohydrates	500 gm	287.90 gm	212.10 gm
Calcium	—	0.40 gm	
Iron	20 mgm	12.70 mgm	7.3 mgm
Phosphorous	—	1.30 gm	
Vitamin A	3 000 IU	3 000.00 IU	
Vitamin B	350 IU	50.00 IU	300.0 IU
Vitamin C	600 IU	650.00 IU	

The above survey gives an estimate of monthly consumption of foodstuffs for an average size of a household, that is, equivalent to 2.6 adults. The sample was drawn

Table 4.5 *Cost of living estimates and wage rates in Dar es Salaam, 1928–58* (Selected years)

Year	Cost of living estimate (Shs.)			Wage rates	Estimated by
	Bachelor	Husband + wife	Family of 4 children		
1928	23.16	30.83		Government (unskilled): 77 cents to Sh. 1 per diem Lighterage Co.: Shs. 2[a] per diem (unskilled) Skilled/semi-skilled & domestic servants: Shs. 30–80 per month	District officer (A)
1939		31.54			Baker's report (B)
1942	27.50	41.47	48.35	Government (unskilled): Shs. 20–60[b] per month Private (unskilled): Shs. 12. 50–15 per month	Report of Enquiry into Wages and Costs of Living of Low Grade African Government Employees in Dar es Salaam (C)
1944	53.00			Domestic servants: Shs. 35–45 per month	Governor (D)
1944	53.47			Semi-skilled/unskilled: Shs. 30–35 per month Skilled (around 1940): Shs. 30–100 per month(F)	C. Kirk (E)
1958	103.97			Minimum wage under the DSM Minimum Wage Order 1957, Shs. 81. 90 per month for adult male over 18 years. Government daily rate: Shs. 3–4 per day	Chesworth Report (G)

Notes: [a] Since the casual labour in the Lighterage Co. would not get work throughout the month, its monthly income would not necessarily amount to Shs. 60 per month.

[b] Almost 90 per cent of the survey sample were receiving less than Shs. 40 per month.

Source: A. District Officer to PC, Eastern Province, 10 January 1928, TNA 11625/I.

B. Baker E. C., 'Sociological conditions in DSM', August 1939, cited in 'Report of Enquiry into Wages and Cost of Living of Low Grade African Government Employees in DSM', p. 6, TNA 30598.

C. *op. cit.* D 29 November 1944, TNA 32744.

E. Kirk to Creech Jones, 7 December 1944, FCB 112/1/41–2.

F. Jerrard, R. C., 'Labour Conditions in Tanga', 21 March 1940, TNA 25971.

G. *Report of the Territorial Minimum Wage Board* (DSM: Government Printer, 1962), p. 20.

from families earning approximately Shs. 75 per month which was far in excess of the average earnings of a large majority of Dar es Salaam workers, and yet it shows deficiencies in calories, proteins, fat and almost all vitamins. As the 1942 Report noted: 'Any reduction on expenditure is bound to take the form of saving on the already meagre diet on which the average lowly paid native exists. It is no misstatement to say that because of this lack of proper food a considerable portion of the population of Dar es Salaam are becoming unemployable. Crude mortality figures for the township for the period 1st January to 24th August, 1942 show a death rate of 10.38 per thousand for the African population.'[95] True, through their struggles and organization in the 1950s, to be discussed in the next chapters, the more militant sections of the urban working class managed to get a considerable raise in their monetary wage rates. Yet the overall wages hardly kept pace with the ever-rising cost of living. The Chesworth Report once again noted the extremely poor diets of the working class. In the board's survey of ninety-nine wage-earners drawn from the building, transport, commerical and catering trades, only six were found to be free from signs of malnutrition.[96]

Therefore the sheer struggle to keep body and soul together drove the workers to 'steal' and borrow. In one letter, the District Officer of Dar es Salaam noted that 'much of the serious and petty thieving in this town is due to want' and according to him the 'starvation scales' of wages were responsible for it.[97] The Resident Magistrate of Dar es Salaam in his letter to the Provincial Commissioner dated 10 December 1946 had the following to say:

From a rough survey which I have made, I find that of approximately 365 charges of stealing (and kindred offences) laid in the last five months, at least 60 were perpetrated as a result of genuine hunger conditions. I have made a point in connection with all petty theft charges to ascertain the motive for the crime and have, where hunger was the plea, made enquiries to the extent of the efforts, if any, which the accused persons have made to obtain employment. And I am satisfied that those 60 Africans mentioned above had all made their maximum effort to obtain work.[98]

Indebtedness was noted in a number of budget surveys of the working class. The 1942 report, already quoted, noted that some 1,726 employees or almost 60 per cent out of the total sample of 2,901 government employees analysed admitted to being in debt to the extent of more than a month's pay. A survey of family budgets of Tanga workers done in 1958 also brought out the prominent role of borrowing and lending transactions in the income and expenditure of African workers.[90] Table 4.6 gives a summary of the receipts and payments where, as can be seen, borrowing contributes anything up to 40 per cent of a worker's income while some 20 per cent of his expenditure is for repayment of loans.

Whereas in Tanga borrowing was mainly from friends, in Dar es Salaam pawn-broking played a very important role. Leslie's survey of Dar es Salaam in 1958 found some eighteen pawnshops in Dar es Salaam tightly controlled by merchants.[100] The articles pledged included everyday items such as *khangas, kanzus,* shirts, shorts, trousers, vests, stoves and shoes. The loans were usually small, less than Shs. 15: 'in a sample of 3,000 consecutive entries the mean value of the loans granted was 3 Shs. 94 cents'.[101] The pawnbroker charged interest and if the article was not redeemed within the given time the pledge was sold through either the pawnbroker's own shop or a public auction at a very high rate of profit. According to one survey, 'the pawnbrokers' rate of profit on the sale of unredeemed goods often amounts to 400 per cent or more'.[102] The business was brisk, highly profitable and almost without risks but at the expense of the working class. Leslie estimated that some third of a million small loans were granted every year in Dar es Salaam.

The monthly cycle of the business reflected the violent vagaries in the income and expenditure of its clientele:

[On] about the fourth of each month the pawnshops begin to fill up as the salaries received at the beginning of the month begin to come to an end (most of them having been applied to liquidate advances, debts and rent owing, and to have a bit of a splash while the going is good); from the 4th to the 13th there is a steady rise in the number of pledges as more and more run out of money; then there is a recovery as a large number receive fortnightly pay or the 'subsistence' advance at mid-month which most prefer; then on about the 20th the queue begins again in earnest, reinforced by the monthly paid, until at the 23rd or so the nadir is reached: this is the true *siku za mwamba*, the 'tight-stretched days'; thereafter it is possible to borrow on the strength of the near approach of payday, and the queues at the pawnshops are relieved. At payday long queues may be seen at every pawnshop, this time with money in hand, and the pledges are redeemed.[103]

Table 4.6 *Average receipts and payments per worker, Tanga, 1958*

| | Receipts | | | | | |
| Source | Single | | Married | | Total sample | |
	Shs.	%	Shs.	%	Shs.	%
Income						
Regular employment	70.36	59.8	85.88	50.4	80.70	52.8
Casual employment	3.35	2.8	2.51	1.5	2.79	1.8
Sales	2.31	2.0	5.06	3.0	4.15	2.7
Other receipts						
Gifts	2.82	2.4	6.58	3.9	5.32	3.5
Borrowing, etc.	38.82	33.0	70.25	41.2	59.78	39.2
Total	117.66	100.0	170.28	100.0	152.74	100.0

| | Payments | | | | | |
| Item | Single | | Married | | Total sample | |
	Shs.	%	Shs.	%	Shs.	%
Food, drink, tobacco	67.39	57.4	96.51	56.7	86.75	56.8
Household items	10.29	8.8	12.33	7.3	11.55	7.6
Clothing	3.35	2.9	7.27	4.3	5.96	3.9
Transport, medical & entertainment	2.68	2.3	2.84	1.7	2.79	1.9
Rent	8.30	7.1	12.26	7.2	10.94	7.2
Gifts and remittances	2.05	1.7	3.13	1.8	2.76	1.8
Taxes	—	—	0.15	0.1	0.10	0.1
Repayment of loans, etc.	23.25	19.8	35.59	20.9	31.48	20.7
Total	117.31	100.0	170.08	100.0	152.33	100.0

Source: EA Statistical Department (Tanganyika Unit), *The Pattern of Income, Expenditure and Consumption of African Workers in Tanga, February 1958* (Dar es Salaam: Central Statistical Bureau, 1958).

So there it was: while the employer squeezed every ounce of a worker's energy at the work place, the landlord, the pawnbroker and the shopkeeper fleeced him of the last cent in his pocket, ensuring that he would always be a worker and always in debt to them.

That brings us to the role of the state in regulating (or otherwise) wages. This can best be investigated by analysing the history of minimum wage legislation which was perhaps the most important statutory intervention of the state on the question of wages.

The history of Minimum Wage legislation in Tanganyika goes as far back as 1939 when the first Minimum Wage Ordinance[104] was enacted. The government still believed that wages should be fixed and regulated without interference from the state. The passing of this legislation was therefore not because of any change of policy on the part of the government, but was rather to comply with the ILO Convention and to ward off international criticism. The International Convention on Minimum Wage-Fixing Machinery (No. 26) was adopted in 1928 and was ratified by the United Kingdom. The Convention required the signatories to create necessary machinery for fixing of minimum wages statutorily in trades or parts of trade where no effective machinery existed and the workers were not organized enough for collective bargaining.

The Minimum Wage Ordinance which attempted to give effect to this Convention provided that the Governor in Council, by order, may 'fix a minimum wage for any occupation in any township, minor settlement, district, or other area in which he is satisfied that the wages for that occupation are unreasonably low and such order may including the fixing of minimum wages for piece work, time work, the minimum wages to be paid to any special classes of employees within the occupation, exceptions or any other matter which requires to be inserted in the order' (s. 3). The governor was to make such order after obtaining advice from the wages board appointed by him for a particular occupation. A wage board was to consist of members representing employers and employees respectively in that particular occupation in equal proportion and other appointed members (s. 4). The order would not be effective until it had received the approval of the Legislative Council (s. 3).

When the Bill was presented to the Legislative Council, virtually all the unofficial members, mostly representatives of the employers, opposed it. Mr Stone argued that the Bill would work against the interest of the employees because it would be difficult to appy such legislation in a country 'which is mainly agricultural, and where at the moment it is established that somewhere in the region of half a million adult males are unemployed . . .'[105] Dr Malik arrived at the same conclusion by offering a completely opposite reasoning. He argued that wages depended on supply and demand and since there was a shortage of labour there was no danger of the employees being paid low wages: 'very low wages would be paid when there is excessive labour, but if there is a deficiency of labour, if we cannot get labour, the industrialist has to pay the maximum wage that he can economically stand'.[106] Therefore, he argued, there was no need of such a legislation. So whether because of unemployment or full employment, either way, the employers wanted the state to keep off the question of wages. Other members went so far as to suggest that such a legislation could have been drafted only by 'a totalitarian Government and not one professing democratic ideals'.[107]

The Acting Chief Secretary in his introduction as well as in his response made it amply clear that the state had no intention of interfering with the freedom of the employers. The real purpose of the Bill was simply to put it on the Statute Book so as to comply formally with Her Majesty's international obligations. As a matter of fact, the Acting Chief Secretary said, the government did not think that the wages were 'unreasonably low' and therefore the legislation would not have to be used very soon.[108]

In practice, the government kept its promise for almost twenty years. The first Minimum Wage Order was not made until 1957, fixing a minimum wage for the township of Dar es Salaam. The truth was that the colonial officials did not even believe that the machinery as provided under the 1939 Ordinance was workable. Three main reasons were given for this: first, that the wage boards would have to be established for each industry, that is, on an industrial basis rather than geographically, and this would be cumbersome; secondly, that it was difficult to find authentic representatives of employees; and thirdly, that the Order would have to be approved by the Legislative Council and this would cause much delay.[109] In spite of this, serious discussion for amending the Ordinance did not begin until 1946. Two factors were responsible for the revival of interest in minimum wages. First, the war had very dramatically affected the living conditions of the working class. Report after report, as we saw, observed that the cost of living had far outpaced wage rates and that the workers were living in deplorable conditions. This in itself would have probably not done much beyond moving the hearts of a few colonial officials. But then the second factor was the organized resistance of the working class itself, dramatically expressed in a spate of strikes, particularly among the dockworkers. In 1947, as we shall see in the next chapter, the situation came close to a general strike. It was in response to this situation that the minimum wage machinery, after a stop-gap measure of 1947,* was completely revamped in the Regulation of Wages and Terms of Employment Ordinance of 1951.[111]

Introducing the Bill, the Labour Commissioner assured the members that, if the Bill were enacted into law, there was no intention of 'following it up by the issue of a spate of orders establishing Wages Boards and Wages Councils throughout the Territory'. He emphasized that the idea was to establish a machinery to enable employees to have legitimate channels of forwarding their grievances. Although, he said, hitherto the industrial situation had been relatively peaceful, this should not 'lull us into a false sense of security, because I consider that the basis of the structure of our system of Industrial Relations is not sound'. He continued:

All the world over today you can see examples that labour is demanding a greater say in the management of their working conditions, not only in the metropolitan territories but in the colonies, and employers must be prepared to adapt themselves to these changing conditions and influences. As I have said, there is need for machinery whereby employees in various undertakings have a channel for voicing grievances and bringing them to the notice of their employers.[112]

The government had no doubt read the writings on the wall in the dockworkers' strikes. The policy now was to create the official machinery to co-opt, channel and supervise workers' discontent so that it did not assume independent forms which would have threatened the established order. This can be seen in the speech of the commissioner summarized above. The Bill was passed without dissent.

In the Minimum Wage Ordinance of 1939 the criterion for establishing a minimum wages board was an unreasonably low standard of the wage of any employee or class of employees. This was one of the reasons cited to argue that the Ordinance would have been difficult to implement since the test of 'unreasonably low' was subjective. The 1951 Ordinance therefore incorporated the principle of the UK Wages Council Act of 1945 in which the criterion for fixing wages and conditions of employment was not that wages were unreasonably low but that there was an absence of any machinery for an effective regulation of wages and conditions of employment. The rationale behind the UK Act was to provide for a machinery in trades and occupations where the workers were thought to be relatively unorganized and therefore too weak to 'protect' themselves through collective bargaining. Thus initially statutory minima were fixed in 'sweating' trades, and later the establishment of wages councils was confined to relatively small concerns.[113] The statutory machinery was therefore never considered a substitute for free collective bargaining; rather it was supposed to help in the process of strengthening it. As soon as the workers' organizations were strong enough, wages

* In 1947 the Minimum Wage (Amendment) Ordinance[110] repealed and replaced ss. 2, 3, and 4 of the Principal Ordinance. In providing for a wages council and not requiring the approval of the Legislative Council, it closely followed the UK Wages Council Act of 1945.

councils were abolished. It is for this reason that in Britain statutory minimum wages have never been fixed territorially, and nation-wide.

In the situation in Tanganyika, on the other hand, the problem was one of really extremely low wages in the country as a whole. So, although ostensibly the criterion adopted was of the 1945 UK Act, in practice the minimum wage-fixing machinery was used to fix territorial minimum wages.

Under the Ordinance, the member in charge of labour matters was empowered to appoint a wage board or wages council. The object of a wages board was to fix basic minimum wage for the lowest paid workers in any area. Its proposals would be sent to the member, who, with or without modification, might make a wages regulation order which had the force of law.[114] The procedure with the wages councils was the same, except that they were established when, in the opinion of the member, 'no adequate machinery exists for the effective regulation of the remuneration or the terms of employment of any employees or any class of employees . . .' (s. 6).

Both the board and the council were tripartite bodies with not more than three independent members and equal representation from the employers' and employees' sides.

Under section 12 of the Ordinance, a statutory minimum wage became part of the contracts of employment of the employees concerned and it was a criminal offence to pay less than the statutory minimum.

After the *ad hoc* regulation of wages of government employees during the war,* the first ever minimum wage order fixing wages for the Dar es Salaam municipality was made in 1957.[116] Under that order hourly rates were fixed for adult males (18 years and over); male young persons (different rates for the ages of 15, 16 and 17 years); adult females and female young persons, the ages being the same as those in the case of males. Lower rates were prescribed where the employees were given free housing and piped water. It is interesting to note that this Order continued with the tradition of discrimination in wage rates against women. For example, the rate for an adult male (42 cents per hour) was some 30 per cent higher than that of an adult female (32 cents per hour), while that of a male young person of 17 years of age was 8 cents more per hour than that of a female young person of the same age (24 cents per hour).

Overall, the 1957 Minimum Wage Order was said to have benefited some 20 per cent of the 22–25,000 workers employed in Dar es Salaam. The Order increased the daily rates from the prevailing Shs. 2–2.50 for unskilled workers to the statutory rate of Shs. 3.36[117] (that is, eight hours at 42 cents per hour).

To a certain extent the benefits of the statutory minima by-passed substantial numbers of workers because of the problem of enforcement, which was noted by the Chesworth Report. The Tanganyika Federation of Labour in its evidence to the Chesworth Board said that 'the terms of the order were ignored by large numbers of employers, particularly in the fields of retail distribution, smaller hotel and bars, casual work, and domestic servants employed by certain classes of the community'.[118] A spot check by the board itself in Dar es Salaam discovered eight alleged breaches in half an hour. 'When the employers were interviewed, not only was underpayment cheerfully and indifferently admitted, but the provisions that records must be kept of all persons covered by the order for a period of two years were entirely ignored.'[119] In the face of what appeared to have been a widespread breach of the order, it is interesting that the

---

* *Ad hoc* tribunals were set up under the Emergency Powers (Defence) Acts, 1939–40, to keep wage rates and cost of living under review.[115]

Chesworth Report discovered only one prosecution under the Ordinance for the contravention of the Minimum Wage Order. In a situation of general unemployment, a weak and legally not so conscious trade union movement and a poor labour inspectorate, it is no wonder that the enforcement of a minimum wage legislation would always face problems.

The Dar es Salaam order was the only one to be promulgated during colonialism. The next one came after independence. As we noted earlier, the independent government adopted the policy of stabilizing the labour force by providing for relatively higher wages and, in particular, wages adequate for a family. That policy was not only in accord with the government's plans for import-substitution industrialization but also an inevitable response to the mounting trade union pressure and working-class militancy.

The Territorial Minimum Wages Board under the chairmanship of D. P. Chesworth was appointed on 4 August 1961 to investigate and recommend to the government on the establishment of a basic minimum wage. The board gave a comprehensive report in which it noted the deplorable and squalid conditions of the working class. It rejected the Poverty Datum Line as a basis on which to fix minimum wages and took the view that its recommendations for initial statutory minimum wages should be based on the apparent maximum capacity of employers to pay. Nevertheless the board did make a calculation of the Poverty Datum Line on a bachelor basis for Dar es Salaam and came to the conclusion that simply to provide accommodation, food, clothing, fuel, light, soap and taxes came to Shs. 103.97 per month.[120] This compared extremely poorly with the prevailing wage rates of Shs. 60–90 per month. It was obvious that the minimum needed to be raised substantially. The board recommended basic minimum wages on a differential basis for Dar es Salaam and Tanga and for other townships. For Dar es Salaam and Tanga the monthly minimum for an adult person* was to be Shs. 150 per month. This was a rise of over 65 per cent over the 1957 minimum for Dar es Salaam. The board's proposals were adopted by the government.[121]

Following the Territorial Minimum Wages Board, a wages board was established[122] to look into and make proposals for prescribing a basic minimum wage for non-plantation agricultural workers. Later a number of wages councils were set up to fix minimum wages for particular trades.

The most important effect of the wage rise was to stabilize the working class. As we have already seen, the trend towards greater stability began in the 1950s but picked up dramatically after the independent government made a conscious decision to provide wages adequate for supporting a family unit. Sabot, in his detailed study, finds that unlike the colonial migrants the migrants of the later period were either accompanied by their wives or very soon joined by their families, and many of the female *migrants* came as dependants.[123] 'The stabilization of the labour force has become an important factor in sex selectivity in migration as it has resulted in an increase in the proportion of migrants who bring their wives to town.'[124] In his study Sabot also notes that the post-independence migrants stayed longer and in fact had become urban residents. 'These newly settled urban residents have severed three of the threads that tied them to the countryside: their locus of residence has shifted from the rural to the urban areas; they no longer derive income from economic activity in their home areas; and they no longer

---

* It may be noted that no distinction is made between male and female employees. This was a clear break with the colonial heritage of embodying different wage rates for male and female workers *in law*. Of course, this should not be taken to mean lack of discrimination against women workers in practice.

maintain their immediate families in the rural areas.'[125] In short here we have a description of a *proletariat* in the fullest sense of that term.★

The second most important effect of the wage rises was the rise in productivity as the employers reorganized their work process, thus increasing tasks and introducing some mechanization.[126] Increased wages were therefore more than absorbed by higher productivity.

Housing

The housing of the urban working class, unlike the semi-proletariat, was not regulated by law. It will be recalled that in the case of the migrant worker on the plantations and elsewhere, the employer had to comply with certain minimum standards for the housing he gave his workers. In the case of urban labour, the worker had to cater for himself so far as housing was concerned. Accommodation, type of housing and the general conditions of the worker's dwelling place were all very much the function of urbanization and the problems this gave rise to rather than a reflection of any legal standards. The most typical centre of the housing problems was the national capital, Dar es Salaam.

The African population in Dar es Salaam and Tanga almost doubled during the war.[127] This gave rise to enormous problems of accommodation and concomitant growth of shanty towns and slums. Around 1943, one source estimated that there were some '3,123 native houses in the township, which indicates that an approximate density of 10 persons per house has risen to 15 and that slum conditions have been accentuated'.[128] The 1949 Annual Labour Report observed that whereas some 15,000 houses were needed to provide accommodation to some 70,000 Africans residing in Dar es Salaam, there were only 6,000 houses of the usual type, of which only 3–4,000 were considered of adequate standard.[129]

The type of housing in which the Dar es Salaam working class lived was the typical housing in, to use the colonial parlance, zone three — that is, the African area. The city was divided racially and each racial zone had its own housing characteristics and architecture.

The African area, the main hub of which was originally Kariakoo, later extending to Ilala and Magomeni, was dominated by the Swahili type of housing. Leslie has described the Swahili type house in the following terms:

The Swahili type of house which shelters nearly three quarters of the African population of Dar es Salaam is built very much to a single design. There is the main house itself, divided by a central corridor off which are three rooms each side. There is thus a single front door, opened and shut first and last thing by the landlord (if he lives in the house) or his agent. Once inside one looks straight through to the courtyard, half as big as the house, where all the laundering, dishwashing and general chores go on. At the back of the courtyard are usually three rooms, which are latrine, kitchen and store when the house is comparatively empty (or when the house is of the better-than-average type), or all three may be used for sleeping and rented out, the latrine and kitchen being set at one side instead.[130]

The old-style houses used mud and poles for their walls, in some cases with a smooth finish and whitewashed. The newer type had cement floors and iron roofs with, of

---

★ Strangely, Sabot appears to doubt if they can be described as proletarians on the ground that they still maintain contacts with rural areas in terms of paying visits and making infrequent remittances. In our opinion, this is only a lingering remnant of traditional extended family set-up and in no way detracts from their *proletarian* character. The decisive point is that they have no substantial *economic* ties with rural areas.

course, higher rents. But in all cases the design remained the same. A typical single room would generally be 12 feet by 12 feet with small windows. Ventilation was through the open airspace between the roof and the walls. These houses had no piped water nor water-borne sanitation and no electricity. The occupants bought their water from either central kiosks or from water pedlars. 'In July, 1944 only 24 street lights and 16 water kiosks served the African townships.'[131]

It is in the single rooms of such houses that the large majority of working-class families lived. In a space of 12 by 12 feet they slept, ate and bred and kept all their furniture and household goods. They lived more like lodgers than as settled families. Nevertheless, for the colonial state the Swahili type house was a great blessing. It relieved the housing problem, as Molohan noted in regard to this type of housing: 'it is designed for the accommodation of lodgers and there is no doubt that the existence of this type of housing has assisted towards relieving the housing problem in towns'.[132] Vestbro in fact argues that the colonial state encouraged this type of housing for several interrelated economic and political reasons. First, the Swahili type of house was cheap to build and relied heavily on local material and traditional architecture. This meant that it was within the rearch of African small traders and artisans who through savings could build such houses and eventually become landlords. Secondly, although Africans were free in choosing the style of housing, the state controlled the allocation of plots thus achieving both 'control' as well as 'low costs'. Thirdly, it created a stable nucleus of African landlord class to which the colonial state paid much importance after the war. It was from such groups that the colonial ruling class expected political moderation and, eventually, protection for their economic interests.[133]

Be that as it may; the point is that meanwhile workers paid some Shs. 10–30 per month for such rooms accounting for 10–15 per cent of their total expenditure. A survey by the Chesworth Board showed that around the time of independence, rents for a single room in privately owned houses in urban areas ranged from Shs. 15 per month (lowest) in towns like Dodoma, Mbeya and Morogoro to Shs. 30 (highest) in Moshi and Arusha.[134] The description of working-class housing by the Chesworth Report is worth quoting at length:

The Board heard evidence from Government officers, Trade Union representatives, parochial clergy and medical practitioners, describing the squalid conditions of urban housing as well as the high rents invariably paid. It unanimously came to the view that, at the existing rent levels — the majority of urban workers are paid too little to enable them to obtain accommodation which is acceptable by any standard. It is customary for one, or at the most two, rooms to be rented — unlighted, poorly ventilated, often not weather-proof, without a water supply and with unsanitary communal latrines. The chairman and members of the Board visited such accommodation in a number of urban centres. It was note-worthy that many people living in such unattractive conditions, often with water only available from a waterpoint a quarter of a mile away, were making courageous but near-impossible attempts to maintain a decent standard. In contrast to rural housing, there is often great overcrowding in urban areas, the inevitable result of shortage of accommodation and high rents. With such overcrowding it is not surprising that in the towns tuberculosis rates, already high, are on the increase.[135]

Besides the Swahili type of house, another type of house came into being after the Second World War. This was the 'Quarter' as it was and is popularly called. To combat heavy shortage of housing and proliferation of slums after the war, the colonial government applied resources from the Colonial Development and Welfare Fund to build low-cost quarters.[136] These were in the form of one-room, two-room and three-room bungalows in Ilala or semi-detached villas in Temeke or terraces in Magomeni. They were single-family units characterized by greater privacy, each flat being self-contained with its kitchen, latrine, front and back doors.

Initially the city council gave preference to applicants earning a wage of Shs. 150 or more a month.[137] This, and the fact that these houses offered greater privacy, attracted a certain type of tenant — mainly Christian, married and educated couples from clerical and artisan groups. They were mainly from up-country 'tribes' like Pare and Chagga or 'foreigners' like Luo from Kenya and generally employed by the government or the East African High Commission. In short, this type of housing really catered for the up-coming petty-bourgeois intelligentsia generally and the civil servants in particular. Around 1957, only about 6 per cent of the population in Dar es Salaam lived in Quarters.[138]

After independence the government embarked on a slum-clearance programme. Following expert advice from an Israeli firm, a tenant purchase scheme was worked out. Houses built by the National Housing Corporation (NHC), which was in charge of this scheme, were essentially of the Swahili type but with concrete blocks and factory-made joineries. Overall this type of housing provided a better standard but the NHC was far from satisfying the great demand for housing. In 1964–9 some 5,000 mud-and-pole houses were supposed to be pulled down in Dar es Salaam but the target was fulfilled only in Magomeni, where by 1967 some 1,200 units were replaced.[139]

That the housing for the working class remained grossly inadequate was witnessed by the continual growth of shanty towns and slums in Dar es Salaam and other urban areas. Thus a large majority of the working class were housed in the Swahili type of houses and the mud-and-wattle structures that they continually put up in peri-urban areas. The official Labour Report of 1964/65 saw no solution to the problem and threw up its hands in despair:

In common with most developing countries, it would, however, appear that the problem of finding enough adequate housing for all urban employed populations is a problem which will take many years to solve. The present housing shortage is emphasized by the high rents which have to be paid by urban dwellers and has caused a number of those to move into the peri-urban areas.[140]

So that is how the worker and his family were sheltered. Let us now see what the worker was exposed to in the factory where he spent the greater portion of his life. In other words, we examine 'the conditions of the production process' which in the apt words of Marx are the worker's 'conditions of . . . active living process, or his living conditions . . .'[141]

Conditions of the production process (industrial safety)

Marx likened the 'gigantic workhouse for the industrial worker' called the factory to the 'house of terror' dreamed up for paupers in England in 1770.[142] That workhouse with its propensity to kill and maim became a prominent feature of Tanganyikan working-class life in the 1950s and 1960s. At the time that the Factories Ordinance[143] was passed in 1950 it was estimated that it would cover about 2,500 establishments.[144] By 1965 the number of registered factories had increased by two and half times.[145] In 1965 some 89,399 persons were employed in factories, constituting over one-fourth of the total wage-employment (excluding domestic servants), compared to 56,147 or 13 per cent of the wage-employment in 1953.[146] Together with the expansion of factories the working class was exposed to increased and newer hazards to its life and limb. The 'workhouse' was also the slaughter-house where a worker's very flesh and blood were offered at the altar of capital.

Every organ of sense is injured in an equal degree by artificial elevation of the temperature, by the dust-laden atmosphere, by the deafening noise, not to mention danger to life and limb among the thickly crowded machinery, which, with the regularity of the seasons, issues its list of the killed and wounded in the industrial battle. Economy of the social means of production, matured and forced as in a hothouse by the factory system, is turned, in the hands of capital, into systematic robbery of what is necessary for the life of the workman while he is at work, robbery of space, light, air, and of protection to his person against the dangerous and unwholesome accompaniments of the productive process, not to mention the robbery of appliances for the comfort of the workman."[147]

It is this robbery of the comfort, health and safety of the workman in a factory that we propose to document briefly in this section. We would also discuss the important legislation — the Factories Ordinance and the Workmen's Compensation Ordinance[148] — which were at the same time a result of class struggle as well as an attempt by the collective capitalist, the state, to curb the excesses of the said robbery.

The Factories Ordinance was enacted in 1950. Its history however goes as far back as 1936. In that year the Secretary of State recommended to the colonies a draft factory legislation based on the existing law in Trinidad and the 1901 Factory and Workshop Act of the UK. Discussion on the draft was deferred in view of the impending replacement of the Factories Legislation in the UK. The new Factories Act of 1937 reopened the discussion on its possible adoption in entirety while the Chief Inspector of Labour suggested that some parts of the UK legislation, especially Part VI dealing with juveniles, be omitted. That discussion, however, was put to rest by a decisive minute of the Chief Secretary in which he said that the proposed Factories Bill 'falls into the academic category when the interests of juveniles have been safeguarded . . . Further consideration of the general legislation proposed can be postponed, say, for 12 months, without detriment.'[149] Subsequently, for nearly ten years, official discussion raged on whether the country needed an elaborate factories legislation or just a simpler enabling Bill.[150] It was not until 1950, therefore, that a fairly comprehensive Bill was presented to the legislature.

There were two basic reasons behind this dilly-dallying: first, the fact of the very absence of elaborate industrialization and, secondly, the resistance of employers expressed through their representatives in the state. And in the absence of organized resistance and militancy on the part of the working class the colonial bureaucracy felt little pressure to expedite such measures. It was only in the late 1940s and early 1950s that such pressure began to be felt and the colonial state set itself to forestall its radicalization by chanelling it along 'acceptable lines'.

Thus the Bill was finally enacted in 1950. Even then its operation was deferred by almost two years in compliance with the wishes of the TSGA.[151] The TSGA put up a stiff resistance at the Select Committee stage, arguing that the sisal industry had its own peculiar problems and therefore should have its own factories legislation. This was not accepted but a number of other recommendations of the TSGA were incorporated in the Select Committee's report. For example, a proviso was added to the definition of 'factory' allowing the governor to 'except any premises or part of any premises being a factory as hereinbefore defined from the application of all or any of the provisions of this ordinance' (s. 5(1)). This proviso was a compromise solution adopted by the Select Committee in response to TSGA's argument that 'drying lines' on the sisal estates should not fall within the definition of 'factory'. Another concession that was made to the employers was to give four years' period of grace to the establishments which did not comply with the section on overcrowding (s. 14(4)).

As a matter of fact, when introducing the Bill, the Labour Commissioner went to great lengths to reassure the employers that in the long run the factories legislation was in their interest. After all, it would reduce the amounts that had to be paid out in compensation. In any case, there was a need of minimum standards, standards which would not be far behind those acceptable in industrialized countries 'although, of course, we cannot hope to attain at once the degree of perfection that has been achieved elsewhere'.[152] All the same, the commissioner continued, the standards must be set 'because of the number of new industries that are opening up here. I myself receive numerous inquiries from persons, newcomers to this Territory, who wish to open up factories, and it is only fair to them that they should know what standards they have to accept here. I think that a Bill of this nature will be a protection for the good employer against unfair competition.'[153]

As we shall see, the standards themselves were often breached, yet it was an achievement of the working class to have such standards placed on the statute book at all. Marx argued that the UK Factories Acts were a result of persistent class struggle and no doubt the Factories Ordinance of Tanganyika, which was based on the 1937 UK Act, embodied the victories of that struggle. In the words of Marx: 'The English factory workers were the champions, not only of the English, but of the modern working class generally . . .'[154]

Let us now examine the Ordinance itself, its practical operation and the state of industrial safety and health during the period under investigation. The very definition of 'factory' in the Ordinance gave rise to problems of interpretation. For example, in the appeal of *The Attorney General* v. *Patel Farmers*[155] Justice Abernathy was faced with the problem of whether a tobacco barn where tobacco was dried, cured and sorted for sale fell within the definition of 'factory'. He reluctantly decided that it did, although he wondered 'if the Legislature ever intended the Factories Ordinance to apply to premises of the nature of the premises now under consideration'. Probably the more important question than the problem of interpretation was that the definition left out building operations from its purview. A common accident in building resulted from the very dangerous way in which the scaffolds were erected. The colonial labour officers gave it the name of 'Tanganyika scaffold' and often made strictures against it in their accident reports. Reporting an accident in 1958 in which three workers sustained multiple injuries including a fractured elbow, sprains and back strains, a labour officer remarked: 'The scaffolding in use was typical Tanganyikan style poles roped together in rather haphazard fashion and planks of varying length and strength, one plank in use was split over half its length and had been 'strengthened' by wooden battens crossways.'[156] Yet this practice appears to have continued for there were no regulations covering such cases.

Part III of the Ordinance provided for registration of factories while Part IV dealt with general health. The latter included provisions on cleanliness, overcrowding, ventilation, lighting, drainage of floors, sanitary conveniences and so on. These provisions were important for both the safety and health of the workmen. Accidents often occur because of a slippery floor or lack of floor-space. Section 14(2) provided that each workman employed in a workroom should have a space of at least 350 cubic feet and a workroom should have adequate ventilation to ensure a free circulation of air. Often, in particular among small employers, these provisions were breached. Referring to one tailoring establishment in Tanga which employed six people a labour officer observed:

This workroom is situated above a display window, and measures 6′ 3″ high by 13′ 6″ long, by 10′ 3″ broad. I haveinformed the occupier that this premises is not in compliance with Section 14 of the Factories Ordinance in that it is less than 9′ high, and that the only means of access to it is a practically vertical ladder.[157]

The response of the employer was to engage an advocate who pleaded that his client's undertaking be exempted under the proviso to section 14(3).* Another tailoring undertaking employed seven people in a room measuring 9ft 3in. by 10ft 6in. by 13ft 0in, which was considered adequate for only three people.[158] As the contravention letters of the labour officers show, sanitary provisions, especially those on providing adequate washing facilities and latrines, were also breached with fair regularity.[159] As a matter of practice, labour officers wrote contravention letters in cases of such breaches rather than prosecute the offenders. In some cases this author found documents showing some contraventions occurring at every inspection and yet no action being taken. For example, inadequate ventilation was noted in the case of African Cashew Processors Ltd, in the letter of 14 January 1958; it was again remarked on in the letter of 26 October 1963 and once again made a subject of elaborate advice to the employer in the letter of 23 November 1965.[160] In the case of Vadgama Construction Company,[161] contravention letters drawing attention to inadequate height of the workrooms, inadequate and dirty sanitation and insufficient fencing of dangerous machinery were the subject of numerous contravention letters between 1958 and 1974, and yet no legal proceedings appear to have been taken. We shall come back to this reluctance to prosecute later in our discussion. For the moment let us turn to the safety provisions of the Ordinance.

Part V of the Ordinance dealt with the fencing of dangerous machinery and provision of guards where possible. It also provided for guarding against dangers emanating from lifting machines and equipment such as ropes, chains, cranes and tackles. There were provisions to guard against fire, poisonous liquids, inflammable dust, gas, vapour and so on. In short, this part of the Ordinance was fairly comprehensive so far as safety at the workplace was concerned and theoretically should have played an important role in safeguarding the life and limb of the workmen. But in practice matters stood differently.

Examination of reported industrial injuries showed that accidents resulting from unguarded and unfenced machinery were not uncommon. In wood workshops common accidents — ranging from simple cuts and lacerations to amputation of fingers and hands — resulted from circular saws and power-driven planing machines.[162] The following accident[163] which occurred at a saw-mill in Tanga some time in 1964 illustrates some of the points made above. Hassani Rashidi, a carpenter of over three years' service, was planing a piece of timber on an electric planing machine known as a 'thicknesser'.

Usually when planing a helper is provided to pull the timber from the other end (rear) of the machine. On this particular time the helper had been allocated some other work to do and injured told to do the work alone. As he went round the rear of the machine to pull out the piece of timber he slipped on the ground as there were much rubbish from the planer. As he tumbled his left hand landed on the machine and was caught between the revolving planer . . . and the roller . . . resulting into all his fingers being cut off.[164]

Later the worker's hand was amputated at the wrist. The factory inspector observed that the opening between the roller and the revolving planer was too wide and the occupier was advised to reduce this gap. In this incident there is little doubt that the occupier had not bothered to have the floor cleaned of the rubbish, contrary to section 13 of the Ordinance, had indulged in dangerous practice by removing the helper and had provided inadequate and insufficient guard contrary to section 23, and yet he was

---

* In this case the LC refused to exempt and ordered the employer to rectify the contraventions.

not prosecuted. The Factory Inspector opined that the occupier had not been warned previously* as to the dangers of the 'wide opening' referred to above and that in any case, 'No negligence is proved or can be proved against the employers'!

Accidents often occurred in the decorticating and brushing machines on the sisal estates. We came across a number of reports of gruesome accidents resulting from an injured person's clothes (lack of proper uniforms?) or sisal fibre getting wrapped round unfenced revolving shafts or a workman's hand getting pulled under rollers and unguarded pulleys. In a report from Mwanza made in 1953 a labour officer noted that some progress had been made towards adequately guarding the most dangerous machinery. However, he continued:

It is doubtful if the majority of factory owners and occupiers realize how dangerous fast revolving shafts and belts and pulleys can be and what is the purpose of the ordinance. There was a most unfortunate episode at Bariadi where a child was killed through a line shaft being unguarded and the sisal fibre he was holding becoming wrapped round the shafts. The child received multiple injuries and died almost immediately.[166]

The employer was prosecuted and fined Shs. 2,000, the maximum in the District Court. In another accident at the Fili Sisal Estate a raspador attendant's clothing became wrapped round an unguarded revolving shaft. 'The man was dragged into the transmission machinery and decapitated.'[167] Asuma fractured his left humerus when clearing the feed table in a sisal decorticating machine. He was attempting to remove grass from the section of the moving first roller between the two endless belts when his left hand was caught up by grass and pulled in and jammed between the roller and the feed table structural cross-member.[168] Bambuje lost a phalanx of his left forefinger in the service of Mtotohovu Estate. The injured person, according to the inspector, 'somehow but seemingly from mental aberration interrupted his normal ryhthmical method of removing fibre and walked along with fibre until it was almost on the in-running nip of the off-take rope terminal pulley, when he tried to scoop up an inordinate handful of fibre which carried into the nip of the unguarded pulley and rope carrying his hand with it'.[169] Regardless of mental aberration, the accident would probably have not happened if the employer had provided a guard for the pulley. And yet the Factory Inspector did not feel obliged to prosecute.

One could go on and on citing incident after incident of such and other accidents. But that is not necessary. Suffice it to say that an ever-increasing list of maimed, mutilated and dead workers continued to appear in spite of the Factories Ordinance. Official figures show that the rate of industrial injuries increased three-fold from 5.6 per thousand wage earners in 1953 to 17.2 in 1965.[170] This refers only to those injuries disabling a workman for more than three days since under section 3 of the Accidents and Occupational Diseases (Notification) Ordinance[171] only such accidents need be notified. During this same period a total of 1,180 workers lost their lives and over 7,000 were permanently incapacitated, some totally and others partially.[172] Although the rate of fatal injuries fluctuated around 0.2 per thousand during the period, industrial accident as the cause of death compared to other causes among workers increased steadily over the period as Table 4.7 shows. Thus, relatively, deaths caused by

---

* To an argument on a similar ground in the case of an accident in 1962, the then Acting Labour Commissioner responded by quoting an English judge who had observed in an English case that 'it is a little wearisome to find employers urging again and again, and with success, that they can make a new statute and that it is enough for them if they give particular instructions to their workman or if they can say: "This has passed muster with the Factory Inspector for so many years. . . ." '[165]

accidents had shown a rise. This was probably because with the increase of real wages in the early 1960s and greater urbanization and stabilization, deaths resulting from nutritional, infective and other diseases (which used to be a common cause of deaths among plantation workers) decreased.[173]

Table 4.7 *Deaths of employed persons by accidents as % of total deaths, 1953–69*

Period	Average per year	Average %
1953–56	127	15
1957–60	155	26
1961–65	96	26
[1966–69	102	35]

Source: Annual Reports of Labour Department.

From our foregoing discussion it is clear that many industrial injuries were preventable and would probably have been prevented if the Factories Ordinance had been scrupulously applied and thoroughly enforced. The question therefore is: what had been the problems in the application and enforcement of the Factories Ordinance? There are a number of interrelated socio-economic factors that have to be considered in attempting to answer this question.

First, a piece of legislation like the Factories Ordinance embodied in it an important contradiction between capital and labour. Provision of safeguards and safety measures meant that an employer had to increase his constant capital thereby affecting his rate of profit. Employment of workers to keep the work-place clean would also mean spending on unproductive labour which for the capitalist was wasteful. Adopting such safe working practices like stopping machines when oiling* and cleaning was done or reducing speeds to levels which were safer would all mean loss of valuable production time to the capitalist, time during which surplus-value would not be produced and machines would be lying idle. As Marx put it:

Since the labourer passes the greater portion of his life in the process of production, the conditions of the production process are largely the conditions of his active living process, or his living conditions, and economy in these living conditions is a method of raising the rate of profit; just as we saw earlier that overwork, the transformation of the labourer into a work horse, is a means of increasing capital, or speeding up the production of surplus-value such economy extends to overcrowding close and unsanitary premises with labourers, or, as capitalists put it, to space saving; to crowding dangerous machinery into close quarters without using safety devices; to neglecting safety rules in production processes pernicious to health, or, as in mining, bound up with danger, etc. Not to mention the absence of all provisions to render the production process human, agreeable, or at least bearable. From the capitalist point of view this would be quite a useless and senseless waste.[175]

What has been said above can be best illustrated by the example of brush machines in the sisal estates. We have already seen that workers working at these machines had often had their hands and arms torn off by being pulled in through the feed apertures. Labour officers advised employers to reduce the width of the feed gaps so as to minimize this danger. However, the effect of such reduction would be to slow down the speed of work, which was resented not only by the employers but even by the workers. The workers would have had to spend more time to complete the same task. Hence, around 1960

---

* Cf. the case of Herbert Karata whose throat was compressed by a saw frame when, to save time, he attempted to oil the saw guides while the frame was rising.[174]

there were a number of strikes on the issue. The employers and even the labour officers were only too ready to blame the union and workers as opposing safety measures, typically making the victim the cause of his misfortune. But the issue was not so simple. More enlightened labour officers in fact noted that the problem was not primarily a union matter but a question of engineering. In fact a number of sisal estates had managed to design *curved* guards which would be protective without reducing the speed of work. This would have involved time and money on research to design and fit appropriate guards, a process in which the capitalists were of course least interested. When pressed by the Factory Inspectors they resorted to the simpler and cheaper method of reducing feed gaps without, it must be emphasized, reducing tasks, thus arousing industrial unrest and in turn using it as an excuse not to effect safety measures.[176]

The point, therefore, is that whenever possible employers would invariably breach safety regulations if they could get away with it. This brings us to the important issue of the enforcement of the Factories Ordinance.

The Ordinance placed the responsibility of its administration and enforcement on the Labour Commissioner (s. 67). It also provided for the appointment of a chief factory inspector and other inspectors who were given fairly wide powers of inspection, examination and investigation as well as prosecution in law courts for non-compliance of the Ordinance (ss. 68, 69 and 70). Undoubtedly, therefore, a very strong, skilled, experienced and honest inspectorate was an essential condition for the Ordinance to be effective. An examination of the Annual Reports of the Labour Department shows that the factory inspectorate had been lacking in all these qualities. In 1964, for example, there was only one factory inspector to assist the Chief Factory Inspector although the authorized establishment of the inspectorate was five.[177] In 1965 another inspector was recruited, and these two inspectors continued to shoulder the burden until 1969 when for the first time the Labour Department had all five authorized posts filled.[178] Therefore, on an average, there had hardly been even one inspection per factory per annum. In 1964 effective visits amounted to 620 while in 1965 there were a total of 1,400 inspections, in both cases the inspections being far less than 50 per cent of the number of registered factories. This in itself shows that the state had cared little to give teeth to the Factories Ordinance.

Next we come to the problem of effecting compliance of the legislation by the existing inspectorate. Here one cannot help noting an employer-biased attitude of labour officers, to say the least, particularly when it came to instituting prosecutions. A random sample of fifty-five industrial accidents notified to the Labour Office over the period of 1956–62, for example, showed that there were only six prosecutions when in three-fourths of these accidents the investigating officer had found the conditions to be 'unsafe'.[179]

The investigating officer, at the end of the form that he filled in after an accident, was required to give his opinion as to whether the employer concerned should be prosecuted or not. Examination of a sample of these opinions illustrates the inspectorate's attitude. In an accident on a sisal estate where a worker lost the phalanx of his left forefinger when his fingers were drawn into the nip of an unguarded pulley, the Factory Inspector said: 'Ordinarily I would prosecute and will do so if you so say, but I do feel that the new owners took the machinery condition as complying with the Ordinance. There is no doubt a lot remains to be done and even at this date the fencing was not secure.'[180] In another accident where there was an 'unfenced gap between the revolving first roller', the officer advised against prosecution '[in] view of the company's record both as an employer, its very low accident rate and the cause of the accident . . .'[181] In another accident on a sisal decorticating machine where it was normal practice to clear the fibre sifter while the machine was in motion, the inspector noted in his remarks: 'the practice is at fault. It is possible to remove the sifter covers and clear the machine properly when it is at rest and I have informed the management to do so. However, their complaint is that this would involve a great loss of production time.' And yet the same inspector advised against prosecution on the grounds that 'the management, which has been taught this malpractice by the previous occupier from whom it was recently taken over, thought this was the accepted practice, and the injury of the workman is slight'.[182] The latter part of the argument was hardly justifiable in law because proceedings for unsafe practice under section 43 of the Ordinance (or prosecution for contraventions of safety provisions under other relevant provisions) were not and need not be linked with injury resulting therefrom. In fact section 75 created a separate offence and penalty where an injury or death resulted 'in consequence of the occupier or owner of a factory having contravened any provision of this ordinance . . .' In the case of *Rajabali Meghji Visram v. R.*, the East African Court of Appeal remarked:

In our view Section 75 does not merely prescribe an increased penalty for an aggravated contravention of a provision of the ordinance, as the High Court thought, but creates an entirely separate and independent offence, which is that some person is injured in consequence of a contravention.*[183]

In one case, where a workman's finger was amputated, the employer had installed a pendulum cross-cut saw in such a way that it ran in a direction away from the workman, opposite to the direction which a pendulumn cross-cut saw was normally accepted as running. According to the inspector's own admission this created a situation where the workman 'always is in risk of his hand coming in contact with the blade'. However: 'This company is a very good employer and I feel that they installed this saw in the best of faith albeit in an extremely dangerous manner and in consideration of the efforts he had made to safeguard the machine, I am loathe to prosecute in this instance.'[184] So much for sympathy for the 'good' employers. What about the 'bad' employers? In an accident where he discovered at least two faults on the part of the employer, the inspector observed: 'Although it cannot be said that this company are the ideal employers and that they are at fault in this case, it is apparent that the injured person was the greatest contributor in the negligence . . .'[185] The opinions cited are typical and illustrate the general bias of the officials in favour of the employers.

But even where the recalcitrant employers were taken to court, they were either acquitted on some technicality or convicted and fined *nominal* sums. In our investigations we came across hardly a single case where an employer was sent to prison for the contravention of the Factories Ordinance. And the fines were so low† that occupiers found it much cheaper to pay the fine year in year out rather than act to comply with inspector's recommendations. Under the circumstances, honest and conscientious inspectors would feel too embarrassed and ridiculed to resort to court action.

The sum result of the problems of enforcement discussed above was that even the

---

* In that case the employer had been charged with two counts: causing injury to a workman by failure to fence contrary to section 75 and failure to fence dangerous machinery contrary to section 23(1). The magistrate had convicted the employer on the first count but did not make a finding on the second. The High Court substituted conviction on the second count for the first. On appeal and cross-appeal, the East African Court of Appeal restored convictions on both counts.

† The maximum fine under the Ordinance was Shs. 2,000 and/or three months' imprisonment (s. 75) and it has been so since the passing of the legislation in 1950.

fewer teeth provided in the Ordinance in practice simply did not bite. One cannot but agree with the remark of a recent researcher of industrial accidents who observed that in underdeveloped countries like Tanzania, 'where enforcement machinery is grossly inadequate, corruption of officials rampant, genuine trade unions virtually absent and democratic traditions weak, the industrial safety legislation may not be worth the paper it is printed on'.[186]

If the safeguarding of a worker's life and limb is weighed against costs of production and rates of profit in capital's books, so is the worth of its loss weighed in the scales of commodity-exchange. Every part of the human body has a price-tag attached to it. In the cool rationality of capital, a worker's body is no more than the embodiment of labour power, which like every other commodity has a definite price in the market-place. And a price-list was neatly provided in the Workmen's Compensation Ordinance.

The Workmen's Compensation Ordinance was enacted in 1948. Once again, as was typical in legislation of this sort, the ball was set rolling as far back as 1937 by the Secretary of State, who had sent a draft model Act to all the East and West African dependencies with a request that such Acts be put on the statute book as speedily as possible. One of the questions that had arisen then was that the proposed Act was non-racial in its application, a point that the colonial employers could hardly stomach in the colonial/racialist atmosphere of the 1930s. Nevertheless, anticipating pressure from international opinion, the British government had decided as a matter of policy that such a legislation could not be racial. The draft, however, was shelved for almost ten years for it was not considered urgent enough to be enacted during the war.[187]

The 1948 Ordinance followed closely the British Workmen's Compensation Act of 1925. Unlike its predecessor, section 29 of the Master and Native Servants Ordinance,[188] this statute embodied the progressive principle of strict liability attained by the English working class after many years of bitter struggle.

The 1948 statute covered all workmen, regardless of the type and duration of their contracts of service whether manual or non-manual, earning less than Shs. 1,400 per month (s. 2). Section 5(1) of the Ordinance provided: 'If in any employment personal injury by accident arising out of and in the course of the employment is caused to a workman, his employer shall . . . be liable to pay compensation in accordance with the provisions of this ordinance.' Although one of the important objectives of this law was to minimize litigation and make the payment of compensation automatic, the interpretation of this section itself gave rise to voluminous litigation. As employers contested payment of compensation so the court cases increased in numbers. Virtually every phrase of that section has been the subject of judicial interpretation and decision, in the process making it more restrictive.[189] We need not go into that: suffice it to mention that the strict liability that the Ordinance purported to impose was to some extent whittled down by the restrictive judicial interpretations of section 5.

The quantum of compensation payable was linked with the type of injury and the amount of earnings of a workman. Thus if a workman suffered death as a consequence of an accident at work, his dependants were entitled to thirty-one months' earnings or Shs. 24,000, whichever was less (s. 6(a)). In case of temporary incapacity which disabled a workman for more than three consecutive days, the injured person was entitled to periodical payments which in the case of total temporary incapacity was half the monthly earnings every month up to the maximum of ninety-six months (s. 9). For total permanent incapacity the compensation payable was forty-eight months' earnings or Shs. 34,000, whichever was less, although the minimum should not be less than Shs. 2,000.

Compensation for permanent partial incapacity was computed by reference to the second schedule. The schedule gave a list of possible permanent injuries against each one of which was given a percentum, to indicate the degree of disablement. More than elsewhere in the compensation law, here was a place where the commodity relations of the capitalist society found their most manifest, if rather crude, expression. Let us take an illustration. If a factory worker earning Shs. 400 per month lost his leg below the knee he would have been entitled to 40 per cent of his forty-eight months' earnings: in this case Shs. 7,680. On the other hand, if a clerk earning Shs. 1,300 per month lost *his* leg also below the knee, he would be paid compensation of Shs. 24,960. Why should a clerk's leg be worth more than a worker's except by the logic of the values of commodities? The labour power of a clerk has a greater value than that of a worker and therefore although the extent of disability is the same (and from the human point of view probably causes the same pain, anguish and suffering), the value of damage done to the commodity labour power is not the same. Thus what was being compensated here was not the injury* or pain or suffering or even loss of future earnings of the workman, but the *damage* done to labour power.

It must be noted that the amounts payable under the Ordinance were small compared to both the cost of living as well as the damages that could be claimed under a legal action in tort. Table 4.8 shows average compensation paid per disabled workman under various categories. The author of this table notes that the increase between 1957 and 1964 was probably a real gain since the price index for retail goods fluctuated little during the period.

Table 4.8 *Average compensation paid per disabled workman according to category of disability*

Year	Death	Permanent incapacity	Temporary incapacity	
			Per worker (Shs.)	Per day (Shs.)
1951	1 307	326	51	1.55
1957	2 091	541	73	3.20
1964	5 016	1 253	87	3.60

Source: Hirji, K. F., 'Accidents at Work: The Case of Motor Vehicle Workshops' (Dar es Salaam: National Institute of Transport, 1980), mimeo, p. 19.

The quantum of compensation under the Ordinance, as we noted, was far below what would be recoverable as compensation in courts for the same injury. The courts were rather more realistic in that, unlike the Ordinance, they took into account the pain and suffering as well as loss of future earnings for the rest of the expected life of the injured worker. The Ordinance, it will be recalled, fixed an arbitrary maximum of forty-eight months' earnings. Hence, as we saw earlier, it was not even compensation for loss of future earning power as such but rather compensation for damage to labour power which had to have an arbitrary ceiling.

Finally, perhaps one of the most serious shortcomings of the Ordinance was its list of occupational diseases for which compensation was also payable. By 1964 the list was completely outdated in that it left out some major occupational diseases. In the words of one researcher:

all the pneumoconioses, i.e. lung diseases caused by inhalation of various types of dusts, are left out in their entirety. There is no mention of silicosis caused by inhalation of silica dust, nor of

---

* Contrary to the title of the Ordinance, which said: 'An Ordinance to provide for compensation to workman for injuries suffered in the course of their employment'.

byssinosis caused by cotton dust nor of asbestosis caused by inhalation of asbestos dust or of farmer's lung which afflicts agricultural workers handling mouldy hay or straw. The multitude of occupational cancers are also left out of the list.[190]

No wonder therefore that the Annual Reports of the Labour Department mentioned only one compensable occupational disease year in year out: anthrax. Anthrax itself was serious enough. During the 1953–65 period there were fifty-six cases of anthrax reported, with three deaths.[191] The death and suffering from other *occupational* diseases was simply not known since they were not compensable.

Conclusion

In this chapter we have traced the development of permanent wage-labour. Three sources, which formed the basis of its development, were identified. Within the semi-proletarian labour small nuclei of skilled and semi-skilled artisans had begun to develop. These were reinforced by relatively more permanent — although casual — wage-labour in the transport sector, particularly in the docks. The begining of import-substitution manufacturing industry after the war further augmented the development of the industrial proletariat.

The development of the industrial proletariat in town had a backwash effect on the semi-proletariat in the primary sector. In the early 1950s, colonial officials openly deplored the wastefulness of the 'migrant' worker and began to take steps to encourage stabilization of the labour force. Stabilization picked up with the trade union struggles and pressure as one of its principal *raisons d'être* — low wages — was gradually eroded by an increasing rise in wages. The neo-colonial industrialization policy together with a decisive rise in the minimum wage finally broke the back of the system of semi-proletarian labour. Thus developed the agricultural and mining proletariat, the second principal component of permanent wage-labour. The third component of permanent wage-labour was the service worker whose origin lay in administrative and domestic services.

Changes in the character of wage-labour entailed changes in the legal superstructure. The Master and Native Servants Ordinance was superseded by the Employment Ordinance in 1955. The Employment Ordinance was a transitional piece of legislation attempting to regulate both the semi-proletarian and the proletarian labour. Its subsequent amendments increasingly shifted the balance in favour of permanent wage-labour as the migrant labour was stabilized. The most decisive change was after independence in the form of the amending Act of 1962 which abolished the *kipande* system and in practice put an end to recruitment.

The semi-proletarian historical background did not augur well so far as the industrial discipline of the industrial proletariat was concerned. The state therefore had to come to capital's assistance by enacting the Security of Employment Act which legally imposed such discipline.

Finally, in the third section of the chapter, we discussed conditions of work, mainly those of the industrial proletariat. The problems of industrial safety and so on discussed herein themselves reflected the changed character of the productive forces. In this section we traced the legal history of three pieces of legislation: the Minimum Wage Ordinance, the Factories Ordinances and the Workmen's Compensation Ordinances. All three were borrowed from Britain and were enacted locally in the late 1940s and early 1950s. They embodied the results of the class struggles of the English proletariat and were locally enacted partly as a culmination of the intense struggles of the

Tanganyikan dockworkers in the 1940s. Thus, unlike the Master and Native Servants Ordinances and various 'care and welfare' regulations made thereunder, which had predominantly an instrumentalist character, the legislation discussed in this chapter had a significant political character. Yet they too ultimately served the interests of capital so long as capital and its state were dominant. In addition, whatever gains that were made by the working class and embodied in the statute books were continually eroded in numerous ways through non-enforcement and biases of the administrators in favour of the employers. These too have been documented in this chapter.

The shift towards the *political* character of law becomes even more pronounced in the legislation dealing with the dispute-settlement machinery and trade unionism. This forms the subject matter of our next three chapters.

NOTES

1. Morton, A. L., *A People's History of England* (Berlin: Seven Seas Publishers, 1965), Chs. VI and XI.
2. ibid., Ch. VI. Huberman, L., *Man's Wordly Goods: The Story of the Wealth of Nations* (New York: Monthly Review Press, 1968), p. 118.
3. Engels, F., *The Peasant War in Germany* (Moscow: Progress Publishers, 1965), p. 177.
4. ibid.
5. Morton, A. L., op. cit., p. 330.
6. Byatt to SS, 22 November 1922, CO 691/58/436–40.
7. Byatt to SS, 13 March 1922, CO 691/82/541–2.
8. See, for instance, Mitchell, P. E., op. cit.
9. For instance, Iliffe, J., 'Wage Labour', op. cit., p. 286.
10. Honey, M., op. cit., pp. 485ff. Rweyemamu, J., *Underdevelopment*, op. cit.
11. Honey, M. op..cit., p. 498.
12. Quoted ibid., p. 496, emphasis in the original.
13. Rweyemamu, J., *Underdevelopment* op. cit., p. 116.
14. Honey, M., 'Asian Industrial Activities in Tanganyika', *TNR*, No. 74 (1974), pp. 55–69.
15. Rweyemamu, J., *Underdevelopment*, op. cit., p. 120.
16. ibid. See also: Barker, C. and Wield, D., 'Notes on International Firms in Tanzania', *Utafiti*, Vol. III, No. 2, 1978 (University of Dar es Salaam); Seidman, A., op. cit.; Schadler, K., *Manufacturing and Processing Industries in Tanzania* (Munich: IFO–Institut für Wirtschaftsforschung, 1969).
17. Foreign Investments (Protection) Act, 1963, No. 40 of 1963.
18. Rweyemamu, J., *Underdevelopment*, op. cit., p. 128. The same source has been used for the information that follows.
19. Barker, C. and Wield, D., op. cit., pp. 318–19.
20. Arrighi, G., 'International Corporations, Labour Aristocracies, and Economic Development in Tropical Africa', in Rhodes, R. I. (ed.), *Imperialism and Underdevelopment* (New York: Monthly Review Press, 1970), pp. 220ff. See also: Tschannerl, G., 'Periphery Capitalist Development — A Case Study of the Tanzanian Economy', *Utafiti*, Vol. I, No. 1, 1976 (University of Dar es Salaam).
21. Rweyemamu, J., 'Major Trends of Macro-economic Aggregates of the Tanzanian Economy since 1954' (mimeo, University of Dar es Salaam, Dept. of Economics, n.d.), Table 1.5, p. 5.
22. In 1965 the manufacturing sector constituted only 4 per cent of the total Gross Domestic Product, and the wage employment in this sector was only 8 per cent. (Tanzania: *Economic*

Survey, 1968/69, Dar es Salaam: Government Printer pp. 9, 29.)

23. Tanzania, *Survey of Employment and Earnings, 1965* (Dar es Salaam: Central Statistical Bureau), App. VIII.
24. Schadler, K., *Crafts, Small-Scale Industries, and Industrial Education in Tanzania* (Munich: Weltforum Vertag, 1968), p. 157. All information on industrial training is from this source, pp. 130–60.
25. ibid., p. 132.
26. ibid., p. 149.
27. Based on my observations and interviews during visits to factories undertaken in 1975.
28. Minute of F. J. Durman, 4 August 1928, TNA 12566.
29. Director of Agriculture's letter, 3 December 1936, TNA 24693/I.
30. Molohan, M. J. B., *Detribalization* (Dar es Salaam: Government Printer, 1957), p. 11.
31. 'A Preparatory Investigation'', op. cit., p. 12.
32. Molohan, M. J. B., op. cit., pp. 61–2.
33. Annual Report of the Labour Officer, 1948, Lake Province, TNA 215/511/V.
34. Tanganyika, *Report of the Territorial Minimum Wage Board* (Dar es Salaam: Government Printer, 1962), p. 7 (hereafter 'Chesworth Report').
35. For 1958 figure see ARLD, p. 65, and for 1965 figure see *Survey of Employment and Earnings, 1965,* op. cit., p. 13.
36. Guillebaud, C. W., op. cit., p. 88n.
37. Tanganyika, *Report of the Non-Plantation Agricultural Workers Minimum Wages Board* (Dar es Salaam: Government Printer, 1963), p. 6.
38. The Employment Ordinance (Amendment) Act, 1962, No. 82 of 1962. Recruitment was formally abolished by the Employment Ordinance (Amendment) Act, 1969, No. 5.
39. Divisional Circular No. 77/62, 13 December 1972, MLH 808/23.
40. Guillebaud, C. W., op. cit., p. 88.
41. Sabot, R. H., op. cit., p. 67.
42. ibid., p. 66.
43. ibid., p. 71.
44. See Table A.4, below. All figures cited in the section are from this table.
45. Annual Report, 1903/04, in Sherrif Files. Cf. Hirji, K. F., 'Colonial Ideological Apparatuses in Tanganyika under the Germans', in Kaniki, M. H. Y. (ed.), op. cit., pp. 270–11.
46. Hirji, K. F., ibid., p. 211.
47. Mbilinyi, M. J., 'African Education During the British Colonial Period, 1919–61', in Kaniki, M. H. Y. (ed.), op. cit., p. 231. Subsequent information on British education is from this source.
48. Byatt to SS, 22 February 1922, CO 691/54/473–94, and 22 November 1922, CO 691/58/436–40.
49. See generally correspondence in CO 691/76/116–21. Local Civil Service was instituted in 1933, see Sams to SS, 23 March 1933, CO 691/130/5136/51–57.
50. Mbilinyi, M. J., op. cit., pp. 264–5.
51. See ARLD 1948, p. 98, and ARLD, 1950, p. 35.
52. Estimate by LC, 9 October 1948, TNA 32744.
53. Domestic Servants' Association, Mwanza, to DC, 28 May 1947, TNA 41/L/1/2.
54. ibid., and other letters in the same file.
55. LC's minute, 11 March 1943, TNA 30136.
56. ibid.
57. No. 9 of 1927.
58. Attorney-General's Report on the Ordinance, 19 April 1927, CO 691/88/18085/19.
59. ALP to CS, minute, 19 October 1939, TNA 25233/II.
60. Proceedings of the Legislative Council, 13th Session, 4 November 1955, p. 74.
61. No. 47 of 1955.
62. The EO (Commencement) Order, 1957, GN No. 16 of 11 January 1957.
63. See also the Employment (Amendment) Ordinance, 1960, s. 2., No. 10 of 1960.
64. The EO (Exemption) Order, 1957, GN No. 19 of 11 January 1957, revoked and replaced

by the EO (Exemption) Order, 1958, GN No. 311 of 20 June 1958. The EO (Exemption) Order, 1961 (GN No. 26), revoked the latter and replaced it with a comprehensive order covering all exemptions without changing the amount of wages.

65.   The EO (Amendment) Act, 1962, No. 82 of 1962, s. 10.

66.   The EO (Amendment) Act, 1969, No. 5 of 1969.

67.   The EO (Amendment) Act, 1962, No. 82 of 1962, s. 7.

68.   As amended by the EO (Amendment) Ordinance, 1960.

69.   Wedderburn, K. W., *The Worker and the Law* (Harmondsworth: Penguin, 1965), p. 143.

70.   The Employment (Protection of Wages) Regulations, 1957, GN No. 10.

71.   (1917) 1 KB 305.

72.   Quarterly Bulletin of Labour Department, October–December 1955, TNA 215/1969/II.

73.   ARLD, 1954–9.

74.   Quarterly Bulletin of Labour Department, October–December 1955, TNA 215/1969/II.

75.   App. O, Memorandum No. 17, 19 December 1955, TNA 21097/I–III.

76.   ibid.

77.   Memorandum of W. Wemban-Smith to PC's Conference, July 1959, dated 14 July 1959, App. 8, TNA 21097/I–III.

78.   No. 10 of 1960.

79.   Memorandum of W. Wemban-Smith, op. cit., pp. 34, 35.

80.   See, for instance, Songea District Council (Cultivation of Agricultural Land) By-Laws, 1965, GN 263/65, and generally James, R. W. and Fimbo, G. M., *Customary Land Law of Tanzania: A Sourcebook*, (Nairobi: East African Literature Bureau, 1973), pp. 638–40.

81.   Section 14 of No. 82 of 1962.

82.   The EO (Amendment) Act, No. 10 of 1960.

83.   No. 82 of 1962.

84.   Proceedings of the Legislative Council, 13th Session, 4 November 1955, p. 741.

85.   See above, pp. 117–18.

86.   No. 62 of 1964.

87.   (1970) EA 557.

88.   See, for instance, *Mishi Sefu* v. *Massawe* (1978) LRT n. 13, where a mere refusal of the employer to take back an employee after being subject of a criminal charge was considered to be an implied summary dismissal.

89.   Molohan, M. J. B., 'Report on Conditions of Employment of Dock Labour in Dar es Salaam', 3 January 1940, TNA 25912, and Jerrard, R. C., 'Labour Conditions in Tanga', 21 March 1940, TNA 25971.

90.   ARLD, 1951, p. 47.

91.   See Chs. 5 and 6 below.

92.   'Report of Enquiry into Wages and Cost of Living of Low Grade African Government Employees in Dar es Salaam', 1942, minute dated 22 October 1942, TNA 30598.

93.   District Officer to PC, Eastern Province, 10 January 1928, TNA 11625/I.

94.   ARLD, 1950, p. 64.

95.   'Report of Enquiry into . . . African Government Employees', op. cit., p. 7.

96.   p. 15.

97.   Cf. note 93 above.

98.   TNA 20217.

99.   EA Statistical Department (Tanganyika Unit), *The Pattern of Income, Expenditure and Consumption of African Workers in Tanga, February 1958* (Dar es Salaam: Central Statistical Bureau, 1958).

100.   Leslie, J. A. K., *A Survey of Dar es Salaam* (London: Oxford University Press, 1963), p. 143.

101.   ibid., p. 145.

102.   Chesworth Report, op. cit., p. 17.

103.   Leslie, J. A. K., op. cit., p. 145.

104.   No. 19 of 1939.

105.   Proceedings of the Legislative Council, 30th Session, 1938/39, p. 146.

106. ibid., p. 149.
107. ibid., p. 150.
108. ibid., p. 153.
109. TNA 20217.
110. No. 14 of 1947.
111. No. 15 of 1951.
112. Proceedings of the Legislative Council, 24th Session, 1949/50, pp. 192–3.
113. Wedderburn, K. W., op. cit., p. 131.
114. Sections 4 and 5 and section 10 as amended by section 2 of the Regulation of Wages and Terms of Employment (Amendment) Ordinance, 1957, No. 7 of 1957.
115. See generally Patel, L. R., 'EA Labour Regimes', op. cit., p. 57.
116. Wages Regulation (Area of the Dar es Salaam Municipality) Order, 1957, GN No. 80 of 1 March 1957.
117. Chesworth Report, op. cit., p. 11. The Regulation of Wages and Terms of Employment (Calculation of Basic Minimum Wages) Rules, 1957 (GN 69 of 1 March 1957) laid down the method of converting prescribed hourly rates to their weekly and monthly equivalents.
118. p. 11.
119. ibid.
120. p. 21.
121. See Wages Regulation Order, 1962, GN No. 508 of 21 December 1962.
122. GN No. 406 of 21 September 1962.
123. Sabot, R. H., op. cit., Ch. III, pp. 89ff. and Ch. VII.
124. ibid., p. 104.
125. ibid., p. 192.
126. See above, pp. 117ff.
127. Memorandum on housing conditions in Tanga, 27 November 1943, and memorandum on housing conditions in Dar es Salaam, 27 November 1943, CO 691/185/42423/1.
128. Memorandum on housing in Dar es Salaam, ibid., para. 7.
129. pp. 18–19, para. 87.
130. Leslie, J. A. K., op. cit., p. 69.
131. Iliffe, J. Modern History, op. cit., p. 386.
132. Molohan, M. J. B., Detribalization, op. cit., p. 46.
133. Vestbro, D. U., Social Life and Dwelling Space: an analysis of Three House Types in Dar es Salaam (Stockholm: University of Lund, Report No. 2, 1975), pp. 31–3.
134. Chesworth Report, op. cit., App. G.
135. ibid., p. 14.
136. Leslie, J. A. K., op. cit., p. 88.
137. Vestbro, D. U., op. cit., p. 38.
138. Leslie, J. A. K., op. cit., p. 89.
139. Vestbro, D. U., op. cit., pp. 35–6.
140. ARLD, 1964/65, p. 15.
141. Marx, K., Capital, Vol. III, op. cit., p. 86.
142. Marx, K. Capital, Vol., I, op. cit., p. 263.
143. Factories Ordinance, 1950, No. 46.
144. Proceedings of the Legislative Council, 24th Session, 10 June 1950, p. 171.
145. ARLD, 1964/65, p. 82.
146. 1965 figure from ARLD, 1964/65, and 1953 figure from Jack, D. T., Report on Methods of Determining Wages in Tanganyika (Dar es Salaam: Government Printer, 1959), p. 6.
147. Marx, K., Capital, Vol. I, op. cit., pp. 401–2.
148. Workmen's Compensation Ordinance, 1948, No. 43 of 1948, as amended by Workmen's Compensation (Amendment) Ordinances of 1949 (No. 41), 1954 (No. 28) and 1957 (No. 4).
149. CS, minute, 26 October 1939, TNA 25468/I.
150. TNA 25468/I.
151. TNA 41111.

152. Proceedings of the Legislative Council, 24th Session, 10 June 1950, p. 170.
153. ibid., p. 171.
154. Marx, K., *Capital*, Vol. I, op. cit., p. 283.
155. Criminal Appeal No. 108 of 1957, High Court of Tanganyika, reproduced in Quarterly Bulletin of Labour Department, April–June 1957, App. A.
156. Labour Officer to LC, 6 March 1958, MLH 4/29/206.
157. Principal Labour Officer, Tanga to LC, 20 October 1960, MLH 4/19/254.
158. ibid.
159. For instance, factory inspection reports on Vallabhdas Dewji & Son (Woodworking), MLH 4/19/189; Magunga Sisal Estate, MLH 4/19/8/II; Ngomeni Estate, MLH 4/19/26/II.
160. MLH 4/29/83.
161. MLH 4/19/189 and 4/19/434.
162. See, for example, MLH 4/29/73 and MLH 4/29/206.
163. Accident Report, Tanga Timber Sales (Saw Millers), 22 August 1964, MLH 4/19/365.
164. ibid.
165. Acting LC to Labour Officer, 6 November 1962, MLH 4/19/205.
166. Quarterly Bulletin of Labour Department, 30 June 1952, TNA 215/1969/II.
167. Quarterly Bulletin of Labour Department, July–September 1953, TNA 215/1969/II.
168. Accident Report, 17 December 1959, Tangoni Sisal Estate, MLH 4/19/17/II.
169. Accident Report, 28 December 1959, Mtotohovu Estate, 4/19/9/II.
170. Calculated from ARLD.
171. Accidents and Occupational Diseases (Notification) Ordinance, No. 25 of 1953.
172. Calculated from ARLD.
173. Hirji, K. F., 'Accidents at Work: The Case of Motor Vehicle Workshops' (mimeo, Dar es Salaam: National Institute of Transport, 1980), p. 13.
174. Accident Report, 9 May 1961, Tanga Timbers, MLH 4/19/206.
175. Marx, K., *Capital*, Vol. III, op. cit., p. 86.
176. Based on my study of the following sources: Quarterly Bulletin of Labour Department 1956, TNA 215/1969/II; Accident Report, 14 July 1959, Marungu Sisal Estate, MLH 4/19/66; Accident Report, 10 September 1962, Mkumbara Sisal Estate, MLH 4/19/44/III; correspondence between Principal Labour Officer and the LC between 1 September 1962 and 10 October 1962, MLH 4/19/3/II.
177. ARLD, 1964/65, p. 13.
178. ARLD, 1966–9, pp. 48–51.
179. Calculated by me from the study of Accident Reports (Form LDF 104).
180. MLH 4/19/9/II. See note 169, above.
181. MLH 4/19/17/II. See note 168, above.
182. Accident Report, 30 October 1959, Dalgety & Co. Ltd, MLH 4/19/184.
183. (1956) 23 EACA 428, p. 429.
184. Accident Report, 5 November 1959, A. G. Hamid, MLH 4/19/200.
185. Accident Report, 4 July 1960, Hollital Co. Ltd, MLH 4/19/186.
186. Hirji, K. F., 'Accidents', op. cit. p. 5.
187. ALP to CS, minute, 19 October, 1939, TNA 25233/II, p. 3.
188. For the discussion of s. 29 of M / NSO see above, pp. 76ff.
189. Wedderburn, K. W., op. cit., pp. 180ff. on similar English section.
190. Hirji, K. F. 'Accidents', op. cit., p. 22.
191. ARLD 1953–65.

5

Working-Class Struggles and Organization: A Beginning

The argument

The system of semi-proletarianization had created only half-workers. Therefore even the objective condition — permanent divorce from the means of production and life-long commitment to wage-labour — for collective action and resistance did not exist. As we have seen above, the resistance of the semi-proletariat was marked by individual action or at best spontaneous, short-lived and leaderless 'downing of tools'. No wonder that the first, even elementary, forms of collective action and organization did not occur, say, among the plantation workers who formed the large majority of the wage-earning class. Rather it was the small nuclei of more permanent wage-labourers — factory hands, transport workers, domestic servants and so on — who led and participated in strikes and took first organizational initiatives.

Official and semi-official historians[1] date the beginning of working-class struggles and organization in the 1950s with the formation of the Tanganyika Federation of Labour (TFL). But, as Iliffe has rightly pointed out,[2] labour movement began long before the 1950s. As a matter of fact, two decades before the formation of the TFL in 1955, and especially the 1940s, saw a very important and distinct phase in the development of the struggles of the working class and its formation as a *class*.

It was in the fire of these militant struggles, with the dockworkers in the vanguard, that the Tanzanian working class began, to borrow the words of Marx, to 'constitute itself as a class for itself'.[3] However, that process of the formation of the working class was cut short from giving birth to its own, independent political expression by a combination of class forces and the conjuncture of class struggles which we shall discuss in this and the next chapters.

In this chapter we deal with what we have called 'a beginning' in the labour movement. This period, roughly between the 1930s and 1950, was characterized by struggles emanating from the work-place itself and throwing up its own leaders from rank and file. Workers learnt from their own struggles step by step and arrived at solidarity and consciousness as a consequence of their own efforts 'from below'. The trade unions or the trade-union type of organization formed during the period bore the stamp of grass-root democracy and militancy.

The second phase of the labour movement, to be dealt with in the next chapter, was

155

distinct in many respects. The decade 1955–64 was a time of well-organized trade unionism. Very often these unions were organized 'from the top' by educated petty-bourgeois elements frequently unconnected with the work-place.[4] They were marked by bureaucratic administration and governed by legalism that only an educated élite could master. They had their international connections with such bodies as the International Confederation of Free Trade Unions (ICFTU) and the British Trade Union Congress (TUC). In short, in many ways, they were a reflection of the economistic, reformist and politically moderate trade union organizations of the capitalist countries.

In this periodization of the labour movement we have closely followed Iliffe. But our agreement ends there. Iliffe goes further and likens these two phases with the development of the Russian labour movement. Following Lenin, he identifies the first phase with essentially 'a 'spontaneous' evolution of solidarity and organization among workers'[5] and the second one with a kind of merger of the working-class movement with radical nationalism. True, he does see certain differences. As he puts it:

The doctrine which the TFL offered to Tanzanian workers was certainly not a developed socialist theory, nor was it offered to a coherent working class. Nevertheless its impact was essentially the same as that of socialism in Russia. The radical nationalism of the TFL offered to the docker — as socialism offered to the Russian worker — the possibility of *control*.[6]

In this analysis by analogy Iliffe fails to see not only crucial differences between the Russian labour movement as analysed by Lenin and its Tanzanian counterpart, but fails to analyse the process by which the Tanzanian working class was gradually brought under the ideological and organizational hegemony of the bourgeoisie.

Towards the end of the nineteenth century and the beginning of the twentieth century the Russian working-class movement was brought together with the social-democratic (socialist) consciousness. This was effected through the agency of a working-class vanguard party which was an organizational expression of the proletariat independent of the bourgeoisie. This was not the case in Tanzania. In fact, as we shall see, the colonial state and the imperialist bourgeoisie systematically forestalled such a development. The net effect was, first, that the trade union movement was closely watched, supervised and led along strictly economistic lines; secondly, the petty-bourgeois leadership of this movement acted as a bridge between the working-class movement and the nationalism of the Tanganyika African National Union (TANU) which was firmly under the organizational and ideological leadership of the petty-bourgeoisie; and thirdly, at the international level, the trade union leadership was organizationally linked with bourgeois bureaucratic trade unions on the one hand, and ideologically associated with bourgeois socialism of the British Labour Party and the Fabians on the other. Thus the possibility of the development of an independent working-class organization with its own socialist ideology was systematically destroyed.

We shall return to these arguments in the course of our discussion in these chapters. Meanwhile, it is time to analyse how the various class forces acted and manifested in legal and other forms to bring about the *results* that we have just mentioned. (For it is important to repeat, if only for clarification, that these results were not a consequence of some 'conspiracy' or well-thought-out blue-prints of the ruling classes and their state; rather they were an outcome of highly complex social struggles, manifesting themselves in different forms, including legal ones which are our main focus in these chapters.)

The pre-1939 period

Before we consider the trade unions, let us investigate the state of trade union legislation at this time. It must be expected that in the absence of serious trade union
organization, the law did not cater for such activities. But that was not the case.
Tanganyika enacted its Trade Union Ordinance[7] as early as 1932. And this was done at
the behest of the Secretary of State. In a confidential circular of 17 September 1930 to
all colonies, Lord Passfield urged colonial governments to give urgent attention to the
question of enacting some form of trade union legislation. The rationale behind this
anxiety was expressed by the Secretary in the following words:

I regard the formation of such associations in the colonial dependencies as a natural and legitimate consequence of social and industrial progress, but I recognize that there is a danger that,
without sympathetic supervision and guidance organizations of labourers without experience of
combination for any social or economic purposes may fall under the domination of disaffected
persons by whom their activities may be diverted to improper and mischieveous ends. I accordingly feel that it is the duty of colonial governments to take such steps as may be possible to
smooth the passage of such organizations as they emerge into constitutional channels.[8]

This concern to 'guide' workers' organizations along proper channels, in other words
forestall the development of an independent, radical workers' movement, gets
expressed constantly throughout the formative period of trade unionism. In this respect
the British colonial state had no doubt great foresight and had learnt its lessons probably from some south-east Asian countries where workers' parties played a big role in
the formation of trade unions.[9]

It was as a result of Passfield's circular that the Tanganyikan government introduced
a simple eighteen-section Trade Union Bill to the Legislative Council. Introducing the
Bill, the Secretary of Native Affairs emphasized that then there were no trade unions
awaiting registration but this simple Bill was as a measure of prudence to take care of
such organizations should they emerge in future. Most unofficial members representing settler and plantation interests opposed the Bill on the grounds that it was
premature and would in fact encourage the formation of trade unions which were in any
case unnecessary.[10] Captain H. E. Rydon rhetorically asked: 'Would any person in their
senses give a child of six a loaded automatic to play with? I scarcely think so, because it is
a dangerous weapon, and the child might injure himself besides injuring those he would
be inclined to use it [sic].'[11] The reply of the Secretary of Native Affairs to these
objections left no doubt as to the real aim of the colonial state behind introducing this
piece of legislation. He assured the members that the aim was not to encourage or
facilitate the formation of trade unions; rather it was to regulate and supervise them if
and when they would be formed: 'it is not designed to facilitate the formation of trade
unions; and practically everything which this Bill is designed to regulate can be done
now without any regulation or control whatever. That is the point: that without this
Bill, all these horrible consequences that some Honourable Members have pointed out
as being likely to ensue, all these horrible things can be done without any measure of
control or regulation at all . . . '[12] 'Control and regulation' — these then were the
watch-words. Let us see how they were translated into law in the Trade Union
Ordinance.*

---

* The Bill passed with 6 unofficial members voting against, and 4 unofficial, including 2 Asian members and
14 official members, voting for.

The Ordinance closely followed the UK Trade Union Acts of 1871 and 1876. It adopted the definition of trade union from those Acts and in section 3 also adopted the provisions concerning civil and criminal liabilities of trade unions. It will be recalled that the 1871 and 1876 Acts of Britain were the outcome of a long and bloody struggle waged for almost half a century by the British working classes against the judge-made doctrines of 'restraint of trade' and 'criminal conspiracy' which always threatened to declare any combination of workers unlawful.[13] This historic gain of the international working class became part of the trade union legislation in many countries including Tanganyika.

In one major respect, however, the Trade Union Ordinance differed from the Trade Union Acts of Great Britain. This was in respect of compulsory registration. Under the British Act of 1871 (s. 6) registration of a trade union was completely voluntary and, except for a few trivial privileges, did not add substantially to the status of a trade union.[14] (In essence an unregistered trade union continued to be the same as any unincorporated body.) But section 5 of the Tanganyikan Ordinance made non-registration a criminal offence. An unregistered trade union could not avail itself of the provisions of section 3; therefore it could be subject to all common law illegalities including 'conspiracy' and 'restraint of trade' doctrines (see s. 3(3)). Furthermore, every member of an unregistered trade union who participated in its proceedings would be guilty of an offence (s. 10).

The law further imposed fairly stringent regulations to be complied with before registration. The rules of a trade union had to make provision for certain specified matters (s. 6(b)). Under section 7, which did not have an equivalent in the British Acts, the registrar, if he thought fit, could require the applicants to supply 'such further evidence or information concerning the trade union and the purposes for which it has been established and as to any other matter relating thereto, as may seem to him necessary'. Officers of the trade union were also obliged, on pain of committing a criminal offence, to transmit to the registrar its statement of annual accounts ' prepared and made out up to such date, in such form, and shall comprise such particulars, as the registrar may from time to time require' (s. 13).

Finally, the registrar was given powers 'if in any case it is in his opinion expedient to do so' to refuse or defer registration of a trade union pending the final order of the governor (s. 8). The registrar also had powers to cancel registration of a trade union if he was satisfied, *inter alia*, that a trade union had violated any of the provisions of the Ordinance (s. 17). The Trade Union (Amendment) Ordinance, 1939,[15] made the decisions of the registrar under sections 8 and 17 appealable to the High Court instead of the governor.

It was the weapon of compulsory registration that the colonial state proposed to employ in keeping trade unions under control, monitoring and regulating their activities. As in many other African countries,[16] as we shall see, in Tanganyika too this weapon was often used by the government to destroy the trade unions and trade union leaders who were not to their liking or failed to follow proper 'constitutional channels'.

So much then for the freedom of association as provided in law. We now turn to the discussion of the development of trade unions and how they fared.

The first attempt to form a trade union as far as can be seen in the extant records was in 1927. During that year African motor drivers and mechanics in Moshi formed a Motor Drivers' Union and even attempted a strike for higher wages. It appears the strikers were quickly dealt with. Not much more is known about the union. From the tone of the official report it may be inferred, however, that the union was looked upon with disfavour. As the report put it: 'little sympathy can be shown with this movement' and 'there are reasons for believing that the whole episode was not the product of African brains alone'.[17]

The next attempt to form a union on the part of African workers was made almost a decade later. Meanwhile sporadic strikes of course did occur as were reported from time to time in the annual reports of the Labour Department.[18]

The African civil servants had meanwhile formed themselves into a staff association on the lines similar to Asian and European civil servants' associations. The Tanganyika Territory African Civil Service Association was founded by the famous Martin Kayamba in 1922.[19] Its aims and activities were in keeping with the ideals of its founder and its white-collar class base. Kayamba believed in an élitist organization devoted to the educational and social advancement of its membership as distinct from indulgence in politics and trade union activities like 'strikes'. In the late 1930s the association was weakened as its members became more active in the African Association. When the African civil servants next entered the trade union stage it was in the 1940s, and then they were organized as a much more militant trade union.[20] Yet the Tanganyika African Government Servants' Association, which was the new name of the former association, put itself forward as a staff association rather than a trade union and was accepted as such by the government.

The more serious trade union initiative during the 1930s was taken by the Asian shop assistants and artisans. The first trade union to be registered under the Ordinance was the Union of Shop Assistants which was formed and registered around the middle of 1933.[21] This union consisted almost exclusively of Asian members and its whole committee was constituted by Asians. In fact by common usage the term 'shop assistants' applied to Asian clerks, bookkeepers, accountants and typists while African shopworkers were mainly engaged as sweepers, tea-makers, *askaris*, messengers and so on.

During the six or so years of its existence, the union's main activity centred around the question of the working day. This struggle has been dealt with extensively by Martha Honey and so we need only summarize the main characteristics here.

Shop assistants constituted numerically a small portion of the Asian adult work force, probably around 10 per cent according to the 1931 census. They worked inordinately long hours — from 7.00 a.m. to 10.00 p.m. — in the shops of mainly Asian wholesalers and big retailers and were paid meagre salaries.

In the 1930s the main struggle was to urge the government to pass legislation regulating hours of opening shops or service hours of the employees, or both. The European commercial bourgeoisie who practised more regular opening hours and the Asian middle-level retailers who did not employ any shop assistants supported any legislation which would regulate shop hours. But the Indian merchant bourgeoisie and upper strata of the petty-bourgeoisie opposed it, and they were successful in preventing its enactment for a fairly long period.

Instead, in 1932, a Shop Assistants Employment Ordinance[22] was enacted. The term 'shop assistant' was defined to mean 'any person employed for hire in a shop as a clerk or salesman' (s. 2). The Ordinance set the maximum hours of work of shop assistants at fifty-four per week (s. 3) and anyone contravening the Ordinance was liable to a fine not exceeding Shs. 40 (s. 9). Besides the fact that the working hours were still very long, it was extremely difficult to enforce the Ordinance. The union therefore continued pressing for more stringent measures through petitions and letter-writing. By the end of the 1930s, when the union appears to have ceased its activities, a new Bill regulating shop as well as service hours was drafted but never presented to the Legislative Council.*

During its short existence the union cannot be said to have been very successful. It was numerically weak and its confinement to white-collar workers of Asian nationality meant that its base was racial and narrow with little economic or political clout. Its method of work — petition and letter-writing — reflected its class base which was essentially the lower sections of the petty-bourgeoisie. Although shop assistants were permanent wage-earners they were too scattered and individualized in their work-processes to mount an effective collective action in the form of, for example, strikes. All in all, therefore, this union did not make much impact on the general development of trade unionism.

Unlike the Union of Shop Assistants was the Asiatic Labour Union, formed in February 1937 in the wake of the depression which had resulted in enormous rises in the cost of living. The union's declared aim was to safeguard the interests of 'Asiatic skilled and unskilled workmen'.[24]

Actually skilled workers — or the proletariat as such — constituted a very small portion of the Asian adult work force, probably much less than even 5 per cent.† These were mainly such workers as carpenters, masons and blacksmiths employed in private construction and building firms, in the Public Works Department and in the railways. Although their salaries were generally low, they were much higher than those of Africans of equivalent skills. Thus within the general working class the skilled Asian craftsmen were set apart not only by their minority nationality but also because of their relative privileges based solely on their race.

The result was that such privileges effectively set apart the Asian proletariat, numerically minuscule as it was, from their African brethren. And generally dominated by the bourgeois ideology of racial superiority fostered by the colonial state and buttressed by material privileges, the Asian proletariat was determined to defend its position. It called its trade union 'Asiatic', its membership was confined to Asian workmen and its committee was totally Asian. Indeed, in its letter to the government announcing the formation of the union, its president and secretary assured the government in the following words: 'The name given to this organization is 'The Asiatic Labour Union' and every care will be taken not to keep the African communities into touch with this movement.'[25]

The main demands of the union revolved around increase of wages and shortening of the working day to eight hours. It had already declared that if its demands were not met it would go on strike. The reaction of the employers was swift. The president of the union was without employment and the services of the vice-president and the treasurer — both employed by one of the large Asian construction firms of Keshawji Ramji — were terminated because of their connection with the union. Within hardly a month of its formation the union called a strike — probably the first organized strike called out by a trade union.[26]

The strike lasted some ten to twelve days. It even received material and moral support from the Labour Trade Union of Kenya. At the end of the strike, it had

---

* The new law, the Shop Hours Ordinance,[23] was not passed until 1945, by which time the Asian commercial bourgeoisie had dropped their opposition — not because of labour protests but because of market conditions, as a result of which most shops opened only about 49 hours per week.

† Honey's estimate of 5 per cent includes self-employed and part-employed.

achieved both its demands: that of increase in wages as well as an eight-hour working day.[27] In spite of its success, the union did not last long. It was not even registered under the Ordinance and appears to have turned into some kind of a welfare society. Its base was too slender and its ideology too divisive to enable it to survive the ideological onslaught of the bourgeoisie. Most probably therefore its membership was reabsorbed into the racial and communal fold of the bourgeois and petty-bourgeois dominated racial organizations and 'associations' of the Asian nationality.

The only other trade union which was ever registered under the Ordinance during this period was the Labour Trade Union of East Africa. This union began in Kenya in the middle of 1930s, originally as Kenya Indian Labour Trade Union. It was started by Asian artisans, who were much more numerous in Kenya than in Tanzania. Within two months of its formation, the union changed its name and became non-racial on the advice of Makan Singh, who became its general secretary. The constitution of the Labour Trade Union of Kenya, as it was now called, announced that its aim was to organize all labourers in Kenya on a 'class basis'.[28] One of the duties of a member as stipulated in the constitution was:

To attain a class consciousness and for the betterment of the labour class to promote such class consciousness in others and never to miss an opportunity of gaining their trust. (Class consciousness is that stage when a worker begins to feel the difference between a capitalist and himself; when he comes to know that in fact he is being robbed by capitalists and when he begins to make propaganda against such robbery.)[29]

The ideological consciousness of the leadership was probably far ahead of the membership of the union. The membership to a large extent remained Asian although towards the end of the 1930s Makan Singh was somewhat successful in making contacts with African organizations and even managed to have two African trade unionists on the executive committee of the union.[30]

In 1937, the Labour Trade Union of Kenya changed its name to the Labour Trade Union of East Africa 'to meet the demands for membership from Uganda and Tanganyika workers'.[31] In 1939 it was registered in Tanganyika under the Trade Union Ordinance.[32] However, beyond writing letters, making a few protests* and passing resolutions[34] it does not appear to have been very active in Tanganyika. In Kenya, on the other hand, it led a very active and militant existence organizing huge processions and one of the longest strikes which lasted sixty-two days.[35] In spite of intense opposition from the colonial state[36] and racial divisions which no doubt beset the union and its militant general secretary,[37] the Labour Trade Union of East Africa probably had a much greater impact on the Kenyan working class in popularizing trade unionism and especially the strike technique than the 'Asiatic Trade Union' of Tanganyika. The Labour Trade Union of East Africa almost ceased its activities during the war and was finally removed from the register in 1947.[38]

Martha Honey has summarized the impact of the trade unionism of Asian workers as follows:

the Asian Labour movement in Tanganyika appears as a mere footnote within the broader proletarian struggle. The 1930s represent the most active period for Asian workers in the Territory. Intra-Asian class antagonisms which surfaced during this decade — between the semi-proletariat [sic!] and the commercial classes and . . . between the commercial petty bourgeoisie

---

* For example, it asked to be represented on the Committee of Enquiry into the dispute in the Tanga port in 1939 but was not considered a 'suitable labour organization' which could have nominated representatives.[33]

and the bourgeoisie — were short-lived. Large Asian capital was in the process of successfully consolidating its economic and ideological hold over the other Asian classes. In the 1950s the few Asian wage labourer organizations were essentially welfare societies and most were officially registered as 'associations' rather than unions.[39]

Iliffe, however, believes that the Asiatic Labour Union may have had some influence on the formation of the African Labour Union, formed in the same year (1937) as the former.[40] Be that as it may; it was the African Labour Union formed among the dockworkers which was really the curtain-raiser of the 'broader proletarian struggle', of the intense strikes and collective organization of the working class that characterized the decade of the 1940s. In many ways, the African Labour Union was the first, elementary attempt on the part of the rank and file workers to form their own organization. It therefore deserves some discussion.

The African Labour Union was formed on 7 August 1937 with some forty members, all of them employed by wharfage companies.[41] It consisted of the president, vice-president, secretary and treasurer among whom only the secretary and treasurer could read and write Kiswahili while the president and his vice-president knew only the Arabic script. The name 'Labour Union' was picked up by its office-bearers from their experience in South Africa where they had seen similar organizations. Otherwise the office-bearers confirmed that they had no intention to try and influence 'the employment and control of labour'. This was further borne out by their rules which emphasized mainly social welfare functions of mutual help during sickness, burial and unemployment.[42] The rules provided that every member had a duty to obey his employer; to attend his work in time and not to leave it before time without the permission of his employer. Every member was obliged to learn to read and write; to pay his debts before demand; to pay his government taxes and to keep some deposits in the savings account. The rules further provided for conduct at meetings: to speak in turn; not to repeat what has been already said and to observe general discipline.

The monthly subscription for every office-bearer and committee member was Shs. 1.50 per month and for ordinary members Sh. 1. At the time of its formation it had collected a total of Shs. 45 which had been deposited in the Standard Bank of South Africa.

The union resembled a friendly society, a kind of first hesitant step in the direction of collective organization on the part of workers. It is significant that it was formed by dockworkers because it was they who were to lead the subsequent struggles which forms the subject matter of our next section.

1939–50: a beginning

The decade of the 1940s for the first time saw the formation of African trade unions which were moreover registered under the Trade Union Ordinance. Almost all of these trade unions were formed by permanent workers in transport, domestic servants and tailors. According to the 1947 Labour Report there were four registered trade unions: the Stevedores and Dockers' Union, the African Cooks, Washermen and House Boys' Association, the African Tailors' Association and the Dar es Salaam African Motor Drivers' Union.[43]

The story of the dockers' union, which was formed at the climax of a long-drawn-out intense struggle, will be dealt with later. The Unions of domestic servants, drivers and tailors all had rather chequered histories illustrating both their own objective shortcomings as well as the state's attitude towards trade unions in general and militant unions in particular.

As we have already seen, the first attempt, which was unceremoniously put down, by African drivers to form a union was as far back as 1927.[44] Again, around 1944, drivers working for the railways in Southern Highlands, having picked up the idea while serving in the army, formed a fairly well organized association. Their main demand was for higher pay and a 'closed union shop'. Their territorial organization, the Amalgamated African Motor Drivers' and Commercial Road Transport Workers' Union was registered in August 1948, with a membership of 340.[45] Two years later its certificate of registration was cancelled by the registrar because apparently its membership had dwindled to nothing owing to (according to the Labour Report) lack of experience of its officers.[46]

The tailors in different urban areas, including especially Mwanza, Tanga and Tabora,[47] made concerted efforts to form unions and put forward their grievances. The fate of the Lake Province Tailors' Association is illustrative of the tailors' unions.

The Lake Province Tailors' Association applied to be registered in 1948 and was finally registered on 11 February 1949 with a paid up membership of under fifty.[48] By the later part of 1950 it had branches at Musoma and Ukerewe and two small settlements in the Geita District. According to the Labour officer of the Lake Province, 'one noticeable feature of this Union was that all the officials were working members of the trade and no full time outside persons were employed in any way.'[49]

In Mwanza, the association prepared a draft of service conditions but no effort was made to approach the employers. 'Some of the conditions were such that it was very doubtful if any employer would agree to them. For example the Union expected three months' notice on either side to be given and moreover the equivalent of a 'closed shop'.[50] That a Labour Officer should think these demands to be exaggerated goes some way to show the disfavour with which the unions were held by the government officers.

The association did not last long. In February of 1951, it was warned because of its 'unsatisfactory' administration and five months later its certificate was cancelled. Its treasurer was prosecuted and sentenced to six months' imprisonment with hard labour and fined Shs. 371 apparently for failing to produce the funds. The president of the association's branch at Katunguru in Geita District was sentenced to five months' imprisonment with hard labour and a fine of Shs. 300 for offences of 'intimidation'* (ss. 23 and 24) under the Trade Union Ordinance.[51] The Labour Officer's comment on this is revealing: 'In the words of the Geita magistrate 'a reign of terror existed in Katunguru' at the time. The dictatorial methods adopted by this branch demonstrated clearly how little Trade Union principles were understood. In fact the general idea was that a trade union was a legal organisation supported by the Government for the simple purpose of stirring up trouble.'[52]

There can be little doubt that the state was bent on using its powers under the Trade Union Ordinance and the weapon of criminal sanctions against any trade union or trade

---

* Immunity of trade unions from actions in tort for tortious acts done in furtherance of trade disputes was introduced by the Trade Unions (Amendment) Ordinance, 1941. While allowing peaceful picketing the Ordinance made it an offence to intimidate or to do any act calculated to intimidate, even if this was in furtherance of a trade dispute. The Ordinance introduced a very wide definition of 'intimidation' which did not require 'personal violence' or 'threat of personal violence'. A 'reasonable apprehension of injury' was enough to constitute intimidation (see *R.* v. *Valambia*, (1963) EA 12.) Thus picketing in *such numbers* or in such a manner "calculated to intimidate" was an offence (s. 24(2)).

union leaders who would not toe their line. By the end of 1951 hardly a single tailors' trade union had survived.

The fate of the African Cooks, Washermen and House Boys' Association was not very different. Originally probably formed in 1939 in Dodoma as Chama cha Wapishi na Maboi, it spread to other urban centres.[53] By 1944 the association had drafted considerably clear rules and sought government's help.

One of its outstanding leaders was Saleh bin Fundi, whom Iliffe calls 'Tanganyika's first African labour leader'.[54] He organized openly, called public meetings and addressed them and seems to have had a clear view of trade union tactics. In one public meeting he asked his audience what they would do if the whole committee was locked up by the government for allegedly teaching them 'wrongful ways'.

'If that happens we shall refuse to work,' said his listeners.

'No,' said Saleh, 'if you do not know I will tell you.

'In such a case, all of you, boys employed by Europeans as well as those employed by Indians, should go to the Chief Secretary and ask to be locked up.'[55]

Such militancy was completely out of step with what the state considered as proper trade unionism. One labour officer commenting on the formation of the association's branch in Tanga opined: 'S. Fundi is not a desirable character to have at the head of such an association.'[56]

Domestic servants' demands revolved mainly around the question of higher minimum wages, short and more systematic hours of work and a kind of 'closed union shop'. These demands were, for example, clearly spelt out in a letter from the Domestic Servants' Association of Mwanza to the District Commissioner. It requested the government to look into their low wages because 'the domestic servants are left to die of starvation due to inadequate payments'.[57]

In these demands and especially that of a 'closed shop' the Association ran up against the Women's Service League. The league appears to have been an organization of white officers' wives controlling the employment of domestic servants. Both the league and government officers looked with great disfavour on the activities of the association. 'This association' one official report noted with great venom, 'has few ideas beyond more pay and less work and it is hoped it will die a natural death, as it is anything but satisfactory. It is very keen to take over the functions of a Domestic Registry from the Women's Service League and this would lead to an even further supply of false chits, it is hoped that the Women's Service League will manage to continue the good work that they are doing.'[58]

In June 1949, after hardly four years of existence, the African Cooks', Washermen and House Boys' Association was struck off the register 'for continual failure to comply with the directions of the Registrar of Trade Unions'.[59] The official who had hoped for its 'natural death' a year earlier gleefully noted: 'The African Cooks, Washermen and House Boys' Association ceased to function on the cancellation of its registration as a Trade Union and since then servants are offering themselves for employment at rates more commensurate with their employers' pockets.'[60]

The case studies of these three unions illustrate a number of significant points. First, all of them were formed by permanent, relatively skilled or quasi-skilled workers whose occupations brought them into contact with the urban milieu. Secondly, they had their own leadership with a varying degree of sophistication yet unable to meet the legalistic and bureaucratic demands of the state which would give them legitimacy in the eyes of the law. Thirdly, their membership, besides being small, was highly *individualized*, too scattered or mobile by the very nature of its occupation to mount an effective collective action beyond letter-writing and public meetings. (Thus none of these unions ever made use of the weapon of strike.) This last enabled the state to suppress them without much ado. In short, their collective organization was not matched and backed by effective and sustained collective action.

During this same period, however, there were collective actions — trade disputes and strikes — among other more concentrated groups of workers. For example, in 1948 there were thirteen strikes involving some 1,700 workers. Most of these strikes were of short duration lasting under four days. In almost all, the workers returned without their demands being met; in some cases their services were terminated and in others their leaders were arrested and convicted.[61] Even in the case of Geital Gold Mining Co. Ltd, where some 500 workers struck for ten days, the concessions from the employers were minor. In fact, all the workers who belonged to one particular 'tribe' and who were considered to be agitators were discharged.[62] So in these cases — transport, industrial establishments, plantations, mines and so on — while there was a concentration of workers and therefore an objective possibility of the use of the strike weapon, there had not yet developed effective collective organization (trade unions) to lead and sustain such collective actions successfully.

Both these conditions — concentration and the development of collective organization — were met among the dockworkers. It is the dockworkers who mounted a sustained struggle in the heat of which was born the most militant trade union organization of the decade. Between 1939 and 1950 the dockworkers organized four major strikes, each one of which was at a higher level of solidarity and consciousness reflecting a dialectical relationship between collective action and collective organization. The dockworkers learnt and formed themselves as a class in the process of this struggle: in this they gave a lead and marched in the van of the rest of the working class. It was also in the process of this struggle that the state refined its legal instrument and other means of class struggle. All this then can be best analysed and understood by reviewing the four major strikes, their implication and consequences at each stage and what each one of them meant both for the working class as well as the ruling class.

1939–50: the dockworkers in the van

Conditions

Conditions of urban wage-labour and other working people in urban areas just before the war had reached their nadir. The low wages of the depression period continued to reign in spite of the fact that capital had made considerable recovery and was reaping substantial profits. For the first time official reports began to talk about unemployment, particularly in Dar es Salaam and Tanga. This was one more sign of the fact that a small *permanent* wage-labour force wholly dependent on wages had come into being and was there to stay.[63]

One report on labour conditions in Dar es Salaam just around October 1938 estimated that some 1,500 people were unemployed. Wages had slumped below subsistence level. 'Certain cases have come to notice where the rate of pay is Shs. 10 per kipande (without food) of 30 days' work for a 10 hour day. In Dar es Salaam Shs. 10 per calendar month (i.e. 26 working days average) is the barest minimum on which a man can support subsistence for himself alone. It is obvious that wages have now reached a sub marginal limit.'[64]

Similar observations were made as regards conditions in Tanga. There was a great influx of people from surrounding villages seeking employment. The main employment was at the docks which employed about 300 people while others were employed by the Public Works Department, the railways and as domestic servants. Wages, the investigator Mr R. C. Jerrard reported in 1940, were below living wage. Even PWD paid only Shs. 15–18 per month which was less than 75 cents per day, the minimum necessary according to R. C. Jerrard. Many failed to find wage-employment; nor could they return to the land, of which there was a shortage around Tanga.[65]

Besides low wages, shortage of housing, high rents and shortage of consumer goods were also prevalent. In Tanga rents for a single room varied from Shs. 3 to Shs. 6 while land rent for crown land per plot was Shs. 6 per year. But there was not much crown land since 'about 40 per cent of that was occupied by non-natives'.[66]

Grievances therefore were widespread and affected virtually the whole of the urban working population. But it was the concentrated group of the proletariat — the dockworkers — being employed in the nerve centre of the colonial economy who were best placed to react. And they reacted.

The 1939 strikes: the first stage

In the two months of July and August 1939, two major strikes took place in Dar es Salaam and Tanga ports respectively. On 17 July, casual workers at the Dar es Salaam port stopped work. Apparently the permanent workers did not join in. After being addressed by the District Commissioner the strikers formulated their demands two days later. These included a rise in daily wage from Shs. 1.50 to Shs. 2 per day, which was the rate before the depression; Shs. 3.50 for night work; compensation for sickness and accidents as in the case of permanent workers; and finally, better treatment on the job. The petition of the workers to the commissioner stated that if the above demands were accepted by the companies 'we shall be ready to do their work, provided that they will agree with what we have written above and sign the agreement before you, sir.[67]

The employers were in no mood to give in. The strikers were all casual employees and they could be easily replaced, which the companies actually threatened to do if the strike continued. Eventually, the Provincial Commissioner advised the workers' representative to resume work. Pickets were removed and gradually the strikers returned without having made any material gains. In fact, some of them were even victimized by the employers and yet the workers were not united or organized enough to do anything about it.

According to Iliffe, the strike did not have a known leadership. It appears to have been spontaneous and loosely organized. Its greatest weakness was that it involved only casual workers. At best therefore it was only a first stage, an elementary attempt at collective action.

The Tanga strike was much more protracted and engulfed other workers as well as the dockworkers. On 6 August the workers loading the *Llanstephan Castle* refused to work but were persuaded to do so by the offer of an extra 60 cents per man. The next day, workers refused to load other ships and on 8 August the strike began, following a breakdown of negotiations with the employers. The main demand of the workers was an increase in daily wage from Shs. 1.50 to Shs. 2 and the night wage from Shs. 2 to Shs. 3.[68] Initially this was the demand of the workers employed by the Tanganyika Lighterage and Stevedoring Co. only. Later, workers of other companies put forward their own differing wage demands. Eventually, on 9 August, the strikers were able to put much more coherent and definite demands in a letter addressed to the District Officer, Tanga.[69] That letter was written on behalf of the African workers — watchmen, boatmen, drivers, skilled labourers and casual workers — of the East African Lighterage and Stevedoring Co., the Tanganyika Landing and Shipping Co., the Tanganyika Boating Co., Thomas Co. and Unga Mill. Besides demanding rates of wages similar to 'those of our countrymen engaged elsewhere' and 'such as are obtainable in Mombasa and Dar es Salaam', the letter also asked for sick pay, compensation for injury at work and leave. The letter ended by saying: 'We earnestly put forward these requests and if they are met we are ready to work, but if not we do not desire to do any work for the companies whether we be skilled labourers or drivers or follow any other of the professions stated above. That concludes this letter and we pray we may be answered by our king, King George VI.'

On the day of the strike, the labour officer intervened and persuaded some thirty representatives of the strikers to resume work. He could not, however, assure them that their demands would be accepted 'for he as the representative of the Government was in the position of a referee in a football match between them and their employers. He would do his best to bring about an agreement acceptable to both parties, but he was not in a position to dictate to either what they should offer or accept.'[70] Although the representatives agreed to resume work on this basis their fellow workers shouted them down as soon as they had stepped out of the labour officer's office. They said they would not only refuse to work the next morning but would also prevent other persons going to work in the docks or elsewhere in the town.

Both on 8 and 9 August everything was quiet. There was no evidence of violent picketing whatsoever. Yet the state had begun to flex its muscles by a show of arms. On the morning of the 9th, mobile police patrols were out parading in the streets.

Worse than this veiled intimidation and obvious provocation was the decision to supply blackleg labour that was undoubtedly responsible for sparking off workers' subsequent anger. In the evening, the Manager of Landing and Shipping Co., accompanied by the labour officer, visited the Provincial Commissioner and made a request for a minimum of 130 men to unload SS *Jagersfontein* which was then in the harbour. The commissioner declined to supply forced labour which would be against the law. But he was not wanting in his advice and suggestion which would be within the *letter* if not the spirit of the law. Let the story be told in the Provincial Commissioner's own words:

After discussion it was suggested to him [i.e. the manager] that there were some 100 men in the Maweni Labour Camp, 7 miles from Tanga, who were performing tax labour, and that, if he was willing to see them in the morning and offer them the work and if they accepted, he was at liberty to advance to them the money which each owed for the completion of his obligation in respect of arrears of tax. If then this money was tendered to the Tax Officer he would have no alternative but to accept the money, issue them with a tax receipt and allow them to go. It was no concern of Government where the men got the money or under what conditions. If it was tendered, it must be accepted and the men allowed to go. This was provided for under Section 11(4)* of the Native Tax Ordinance, 1934 . . .[71]

The manager promptly acted on the suggestion. Next day some 100 Maweni prisoners began working at the harbour under police guard. Arrangements were made for them to sleep on board or alongside the ship in lighters.

The insult thus added to the injury was unbearable. Apparently the striking workers

---

* That section provided: 'Any person required to pay his tax by labour may at any time tender the equivalent in cash of the period of labour which remains to be performed by him together with the value of any rations which he has received, and thereupon he shall be granted a tax receipt and shall be discharged from such labour.'

had taken the role of the state as a referee seriously. But here, in front of their own eyes, that ostensible role had been thrown overboard and, as one witness to the official Commission of Enquiry put it: 'the Government had promised to act as a referee and now by this action it had violated its word'.[72]

In the afternoon a group of workers rushed to the docks with the apparent aim of preventing the blackleg labour from working. But in this they were frustrated because the blacklegs were on the ship and those who were working on the shore were quickly put afloat in a lighter. The workers instead rushed through the town armed with sticks. The police continued to be reinforced and some arrests were made. Eventually the military (the King's African Rifles) and special constables were called in. Reinforcements were summoned from Dar es Salaam and Moshi as well.[73] By 10 August the strike had spread to railway and Public Works Department workers. Meanwhile the police continued making numerous arrests. Armed soldiers and special constables were guarding entrances to the commercial areas and the residential areas of non-Africans as well as petrol stations and other strategic places. Picketing continued throughout the day but according to the Provincial Commissioner himself there were no acts of aggression or violence 'apart from the running about and the pushing given to individual natives standing by. These pushes were accompanied by warnings that there should be no work in the morning.'[74]

The police nevertheless kept up their offensive. On this same day they made thirty-two arrests. On the next day, 10 August, picketing had ceased and everything was quiet. But: 'It was decided to take initiative against the mob which was expected to begin to gather soon after day break.'[75] The police marched into the African quarters and were surrounded by some 1,500 people. On refusal by the crowd to disperse, they opened fire injuring tens of people and killing one.[76]

The workers were neither united nor organized enough to withstand this extent of state force. The situation began to quieten down and the next day there was an almost 50 per cent turn-out at work-places. Meanwhile, marches by the police and KAR through the streets continued, and more arrests were made. Even a military plane was flown over surrounding areas as a show of strength to dissuade other workers, especially those in the sisal estates, from joining. The strike does not appear to have spread much to the sisal estates although there were one or two incidents. For example, some 200 men had walked out at the Amboni estates demanding higher wages. When they were asked how much they expected they replied that they did not know but must first ask the people in Tanga. This shows that there was some communication between the workers at Amboni and those in Tanga.

Unfortunately we do not have any independent evidence to be able to analyse the extent of organization, solidarity and consciousness among the dock workers and between the dockworkers and other town workers. We therefore have to read between the lines of official reports. One thing, however, is clear: that the strike was the result of 'smouldering discontent and unadjusted grievance', to use the words of the official commission.[77] In addition, the Mombasa strike which had taken place earlier no doubt was influential and played a role by force of example, but the cause lay in the very conditions of work.

There does not appear to have been a coherent, recognized leadership although a certain amount of co-ordination and underground communication cannot be discounted. Yet there is no evidence of a premeditated organization for a general strike. What brought out other town workers on the streets was more the armed provocation of the state rather than a conscious show of solidarity with dockworkers. In fact, at no point did these other workers put forward any concerted demands. The workers lacked that general unity, organization and direction which would have enabled them to withstand the armed repression of the state. And the state in turn was determined to forestall such a development by instilling fear, which it did successfully by use of intimidation and force.

The whole episode had probably one objective lesson to teach. It exploded the illusion of the neutrality of the state. Close alliance between the state and the employer was there for everyone to see. But seeing, on the one hand, and perceiving and conceptualizing, on the other, are different things. While such experiences no doubt become part of the general consciousness of the working class, it is doubtful if they were also converted into theoretical knowledge to act as a guide to future action in the absence of a working-class organization. No such organization nor even a trade union was born as a result of the 1939 experience. That had to await the more united action of 1947.

Even at the level of economic struggle the 1939 Tanga strike achieved very little. The government appointed a Commission of Enquiry which made very general recommendations such as that investigation should be made into the question of land tenure and high ground rent; that there should be uniformity of scale of wages at Mombasa, Dar es Salaam and Tanga ports; that the wages of Tanga Township Authority workers should be increased by 10 cents per day, and finally, that the government should repatriate Africans from other areas residing in Tanga to alleviate the unemployment problem.[78] These recommendations were neither here nor there, and in any case, with the breaking out of the war most of them were shelved.[79]

Nevertheless the struggle of the dockworkers, especially those at Dar es Salaam, continued unabated. The main reason for this was that deterioration in their conditions had also continued unabated as the wartime inflation gathered momentum. As the radical paper of the time, *Kwetu*, put it: 'Our chief lamentation today is pay, every corner, official and unofficial, skilled and unskilled office and field, house and kitchen, grumble for better pay.'[80] It was against this background that the 1943 strike took place.

The 1943 strike: 'unity is strength'

General discontent and particular grievances among wharf labour had been of long standing. As early as June 1943 the workers of the Tanganyika Boating Co. had complained to the Chief Secretary.[81] Their main complaint was that they did not get rations or a war bonus like the government employees.[82] On 31 July 1943 they had refused to accept wages on the ground that poll tax was being illegally deducted from their pay. They stopped work for three days after which they were refunded tax deductions.

The District Commissioner advised the four companies to standardize their rates, which was done. But when these were announced on 13 August, the workers refused to accept them.[83] And two days later they presented their own demands on which the companies refused to negotiate. On 22 August, the workers met and decided to strike the next day. The strike involved some 800 men: all the casuals from the registered 'pool', some 300 outside casuals and 170 of the 250 permanent workers.[84] Thus the strike was almost complete except the headmen who nevertheless acted, in some cases, as the strikers' spokesmen.

The demands of the permanent workers were: (a) increase in wages of some 15–20 per cent; (b) grant of cost of living allowance; (c) removal of inequities in the system of wage deductions for unauthorized absence; (d) medical treatment and sick pay; (e) annual leave, and (f) gratuity on retirement.[85] The casual workers demanded increase in wages;

medical treatment and sick pay and free food during working hours. The workers who appeared before the tribunal later also mentioned ill-treatment, badly cooked and dirtily served food and assaults by some European overseers as additional causes of discontent.[86]

Although at least one employer thought that the strike ought to be broken as was done in 1939, there was no serious attempt to employ blackleg labour. The skilled and semi-skilled labour could in any case not be easily replaced.[87] However, the government did supply military recruits under police protection to do essential work.[88] Meanwhile the companies continued pressing the government to use defence regulations to break the strike.

Failing to persuade the workers to return to work in spite of threats, the governor finally promulgated the Defence (Trade Disputes) Regulations, 1943,[89] on 27 August. The regulations empowered the governor to make an order establishing a tribunal, to effect settlement of a trade dispute referred to it (reg. 3(a)). It also empowered the governor to make an order 'prohibiting . . . a strike or lockout in connection with any trade dispute' (reg. 3(b)). Anyone contravening the orders made under the regulations was guilty of an offence (reg. 5).

On the same day the governor made the Defence (Lighterage Dispute) Order, 1943,[90] to take care of the existing dispute between the four companies and its workers. A tribunal composed of five people under the chairmanship of Judge Wilson was appointed and it was charged with inquiring into and determining,

(a) The reasons why the said labourers have left their said employment, and why other labourers who have hitherto been employed from time to time by the said companies as casual labourers are unwilling to present themselves for work although they have been notified that such work is available.[91]

(b) subject to what terms and conditions the said labourers shall continue in their said employment, and subject to what terms and conditions it would be reasonable to require the said casual labourers to present themselves for work when notified as aforesaid.[92]

The order also obliged the workers to resume work 'forthwith' and to remain in their employment upon the same terms and conditions that prevailed at the time they left their employment (reg. 3).

But the workers were adamant. In their meeting of 28 August they resolved to continue until their demands were met.[93] According to some evidence, 'strikers had bound themselves by religious oath not to return to work except on own terms . . . '[94]

Next day no workers turned up. The governor authorized arrests, and 143 workers (all of them permanent) were arrested, 115 appearing before the magistrate charged with disobeying the above-mentioned order. They were bound over to appear for judgement on 5 September, when they were sentenced to one day's imprisonment.[95]

As a result of this action workers began to return. By 3 September, 205 out of 230 permanent workers were back and casual employees had also resumed work.[96] Thus the strike which had lasted twelve days was finally broken.

The tribunal published its award on the 6 September. Besides some rationalization and slight improvement in terms and conditions of work, including granting of wartime temporary cost of living allowance, the award closely followed the offer that had been made by the employers before the strike. In material terms therefore the workers did not gain much.

However, they did gain in their consciousness. The strike had lasted twelve solid days during which the workers had displayed great solidarity and unity. Unlike the 1939 strike the workers appeared to have had some definite leadership, probably of skilled workers, which was always at hand to negotiate. And if finally they gave in it was because they had come up against the state itself. Without an organization they were not yet in a position to take on the state. They were powerless even to prevent victimization of some of their comrades who had given evidence before the tribunal, three of whom were dismissed without compensation.[97] In Iliffe's apt remark: 'Just as in 1943 they had learned that an effective strike required unity between permanent and casual workers, so they learned from this victimization that striking without union organization was dangerous.'[98] Nevertheless, the 1943 strike displayed much greater sophistication than the 1939 one. Throughout it was orderly and well organized and gave no excuse to the state to use overt force.[99]

The strike was one more experience which was put to good use in the next stage of the struggle, the 1947 general strike.

The 1947 general strike: organization is born

If the war-time inflation and shortages had annoyed and irritated the urban population, the post-war years angered and embittered them, for this was the worst period in the history of urban people.[100] The African population of Dar es Salaam almost doubled during the war while the number of houses actually fell. Rents were high. Inflation had eaten away wages while necessary consumer goods were in extremely short supply.[101] Hunger and unemployment were rampant. These conditions affected not only the working class but also other working people like small tradesmen and craftsmen. The economic situation was explosive and it needed only a spark to ignite. That spark was provided once again by the dockworkers.

On 22 August 1947 the dockers had already given their employers advanced notice of a strike if their demands for substantial improvements in wages and other conditions of work were not fulfilled within a week. After a fortnight the employers made an offer but by this time the workers were already on the warpath. On 7 September 1947 they went on strike.

Just before the strike and in its anticipation the government had rushed through the Legislative Council a new Ordinance setting up for the first time a dispute-settlement machinery. The Trade Disputes (Arbitration and Enquiry) Ordinance, 1947,[102] was enacted on 27 August 1947 without much debate in the Legislative Council and was brought into force on 5 September 1947. Hitherto, the colonial officials had been complacent about setting up a dispute-settlement machinery. As early as 1938, the Secretary of State had circulated a copy of the Trinidad and Tobago Trade Disputes (Arbitration and Enquiry) Ordinance which he said could act as a model for other dependencies. But the colonial officials as well as the Executive Council had felt that the 'introduction of such legislation to this Territory was premature . . . ' and that 'time had not arrived when legislation on the lines indicated was necessary'.[103]

Both the 1939 and 1943 dockworkers' strikes had demonstrated that the days of individualized resistance were fast coming to an end and that collective action had not only begun but was there to stay. As we have seen, the 1943 strike was taken care of by the Defence (Trade Disputes) Regulations which were enacted under Emergency Powers. They had been so effective that they were preserved during the whole of the war period. But the draconian provisions of the Defence Regulations could not be used during 'peace-time'. They were not adequate, and nor could they stand the criticism of international opinion. And therefore they had to be replaced by the 1947 Ordinance.

In the history of dispute-settlement machinery in Tanzania, the 1947 Ordinance was the first and, although the machinery has undergone many and varied changes since then, some of the basic concepts used therein have survived.

The Ordinance set up a two-stage machinery for settlement of a trade dispute, conciliation and arbitration. As soon as an existing or apprehended trade dispute* was reported to the Labour Commissioner by either of the parties to the dispute, he would endeavour to conciliate the parties as a first step (s. 3). (It is interesting to note that this procedure of conciliation was a peculiarly Tanganyikan innovation for it did not exist in the model Trinidad and Tobago statute.)[104] If he succeeded the settlement was deemed to be an award. On the other hand, if he failed to conciliate the dispute it was referred to the governor who 'if he thinks fit and if both parties consent' would authorize the Labour Commissioner to refer the matter for settlement to an Arbitration Tribunal. However, the Labour Commissioner would not resort to arbitration procedure before first exhausting any voluntary dispute-settlement machinery that might exist between the employers and employees and only when such machinery had failed to effect settlement and when both parties consented that the statutory arbitration machinery would be invoked. Thus, following the footsteps of UK dispute-settlement tradition[105] the state at this juncture kept statutory intervention to the minimum. The aim still was a liberal one: to provide a standing statutory machinery not as a substitute but in addition to collective bargaining and other methods of voluntary settlement. This liberalism did not last long. Within three years it was to be replaced by the notorious 'essential services provisions' involving compulsory arbitration. But let us not jump ahead of our story.

The Arbitration Tribunal was to consist of one of the following: (a) a sole arbitrator appointed by the Labour Commissioner; (b) an arbitrator appointed by the commissioner and assisted by one or more assessors nominated by or on behalf of the employers concerned and appointed by the commissioner; (c) one or more arbitrators nominated by the employers and workmen concerned and an independent chairman, all appointed by the commissioner. In the case of (b) it was the arbitrator who made the final decision, and in (c) where the members of the tribunal failed to agree, the chairman was to decide as a sole arbitrator (s. 4(2)).

The most interesting provision of the Ordinance was on the question of the effect of the award. There had been some discussions among colonial officials to impose criminal sanctions for breach of an award. But this would probably have been politically embarrassing. The same result was, however, reached in an indirect way. Section 8 of the Ordinance made the award part of the contracts of service between the employers and workmen concerned. This automatically made the terms of the award enforceable under the Master and Native Servants Ordinance which provided for penal sanctions for certain breaches of contracts of service. [106]

This was then the machinery which was hurriedly set up to deal with the impending dockworkers' crisis. Meanwhile, the spark lit by the dockworkers' strike had begun to spread like prairie-fire. Within two days all dockworkers, including casual workers and headmen, had come out demanding an increase in the daily rate from Shs. 2.30 to Shs. 5 and a general rate of Shs. 100 per month for skilled permanent employees. On 10 September the railwaymen, led by their Railway African Association[107] which was 2,000 strong, walked out. The strike began to spread along the central railway line. Railway workers in Morogoro, Dodoma, Kilosa and Tabora also walked out 'apparently on instructions from a central strike committee in Dar es Salaam'.[108] By the 13th

---

* 'Trade dispute' was defined to mean 'any dispute or difference between employers and workmen, or between workmen and workmen, connected with the employment or non-employment, or the terms of the employment, or with the conditions of labour, of any person' (s. 2(1)).

the Tabora strike had become general and was joined even by the African teachers of two government schools. The government servants and the white-collar-dominated Railway African Association in Tabora took the occasion to raise a more democratic demand of equal treatment of African and Asian employees: an end to 'colour bar' and discrimination and 'equal pay for equal work'.[109] Similar demands would occupy a much more important place in the struggles of the 1950s and early 1960s, in particular the struggle of the petty-bourgeoisie.

Meanwhile, having failed to persuade the dockers to return to work on the promise that a tribunal would be appointed to look into their grievances, the government began to put into effect sterner measures. Lorries under police protection moved into the African town to transport those willing to work. The government warned its employees that if they did not turn up for work on the 15th they would be considered as having given notice. Furthermore, no public servant who was absent during the period of strike would be paid wages for those days.[110] This no doubt had the desired effect. Half the strikers in a meeting on 14 September voted to return. The next day, pickets were removed and the situation began to return to normal in Dar es Salaam.[111] On the same day a tribunal chaired by G. W. Hatchell was appointed under the provisions of the 1947 Ordinance.

The general strike in the capital was over, but up-country it was only just beginning. Kigoma and Mwanza struck on 15 September. The Kigoma strike was headed by railway clerks while in Mwanza the dockers struck first and then moved through the town calling out other workers, and stoning Barclay's Bank. The strike then spread to trading settlements in Bukumbi and Masungwe. Two days later the situation was normal again in both Kigoma and Mwanza. Workers on the Kongwa Groundnut Scheme struck 15 September for ten days. There was a brief stoppage in Arusha on 17 September, while saltworkers at Uvinza remained out until 22 September. The final incident took place on 6 October at Uruwira lead mines in Mpanda. The strike had taken precisely a month to spread from Dar es Salaam to Mpanda.[112]

No wonder the historian Iliffe calls this 'Tanganyika's most widespread protest since the Maji Maji rebellion'.[113] It could not fail to make an impression on the tribunal. After some six days of sitting the chairman of the tribunal published the award which was his own since the workers' and employers' representatives had failed to reach agreement. The award was a resounding economic success for the dockers. Wage increases of some 40–50 per cent were granted; casual daily wage was raised from Shs. 2.30 to Shs. 3.90. The award also introduced a bonus for regular work, regular free meals and free hospital treatment. Hatchell's explicit aim was to create a regular labour force, 'a professional class of waterfront workmen'[114] — and hence considerable increases in wages. Other employers too fell in line which resulted in overall wage increases.

The 1947 general strike, besides being an economic success, was a great lesson in struggle to the proletariat. The dockers and their fellow workers had managed to paralyse the heart of the colonial economy and administration for two days.[115] They had managed to lead and arouse the sympathy of the working people almost throughout the country. Even by official accounts, the strike was generally well organized, led by skilled workers, and maintained good co-ordination and liaison 'by bicycle'![116] All this could not have been achieved without considerable organization. There appears to have been a 'central strike committee' in Dar es Salaam which operated clandestinely.[117] But this organization had been only *ad hoc*. Its success immediately taught the workers the need for a more permanent organization which would guard the gains of the struggle. Hence was born the Stevedores' and Dock workers' Union with a paid-up membership of 1,500.[118] Literally, the organization of the workers was born in the womb of the struggle.

The Stevedores' and Dockworkers' Union was formed and led by the workers themselves.[119] The Labour Commissioner later admitted that the Labour Department was not responsible for forming this union. 'The Labour Department had no knowledge of this union until it actually applied for registration.'[120] However, once the union was formed the state promptly mounted a two-pronged attack to bring it under its control. First, a labour officer, one Hamilton, was quickly assigned to advise it. The 1947 Annual Report of the Labour Department observed that the union was 'being guided on correct lines by a Labour Officer who has been studying the port labour problem in Dar es Salaam'.[121] Secondly, the government intrigued to foist a petty-bourgeois leadership on the union. Around February 1948 Abdul Sykes, son of a well-known African businessman, was asked by the government to become the secretary of the dockworkers' union.[122]

Abdul Sykes did not come from among the dockers nor even from the working class. His father, Kleist Sykes, had risen from being a soldier through a civil servant to become a businessman. Kleist Sykes was essentially moderate in his views, believing 'strongly that business was the only thing that could uplift a man economically'.[123] It is clear, therefore, the type of leadership that the state preferred for trade unions.

But Sykes did not last long. He could not understand the militancy, enthusiasm and grass-root democracy that characterized the union. 'Abdul Sykes later recalled the horror with which his dignified, respectable father used to witness meetings of the executive in his house, often while union members danced an ngoma outside.'[124] Within a few months Sykes was forced to resign and the leadership passed into the hands of Erika Fiah, Sykes's arch-opponent.

Fiah originally came from Uganda. He represented militant black nationalism which was disliked not only by the government but also by the moderate wing of African civil servants and businessmen. Fiah edited a fiery paper called *Kwetu* in which he often attacked the so-called educated Africans who denied being Africans.[125] No wonder that he was eventually ousted from the union's leadership by government intrigue.[126]

Meanwhile, Hamilton tried to work closely with the union to bring about decasualization of dockworkers and create a more regular labour force. To a certain extent he succeeded in doing this by installing a system of registration under which some 1,800 dockworkers were registered by May 1949. Then he went on leave and the employer turned the system which was meant to introduce regularity into an instrument of discipline: any registered dockworker who was absent from job for more than six days in a month would lose his registration card and therefore his right to work in the port. Most probably this was one of the major grievances behind the 1950 strike.

By 1950, therefore, it was clear to the state that they had not succeeded in bringing the union under their control. In fact, the state throughout feared that the union might fall under radical influence and Fiah's ascendance to leadership may have accentuated that fear.[127] The 1950 strike was a god-sent opportunity which the state grabbed with both hands to ban the union.

The 1950 fatal strike and its effects

Although there is not enough evidence, it appears the cause of the 1950 strike was the discontent generated by the registration scheme. It is clear that the scheme would not only effect regularity and in the process reduce the numbers employed but could also be used by the employers for control and discipline. The immediate reason for the strike was the order of the employers to use the new entry gate and call-on stance. On 31 January 1950 the union executive instructed its members not to use the new gate and on

1 February the strike was complete. In fact the workers, probably rightly, guessed that the opening of the new gate was the beginning of bringing the registration scheme into force. 'The union had been apprehensive that the intention behind the use of the new gate was to introduce a scheme of control for port workers in order gradually to weed out the less regular workers and create a more efficient working force.'[128]

Under the leadership of the union the strike would have probably been as orderly as the previous ones. But that was not to be. There is a belief among those who participated and some evidence to show that the state had been waiting for just such an opportunity to destroy the union which it had intensely disliked.[129] The state promptly intervened — almost on the day of the strike — by show of force: steel-helmeted police were posted to guard the port. The employers, no doubt with the connivance of the government, added insult to injury by employing blackleg labour. On the day of the strike some 300 'volunteers' were at work and by the next day the number had doubled.[130] Even other employers showed their solidarity by detailing *their* labour to work the port. Under the circumstances, peaceful picketing would have been virtually impossible. Even then the union actually warned the employers beforehand to cease breaking the strike by the employment of blackleg labour.

On the morning of the 3rd the pickets were confronted by a police detachment and in no time there were physical skirmishes. An assistant superintendent was injured and some thirty arrests were made on the same day. More clashes occurred while arrests continued. KAR detachments were called out and HMS *Loch Quich* was assigned to guard the port area. 'By the evening of the 3rd over eighty arrests had been made and all members of the Dockers' Union Executive had been apprehended.'[131] According to one report two strikers had been killed as a result of the clashes.[132]

The reprisals by the state were unprecedented in the history of Dar es Salaam's dockworkers. Some 145 men were charged with offences in connection with the strike.

Eight members of the union executive charged with unlawful assembly and conspiring to prevent casual labourers from exercising their occupation were released for lack of evidence. Of those charged with offences arising from the riot, one was sentenced to ten years for attempted murder, and nine others — including one described as a union official — were imprisoned for lesser crimes. Another 77 were convicted of offences in other incidents.[133]

Meanwhile the port continued to work with 'volunteer' labour. By the 5th the situation had returned to normal and many casual workers had filtered back. However, skilled permanent workers never returned, and with their departure the dock working class temporarily lost the heroic tradition of initiative and leadership in the struggle.

On 2 June 1950 the dockworkers' union was dissolved by a High Court order and its property — a half-completed building and Shs. 24,000 in cash — was confiscated by the state. Thus ended the first important collective organization of the working class which also brought to a close an important and distinct phase in the history of working-class resistance and organization.

By 1951 there was not a single trade union — except the Dar es Salaam Asian Commercial Employees' Association — on the trade union register. The state which had been so much responsible for the collapse of these early unions now unequivocally blamed the workers. 'Government were of the opinion that the African was at the present time quite unable to accept responsibility in a Trades Union sense and were doing absolutely nothing to encourage Trade Unionism at this time', declared Hamilton.[134] The Labour Commissioner chimed in by saying that the experience of dockworkers had shown that 'the vast majority of workers here are at present completely incapable of comprehending the principles and concepts of trade unionism . . .'[135]

Therefore the present stage, as was emphasized in the 1951 Labour Report, was to encourage elementary joint consultation at workshop and enterprise level where 'the employers must provide opportunities for his employees to meet him or his representative to discuss matters of common interest'.[136] The paternalism of the simple joint consultation machinery, then, became the guiding policy of the Labour Department for the next five years.

The lessons learnt by the state from the intense class struggles of the 1940s were put to immediate use to strengthen and consolidate capital. The immediate measure taken was to try and forestall the kind of strikes that occurred in the 1940s. The result was the passing of a new legislation on dispute-settlement machinery.

The Trade Disputes (Arbitration and Settlement) Ordinance, 1950,[137] introduced the notorious 'essential services' provisions. In other respects it more or less repeated the provisions of the 1947 Ordinance but provided for special procedures for 'essential services'. Section 10 provided that any existing or apprehended trade dispute might be reported to the Labour Commissioner who would first attempt to settle it by conciliation. On failure to settle it by conciliation, or on failure to reach settlement through any other machinery that may have been involved or where in the opinion of the Labour Commissioner a settlement was unduly delayed, 'the Labour Commissioner shall cancel any reference, if made, and report to the member who may refer the trade dispute for settlement to a Tribunal' (s. 10(1)(d)). The member in charge of labour matters was required to make the reference to the tribunal within twenty-one days or within such extended period that the member, in writing, had allowed. The tribunal was to consider the trade dispute referred to it and make an award which was binding on the parties and was implied in the contracts of service of the concerned employees (s. 21(1)). Such an award was to remain in force for six months before an application to vary it could be made (s. 21(2)).

Coupled with the above provisions were those making strikes and lock-outs criminal offences unless the procedure set out above was exhausted and no settlement had been reached. Section 12(1) provided:

No employer shall take part in a lock-out, and no workman shall take part in a strike, in any essential service, unless a trade dispute exists and has been reported to the Labour Commissioner in accordance with the provisions of Section 10 of this ordinance and twenty-one days, or, if a further period has been allowed by the member under sub-section (4) of that section, twenty-one days and such further period shall have elapsed since the date of the report and the trade dispute has not during that time been settled or been referred to a Tribunal for settlement in accordance with the provisions of that section.

In practice, therefore, strikes and lock-outs in 'essential services' were made virtually illegal and at the same time statutory arbitration was made compulsory.

'Essential services' were defined as those stated in the schedule (s. 2) and the Governor-in-Council was empowered to add any service to the schedule (s. 29). Thus carte blanche was given to the executive to control the collective resistance of the workers virtually in any sector. The original schedule contained water, electricity, health, hospital and sanitary services including transport services necessary for their operation. Public transportation, telecommunications and, of course, ports and dock services were also included. Around 1960 this list of some ten services had been lengthened to eighteen covering virtually all *industries* except agriculture and mining.[138]

Originally the 'essential services' provisions were introduced in the United Kingdom during the Second World War. There the efforts of the state to continue to apply them in the post-war period were frustrated by the concerted resistance of the working class resulting in the repeal of those provisions.[139] In Kenya too, although similar provisions, passed in 1950, remained on the statute-book, their enactment was greeted with mass meetings, arrests and strikes of workers.[140] In Tanganyika, on the other hand, there was not even a ripple of resistance. As we saw, the vanguard of the working class — the dockworkers — had been completely crippled with the destruction of their union and the decapitation of their leadership.

Armed with this legal weapon on strikes and having destroyed the workers' organizations, the state was all set to squeeze the maximum out of the workers. In 1953, Hamilton's informal efforts of the late 1940s at establishing a registration scheme for dockworkers were converted into law. The Dockworkers (Regulation of Employment) Ordinance, 1953,[141] empowered the member in charge of labour matters to establish a scheme for dockworkers providing, *inter alia*, for regulating the recruitment and rates of remuneration and conditions of dockworkers; for their registration and training and for various other related matters (s. 3). Under that Ordinance, the member made an order establishing the scheme for Dar es Salaam dockworkers which came into effect on 1 July 1955.[142] Actually, the scheme had already functioned informally for some time. By the time the Ordinance was enacted in 1953, there were already some 3,000 dock-workers on the register in respect of whom all the documentation — including identification, photographing and so on — had been completed.[143]

The objects of the scheme, in the words of the order itself, were 'to ensure greater regularity of employment for dockworkers and to ensure that an adequate number of dockworkers is available for the efficient performance of dock work' (para. 1(2)). The scheme was to be administered by a registration officer appointed by the Labour Commissioner. There was also established an advisory committee under the chairmanship of the registration officer and consisting of representatives from employers' and workers' sides appointed by the member from among panels nominated respectively by the employers' and workers' organizations.

The registration officer was required to maintain a register of 'daily workers' and a register of employers. It was his task to allocate 'daily workers' on the register to the registered employers according to the latter's daily requirements. Among other things, the registrar had powers to remove a dockworker from the register on several grounds including 'that the number of registered dockworkers exceeds a number which would ensure regular work for all the dockworkers so registered' or 'that the registered dockworker has been guilty of serious misconduct arising out of his employment or has persistently acted in breach of the provisions of this scheme' (para. 15(a)(b)). The scheme was thus an instrument not only to regularize and professionalize dockworkers and maintain an adequate supply of labour for the employers, but also to discipline the labour force employed in the port. All this was what the dockworkers had resisted in their spirited opposition of 1950. But in that battle they had been vanquished, and now the victor was making maximum use of the workers' defeat to bring them under complete control. The fruits of that control were seen in the rise of dockworkers' productivity between 1952 and 1954. Average tonnage handled per man, per month, in the first quarter of 1954 was almost 45 per cent higher than that during the same period in 1952. On average, some 1,486 men were employed in the first quarter of 1954 compared to some 1,773 employed during the corresponding period in 1952, the result being that some 300 persons had lost their jobs.[144]

Conclusion

In Chapter 4 we discussed at length the development of permanent wage-labour. It is a section of that wage-labour — in particular the skilled and semi-skilled proletariat — which in the 1940s took initial steps in collective action and collective organization. In this the dockworkers played a leading role. In absence of, as yet, a strong manufacturing sector, the dockworkers formed the most concentrated section of the working class. They were permanent, although irregular, and urbanized, occupying a strategic position in the export-oriented colonial economy. These objective factors formed the material basis of the collective struggle and organization of the dockworkers.

Our study of the dockworkers' struggles throws into sharp relief a number of theoretical propositions in regard to state and law. First, once the workers took up *collective* action, the role of the state between capital and labour became much more directly interventionist as opposed to being simply regulatory. This was seen in the case of all strikes and in particular the 1950 strike. Also the state provided itself a much more prominent role in the 'settlement' of collective disputes. Strike action is clearly a semi-political *class* action on the part of a working class because it is a conscious, collective act to withdraw labour power, the life-line of the capitalist system. With trade disputes and strike action we leave the realm of commodity-exchange — epitomized in a legal contract — and enter the realm of the production of surplus-value.

Secondly, corresponding to the development of collective struggle there developed the necessary legislation to control and supervise it; the legislation on dispute-settlement machinery and trade unions. These pieces of legislation embodied the results of class struggle including certain gains made by the working class — for example, trade union recognition — while at the same time attempting to assist capital in maintaining its dominance over labour. In this respect therefore this legislation exhibits the *political* character of law. As a matter of fact, in this legislation we also begin to witness the ideological character of law. Such notions as conciliation between capital and labour when capital–labour relation is inherently contradictory, or setting up of tripartite arbitration tribunals which assume equality between capital and labour on the one hand and neutrality of the state on another, are eminently ideological in character.

These propositions are further illustrated and fortified in our study of trade unionism in the next two chapters.

NOTES

1. Tandau, A. C. A., *Historia ya Kuundwa kwa TFL. 1955-1962 na Kuanzishwa kwa NUTA, 1964* (Dar es Salaam: Mwananchi Publishing Co.,). Kawawa, R. M., 'The TFL, TANU and Unity', *Spearhead* (The Pan-African Review), Vol. I, No. 2, December 1961, pp. 14–16.
2. Iliffe, J., 'A History of the Dockworkers of Dar es Salaam', *TNR*, No. 71, 1970, pp. 119–48.
3. Marx, K., *The Poverty of Philosophy* (Moscow: Progress Publishers, 1955), p. 150.
4. See below, Ch. 6, and Friedland, W. H., 'The Institutionalization of Labour Protest in Tanganyika and some Resultant Problems', *Sociologus*, Berlin, Vol. 2, No. 2, 1961, p. 132.
5. Iliffe, J., 'Dockworkers', op. cit., p. 120.
6. ibid., p. 121.

7. No. 23 of 1932.
8. Passfield to Colonies, 17 September 1930, TNA 19335/I.
9. See, for instance, Morgan, M., 'The Rise and Fall of Malayan Trade Unionism, 1945–50', in Amin, M. and Caldwell, M. (eds.), *Malaya, the Making of a Neo-colony* (Nottingham: Spokesman Books, 1977), p. 152. In Malaya the first trade union was formed by the members of the Malayan Communist Party. The intense struggle in the British West Indies in the 1930s was another lesson that the British did not want to be repeated in Africa. See Woddis, J., *The Lion Awakes* (London: Lawrence & Wishart, 1961), pp. 43–6.
10. Proceedings of the Legislative Council, 7th Session, 7 November 1932, pp. 195–6.
11. ibid., p. 196.
12. ibid., p. 200.
13. Wedderburn, K. W., op. cit., Ch. VII, and Morton, L., op. cit., Ch. XIV.
14. See Wedderburn, K. W., ibid., pp. 225–6.
15. No. 7 of 1939.
16. Woddis, J., *The Lion*, op. cit., pp. 65ff.
17. ARLD, 1927, para. 153.
18. See, for example, Northern Province Labour Report, 1935, TNA A 23217, and Quarterly Labour Report of Tanga Province, 30 June 1937, TNA 11168/I.
19. Iliffe, J., 'The Spokesman: Martin Kayamba', in Iliffe, J. (ed.), *Modern Tanzanians* (Dar es Salaam: East African Publishing House for the Historical Association of Tanzania, 1973), p. 73.
20. Iliffe, J., *Modern Tanganyika*, op. cit., p. 396.
21. The information on shop assistants, unless otherwise stated, is from Honey, M., *Indian Merchant Capital*, op. cit., Ch. VIII.
22. No. 33 of 1932.
23. No. 25 of 1945.
24. 'Information on the Asiatic Trade Union', 26 February 1937, TNA A 24829. The rest of the information on this union is from this source.
25. President of the Union to CS, 16 February 1937, TNA A 24829.
26. *Tanganyika Herald*, 6 March 1937, in TNA A 24829.
27. Singh, M., *History of Kenya Trade Union Movement to 1952* (Nairobi: East African Publishing House, 1969), p. 59.
28. 'Constitution of the Union', copy in TNA 27259/I–II.
29. ibid., p. 4.
30. Clayton, A. and Savage, D. C., *Government and Labour in Kenya, 1895–1963* (London: Frank Cass, 1974), p. 213.
31. Singh, M., op. cit., p. 59.
32. ibid., p. 70.
33. General Secretary, TUC, to SS, 18 August 1939, CO 691/174/42191/13/18, and SS to General Secretary, TUC, 30 September 1939, CO 691/174/42191/13/9–10.
34. See ibid. and Singh to Colonial Secretary, Tanganyika, 6 May 1937, TNA A 24829, and Singh to EA governments, 31 July 1938, TNA 27259/I–II.
35. Singh, M., op. cit., p. 63.
36. Wade to SS, 20 May 1937, TNA 27259/I–II.
37. Clayton, A. and Savage, D. C., op. cit., pp. 213–14.
38. ARLD, 1949, p. 28, para. 136.
39. Honey, M., 'Draft Thesis' (this paragraph has been omitted in the final version of her thesis).
40. Iliffe, J., *Modern History*, op. cit., p. 400.
41. TNA 25201.
42. Copy in TNA 25201.
43. ARLD, 1947, p. 22.
44. See above, pp. 158–9.
45. Iliffe, J., *Modern History*, op. cit., p. 399.
46. ARLD, 1950, p. 18, para. 94.

47. Annual Report, Lake Province Labour Office, 1948 and 1950, TNA 215/511/V; *PC's Annual Report, Western Province*, 1952 (Dar es Salaam: Government Printer), p. 187.
48. ARLD, 1949, p. 28, para. 132.
49. Annual Report, Lake Province Labour Office, 1950, TNA 215/511/V.
50. ibid.
51. Trade Unions (Amendment) Ordinance, 1941, No. 30 of 1941.
52. Annual Report, Lake Province Labour Office, 1950, TNA 215/511/V.
53. Iliffe, J., *Modern History*, op. cit., p. 397.
54. ibid., p. 398.
55. ibid.
56. Labour Annual Report, Tanga and Pangani Districts, 1948, TNA 4/962/9.
57. Letter dated 28 May 1947, TNA 41/L1/2.
58. Labour Annual Report, Tanga and Pangani Districts, 1948, TNA 4/962/9.
59. ARLD, 1949, p. 28, para. 132.
60. Labour Annual Report, Tanga and Pangani Districts, 1949, TNA 4/962/9.
61. ARLD, 1948, p. 83, App. K.
62. Annual Report, Lake Province Labour Office, 1948, TNA 215/511/V.
63. See, generally, Freyhold, M., op. cit., p. 40.
64. District Officer to PC, Eastern Province, 31 October 1938, TNA 25912.
65. Jerrard, R. C., 'Labour Conditions in Tanga', 21 March 1940, Part II, TNA 25971.
66. Tanganyika, *Report of the Commission Appointed to Enquire into the Disturbances which occurred in the Port of Tanga during the month of August 1939* (Dar es Salaam: Government Printer, 1939), pp. 22–5, Apps. A–C. Hereafter cited as *Commission Report, Tanga Strike*.
67. Quoted in Iliffe, J., 'Dockworkers', op. cit., p. 127.
68. *Commission Report, Tanga Strike*, op. cit., p. 8.
69. ibid., App. D.
70. Foster, L. H. L., 'Tanga Dock Strike and Riots, August 1939, Report and Diary of Events', p. 2, CO 691/174/42191/13/24–54. Hereafter cited as 'Diary'. Rest of the information on this strike is from this source unless otherwise indicated.
71. ibid., p. 3.
72. *Commission Report, Tanga Strike*, op. cit., p. 13.
73. Governor to SS, 10 August 1939, CO 691/174/42191/13/67.
74. 'Diary', op. cit., p. 9.
75. ibid. p. 13.
76. Governor to SS, 11 August 1939, CO 691/42191/13/62, and *Daily Telegraph*, 11 August 1939, clipping in CO 691/174/42191/13/61.
77. *Commission Report, Tanga Strike*, op. cit., p. 10.
78. ibid., pp. 20–1.
79. Young to SS, 28 February 1941, CO 691/183/42191/13/6.
80. Quoted in Iliffe, J., 'Dockworkers', op. cit., p. 108.
81. 'Record of Proceedings: Lighterage Dispute Tribunal', 30 August 1943, p. 14, CO 691/183/42191/13. Hereafter cited as 'Tribunal Proceedings'.
82. ibid., p. 19.
83. Iliffe, J., 'Dockworkers', op. cit., p. 129.
84. ibid.
85. ARLD, 1943, pp. 7–8 and 'Tribunal Proceedings', op. cit., App. A.
86. 'Tribunal Proceedings', op. cit., pp. 4–5.
87. ibid., p. 12, and Iliffe, J., 'Dockworkers', op. cit., p. 129.
88. Governor to SS, 30 August 1943.
89. GN No. 279 of 27 August 1943.
90. GN No. 280 of 27 August 1943.
91. As amended by the Defence (Lighterage Dispute) (Amendment) Order, 1943, GN No. 281 of 30 August 1943, which added the provision on casual workers.
92. Reg. 4(a) and (b) as amended.
93. Iliffe, J., 'Dockworkers', op. cit., p. 130.

94. 'Tribunal Proceedings', op. cit., p. 2.
95. Governor to SS, 3 and 7 September 1943, CO 691/183/42191/13/telegrams 781 and 793.
96. ibid.
97. Iliffe, J., 'Dockworkers', op. cit., p. 130.
98. ibid., p. 131.
99. ARLD, 1943, p. 24.
100. Iliffe, J., 'Dockworkers', op. cit., p. 131.
101. Chairman, Economic Control Board, to CS, 27 December 1945, TNA 11127.
102. No. 11 of 1947.
103. Papers in TNA 25911/II.
104. ibid.
105. See Wedderburn, K. W., op. cit., pp. 122ff.
106. TNA 25911/II.
107. This was considered a 'staff association' and therefore was not registered under the Trade Union Ordinance although formed in 1945.
108. Annual Report of the PC, Eastern Province, 1947, p. 38 (Dar es Salaam: Government Printer.)
109. Iliffe, J., *Modern History*, op. cit., p. 403.
110. Government Circular No. 16 of 1947, 16 September 1947, in TNA 36490.
111. Telegram from Dar es Salaam to Tanga, 15 September 1947, TNA 4/652/70.
112. Iliffe, J., 'Dockworkers', op. cit., p. 133.
113. Iliffe, J., *Modern History*, op. cit., p. 402.
114. Hatchell's award is reprinted in ARLD, 1947, App. J., pp. 44ff.
115. See Annual Report of PC, Eastern Province, 1947, op. cit., p. 38.
116. ibid.
117. Freyhold, M., op. cit., p. 42.
118. ARLD, 1947, p. 22.
119. Iliffe, J., 'Dockworkers', op. cit., p. 134. Freyhold, M., op. cit., p. 42.
120. Proceedings of the Legislative Council, 24th Session, 1949/50, p. 192.
121. p. 22.
122. Buruku, D. S., 'The Townsman: Kleist Sykes', in Iliffe, J. (ed.), *Modern Tanzanians*, op. cit., p. 110.
123. ibid., p. 109.
124. Iliffe, J., 'Dockworkers', op. cit., p. 136.
125. Buruku, D. S., 'The Townsman', op. cit., p. 103.
126. Iliffe, J., 'Dockworkers', op. cit., p. 136.
127. ibid.
128. ARLD, 1950, p. 19, para. 102.
129. Iliffe, J., 'Dockworkers', op. cit., p. 136.
130. ARLD, 1950, p. 19, para. 102.
131. ibid., p. 20.
132. Annual Report of PC, Eastern Province, 1950, op cit., p. 38.
133. Iliffe, J., 'Dockworkers', op. cit., p. 137. Subsequent information from this source.
134. ibid., p. 138.
135. Proceedings of the Legislative Council, 24th Session, 1949/50, p. 192.
136. ARLD, 1951, p. 21, para. 102.
137. No. 43 of 1950.
138. Woddis, J., *The Lion*, op. cit., p. 70.
139. ibid.
140. Singh, M., op. cit., pp. 248, 268, 271-2.
141. No. 20 of 1953.
142. Dar es Salaam Dockworkers (Regulation of Employment) Order, 1955, GN No. 222 of 10 June 1955.
143. Proceedings of the Legislative Council, 27th Session, 1952/53, p. 244.
144. Quarterly Bulletin of Labour Department, 1954, TNA 215/1969/II.

6

The Rise of the
Trade Union Movement

The year 1950 saw the dissolution of the dockworkers' union and brought to an end the first phase of working-class struggles during colonialism. The prominent actor in delivering the *coup de grâce* was the state itself. It was the state again which, through the instrument of its Labour Department, now set about putting into practice its own version of what capital–labour relations ought to be. The department's policy, to be discussed in this chapter, was essentially two pronged: to guide the infant trade union movement along acceptable lines (which essentially meant to encourage only small, craft-based localized unions and to control the unions so formed) and to establish joint consultative machinery to pre-empt the trade union movement or to co-opt it.

In spite of the state's policy, a strong, militant trade union movement grew up in Tanzania during the second half of the 1950s. To be sure, the movement of the 1950s was distinctly different from that of the 1940s. It was initiated from the top, bureaucratic in its organization and with a petty-bourgeois leadership. Yet, no doubt, its militant economic struggles brought the working class considerable successes.

In the first section of the chapter we shall discuss the development and organization of the trade unions including the character of their leadership and their ideological orientation. The second section will concentrate on the analysis of the strike wave which characterized roughly the decade from 1954 to 1964. In the third section we look at the responses of the employer and the various ways and means employed by the state to control and supervise the bourgeoning working-class movement. And here we discuss at some length the use of law as an instrument of control. Finally, we present a case study of industrial relations in the sisal industry, for it was here that all the important features of the class struggle during the period found their most concentrated expression.

Trade unionism: development and organization

Development

Table 6.1 summarizes the development of registered African[1] trade unions from 1950, when the dockworkers' union was dissolved, to 1964, when the National Union of Tanganyika Workers (NUTA) was born. The years 1950–3 were a kind of interregnum

182

Table 6.1 *African trade unions[a] registered in Tanganyika, 1950–64*

Year	Social character of union			Technical character of union		Area of operation		Total no. of unions	Total estimated membership	Average no. of members per union
	Blue collar[b]	White collar[b]	Mixed	Craft	Industrial	Territorial	Localized			
1950	1	–	–	1	–	–	1	1	33	33
1951	–	–	–	–	–	–	–	–	–	–
1952	2	–	–	2	–	–	2	2	301	150
1953	3	2	–	3	2	–	5	5	687	137
1954	4	2	–	4	2	–	6	6	291	49
1955	15	3	1	9	10	3	16	19	2 349	124
1956	19	1	3	11	12	3	20	23	12 891	560
1957	12	–	3	2	13	11	4	15	33 986	2 266
1958	11	4	3	2[c]	16	16	2	18	44 850	2 492
1959	11	5	2	2	16	15	3	18	78 317	4 351
1960	7	7	2	1	15	14	2	16	91 770	5 736
1961	6	6	2	2	12	12	2	14	199 915	14 280
1962	6	4	2	1[d]	11	10	2	12	182 153	15 179
1963	6	4	2	1	11	10	2	12	147 177	12 265
1964	–	–	–	–	1	1	–	1	217 923	217 923

Notes: a Employees' unions only.
b i.e. predominantly in terms of its membership composition. (This categorization is based essentially on the names of the unions and my inferences from the unions' history.)
c African Medical Workers' Union and Union of African Teachers.
d Teachers' Union.

Source: Friedland, W. H., *Vuta Kamba* (Stanford: Hoover Institution Press, 1969), pp. 157–62. ARLD, 1964/65, p. 73, for 1964 figures.

during which trade union activity was as its lowest ebb. After the dissolution of the dockworkers' union, the only union that existed on the Trade Union Register was the small tailors' union in the Lake Province, with only thirty-three members, which was also to disappear the next year. During this period the Labour Department vigorously pushed its policy of encouraging and establishing joint consultative machinery.[2] At the end of 1953 the Annual Report claimed that some 20,000 workers were covered by joint committees while some 80,000 in agriculture and the mines came under the less formal tribal and headmen's councils.[3] The department was apparently so satisfied with the way it had pushed its two-pronged policy that in its 1954 report it boasted:

Trade unions are still in their infancy in Tanganyika; where they exist they are usually very willing to negotiate dispute settlements rather than to strike in the first place, which is a good sign for the future. Workers are gaining valuable experience in the Joint Staff Committees already mentioned. Government considers it important that organizations should develop from the craft or occupational union upwards, and that higher formations should rest upon these as the only stable foundations. Those wishing to form unions have been advised on these lines and the advice has generally been found acceptable.[4]

But the same year saw a renewed activity in the formation of trade unions. In the next two years trade unionism became labour's battle cry. By the end of 1956, there were twenty-three trade unions, the biggest number ever, boasting a membership of a little under 13,000, a four-fold increase over 1952.[5] What was the source of this new upsurge? To answer this we have to look at two geographical places — Mwanza and Dar es Salaam — and two idealogical and organizational inspirations — nationalist and trade unionist — which for different reasons and under different circumstances became the source of this initial upsurge in the development of trade unions. We investigate each one of these in turn.

On 7 July 1954 the territorial conference of the Tanganyika African Association (TAA), meeting in Dar es Salaam, adopted a new constitution and changed its name to Tanganyika African National Union (TANU). One of the explicit aims of the new organization was 'to prepare the people of Tanganyika for self-government and Independence, and to fight relentlessly until Tanganyika is self-governing and independent'.[6] The Sukuma branches of the former TAA immediately converted themselves into TANU branches and began their activities in earnest. But the government reacted swiftly. In October it refused to register the TANU branches and banned all party activities.[7] It was under these circumstances that the former TAA activists, and now TANU stalwarts like Bhoke-Munanka, turned to the formation of trade unions as a possible vehicle to advance their nationalist goal.[8]

The first attempt, without much preparation or thought, was to register a territorial 'Federation of all workers and Trade Unions'.[9] This was quickly snuffed out by the Labour Department. It was refused registration on the ground that the existing registered unions had not been approached (which was probably true), nor had they shown any desire to participate in such an amalgamation. The organizers therefore turned to forming small and localized craft- or occupation-based unions. By the end of 1954 some ten unions from Lake Province had applied for registration of which seven, with a total membership of 299, were registered in March 1955.[10] These were:

The Mwanza Mechanics' and Fitters' Union
The Mwanza African Road Transport Workers' Union
The Mwanza Hotel Workers' and Domestic Servants' Union
The Mwanza Masons' and Bricklayers' Union
The Mwanza African Carpenters' Union
The Mwanza African General Office Workers' and Clerks' Union
The Mwanza African Tailoring Union

The Labour Department suspected that all these unions, except one, had 'connection with the series of unions formed under the auspices of Mr Munanka and his associates'.[11]

Not much is known about the activities of these unions. There is certainly no evidence to show that the unions embarked on any substantial strike movement.[12] This is probably understandable. Besides being small and craft-based, they also lacked aggressive leadership as the original nationalist 'agitators' turned their attention to the co-operative movement as a more potent weapon in their nationalist struggle.[13] The result was that Mwanza-based leaders like Bhoke-Munanka and their overt nationalist ideology failed to leave any mark on the subsequent development of the trade-union movement. Rather it was the Dar es Salaam-based clerks and civil servants, with an explicit trade-unionist drive, who initiated, organized and led the trade unions as they developed in the late 1950s.

In Dar es Salaam it was mainly the African clerks in private commercial firms and civil servants who provided the initial impetus to the development of trade unions. The civil servants were organized in a number of staff associations formed on the lines of its counterpart Asian and European associations. These were allowed to exist during the interregnum[14] since they were no more than social clubs of the relatively educated elite with little trade union inclination. The most important of these in 1953 were the Tanganyika African Government Servants' Association (TAGSA) (membership: 2,000); the Tanganyika African Postal Union (membership: 404); and the East Africa-wide African Railway Union.[15] The Railway Union changed itself into a trade union and was registered under the Trade Union Ordinance as the Tanganyika Railway African Union (TRAU) in 1955.[16] Latter-day prominent trade unionists like R. M. Kawawa and J. A. Ohanga were connected with TAGSA and TRAU respectively as their presidents.

The African clerks in private firms, on the other hand, were organized under the African Commercial Employees' Association (ACEA). Although formed in 1951, with two prominent trade unionists, M. M. Kamaliza and M. M. Mpangala, as its treasurer and committee member respectively, it was not registered until 1953.[17] At the time of its formation it had about 30–40 members and the maximum membership it reached was 300 in 1953, only half of whom could pay a subscription of Sh. 1 per month.[18] Its leadership was part-time since the union could not afford full-time employees. Besides problems of finance and leadership, it faced determined opposition from the state in its efforts to expand. Around December 1953, the association's application to change its name to Tanganyika African Trade Union Congress was rejected out of hand.[19] The assocation does not appear to have been very active as a trade union body. The only recorded evidence of its activity is a campaign in 1953 for equal treatment with Asians and the publication of a newsletter with the primary aim of recruiting members.[20] Its most important contribution, however, was probably in terms of championing the formation of a central organization and in this respect the most outstanding and devoted figure was M. M. Mpangala.

As early as 1953 Mpangala wrote to the existing trade unions suggesting the formation of a central organization, but received a very cool response. He made a similar effort in early 1955 but a plan to hold a general meeting foundered because the trade union leaders did not have enough money to attend such a meeting.[21] Finally, Mpangala took an active interest in organizing a visit of Tom Mboya from Kenya. Tom Mboya and Henry Gaya, both of them ICFTU workers at the time, paid a visit to Dar es Salaam in June 1955.[22] Mboya had several meetings with trade union leaders, gave them courses on various aspects of trade unionism[23] and addressed a mass meeting attended by some 700 people.[24] All in all, Mboya's visit did much to foster interest in trade unionism and his idea that emphasis for the development of unions had to come 'from the top' was enthusiastically adopted.[25] 'We learnt for the first time', Kawawa was to say later with some exaggeration, 'that trade unions could be organized on an industrial and a territorial basis with a national centre which could affiliate to an international organization such as the ICFTU.'[26]

Immediately after Mboya's departure Mpangala set to work. He resigned from his clerical job with Kettles Roy & Wilson (Insurance) Co. to devote himself fully to trade union work. The seven members of the ACEA's Executive Committee volunteered to pay Shs. 25 each every month for his upkeep.[27] The promised financial assistance was not always forthcoming, but Mpangala persevered.[28] Finally he succeeded in organizing a national general meeting on 7–10 October 1955 at Dar es Salaam where the Tanganyika Federation of Labour (TFL) was born.

The meeting was attended by some thirty delegates. The organizations from outside Dar es Salaam were represented by two delegates each (to reduce expenses) while those in Dar es Salaam by four delegates each. From outside Dar es Salaam came the Carpenters' Union, the Hotel Workers' and Domestic Servants' Union and the African Road Transport Workers' Union, all from Mwanza. The Musoma Drivers' Association, the Kilimanjaro Drivers' Association and the Tanga Port Stevedores' and Dockworkers' Union were also represented. From Dar es Salaam came the Railway African Union, the Tanganyika African Postal Union, the TAGSA, the ACEA and the African Staff Association of the Landing & Shipbuilding Co. of East Africa. Thus over two-thirds of the delegates came from predominantly white-collar unions and staff associations. This was dramatically reflected in the leadership that was elected for the newly formed federation. The president (Ohanga) and one trustee (Kanyama) came from TRAU; the senior vice-president (Jumbe), the junior vice-president (Shaba), the general secretary (Kawawa) and another trustee (Singini) came from TAGSA while the ACEA supplied the vice-general secretary (Mpangala), the general treasurer (Kamaliza) and the assistant treasurer (Odoro).[29]

At its very first meeting the TFL set itself two main tasks: to mount a membership drive and to amalgamate small, similar unions so as to form territorial, industrial and general unions. In its first task, the TFL was highly successful. By the end of 1961 the total trade union membership was almost 200,000. Thus some 42 per cent of Tanganyika's workers had been unionized compared to 8 percent in Kenya and 11 per cent in Uganda.[30]

In its drive for amalgamation TFL was beset with two major problems. First, there was the implicit opposition from the Labour Department which insisted on a scrupulous observation of the relevant provisions of the Trade Union Ordinance, 1956,[31] on amalgamation (ss. 28–30). These required that a secret ballot be taken in the case of each of the proposed trade union where 'the votes of at least fifty per centum of the members entitled to vote thereat are recorded and of the votes recorded those in favour of the proposal exceed by twenty per centum or more, the votes against the proposal'. Before registering, the registrar had to be satisfied that the procedures had been complied with and that the trade union so formed fulfilled all the conditions entitling it to be registered. If nothing else, the Labour Department could at least use delaying tactics to register amalgamations, and this it did. For instance, the registration of the giant Transport and General Workers' Union (TGWU), formed as a result of the amalgamation of the Commercial and Industrial Workers' Union and the Transport and Allied Workers' Union, took some six months. The amalgamation of two government unions to form the Tanganyika Union of Public Employees (TUPE) took a whole year.[32]

The other problem that amalgamation faced was that the leadership of existing unions who had built up independent bases was often reluctant to merge with other unions. Thus the Building and Construction Workers' Union refused to merge with the TGWU and, as a result, was disaffiliated from TFL in 1959.[33] The proposed merger of the Tanga Dockworkers' Union with the Dar es Salaam Dockworkers' and Stevedores' Union and the Railway African Union never materialized, presumably because of the strong leadership of TRAU which the other two feared.[34] Nevertheless, in spite of these problems, considerable success was attained by the TFL in channelling union development along industrial and territorial lines. By the end of 1961, Tanganyika had fourteen registered African trade unions of which twelve were territorial and twelve industrial. (The two localized unions were the Tanga and Dar es Salaam dockworkers' union, while the two craft unions which still persisted were the teachers' and medical workers' unions.) The average membership per union was in the order of 14,000, a far cry from 1956 when it was only 560.[35] The five giant unions — Railway, Local Government, Plantation Workers, Transport and General Workers and Public Employees — boasted a total membership of over 95,000 in 1962.[36]

There is little doubt therefore that at the time of independence the country not only had a strong trade union movement but it could claim to be a *mass* movement with a fairly strong *centre* and little inter-union rivalry in terms of membership and recognition. This was one of the most important factors which contributed to the substantial success of the trade unions on the economic front, which success was often attained by massive strikes, to be discussed in the subsequent section. For the moment let us turn to the objective condition which facilitated the development of a mass-based, united trade union movement.

There are three interrelated factors which may be mentioned. First, as was shown in Chapter 4, Tanganyika's economy was characterized by an extremely low level of industrial development. This meant that the working class was, to a very large extent, undifferentiated in terms of skills, occupations and various other hierarchical gradations that one finds in typical industrial economies. Hence, there was little basis for numerous occupation-based trade unions and inter-union rivalries. This facilitated the development of a single centre without opposition. Secondly, the very fact that the most significant development of trade unions *followed* the formation of the centre and was initiated and organized by it made the centre relatively stronger *vis-à-vis* its individual members. Both the bureaucratic organizational structure of the centre and petty-bourgeois (white collar) leadership made it 'efficient' in terms of quick decision-making and providing guidance and advice. Thirdly, the initial development and successes of the movement were related to the fact that trade unions in urban areas were concentrated in the private sector — manufacturing, transport, services, construction and so on. In these sectors there were a relatively large number of small-scale and unorganized employers[37] which gave the relatively more centralized trade unions a strong bargaining position. Successes in these sectors boosted the overall morale and image of the trade union movement and stood in good stead when it came to confronting stronger employers in the sisal industry and the government sector.

The fourth factor might have been the concurrent development of TANU whose leadership most probably encouraged its members and others to join trade unions. However, there is no evidence that this was the most significant factor in the high rate of union membership.[38]

These conditions which determined the structure and organization of the trade unions and contributed towards their success became in different circumstances and conjuncture of forces a source of weakness. But before we can fully understand this we need to examine the character of the trade union leadership and their ideological orientations.

Leadership

The fact that the trade union movement developed 'from the top' and in circumstances where the initial attempt at development from grass-roots and through struggle had been effectively smashed, lent some distinct characteristics to the trade union leadership. First, it was essentially petty-bourgeois (white-collar) and secondly it had *bureaucratic* rather than democratic orientation towards its constituency — that is, the working class.

As was shown above, the unions that were behind the setting up of TFL were all white-collar whose leadership was predominantly clerical or from civil servants. This was true of the leadership of the unions as a whole. One survey in 1960 showed that, of the full-time leaders interviewed, 83 per cent had clerical (clerk, book-keeper, typist and so on), 15 per cent technical (mechanic, artisan, electrician and so on) and 2 per cent manual (unskilled worker) occupational backgrounds[39] when over 70 per cent of the work force was unskilled.[40] The leadership was Christian,[41] with six to ten years of school education[42] and in the age-group 21–23 years.

That the leadership had a bureaucratic–careerist orientation towards trade unionism as such is shown by a number of significant indicators. Friedland found a rather high leader–member ratio and he attributed this to lack of voluntarism.[43] The unions were run by paid employees who not only did the routine jobs but also determined policy and the overall orientation of their organizations. Of the leaders interviewed, 53 per cent were appointed and only 41 per cent elected; 39 per cent joined the union out of self-interest, 22 joined when they began working for a union and only 30 per cent indicated some altruistic reason for joining.[44] This careerist attitude is further borne out by the high turn-over of leadership and the fact that paid leadership remained in trade unionism for only short periods.[45]

Finally, unlike the leadership of the 1940s these leaders did not emerge from the struggles of the working class. Of the leaders interviewed by Friendland in 1960, 39 per cent were never involved in a strike; only 10 per cent had been involved as strikers and 52 per cent as leaders who had never themselves experienced a strike. As a matter of fact, the leadership bore no continuity with the struggles of the 1940s. A very large number of them, nearly 90 per cent, joined the unions only after 1955.[46]

The overall picture that emerges is that much of the trade union leadership did not bear any intrinsic loyalty to the cause of trade unionism as such.*. It certainly did not arise from struggles and had no organic links with the working class. We shall return to this point when we discuss the dissolution of trade unionism in the next chapter. We now propose to turn another important facet which characterized Tanganyika's trade unions in the 1950s. This is the so-called non-political ideological orientation of the unions.

---

* Of course, there were exceptions but they only proved the rule. One such exception was M. M. Mpangala, the highly devoted and self-sacrificing trade unionist. Unlike many of his contemporaries in the trade union movement he never rose to become a politician–bureaucrat; ultimately he became disenchanted and worked as an industrial relations officer in a private firm.[47]

Ideological orientation

The question of whether Tanganyika's unions during 1956–60 were political or not and the extent to which they participated in nationalist struggles has been given conflicting answers by academic analysts.[48] The situation has been made even more complex by *ex post facto* claims by political leaders in the post-independence period that trade unions were a wing of the nationalist struggle.[49] Before we attempt to answer this issue, let us quickly examine the historical evidence in the wider context of the general ideological orientation of the trade union movement during the period 1956–60.

The model for a non-political trade union movement was set by the Labour Department. This made it clear that trade unions and trade unionists were not supposed to involve themselves directly in political matters, nor were political persons supposed to meddle in union affairs.[50] This, together with the constant cry of political 'wolf' by settler-employers and their mouthpiece, the *Tanganyika Standard*, made trade unionists extremely defensive on the question. They went out of their way to dissociate themselves from political issues and strictly adhered, both ideologically and organizationally, to economic goals. Originally, this may have been for fear lest their unions be suppressed by the state but eventually it became part of the leadership's ideology. Two sources played a crucial, even a decisive, role in reinforcing the economistic ideology. These were the foreign mentors of Tanganyika's trade unionists — the ICFTU, the British TUC, the Fabian Colonial Bureau and the international secretariats of the various western trade unions. The second source of influence was the nationalist movement itself — TANU — which enforced a strict separation between economics and politics, between trade union and nationalist struggles. Each one of these will be examined in some detail.

Tanganyikan trade unionism arose in the period of intense cold-war conflicts and propaganda. In January 1949, the non-Communist trade unions walked out of a session of the World Federation of Trade Unions (WFTU) Executive Bureau to form the ICFTU.[51] Thereafter an intense struggle developed between the WFTU (dominated by the Soviet Union) and the ICFTU (increasingly dominated by the American AFL-CIO) to win the support of trade unions in colonized countries. The ICFTU, together with the British TUC, which had almost exclusive access to the colonized territories, became important influences on the Tanganyikan trade unions.

It will be recalled that Tom Mboya, a representative of the ICFTU, played an important role in the formation of TFL and at its very first conference the TFL resolved to affiliate with the ICFTU.[52] The ICFTU helped the TFL materially and financially, and its leaders often intervened in negotiations and strikes.[53] But more important than its material support was the ICFTU's ideological influence. This came thorough advice and training provided by the ICFTU to the Tanganyikan trade unionists. A number of important Tanganyikan trade unionists attended training courses organized by the ICFTU or its affiliates. For instance, Mpangala went on a three-month ICFTU-organized course to Mexico in 1956, while Kawawa, after becoming the general-secretary of TFL, attended a short course on unionism in England organized by the TUC. A number of other trade union activists attended courses in Israel organized by the Afro-Asian Institute, and appear to have been heavily influenced as their later statements on Israel showed. The most important externally organized training programme were at the ICFTU African Labour College in Kampala which was attended by a substantial number of trade unionists from Tanganyika. Tutors from the Kampala College also held classes within the country.[54]

In the early 1950s, the ICFTU policy towards colonial trade unions was heavily influenced by the British TUC, which took a conservative view of colonial affairs and believed that trade unions in the colonies should not be linked with anti-colonial struggles.[55] 'Every time a British delegate spoke at ICFTU Congresses, he included warnings against Pan-African 'dominance' and 'political unionism', and made his pathetic plea for an understanding of Britiain's colonial mission.'[56] In fact, the TUC was a member of the Colonial Labour Advisory Committee and worked through the colonial machinery. British trade unionists employed as trade union advisers in the colonial Labour Departments advised workers that a trade union was not an organization with political aims, and that its main object was to regulate relations between workers and their employers.[57] No wonder Kawawa cited the ICFTU policy as his authority when repudiating any orientation of the TFL towards party politics.[58]

Although in the later part of the 1950s, as independence approached, AFL–CIO influence in the ICFTU made it more sympathetic to the nationalist cause,[59] this did not go beyond sympathy. The emphasis still was on narrow economic goals rather than any broad political trade unionism.

The other body which exerted ideological influence was the Fabian Colonial Bureau. Virtually all leading trade unionists and even nationalist leaders had links with the bureau, from which they often sought advice and literature, as did Bhoke-Munanka[60] and F. E. Omedo[61] when they wanted to form trade unions in 1954. Similarly, Kawawa wrote to the bureau when he wanted to change the TAGSA into a trade union.[62] The bureau's response was inevitably to send literature produced by the TUC and to give names of local TUC and ICFTU contacts. It even recommended the colonial Labour Department, and its specific advice did not differ very much from that of the local labour officers. The following extract from a letter of the secretary of the bureau to F. E. Omedo who had sought her advice illustrates the point just made:

It is not possible for me at this distance to give you advice on exactly how to form a union, except that I can tell you that it is essential to form a union of workers in a same occupation beginning with those with whom you are working. The job of a union is to negotiate with the employers, and obviously that can best be done in your own jobs. It does not produce good results if you try to organize into one union a large number of people who may live in the same town but do different jobs for different employers . . . The government labour officers know all about formation of trade unions and they are there to help those who want to form them. Mr Williams [of the Labour Department] was particularly interested in this matter, and he was helping the dockworkers at the time I was there.[63]

Mr Omedo knew better. In his reply he said that the labour officers would only rejoice at the suppression of the trade union movement and that he had failed to get any assistance from the Labour Department at Arusha. 'All I can get is the most British liked nick name — "agitator".'[64]

Thus it can be seen that both the TUC and the Fabians had little of their own socialist, egalitarian or radical historical antecedents left in them when it came to colonial labour affairs.* At best they could be categorized as left of the colonial administration and at worst sheer liberals with an opportunist eye on maintaining

---

* The conservative influence of the British TUC on colonial trade unions is brought out in sharp relief when contrasted with the orientations of trade unions in the French colonies. France did not have one single trade union centre. And among the three major centres the most important one was the Communist Confédération Générale du Travail (CGT) to which were affiliated half of all African trade union members in 1955. Following the French experience, their African counterparts of the CGT tended to be overtly political, and this may account for the radical tradition of the working class in the former French colonies.[65]

neo-colonial influence. A reply from the bureau to a conservative settler–critic summed up their opportunism: 'Perhaps we are inclined to pay more attention than you do to the young African nationalist leaders, because although we realize that they sometimes make regrettably extremist statements, we are also well aware that the discredited leaders of today may be ministers tomorrow.'[66]

Another source of ideological influence that reinforced the so-called 'non-political' character of the trade unions was TANU and its variant of nationalist ideology.

The relation between TFL and TANU has to be analysed at three different levels: overlapping leadership, TANU support for TFL's economic struggle, and the political struggles of TFL itself in relation to TANU. The first two have to be clearly distinguished from the third, for it is this writer's contention that the existence of the first two during 1956–60 in itself does not imply or show the third.

There is enough evidence to show that at different periods leading trade union activists participated in TANU activities. ACEA had its office in the same building as TANU at New Street, and Mpangala not only recruited members for TANU but is said to have been a member of its Central Committee.[67] Kawawa also played an important role in TANU and became a member of its Central Committee in 1957.[68] But it is clear that he came to TANU via the trade unions. In his leadership survey of 1960, Friedland found that of the sixty-four full-time union leaders (all of whom were TANU members) only five had previously been employed as full-time TANU officials. Nine of the sixty-four held offices in TANU at the time of interview, and the total having held offices previously was eight.[69]

At various points, especially during strikes, TANU lent its support to the trade unions. In the DMT strike of March–April 1957 and the brewery strike of April–May 1958 TANU played a significant role in organizing and mobilizing the African population to boycott public transport and beer-drinking respectively.[70] And yet both these strikes were economic. This was true of all of the strikes organized by the trade unions between 1956 and 1960, although some of them did have political implications, like the Mazinde one discussed below.

TFL and the trade unions generally would do nothing to oppose TANU as such, but they were not affiliated to the party and took pains to keep their distance. For instance, E. N. N. Kanyama, the general secretary of TRAU, had to vacate his post because he signed the nomination papers of a non-TANU independent candidate, Dr G. M. Daya. The TFL spokesman said: 'The action of Mr Kanyama may show to people that the trade unions are opposed to TANU.'[71] While TFL passed resolutions supporting the general aims of TANU to fight for independence, it never organized a single strike to achieve a specific or general political goal or in support of TANU as such.[72] The separation between economics and politics was in practice so well operationalized that one interviewee was able to explain to Friedland that 'if a worker came to the union to complain of having been beaten by his employer, this was considered within the jurisdiction of the union; if he had been beaten by the police he was referred to TANU'.[73]

This distinction between anti-employer and anti-state activity as falling within the respective spheres of economics and politics squares with what Marx said on the issue:

every movement in which the working *class* comes out as a class against the ruling classes and tries to coerce them by pressure from without is a political movement. For instance, the attempt in a particular factory or even in a particular trade to force a shorter working day out of individual capitalists by strikes, etc., is a purely economic movement. On the other hand the movement to force through an eight-hour etc., *law*, is a *political* movement.[74]

Organization, mobilization and the use of the strike-weapon to force the state to adopt a particular law or to drop some specific legislation are undoubtedly important ingredients of *political* trade unionism. These elements were conspicuous by their absence in Tanzania's trade union movement. Neither the 1956 Trade Union Ordinance nor its amendment in 1959 called forth generalized trade union opposition. Although Kawawa, then member of the Legislative Council, opposed the 1959 Bill, the issue was never taken beyond the walls of the Legislative Council's buildings.[75]

Hence, what dominated the trade union movement was strictly the conservative bourgeois ideology of economism, doggedly resisted by the British trade unionism itself in the early part of this century.*

The trade union movement, in not pursuing any political goals itself but at the same time being sympathetic to TANU, did not evolve its own explicit anti-imperialist, anti-colonial or nationalist ideology. The nationalist ideological formation became exclusively the monopoly of TANU which was dominated by traders and urban salariats without any working-class component.[77] Once again, such an ideological orientation became a source of weakness in the post-independence era and enabled the smashing up of the trade union movement and its incorporation in the state-party without substantial opposition.

The strike wave

The common economic situation of being at one place and being the sellers of the same commodity — labour power — unites workers in combinations. This combination, Marx said, is not only to reduce competition among workers but to wage a 'general competition' with the capitalist[78] which necessitates the maintenance of permanent combinations, the trade unions.

In waging this general competition with the capitalist, the most potent weapon of the working class is strike, that is, the withdrawal of labour power. Strike is a weapon of the collective, for withdrawal of labour power by an individual worker is only a breach of contract which puts an end to *his* employment. 'Strike', as section 2 of the Trade Union Ordinance 1956, recognized, is 'the cessation of work by a *body of persons* employed, acting in combination, or a concerted refusal or a refusal under a common understanding of any number of persons employed to work for an employer . . . done as a means of compelling their employer . . . or to aid other employees in compelling their employer . . . to accept or not to accept terms or conditions of or affecting employment'. The definition is essentially that of an *economic* strike which forms the kernel of economic struggles of workers.

It is true that economic struggles in themselves do not automatically and necessarily lead to the development of a *political* movement ('that is to say, a movement of the *class*, with the object of enforcing its interests in a general form.'),[79] as the Tanzanian experience shows, yet it is the basis and absolutely necessary for the development of a political movement. 'Only struggle educates the exploited class. Only struggle discloses to it the magnitude of its own power, widens its horizon, enhances its abilities, clarifies

---

* In the case of *Amalgamated Society of Railway Servants* v. *Osborne* [1910] AC 87, where a member had challenged his union for devoting its funds to support the infant Labour Party, the House of Lords ruled that it was *ultra vires* and further that a trade union — by virtue of the definition set out in the 1871 and 1876 Acts — could not in fact have a valid political object. The judgement raised an outcry and forced through an amendment in the form of the Trade Union Act, 1913.[76]

its mind, forges its will.'[80] In this regard, the massive strike movement of the 1950s was a great experience in the annals of the history of the Tanzanian working class.

The strike wave of the 1950s went hand in hand with the development of trade unions and in turn helped to develop and organize them. During the interregnum and the pre-TFL period of small craft-unions (1951–5), not only were the strikes small in number but they were essentially spontaneous and sporadic, involving a few workers and lasting only a short time. Most of these strikes were in the plantation sector, often involving rates of remuneration and tasks without any articulate demands or capacity to organize and sustain them.[81]

The strikes of the post-TFL period were of a distinct character as Table 6.2 dramatically illustrates. The average number of strikes in the 1956–60 period was more than twice that in the 1951–5 period. The average number of workers involved was more than eight times that in the earlier period — some 59,457 workers, almost one-seventh of the total average African wage-labour during the period.[82]

Table 6.2   *The strike wave, 1950–64*

Period	Annual average of strikes	Annual average of workers involved	Annual average of man-days lost	Average no. of workers involved per strike	Average no. of man-days lost per strike	Average no. of man-days lost per worker involved
1950	50	7 444	11 006	149	220	1.48
1951–55 (5 years)	60	7 805	11 183	130	186	1.43
1956–60 (5 years)	146	59 457	483 521	407	3 312	8.13
1961–63 (3 years)	113	31 933	234 574	283	2 076	7.35
1964	24	3 582	5 855	149	244	1.63

Source: Jackson, D., *The Disappearance of Strikes in Tanzania: Incomes Policy and Industrial Democracy* (Working Paper series No. 117, University of Aston Management Centre, November 1978), p. 2.

The strikes involved a large number of workers, were well organized and could hold out for long periods. The annual average of working-days lost per worker involved in the strike was eight, the highest being seventeen in 1960. The 1959 Labour Report noted that the number of man-days lost to the industry during the year was equivalent to 0.3 per cent, whereas the comparable figure for the United Kingdom in respect of the first ten months of 1959 was 0.2 per cent.[83]

One distinctive feature of the strike wave of the 1950s, compared to the strikes of the 1940s, was that the dockworkers were pushed to the background from their vanguard role. Although the Dockworkers' and Stevedores' Union was re-formed in early 1955 and boasted a membership of 2,500 in 1960, the dockworkers did not participate in any substantial way in the strikes. One of the reasons for this was that docks were categorized as an 'essential service' within the meaning of the Trade Dispute (Arbitration and Settlement) Ordinance, 1950.[84] This meant that strikes in these services were made virtually illegal and compulsory arbitration was imposed statutorily to settle trade disputes. The result was that it was the workers in the domestic service, in building and construction, private commerce, manufacturing and transport who participated in the strike wave. In the late 1950s they were joined by the plantation workers, particularly from the sisal industry.

Table 6.3 Analysis of 72 strikes, 1957-62

Industry	No. of strikes	No. of workers involved	Man-days lost	Average no. of workers involved per strike	Average no. of man-days lost per strike	Average no. of man-days lost per worker involved	Rate of participation (%)	Duration of strike (%)				Nature of demands[a] (%)		Incidence of success (%)		
								Less than 1 day	1–5 days	6–10 days	Over 10 days	Economic	Democratic	Successful	Partially successful	Unsuccessful
Agriculture	37 (51%)	16,698	15,437	451	417	0.92	60.0[b]	2.7	70.3	21.6	5.4	69	31[c]	19.0	35.0	46.0
Transport	3 (4%)	[d]	7,810	—	2,603	—	—	0	33.3	0	66.7	67	33	0	100.0	0
Manufacturing	10 (14%)	668	2,006	69	201	3.00	77.0	10.0	60.0	20.0	10.0	50	50	44.0	22.0	33[e]
Building & Construction	17 (24%)	1,679	17,240	99	1,014	10.27	98.0	6.3	25.0	6.3	62.5	76	24	14.0	79.0	7.0
Services	3 (4%)	28	93	9	47[f]	3.32	100.0	0	50.0	50.0[g]	0	33	67	0	33.0	67.0
Mining	2 (3%)	950	5,500	475	2,750	5.79	90.0	0	50.0	50.0	0	0	100	50.0	50.0	50.0
Total	72 (100%)	20,023	48,086	278	668	2.40	63.0	4.0	56.0	19.0	21.0	65	35	19.0	46.0	35.0

Notes: [a] For explanation, see text p. 196. [b] For 35 strikes. [c] For 36 strikes. [d] Not available. [e] For 9 strikes. [f] For 14 strikes. [g] For 2 strikes.
Source: Ministry of Labour Files.[85]

Other important features of the strike wave may be gleaned from Table 6.3 where we have attempted to analyse a sample of seventy-two strikes (other than the major ones discussed individually below) that took place between 1957 and 1962. The information on these strikes is collated from Form LDG 164 (see Appendix E) which the labour officers were required to complete on each strike. This writer cannot say with certitude that the table represents a true picture of the strike wave to the last detail, especially when some sectors (for example, transport services and mining) are poorly represented. It cannot therefore be described as a *random* sample in the mathematical sense of the word. However, our study of the individual strikes and perusal of the Labour Department's Annual Reports of specific years do confirm that the table gives a fairly correct *general* picture of the strike wave and its important characteristics.

The first interesting comparison that the table throws up in sharp relief is between the agriculture and the manufacturing sectors. Being the biggest employer of labour, the agriculture sector led both in the number of strikes (51 per cent) as well as the total number of man-days lost (32 per cent). But its superiority ended there. The manufacturing workers showed a greater rate of participation (77 per cent), that is, a large number of workers were mobilized to participate in strikes. This enabled them to hold out much longer and also attain a greater rate of success. The average number of working days lost per worker involved in a strike in manufacturing was almost thrice that in agriculture. And 44 per cent of strikes in the manufacturing sector were able to achieve their demands compared to 19 per cent of the agriculture sector. True, the workers in manufacturing constituted only a small percentage[86] of the total labour force but they represent the most modern processes of production and it is this advanced nature of the character of the productive forces as well as their relatively concentrated form which accounted for the facility with which the manufacturing proletariat in particular, and the urban proletariat in general, was able to use the weapon of strike.

In addition, there are specific reasons pertaining to the Tanzanian situation. The employers in the sisal industry were well-organized in the TSGA and adopted a high-handed policy of not recognizing trade unions,[87] very frequently using police to intimidate workers. In eleven out of the seventy-two strikes in the sample, police intervention was recorded and half of it was in the plantations. This attitude in itself reflected the backward character of the plantation bourgeoisie.

The building and construction workers also showed great tenacity in their strikes. They were led by the militant Building and Construction Workers' Union which was disaffiliated from TFL for refusing to amalgamate with TGWU. The latter, too, claimed the membership of some building and construction workers and called fairly successful strikes.[88] Carpenters, masons and other artisans formed the leading force, and since they could not be easily replaced they held a strong bargaining card against recalcitrant employers.

Two of the strikes recorded in the table under services occurred in hotels. The hotel workers were united under the militant and powerful Domestic and Hotel Workers' Union. Smarting under humiliating oppression and intense exploitation* and at the same time having direct experience of the conspicuous consumption of their employers and other better-off sections, the hotel and domestic workers became very militant — once they were organized. In spite of that, they were not always successful. Their weakness lay in the fact that they were scattered over many small establishments, could be

---

* An investigation of wages and hours of work of hotels and domestic service in Dar es Salaam in 1958 showed that hours of work ranged from 70 to 105 per week while wages were as low as Shs. 40 per month.[89]

easily replaced, or the small hotel establishments often held out for long periods by making use of family labour.[90]

In mining, our sample includes one major strike that took place at the Geita Gold Mining Co. In 1962 some 900 workers walked off alleging that the mine captain, one G. Morlin, had used abusive language! They remained out for six full days until the captain and the shift boss were transferred to another section and a request was made to the government to appoint a board of enquiry.[91]

The other salient feature of the strike wave which needs to be mentioned is in respect of the character of demands. We have categorized these as *economic* and *democratic* demands. Economic demands relate strictly to the realm of exploitation, that is, the terms and conditions of the sale of labour power: for example, wages, hours of work, leave, bonus, job-security. Democratic demands, which fall in the realm of oppression, relate to: (i) recognition and rights of working-class collective organization* (trade unions), including a right to strike in sympathy with fellow workers, and (ii) such powers as are traditionally considered to be the exclusive jurisdiction of the employer/ management: for example, demands for removal of a particular supervisor, protest against inhuman and oppressive treatment, and other similar complaints against management.

As Table 6.3 shows, there was a preponderance of economic as opposed to democratic demands. Even then the volume of democratic demands — a little more than one-third of the total — is not insubstantial. Actually, most of these demands relate to the period immediately before and after independence. In 1962, for instance, there was a wave of strikes, particularly in agriculture, demanding removal of oppressive European, Asian — and in some cases even African — managerial and supervisory staff.[92] The content of democratic demands in agriculture, services (hotels) and mining on the one hand, and that in manufacturing and building on the other, shows a significant distinction. In agriculture and so on, it tended to be against some oppressive supervisory staff, while in all the five cases in manufacturing the strikes were in sympathy with fellow workers of the same enterprise who had been dismissed or suspended.[93] This was the case in two[94] of the four strikes involving democratic demands in the building and construction sector as well. This probably shows greater *class* solidarity in these sectors than in agriculture.

Some of the analyses that we have made above are further borne out and illustrated by five major strikes that we now propose to discuss. These strikes, which took place between 1956 and 1960, that is to say during the high noon of the trade union movement, mark distinct steps in its growth and development.

The 1956 (general?) strike

The TFL was hardly two months old when it faced its first major strike. In October 1956, during Princess Margaret's visit to Tanzania, three waiters of the Kinondoni hotel were dismissed allegedly for being intoxicated while on duty.[95] The remaining forty-five workers immediately came out on strike in protest against the dismissals. In the ensuing negotiations between the employer and the Domestic and Hotel Workers' Union the latter demanded unconditional reinstatement of the dismissed workers and threatened that if all the workers were not reinstated within three days, it would call a territory-wide strike of all hotel and domestic workers.

---

* This is really a hybrid category and could fall under both.

In the subsequent conciliation proceedings conducted by a labour officer, the management offered to reinstate the head waiter as an ordinary waiter and the other three to be reinstated after being given a written warning. The union refused and sought the intervention of the Labour Commissioner. Instead of intervening, the Labour Commissioner simply advised the union to take the case to a magistrate's court, to be dealt with as a complaint against dismissal for misconduct under section 32 of the Master and Native Servants Ordinance. This must have undoubtedly infuriated the union for obviously the problem had passed the stage of individual, contractual dispute and had become a trade dispute. The union ignored the commissioner's advice and called a strike of all hotel and domestic workers on 6 December 1956.

A labour report estimated that some 40 per cent of workers in private households and some 450 hotel employees came out[96] and that all major hotel and catering establishments in the town were affected. On the 7th the Commercial and Industrial Workers' Union and the Eastern Province Building and Construction Workers' Union called out all their members on a two-day sympathy strike. This was well supported and building work in the town was virtually brought to a stand-still. At the peak period it was estimated that some 10,000 workers, or 20 per cent of the total labour force, were on strike.[97]

On 8 December, the Dar es Salaam Dockworkers' and Stevedores' Union gave seven days' notice of their intention to strike in sympathy with the Domestic and Hotel Workers' Union unless the employers agreed to negotiate with the union. 'They were informed that the question of whether the employers of the domestic and hotel servants agreed to negotiate with the leaders of that union was not a matter which could be in dispute between the Dockworkers' Union and the employers of dockworkers and that such a strike being in an essential service would in these circumstances be illegal.'[98] Following that, the dockworkers' union extended its notice up to 29 December 1956 and then cancelled it on 17 December. On the 13 December, the Tanga Port Stevedores' and Dockworkers' Union also gave a notice of its intention to call a three-day sympathy strike from 4 to 6 January 1957 for the same reasons. It was given a similar warning by the Labour Department following which the union cancelled its strike call. Thus, by the use of the 'essential services' provisions of the Trade Disputes (Arbitration and Settlement) Ordinance, the Labour Department was successful in cutting off the militant dockworkers from their brethren. It is also important to note that the dockworkers' unions themselves were prepared to uphold the legalistic outlook of the Labour Department.

Within three days of the original strike domestic workers had begun to drift back to their work. But meanwhile another development took place. When the members of the Commercial and Industrial Union and the Building and Construction Workers' Union presented themselves for work after their two days' sympathy strikes, a number of them — especially in the motor trade — were not taken back. According to the union sources some 5,000 workers remained unemployed. This developed into a trial of strength between the union — now with the full intervention of the TFL — and the employers.

TFL was undoubtedly facing a new situation of which it had no experience. The situation was made worse by the unsympathetic Labour Department and stubborn employers. The immediate thing the TFL did was to send its general secretary, Kawawa, to the headquarters of the ICFTU in Brussels for discussions. From there he flew to London where he had discussions at the colonial office. Apparently, the colonial office assured Kawawa that it would send a telegram to the governor in Tanganyika to intervene, and further it was agreed that workers should report back for work within three days. When Kawawa returned to Dar es Salaam, the authorities concerned denied having any information of Kawawa–colonial office discussions, while the employers stuck to their guns so far as the question of reinstatement was concerned.[99]

A few days later Kawawa left to attend an ICFTU regional meeting in Accra. While he was away the TFL met in an emergency meeting and passed a resolution to call a nation-wide general strike. The resolution was approved by workers at a mass meeting on 20 January 1957 and on the 21st the TFL gave the Labour Commissioner a 21-days' notice of its intention to call a general strike. The general strike was to press for reinstatement of '5,000 victimized workers' and for resumption of negotiations on wage claims. In a subsequent statement to the press (29 January), the TFL gave reinstatement, wages and a protest against twenty-three sections of the Trade Union Ordinance, 1956, as being the purpose for calling the strike. Tandau gives reinstatement, establishment of a negotiating machinery and a demand for statutory minimum wage for Dar es Salaam as being the purpose of the strike. The fleeting reference to the protest against the Ordinance does not appear to have been pursued and certainly did not feature in subsequent discussions.

Characteristically, the state reacted by using legalistic argument against TFL's call for a general strike. In a meeting on 24 January 1957, the Labour Commissioner warned the leaders of TFL that the manner of calling the general strike was unconstitutional. The decision to strike could be made only by individual unions whose rules provided for specific procedure to be followed and that the federation could not call upon workers to go on a strike. It is important to mention at this stage that the trade unions themselves did not have much option as to whether or not to provide for a procedure on calling strikes and the content of such procedure. The schedule to the Trade Union Ordinance made it obligatory on trade unions to include in its rules provisions with regard to taking of decisions by secret ballot in respect of strikes and lock-outs.[100]

The trade union leadership responded rather submissively to such legal arguments and threats. In fact, when Kawawa came back from Accra accompanied by one W. Hood, head of the colonial section of the British TUC, and A. Hammerton, an ICFTU representative in the East African region, all three of them expressed astonishment at the call for a general strike. From the time of their arrival, the initiative seems to have passed into the hands of Messrs Hood and Hammerton. First, they saw top state officials and representatives of the employers' associations without the local trade union leaders. Later, at a meeting between the employers and the TFL, they advised the TFL to tone down its demands for total reinstatement and instead ask only for the reinstatement of long-service workers with more than five years' service, the number being only 142. Whereas the only thing the employers' representatives agreed to was to recommend to the affected employers to *consider* the proposal for reinstatement, the TFL on its part agreed to withdraw the call for a general strike unconditionally.

Thus ended the first major strike handled by the TFL, from whose point of view it was a fiasco. The strike itself did not achieve its demands; the employers came out of it triumphant while the TFL at the end of it was saddled with some thousands of workers without jobs. It had to raise contributions to assist them.* Although following this episode the government, for the first time, established a statutory minimum wage for Dar es Salaam, it was done without taking into account the TFL's recommendations.

---

* Tandau mentions that a sum of Shs. 20,000 offered by the ICFTU was taken back by Hammerton[101] without TFL being informed. Friedland, however, mentions that there was a cash contribution from the AFL–CIO to assist TFL to send back to their homes the strikers who were not reinstated.[102]

In sum, the strike probably taught the trade union leaders a lesson by negative example. Following it they seriously began the work of consolidation by appointing full-time leaders, pushing amalgamations, and even resolved to establish a strike fund within each union.[103] Another thing this strike must have taught them was the need of preparations and advanced organization rather than 'ad-hocism' which was so much the feature of the 1956 strike. Nevertheless, the strike set a legalistic–bureaucratic precedent in terms of handling of strikes, a precedent which put a firm stamp on the trade union movement.

The DMT strike

Towards the end of March 1957, the Transport and Allied Workers' Union called a strike against the Dar es Salaam Municipal Transport Company (DMT) to press a claim for an increase of 75 per cent in wages.[104] The strike was 100 per cent effective. An attempt by the management to use European and Asian blacklegs to keep the services going was frustrated by the union's call (which was backed by TANU) to all Africans to boycott the buses. Another important feature of the strike was that the union did not seek intervention of the Labour Department and doggedly refused to agree to the employer's stand that the workers should resume work pending negotiations. The workers held out for twenty-four days, at the end of which the union won a wage rise of 12½ per cent.

This strike was a success compared to the 1956 one and boosted the morale of workers and enhanced the tactical experience of the unions. The DMT strike was a dress rehearsal for the brewery strike in which all the salient features of this strike were played out on a larger and more intense scale.

The beer strike

In early 1958 the Commercial and Industrial Workers' Union demanded from East African Breweries a minimum wage of Shs. 150 per month for its members. The employer refused to meet the union, thus forcing the latter to call a two-day strike on 16 March 1958. All 270 workers came out, compelling the employer to recognize the union and negotiate with it. However, the negotiations fell through because the employer stuck to his offer of a minimum wage of Shs. 72–80 per month.[105] Therefore the workers again came out on strike on 16 April.

The employer responded with a two-pronged strategy of defence: to keep the production going by employing blackleg European, Asian and Somali labour, and expose the strikers to maximum harassment. Among the strikers many were staying in the company houses around the plant which the company had rented from the government. Now, with the assistance of the District Commissioner, they were evicted and rendered shelterless. Both these actions further united the workers and inevitably stimulated a semi-political response from the unions.

On 24 April 1958 TFL issued a statement calling upon all African residents of Dar es Salaam to boycott the drinking of European beer of any kind. The statement said that this step had been taken because Asians and Somalis were breaking the strike and had ignored the union's call to co-operate. The blacklegs were being paid Shs. 26 per day with free food and beer. 'Why then', the statement asked rhetorically, 'are they failing to pay the African workers only Shs. 5 per day without food and beer?'[106] Nyerere, the president of TANU, supported the boycott, which was very successful in Dar es Salaam and eventually brought the reluctant employer to the negotiating table.

The eviction of the strikers from the company housing infuriated the TFL, which called upon other citizens to assist. The evicted workers were given shelter by other Africans citizens and in revenge a number of African landlords evicted Asians, Arabs and their other non-African tenants. This move frightened the government which tried to make amends but by then the strikers had resolved to boycott completely the company housing. Even after the strike was over many strikers did not return to the company houses.

Beside the role of the District Commissioner in evicting the strikers, there were two other incidents where the state intervened in its characteristic role of the custodian of the employer-class.* A day after the strike Kawawa had approached two clerks who had not gone on strike and explained to them his reasons for the strike. For this he was charged with intimidation and fined Shs. 101. Nyerere, who was present at the trial, paid the fine. Later some 6–800 people demonstrated their support in which TANU was involved.[108] Another incident where the state intervened directly, under the usual 'law and order' disguise, was when the Chief Secretary himself warned the TFL to remove the strikers from near the plant where they used to maintain vigil during the strike, otherwise he would use the police to do so. The TFL obliged for fear of violence and left only a few pickets near the plant.

The strike lasted some six weeks while the boycott was effective for four weeks. The workers came out victorious in that they had attained their two major demands: increase in the minimum wage and recognition of their union. The minimum wage was fixed at Shs. 130 per month. The wages of drivers and clerks were raised to the maximum of Shs. 250 per month, while those of nightwatchmen were raised from Shs. 110 to Shs. 190 per month. The main plank which accounted for the union's success was the use of boycott which was effective in mobilizing the sympathizers not directly involved in the strike. The involvement of TANU on the one hand and the state on other, was a clear sign of the strike's *political* implications, although the demands of the strikes were strictly economic.

The Mazinde strike

The Mazinde strike came at the climax of intense struggle between the plantation workers' union and the sisal employers. With the formation of four provincial unions of plantation workers during 1957 and their amalgamation to form one union in early 1959,[109] the hitherto unorganized workers in the sisal industry entered the trade union stage with a big bang. The sisal employers through their association, the TSGA, refused to recognize the unions and grant them access to their plantations. Rather, it continued insisting on the use of employer-dominated joint consultation machinery. This led to a wave of strikes in the sisal industry during 1957 and 1958, when the sisal industry accounted for 46 per cent of the total disputes, 75 per cent of total number of workers involved and 77 per cent of man-days lost.[110]

The employers' response was to sit out the strikes so as to exhaust the strikers until they returned to work of their own volition.[111] The employers' other action was to constantly threaten the use of police — they used police mobile force to break up workers' meetings.[112] The following account of an incident at the Mjesani estate where a strike took place at the end of October 1958 describes a typical situation:

---

* In a later legislative debate Kawawa said that the government had interfered in the breweries strike by advising the employer against accepting the union wage demand of Shs.150 per month because that would have repercussions on the government wage structure.[107]

On Tuesday, the manager of the estate wanted to disperse the strikers who had gathered at the football field, but was unable to do this. He then called the police, who came immediately. One had a pistol, nine had guns, and the others had shields. The police began their aggression by shooting at our brothers who ran away, and many were hurt. Some women dropped their children, and this caused further deaths. The results of such misunderstandings was due to the fact that the employers do not respect the union at all.[113]

Most of these strikes lasted for relatively short periods, but at Mazinde, where the strike began on 25 November 1958, it lasted for sixty-eight days and involved over 2,500 workers. The estate was managed by David Lead who was also its employer. He was a supporter of the United Tanganyika Party (UTP), a settler-dominated political party created to oppose TANU.[114] He also played a prominent part in popularizing the consultative machinery but came up against stiff opposition from the trade union when he tried to form an estates committee on his estate.[115] Nevertheless, he formed one by by-passing a prominent trade unionist and appointing his own protégé to the committee. This is what led to the stoppage of work on his estate. Lead responded with high-handed tactics, refusing to talk to the trade union officials, and eventually (on 8 December) he dismissed eight members of the union's branch committee.[116] He further announced that from 8 December, if there was no complete return to work, he would terminate and repatriate a hundred workers a day. When he repatriated the first hundred, the TFL intervened. The rest of the 3,000 workers were all ready to go. An official strike and boycott of Mazinde estate was declared. The union hired buses and began transporting workers to TFL and TANU branches. Meanwhile Nyerere appealed to Tanga residents to give the striking workers a shelter.

There were 'rumours' that the Tanganyika Sisal and Plantations Workers' Union would approach the Tanga Port Stevedores' and Dockworkers' Union to boycott imports and exports from the Mazinde Sisal Estate.[117] Apparently this was never done. Although TANU supported the strike, unlike the DMT and beer strikes, an effective boycott was never mounted. Surprisingly, while the TFL was announcing a three-year boycott of the Mazinde Estate, for reasons that this writer could not discover, Nyerere 'pointed out that the conflict was limited to the Mazinde estate and was not a battle between all plantation workers and all employers'.[118]

Removal of the strikers from the estate in the first place (thus leaving only 'loyalists' behind) and the refusal to enlarge the conflict beyond Mazinde considerably weakened the union's bargaining position. It was reduced to requesting negotiations and conciliation with the employer at the conference table, and there too its tactics seem to have been inconsistent and confused.[119] Eventually, the dispute was settled through conciliation between the union and the employer where the TSGA representatives played an important role. Later developments were tied up with the whole question of the consultative machinery in the sisal industry and will be discussed below. Suffice it to mention that soon after the Mazinde confrontation the government appointed a commissioner to look into the state of industrial relations in the sisal industry. His recommendation for greater participation of the union on the consultative machinery to some degree helped to defuse the Mazinde conflict as well.

The 82-day railway strike

The railway strike followed on the heels of a postal strike which had begun on 24 December 1959. Involving some 1,250 workers, it was against one of the agencies of the East African High Commission. Although some 90 per cent of the African employees came out and the strike lasted a very long while, the administration was able to keep the postal services going. Political inaccessibility of the High Commission and its lack of sensitivity to local pressure further exacerbated the union's problems — problems which were to loom large in the railway strike as well.[120]

The East African Railways and Harbours Administration was the largest service of the East African High Commission, an inter-territorial body of the three British colonies — Kenya, Uganda and Tanganyika. The administration was centrally organized and controlled from its headquarters in Nairobi, thus leaving very little powers to the regional representatives in the constituent countries.

Around 1957, following the policy of the Labour Department, the railway administration had instituted organs of joint consultation, the highest body of which was the All-Line Joint Staff Advisory Council (JSAC). JSAC had employers' and employees' representation with the general manager of the administration as chairman. The employees' representation was divided along racial lines with three Africans, three Europeans and three Asians — one in each category from Kenya, Uganda and Tanganyika. Thus Africans, who constituted the large majority of the labour force, were ridiculously under-represented. JSAC, to all intents and purposes, was simply an advisory staff organization, rather than a negotiating body.

The Tanganyika Railway African Union (TRAU) which had originally been a staff association and which was registered as a trade union in 1955, underwent an important change in early 1959. Its conservative general secretary, E. N. N. Kanyama, was sacked after he supported a non-TANU Asian candidate for the Legislative Council election in March 1959 (see above p. 191) In his place was elected a young railway clerk from Mwanza, C. S. K. Tumbo. Tumbo had been with the railways for only a year after completing his course at the Nairobi Railway Training School.[121]

Tumbo was a militant trade unionist with a great capacity for organization and brilliant analytical insights. By the end of that year TRAU's membership had more than doubled and Tumbo had appointed full-time district and regional secretaries, thus putting the union on a new organizational basis. The railway administration would not recognize these secretaries on the ground that they were not elected. Tumbo argued that it was an internal union matter over which the employer had no say.

Only four months after taking office, Tumbo withdrew TRAU from JSAC, giving three reasons: '(1) Europeans and Asians had a majority in the council, and they supported management; (2) the machinery was purely advisory; (3) the chairman of the council should not be the general manager of the railways but some independent person.'[122]

Besides the accumulated grievances to which the employer had shown no positive response, events towards the end of the year made a major strike almost inevitable. In November 1959, major railway strikes occurred in Kenya and Uganda, and by mid-December the negotiations between the management and TRAU had broken down beyond repair. The ultimate result was that Tumbo announced the strike of all railway workers to begin on 9 February 1960.

The union put forward the following major demands:

(1) That the minimum wage should be raised to Shs. 7.75 per day, and that changes be made in the wages of grade C workers;
(2) That there should not be a big difference between the highest and the lowest wages in grade C;
(3) That a commission of inquiry be appointed to look into the following:
    (i)   giving of responsible jobs and posts to Africans;
    (ii) overtime payment rates;
    (iii) shorter working hours;

    (iv) housing for workers;
    (v)   disciplinary procedure; and
    (vi) a board for promotion.[123]

Over 90 per cent of the African workers (some 10,100 people), responded.[124] The non-striking African workers were non-Tanganyikans. However, except for the bus services, the essential railway services continued functioning through the use of European and Asian blacklegs. This undoubtedly added to the stubbornness and insensitivity of the employer.

Negotiations between Tumbo and the administration very quickly ran into an impasse. The latter insisted that no discussion of substantive issues could take place under the pressure of the strike, while Tumbo would not budge from the position that work would not resume unless the management made some moves to settle the major issues. Eventually, the dispute was reported to the Labour Commissioner who appointed his deputy as a conciliator under the provisions of the Trade Disputes (Arbitration and Settlement) Ordinance. But, according to Friedland, the conciliation proceedings which continued throughout the period of the strike were 'fraudulent' from the beginning. The Labour Department showed neither any seriousness nor impartiality in the conciliation process.

The conciliation process was long, involved, and unproductive. The conciliator permitted a situation to exist in which the two parties were unequally matched, for Tumbo was empowered to make commitments on behalf of his union but the representatives of the railway administration had to consult with and await replies from Nairobi. Any agreements tentatively reached in Dar es Salaam were generally overturned in Nairobi.[125]

With the approach of self-government, the political situation was changing very fast. The TFL became increasingly concerned and asked for the intervention of Tanganyika's governor. Meanwhile, the representatives of the ICFTU and the International Transport Workers' Federation arrived in the country. Their approaches to the railway administration in Nairobi were cold-shouldered, so they concentrated on pressurizing the Tanganyikan government. Given the political situation, the latter in turn put pressure on the local representatives of the railway administration. Agreement was finally reached on 29 April after eighty-two days of striking. It was agreed that a commission of inquiry be appointed to report within six months on the state of industrial relations in the railways, that the strikers and non-strikers should not be victimized, and that the wages of grade C be increased, those at the bottom scale getting a Shs. 10 rise and those at the top a Shs. 4 rise per month.

Thus ended the longest and the last strike of the colonial period. It left some of the most militant and vocal trade unionists totally opposed to the supra-national East African High Commission which was to become one of the two serious bones of contention in the post-independence struggle between the state and the trade union movement. The other issue — Africanization — too may have been influenced by the concrete experience of the trade unions in strikes. The willingness with which the Asian and European employees offered themselves as blacklegs made the African union leadership extremely bitter. This is reflected in the following letter written by the assistant general secretary of TRAU in reply to an invitation from the Railway Asian Union to attend the latter's conference. Accusing the Asian union of having acted to the detriment of African workers during their recent strike, the letter said:

It would be useless for us to come together with you and pretend that we are true brothers when we are not.
True brotherhood among the workers could only come by actions not by mere words, particularly

when one was in difficulties and needed help. The Asian Union had completely lost a very good chance of winning the confidence of the African workers. *

The feelings of my members towards your union are so high, that there is no hope of the parties coming into good terms.[126]

Both the High Commission and the Africanization issues pulled the trade union movement into a *political* struggle which we discuss in the next chapter.

Results

The most important result of the strike wave was that for the first time in the history of wage-labour in Tanzania wages and other conditions of work were fixed through collective bargaining rather than unilaterally by the employers. Whereas in 1956 only 4 per cent of the labour force was covered by collective agreements, in 1961 it was 60 per cent.[127] During the period, both the nominal and real wages of workers rose and probably for the first time wages began to bear any relation to the value of labour-power. Table 6.4 shows the movement of average individual cash earnings of African workers. The rapid rise in real wages after 1958 coincides with a meteoric increase in the percentage of labour force covered by collective agreements concluded between the employers and the trade unions. The increase in the real wage of 56 per cent between 1958 and 1961 followed closely on the heels of an increase of 52 per cent of the labour force covered by collective agreements during the same period.

Table 6.4 *Average individual cash earnings (monthly) (nominal and real) of African workers[a], 1953–63*

Year	Nominal (average) wage (Shs.)	Real (average) wage (Shs.)	% change
1953	45	37	
1954	48	41	10.8
1955	53	47	14.6
1956	57	51	8.5
1957	60	51	—
1958	62	50	–2.0
1959	70	58	16.0
1960	80	67	15.5
1961	96	78	16.4
1962	122	101	29.5
1963	165	138	37.6

Note: [a] Excludes domestic servants.
Source: Calculated from the Annual Reports of the Labour Department.

It was also trade union pressure which brought about the establishment of a statutory minimum wage for Dar es Salaam in 1957. Immediately after independence, a territorial minimum wage was established and the workers gained a number of other benefits. A rise in wages effectively contributed towards the establishment of a permanent labour force, thus ending the notorious migrant system which Mkello had once described as akin to slavery,[128] and which his plantation union had fought hard to abolish.[129]

On the eve of independence the country had a strong trade union movement which furthermore had scored substantial victories so far as the economic well-being of its membership was concerned. This came about through struggle with the employers backed by the state. In the ensuing section we proceed to discuss the response of the employers and the role of the state.

State and employer versus trade unions

The growth and development of the trade union movement described in the preceding section were replete with attacks and counter-attacks from the employer-class, the capitalists. Even more decisive was the role of the collective capitalist — the state — in controlling the movement, guiding it along acceptable channels and giving it a particular character. The state did this in two main ways: by encouraging a parallel machinery of joint consultation, and by enacting legislation to control the trade unions.

Joint consultation

Just a year before the final smashing of the dockworkers' union in 1950, the state, through its Labour Department, had begun to toy with the possibility of a substitute for collective bargaining in the form of works councils.[130] Two years later, works councils were given legislative recognition. Part V of the Regulation of Wages and Terms of Employment Ordinance, 1951,[131] defined 'staff committees' and empowered the Labour Commissioner and labour offices to give advice and assistance for the creation and establishment of these committees in any private or public undertaking (s. 25). Section 24 defined a staff committee as 'a body of persons representative of both employer and the employees, set up by an employer in any under-taking after consultation with the employees . . . ' The objects of staff committees were:

(a) giving the employees a wider interest in, and a greater responsibility for the conditions under which their duties are performed;
(b) providing a recognized and direct channel of communication between the employees and the employer on all matters affecting their joint or several interests; and
(c) promoting throughout the undertaking a spirit of co-operation in securing the efficiency of the undertaking and the contentment of the staff engaged therein.

A circular letter to all government departments from the Member for Social Services further elaborated on these provisions.[132] Notes on works committees prepared by the Labour Department gave a model constitution in which the functions of committees were defined as 'purely advisory and consultative'. It also provided for representation from all segments of workers including junior clerical staff, headmen and labourers.

The precursor of joint consultation is to be found in the Whitley Councils of Britain, established during the First World War when capital and labour were temporarily united by a common national purpose. One major difference between the Whitley Councils and joint staff committees of Tanzania was that the former were auxiliary to collective bargaining, while the latter were conceived as a substitute for collective barganining.[133] As a matter of fact, both the Labour Department and the employers saw joint consultation as a way of forestalling collective bargaining, which is based on opposed interests between capital and labour. The philosophy underlying joint consultation was put succinctly by Sir Barclay Nihill, the first independent chairman of the Central Joint Council in the sisal industry. Giving the principles behind the Whitley Committees, he said he would start off by saying what those principles were not:

They were the opposite of the gospel of Karl Marx. That was to say they were the exact opposite of what now formed the basis of communist philosophy. Why was that? Because first of all they rejected the idea of the inevitability of a class war between capital and labour. They insisted that both sides in industry had one overwhelming common interest. That was the successful conduct of that industry so that all who shared in that industry could earn fair return for what they had put into it. It followed from that that no industry could succeed in the long run without harmonious relations between the employer and the employed, and that each side was necessary to the other.

The worker by the skill of his hands produced the product of the industry. The employer, or the management, by the skill of his brains had to find the capital for plant and machinery and a market for the produce. It was the recognition of those truths that caused the Whitley reports to recommend the formation of joint industrial councils for every properly organized industry so that duly elected representatives of both management and workers could meet and discuss their problems together.[134]

This philosophy is eminently the philosophy of capital. Little wonder joint consultative councils were employer's organs to keep out working-class organizations and avoid confrontation. In practice the councils were inevitably controlled by the employers.[135] When the trade unions began to knock on the doors, employers used joint consultation either not to recognize the unions or simply to give them equal representation with other employee members of the councils, thereby denying the unions the monopoly of being the workers' representative.[136] Unions therefore became the sworn enemies of joint consultation, the most acute expression of which antagonism was felt in the sisal industry, to be discussed later.

State control of trade unions

In his circular cited above, the Member for Social Services made a lukewarm reference to trade unions saying that labour officers may assist trade unions with advice 'although such assistance should not go to the length of the active organization of associations'. And as we saw above, the state's policy was to channel trade unionism into the formation of small craft unions functioning on a limited scale in localized areas. However, once the development of trade unions began it had to come up with a comprehensive piece of legislation to control them. Thus was enacted the Trade Union Ordinance, 1956, hardly a year after the formation of TFL.

The 1956 Ordinance repealed the 1932 Ordinance which was felt to be inadequate and too simple to 'ensure that . . . trade unions continue to develop and establish themselves on a sound basis'. It was believed that the Ordinance would also rectify the deteriorating industrial relations.[137]

The Ordinance retained the principle of compulsory registration (s. 7), this being the characteristic weapon in the armoury of the colonial state to control and keep track of the trade unions. Non-registration rendered a trade union illegal and its officers liable of being convicted of a criminal offence (s. 7(3)). Two conditions had to be satisfied before a combination could be considered an employees' trade union under the Ordinance: (1) it had to have at least twenty members and (2) its principal purpose had to be to regulate relations between employees and employers or employees and employees (s. 2).

A trade union had to comply with all the provisions of the Ordinance, for non-compliance could be one of the grounds for the registrar to refuse to register a trade union or, if it was registered, to cancel its registration (ss. 13(1)(a) and 14(1)(e)). Another ground for refusing registration was if the applicant trade union 'is an organization consisting of persons engaged in, or working at, more than one trade or calling, and that its constitution does not contain suitable provisions for the protection and promotion of their respective trade interests . . . ' This provision was probably to empower the registrar to refuse to register industrial or general trade unions as opposed to craft unions.

Three areas where the registrar exercised close control and supervision over unions were with respect to the funds, appointment of officers and the rules of a union.

First, the funds of a union could be spent only for objects specified in section 40 of the Ordinance. These objects included administrative expenses, expenses relating to the conduct of trade disputes and other activities (cultural, educational, medical and so on) of direct benefit to its members. Notable omission from this list of objects was spending of funds for any political purpose. This was one way by which the colonial state sought to keep the trade unions separate from politics, which in this context would be nationalist politics. Secondly, the officers of a union were required to keep books (s. 42) and its treasurer or any other officer was required to render accounts every year or at any other time when called upon by the registrar to do so (ss. 43(1) and 44(1)). The amount had to be audited by a person approved by the registrar (s. 43(3)). The registrar had further powers of inspecting a union's books and membership and calling for detailed accounts for any period at any time (ss. 46 and 47). Thus the life-line of a trade union - finance - was closely supervised by the state, and all financial transactions had to be conducted in full view of government officials.

As regards officers, section 25(2) provided that all officers except one of a union had to be engaged in or employed in an industry or occupation with which the union was directly concerned.[138] The registrar was given further powers to disqualify any person from the office of secretary or treasurer if he was of the opinion that such a person had not attained a standard of literacy sufficiently high to perform his duties. This imposed a definite educational qualification for these posts and, coupled with the various requirements of the ordinance, all of which called for certain legalistic and bureaucratic orientation (keeping of records, making returns and so on), it further reinforced the elitist leadership in the unions.

The rules of a union, a copy of which had to be registered with the registrar, had to provide for matters specified in the schedule. Among other things, the rules had to provide for taking of decisions by secret ballot in respect of (i) election of officers; (ii) amendment of rules; (iii) strikes or lock-outs; (iv) federation or affiliation; and (v) amalgamation or dissolution (s. 33 and schedule, rule 5). The Labour Department drafted a model constitution which many trade unions adopted for lack of their own expertise to satisfy all the requirement of the Ordinance. The necessity to master the stringent requirement of the Ordinance was probably also responsible for making many trade unionists attend courses organized by the Labour Department. In 1956 alone four short courses were organized, attended by a total of some fifty-five trade unionists.[139] This was another channel of influence for the department to propagate its policy. But it does not appear to have been very effective. Kawawa was to say later that while they were taught 'how to keep accounts and how to compromise, we were never taught the essentials of trade unionism — how to bargain with the employer, how to organize'.[140]

Another area where the state attempted to control trade unions was in restricting the use of its main weapon — strike. The dispute-settlement machinery under the Trade Disputes (Arbitration and Settlement) Ordinance provided a standing statutory machinery for conciliation. The assumption behind such machinery was, once again, neutrality of the state. In practice, more often than not, state officials leaned on the side of the employer (see the railway strike above). Trade unions therefore preferred strike action rather than conciliation. But the Ordinance made strikes in 'essential services' illegal and provided for compulsory arbitration. When the Ordinance was first passed, it contained ten essential services including public transport provided by the East African Railways and Harbours Administration and Telecommunications, Posts and Telegraphs (schedule under section 2). In December 1956, with the beginning of trade union development, the governor added five more services to the schedule.[141] It was not until 1958 that the list was reduced to seven because of trade union pressure.[142] In addition to making strikes illegal, the 'essential services' provisions had the effect of dividing workers. For the 'essential services' could be in the private or public sector and within the same undertaking some workers could fall within essential services. Thus, for example, if workers in a sisal estate went on strike, those providing electricity could not because theirs was an 'essential service'. Such legislation therefore often aided individual employers to apply the time-honoured tactic of divide and rule. Besides, the coercive machinery of the state in the form of penal sanctions was always at hand. Those participating in illegal strikes were subject to conviction. The provisions on picketing defined 'intimidation' and 'injury' so widely that this legitimate activity was very risky to undertake.[143] Furthermore, while section 49(a) made peaceful picketing lawful, paragraph (b) of the same section considerably reduced its scope. Picketing was not lawful if the pickets attended at or near the place of work 'in such numbers or otherwise in such manner as to be likely to intimidate any person in that place . . . or to lead to a breach of the peace'. As we saw in the case of the beer strike, Kawawa's approach to the blacklegs was sufficient to convict him of 'intimidation', while the sitting of the strikers a few yards from the plant was considered by the authorities as likely to lead to a breach of the peace.[144] The legal armoury of the colonial state was definitely not lacking in putting down the unions and their struggle. If it could not always make use of this weapon it was because of the *social* struggle, strength and resistance of the working class.

Non-recognition

The employers' immediate reaction to the development of trade unions was simply not to recognize them. They were used to a patronizing attitude towards their employees and could not now sit at the same table with their employees' representatives. The Acting Senior Labour Officer of Tanga, for example, stated in his monthly report of June 1957:

Mr Hawkins — Industrial Relations Officer for the Shell Company — visited the Ag. Senior Labour Officer on the 19th June. He stated that his company's policy in all three Territories would be one of non-recognition of any trade union as a negotiating body until such time as the trade unions achieved more responsible leadership. I gained the impression that some reliance is placed upon the belief that Government would take action in the event of a serious disruption of the essential services.*[145]

In some cases the employers endeavoured to integrate the trade unions within the structure of joint consultation. The constitution of the Tanga Town Council's Joint Staff Consultative Committee provided that if and when a trade union containing the council's employees was recognized by the council the trade union would have a right to nominate two persons to the committee as against two nominated by the council. In this particular case therefore the staff committee would contain six employees elected from various segments of the workers together with two nominated by the union.[146] The effect of such a tactic was to place the union on a par with elected employees and reduce direct negotiation and confrontation between the employers and the union. The unions had to resort to strike action and boycott of staff committees to force recognition, as they did in the case of Tanga Town Council in early 1959 when some 330 workers struck for two weeks.[147]

Besides the frequent use of mobile police, particularly in the plantations, to intimidate strikers, employers also resorted to the use of blackleg labour. And here they cunningly made use of the European and Asian staff, thus dividing employees on

---

* Supply and distribution of oil and petrol was scheduled as an 'essential service' (s. 2).

nationality lines. The case of the Metal Box Co. illustrates the point. Some 170 African workers of the company struck on 18 October 1956 to force recognition of their union and also demanding the reinstatement of a leading union activist who was dismissed by the employer for leaving his machine unattended when, as a union representative, he had gone to see the manager. The strike lasted for some eleven days but production was maintained by temporary Asian employees who were being paid Shs. 20 per day as opposed to the Shs. 3 pay of the African workers![148]

Occasionally, the Labour Department itself was accused by the unions for supplying blackleg labour under various pretexts. 'With very much regret', protested the Regional Secretary of Tanganyika Transport & Allied Workers Union, Tanga branch, to the Senior Labour Officer, 'it has come to the knowledge of this union that you are finding employment for some people — Drivers, Mechanics, Turn-boys etc., in place of those who are at the present under the strike.' The labour officer cynically replied that it was his department's duty to put those seeking employment in touch with potential employers. 'Your complaint would, therefore, appear to be that employers among the transport industry are employing drivers, mechanics and turnboys etc., as their normal staff are on strike. If this is so, you should convey your protests to the employers concerned and not to this office.'[149]

In spite of the various delaying tactics, eventually employers had to come to terms with trade unions and negotiate with them. They, too, realized that they had to put up a common front. Hence the development of trade unions saw a parallel growth in the formation of employers' associations.

Employers' organizations

Until the development of trade unions, whatever employers' associations that existed were semi-monopoly combinations for consultation and advice to their members rather than negotiating bodies for collective bargaining with labour. It was only with the development of trade unions that an objective need arose for the employers to present a united front.[150] Even then the employers were reluctant to form their trade unions as such and this was particularly true of larger employers in agriculture. Table 6.5 gives a summary of the development of employers' associations which were registered as trade unions under the Trade Union Ordinances.

In 1952 there was not a single employers' trade union. There were a number of employers' associations including the powerful TSGA. But these were not negotiating bodies. In the year of the formation of the TFL was also formed the Dar es Salaam Employers' Association with a membership of thirty-four.[151] As the trade union pressure mounted the tendency was to form localized or geographical associations in big towns or territorial associations in such economic sectors as commerce, services and transport. Usually it was the smaller employers in urban areas who felt the need to come together once they were pressed by strike action.[152] In this, employers were assisted and encouraged by the Labour Department officials.[153]

The agricultural employers were most sluggish in coming to terms with the trade unions. A committee was formed in 1958 by the Northern Province Convention of Associations 'to consider and report on how employers can be brought together to protect their economic and political interests in view of the obvious threat to these interests from trade unions and political associations'.[154] The committee was reluctant to recommend the formation of an employers' trade union because, among other things, of the 'unpleasant fact that an employers' organization, its function being to *negotiate* agreement, would have to register as a trade union'.[155] The committee therefore

Table 6.5 *Employers' associations registered as trade unions, 1952–63*

| Year | Sectoral distribution | | | | | Area of operation | | Total no. of associations | Total membership | Average membership per association |
	Agriculture	Industry	Transport	Commerce & services	Mixed	Localized	Territorial			
1952	–	–	–	–	–	–	–	–	–	–
1955	–	–	–	1	1	1	–	1	34	34
1958	–	2	1	1	1	4	–	4	88	22
1960	3	3	2	2	5	9	5	14	593	42
1963	2	3	1	4	4	8	6	14	416	30

Source: Annual Reports of Labour Department.

recommended a consultative organization to advise local associations. It was not until 1959 that the first two associations of agricultural employers — the Southern Highlands Agricultural Employers' Federation and the Tobacco Employers' Association — were registered as trade unions. And only in 1960 was a territory-wide association of agricultural employers formed and registered with a membership of 176.[156]

Our discussion so far of the various ways in which the state and the employer responded to the development of trade unionism is illustrated in a most concentrated form in the case of sisal industry. To this we now turn our attention.

Industrial relations in the sisal industry: a case study

Until the middle of 1950s, the sisal growers enjoyed a heaven so far as industrial relations were concerned. The terms 'negotiations' and 'collective bargaining' did not exist in their vocabulary. The powerful TSGA unilaterally set the wages and terms and conditions of employment while sporadic and spontaneous strikes of workers were put down with the ever-forthcoming assistance of labour officers and frequently the police. The furthest that the estates had gone was to institute councils of *wazee* on their estates along tribal lines to help resolve disputes over 'women, petty thefts, brawls, etc.' which 'were dealt with by the headmen or elders, sometimes being referred for a decision to the manager of the estate or the local African Authority'.[157] The councils were picked and chosen by the management, met only irregularly and had no more than advisory functions. With the development of trade unionism they collapsed like a pack of cards.[158]

The joint consultation model evolved by the Labour Department did not make any dent on the sisal industry until towards the end of 1957 under the pressure of the government, which was quick to see the threatening clouds of trade unionism gathering on the horizon. The policy of the state in this respect was put in a memorandum by the Member for Social Services to the Provincial Commissioners' conference held in January 1957. The memorandum summarizes the analysis of trade unionism by the state and its strategy for confrontation with such clarity that it bears quotation at length.

The recent rapid growth of Trade Union development in Tanganyika has so far confined itself largely to urban industrial conditions. But there are indications of a movement to recruit support for a general agricultural workers' union, covering paid workers on estates and farms generally, and of a separate movement among workers on sisal estates in particular.
2. *When applications arise, the Labour Commissioner would enforce the limitation of individual union organization to specific industries or occupation groups under the provisions of the Trade Union Ordinance 1956, and also initially to specific areas. e.g. the Eastern Province Sisal Workers' Union.* But, in one form or another, this development is likely to be a fairly imminent contigency. It is, of course, true that the transient nature of a sisal labour force may militate against this to some extent. But labour forces tend to become gradually more permanent, the skilled workers in particular. Apart from this, there seems little reason to expect that embryo trade unions on estates and farms will escape the teething troubles experienced by pioneer trade unionism in urban areas. The risk of interruption of production is thus not inconsiderable.
3. Against this background it is conspicuously noticeable that the sisal industry, unlike other industries such as mining, has made no move in the direction of forming works committees or any other form of consultative machinery as it was advised to do by MSS Circular No. 1 of 1953, precis of which were distributed on a wide basis to all substantial private, industrial and commercial employers of labour throughout the Territory. Many large sisal estates have their 'Camp committees' primarily for the settlement of domestic matters but these bodies exist by favour and not by acknowledged right.

4. It is thought that the eventual development of trade unions covering sisal workers is inevitable and probably not far distant, and that *the prior introduction, on the initiative of employers, of works committees or some other form of consultative machinery*, could do much to ensure that such development took place with the minimum of misunderstanding and disruption of productive effort.[159] (My emphasis).

The memorandum in clearer terms than any analysis, shows: (1) the longer time-horizon, that is, the farsightedness that the state has compared to the class or sections of the class it serves; (2) how the state, in enforcing particular policies, in this case enforcing geographical unions, assists particular interests of the capitalist class; and (3) if one reads between the lines, the state's policy to weaken and (it hopes) to co-opt the unions in the joint consultative machinery. Thus the ensuing confrontation between the union and the sisal employers - which lasted at least five years — deeply involved the state on the side of the employers, although it may seem to have been a neutral referee.

As a matter of fact, the above-quoted memorandum went on to ask the Provincial Commissioners if the government should not exercise pressure on the sisal industry to take appropriate steps. The Provincial Commissioners recommended in the affirmative, and in their July conference of the same year they went further and argued that it was not enough to pressurize individual estates to institute joint consultation, but the 'controlling interests in the sisal industry' should be persuaded to accept the need for joint consultation.[160] It was probably as a result of such pressure that C. W. Guillebaud, who had been invited by the TSGA to do an economic survey of the sisal industry, was asked to make recommendations on the form of joint consultation.[161] Guillebaud's recommendations were in principle accepted by the TSGA in October 1957 and the latter set to institute joint consultation.

Meanwhile a parallel development was taking place on the side of labour. Mpangala of the TFL went round the country in early 1957 to encourage the formation of a plantation union.[162] As a result two provincial unions — Eastern Province Agricultural Workers' Union and Tanga Province Plantation Workers' Union — were registered in June and August 1957 respectively.[163] The Northern Province Plantation Workers' Union and the Southern Province Plantation Workers' Union were registered in March and April 1958 respectively.[164] Under the aegis of the TFL and with the assistance of Tom Bavin of the Plantation Workers' International Federation, a territorial union of the plantation workers (National Union of Plantation Workers) was formed, although it was not registered until several months later.[165]

Immediately the union faced two major problems, those of recognition and access to the estates, both of which the employers persistently denied. The unions therefore resorted to strike action, some fifteen occurring in the first quarter of 1958 alone.[166] This forced the TSGA to begin discussions with the TFL and the plantation union on the issue. The TSGA set several conditions for recognizing the union. Initially, the union rejected these conditions as being interference in their internal affairs. Eventually, however, after pressure* being brought on its officers, the following agreement was reached. The union agreed: (1) to change its name to Tanganyika Sisal and Plantation Workers' Union; (2) to have its headquarters in Tanga; (3) that its officials appointed to negotiate with sisal employers would come from the sisal industry; and (4) that 90 per

---

* It appears that initially Tom Bavin and later David Barrett, both of the Plantation Workers' International Federation, played an important role in these negotiations and may have put considerable pressure on the Plantation Workers' Union, directly and indirectly through the TFL.[167]

cent of its executive board would be from the sisal industry. The TSGA in turn, agreed to recognize the union; to *recommend* to its members to permit union officials access to their estates and to grant the union the right to nominate three representatives to the employees' side of the central joint council.[168]

In the meantime a joint conference of the management and the employees of the sisal industry to establish the Central Joint Council (CJC) and its dependent machinery was held on 10 April 1958.[169] It was chaired by Sir Barclay Nihill, one-time judge of the East African Court of Appeal and the speaker of the Legislative Council. He later became the first chairman of the CJC.

The constitution of the 'Central Joint Council and dependent consultative machinery for the Tanganyika sisal industy' (as it was called) enumerated the functions of the CJC in Article 2 as follows:

(i)   To secure the largest possible co-operation between Management and Employees for the development of the sisal industry and for the improvement of the conditions and prosperity of all engaged in that Industry.

(ii)   To give employees a wider interest in and greater responsibility for the conditions under which their work is performed.

(iii)   To promote a proper understanding between management and employees in order to ensure efficiency and contentment by mutual agreement.

(iv)   Consideration of working conditions and wages in the Industry as a whole.

(v)   Consideration of health and welfare conditions and other services obtaining on the Estates.

(vi)   To make representations to Government in the needs and opinions of the industry.

(vii)   Other matters of joint interest.[170]

The list of functions reflects fairly accurately the philosophical–ideological basis that underlay the doctrine of joint consultation. To recall Sir Barclay Nihill's opening remarks at the joint conference,[171] this philosophy rejected the inevitability of class war between capital and labour and insisted on both sides of the industry having a single overwhelming common interest.

The dependent consultative machinery too was organized accordingly. A hierarchy of consultative bodies was established from estate level to industry level. Subordinate to the CJC were established four regional consultative councils, one in each of the four sisal-growing regions: Tanga, Central Line, Northern and Southern Provinces. Under the Tanga Regional Consultative Council there were four area consultative committees, while under the Central Line Regional Consultative Council there were three. No area consultative committees were established in Northern and Southern Provinces. The provision on estate consultative committees, the foundation on which rose the whole machinery of joint consultation, was a piece of employers' genius. Article 18(v) stated: 'Those estates desiring to be represented on any Area Consultative Committee or Regional Consultative Council *must first form* its own Estate Consultative Committee composed of one or more representatives of the Management and Employees representatives as far as possible of all categories of work.' Thus (1) it was left to the individual employer to decide whether or not he wanted to participate in the joint consultation and if he did (2) how to constitute his estate committee, that is, through selection, election, nomination and so on. And yet it was the management and employee members of the estate consultative committees who each elected separately their own representatives in equal numbers to the appropriate area consultative committee which in turn elected representatives in a similar fashion to the appropriate regional consultative council (Article 19). The CJC was composed of forty-two members elected by the four regional consultative councils from amongst their members: one half elected from and by the management side and the other half from and by the employees' side in proportions stated in the constitution (Article 3). When the trade union was recognized it nominated three members, and three members were nominated by the TSGA thus bringing the total membership of the council to forty-eight. Article 6 provided for an independent chairman for the council elected by a majority vote on both sides of the council. It is doubtful if the *independence* of the so-called independent chairman could have been anything more than a formality in practice. At least the council's first chairman, Sir Barclay Nihill, appears to have been on first-name terms with the leaders of TSGA and held definite views *vis-à-vis* the union as the following extract from his personal letter to one of the employers' representatives on the council from TSGA indicates. After saying that he had a conversation with the governor and had agreed that he could not continue as the chairman because of his post as the speaker of the Legislative Council, Nihill went on:

I have had a telephone conversation with Sir W. Lead [founder and president of the TSGA] and he is aware of the position — we also discussed a possible successor and he is taking certain actions.

I am very sad that we were not able to arrive at even an interim settlement of the wage claim. I believe had Barrett [presumably, David Barrett of the Plantation Workers' International] been about we should have done so, as he would have provided a bridge between us and TU boys. At the same time I blame myself somewhat to underestimating the TU influence on the rest of the employees' side.[172]

This leaves no doubt as to the side on which the independent chairman leaned. However, this was not the most important issue so far as the struggle of the union was concerned.

There were four major features of the joint consultation machinery around which the struggle between the Tanganyika Sisal and Plantations Workers' Union and the sisal employers revolved subsequent to the formation of the CJC.

First, there was the fact that the constitution did not say how the estate consultative committees were to be constituted and left the whole matter to the discretion of the employer. Secondly, the union had no direct representation as a union on the estate, area and regional consultative organs. Thirdly, at the level of the CJC itself, the union was only one among the representatives of workers. It did not have an exclusive monopoly of representing workers. Finally, the very conception of the joint consultation machinery and the way it was structured tended to destroy the *raison d'être* of a trade union. The union could not negotiate and bargain at the *estate* level for the estates legitimately claimed that they could not by-pass their consultative committees which the union recognized as part of the consultative machinery. The union could not negotiate and bargain at the *industry* level because the TSGA consistently and stubbornly maintained that it could not enter into agreements on behalf of its members. The farthest it could go was only to make recommendations to its members. And in the CJC itself the union could not negotiate and bargain for there it was not the only representative of workers. The result was that the union was left in the lurch: recognized by the employers but unable to carry out its union function of negotiation and collective bargaining. Any trade union worth its name could not accept such a situation.

The struggle, however, did not develop at one go. Rather it developed piecemeal around specific issues, manifesting itself in concrete, practical demands. Yet its movement was clear: from demands for changing specific features of the consultative machinery to the ultimate challenge to its very existence. This struggle, which lasted exactly four years — from June 1958 when the CJC held its first meeting and adopted the constitution, to 4 July 1962 when the TSGA changed its Articles of Association to become a negotiating body on behalf of the employers — is in itself an important chapter in the annals of the Tanzanian trade union movement and bears closer examination.

At the second meeting of the CJC held in August 1958, the employees' side presented a carefully prepared demand for a wage increase on the grounds that the cost of living had gone up since the last general revision of wages which took place in 1951. (Official figures show that the cost of living had gone up by 23 points between 1957 and 1958.)[173] The employers made an offer of a 5 per cent increase which was rejected by the employees' side. Meanwhile, at the estate level, strikes and stoppages — many of them spontaneous — began to gather momentum as the union considerably enhanced its activities. At the third meeting of the CJC, the employers made a revised offer of a 10 per cent increase,[174] which was accepted by the employees' representatives but rejected by the union's nominees. This brought to a head the simmering crisis. Within three days of the meeting, strikes began on many estates. In the period until 12 December, there were twenty-four work stoppages involving 15,000 workers and a loss of 105,000 man-days.[175] Many strikes were directed towards the dismissal of the employees on the CJC who had accepted the wage offer.[176]

On 21 November 1958, the union' executive committee passed the following resolution:

That this Council does not recognize the wages increase offered by the TSGA which was accepted by 21 employees nominated by the estate managers and who had no mandate from the workers to negotiate on their behalf; it further resolves that the TSGA which is responsible for the nomination of the 21 employees in the Central Joint Committee would arrange within two months from today's date a proper election of workers' representatives in all joint consultative and negotiation machineries existing at the moment in the sisal industry; and it further demands that the elections in every single case should be observed by representatives of the Labour Department and the Tanganyika Sisal and Plantation Workers' Union.[177]

Besides raising in effect the question of the composition of estate committees on which the rest of the superstructure was based, the union also complained that it was not being given access to many estates. The TSGA's response to both these issues was typical, it issued a circular to its members recommending. the procedure to be followed in constituting estate committees. This contained four essential points: (1) that a consultative committee may consist of any number of members from the employees' side but all categories of workers should be represented and efforts should be made so that as many tribes as possible were represented; (2) that candidates for election and voters should have worked for more than twelve months for the estate concerned; (3) that a labour officer should be invited as an observer; and (4) that the election should be conducted as independently as possible by the workers without intervention or interference from the management or from the union.[178] On the question of access to estates, the TSGA maintained that it had no jurisdiction over estate managements and that it was the managements' discretion whether to allow union meetings on their estates. Yet it was the TSGA which had earlier imposed a ban on the holding of union meetings on estates, which ban was lifted after the union was recognized. Such a double standard could hardly endear the TSGA to the union. To add insult to injury the TSGA refused to meet the union as requested by the latter.[179]

In the meantime, the strike wave continued unabated, culminating in the famous Mazinde strike discussed above. Eventually the government intervened by appointing Professor D.T. Jack to enquire into the state of industrial relations in the sisal industry. Among other things Jack recommended that employees' representatives to estate committees should be elected and that the union should have one seat on each area consultative committee and regional consultative council but 'no direct representation, however, should be given to the Union on Estate Committee'. Jack's tinkering with the consultative machinery left two major issues unresolved: the question of union representation on estate committees and the wider question of the co-existence of joint consultation and the union.* On the first issue, the union won a further concession after threatening to boycott the proposed fourth meeting of the CJC. It was agreed that the elections of estate committees would be conducted by three observers: one management's representative, one union's representative and one independent observer elected from a panel of names drawn up in agreement between the TSGA and the union.[180] Yet it did not solve the problem and this issue kept being raised by the union in the subsequent meetings of the CJC. At the fourth and fifth meetings, the union gained further concessions and at the sixth meeting held in August 1960 a complex wage agreement was accepted.[181]

Around September 1961 negotiations became due for a new agreement to replace the 1960 agreement. At the September 1961 meeting of the CJC, the union's wage claims were rejected by the employers on the ground that the government's investigation into minimum wages was in progress. Another point of dispute was the union's demand to be the sole representative of the workers on the CJC. A deadlock ensued and the workers' side led by Mkello staged a 'walk-out'.[182] The union refused to attend the CJC's next meeting in March 1962 and instead threatened to launch their 'secret plan' to press their demand for wages and revision of the negotiating machinery. The first stage of the 'secret plan' was due to start on 4 June 1962 and it called upon all African employees, inside and outside the sisal industry, not to transport sisal bales. By this time, the country had attained independence and some of the former trade unionists were now occupying important state posts. Kamaliza, the former president of TFL, was now the Minister of Labour. He immediately tried to have the 'secret plan' called off, warning the trade unionists that the government would not tolerate any law-breaking resulting from the implementation of the plan.[183] Eventually he succeeded in bringing the two sides together but not until after the first stage of the plan had been in operation for eight days.[184] As a result of pressure from the Ministry of Labour, the TSGA altered its Articles on 4 July 1962 so as to enable it to enter into negotiations with the union directly.[185] 'This in effect meant the end of the Central Joint Council of the Sisal Industry — a matter which we cannot but regard with considerable regret',[186] mourned the chairman of the TSGA in his Annual Report.

Subsequent events are tied up with the fate of the trade union movement as a whole where the arena of struggle had shifted to the level of the state. This we shall discuss in the next chapter. Suffice it to say that increased militancy of the trade unions and a spate of strikes in the sisal plantations met with heavy repression from the new, independent government. The activities of the Plantation Workers' Union in the Tanga Region were banned,[187] and Mkello, who was now also the president of the TFL, was rusticated to Sumbawanga.[188] During his absence the union accepted an agreement with the TSGA at the end of the negotiations which were chaired by the Minister of Labour himself. When Mkello returned from detention he refused to sign the agreement but was pressurized to do so by the Minister of Labour. Under that agreement a new

---

* Not that Professor Jack was unaware of it, but the ideological blinkers of the dominant class prevented him from seeing further than joint consultation. After raising the fundamental question: 'To what extent is the recognition of the union compatible with the functioning of the new joint consultative machinery?' (p. 9), he drowned it in such homily as that 'the attempt by the TSGA to set up the Central Joint Council and its dependent bodies was . . . an imaginative effort which should be supported' (p. 15).

National Joint Council for the Sisal Industry was established, consisting of seven representatives from the TSGA and seven from the union with an independent chairman. Ten regional committees composed of four representatives from the TSGA and four from the union were also set up. The former estate committees were replaced by the union's shop stewards.[189] In effect the union had achieved its basic demands: to be the sole representative of the workers and confront the employers directly, and to have the employer-dominated joint consultative machinery scrapped. For these demands the union had waged a four-year-long struggle out of which it had emerged victorious.

But this victory was illusory. By this time the arena of struggle had shifted to the level of the state. In this arena the trade union movement as a whole very rapidly lost in the law-making chambers of the state what it had gained from the employers at the negotiating table. This ultimate confrontation forms the subject matter of our last chapter.

NOTES

1. Non-African unions were very few, and membership was overwhelmingly white-collar. We could obtain full figures only for African unions which are the subject of discussion in the text.
2. See ARLD, 1953, p. 21.
3. ibid.
4. ARLD, 1954, p. 14.
5. See Table 6.1.
6. Iliffe, J., *Modern History, op. cit.*, p. 512. Bienen, H., *Tanzania: Party Transformation and Economic Development* (Princeton: Princeton University Press, 1970), p. 29.
7. Iliffe, J., *Modern History, op. cit.*, p. 514.
8. Quarterly Bulletin of the Labour Department, July–September 1954, TNA 215/1969/II, and Annual Report of the Labour Officer, Mwanza, 1954, TNA 215/511/VII.
9. Annual Report of the Labour Officer, Mwanza, 1954, TNA 215/511/VII.
10. Quarterly Bulletin of the Labour Department, January–March 1955, TNA 215/1969/II. ARLD, 1955, p. 15.
11. Annual Report of the Labour Department, Mwanza, 1954, TNA 215/511/VII.
12. ibid.
13. Saul, J., 'Marketing Co-operatives in a Developing Country: The Tanzanian case', in Cliffe, L. and Saul, J., *Socialism in Tanzania*, Vol. II (Nairobi: East African Publishing House, 1973), p. 143.
14. See above, p. 182.
15. ARLD, 1953, p. 86.
16. Quarterly Bulletin of the Labour Department, October–December 1955, TNA 215/1969/II.
17. Tandau, A., *Historia*, op. cit. p. 5.
18. ibid.
19. ibid., p. 7. Quarterly Bulletin of the Labour Department, January–March 1954, TNA 215/1969/II.
20. ibid (Quarterly Bulletin).
21. Tandau, A., *Historia*, op. cit., pp. 7, 10.
22. Quarterly Bulletin of the Labour Department, April–June 1955, TNA 215/1969/II.
23. Tandau, A., *Historia*, op. cit., p. 12.
24. Quarterly Bulletin of the Labour Department, April–June 1955, TNA 215/1969/II.

25. Iliffe, J., *Modern History*, op. cit., p. 538.
26. Kawawa, R. M., 'The TFL, TANU and Unity', op. cit., p. 14.
27. Tandau, A. *Historia*, op. cit., pp. 13–14.
28. Friedland, W. H., *Vuta Kamba: The Development of Trade Unions in Tanganyika*, (Stanford: Hoover Institution Press, 1969), p. 194. (The biography of a union leader under the pseudonym 'Martin' is certainly that of M. M. Mpangala as many details coincide.)
29. Tandau, A., *Historia*, op. cit., p. 20.
30 Scott, R., 'Trade Unions and Nationalism in East Africa', *Proceedings of East African Academy*. Vol. III (1965), EAF, p. 130.
31. No. 48 of 1956.
32. Friedland, W. H., *Vuta Kamba*, op. cit., p. 52.
33. *Tanganyika Standard*, 23 January 1960.
34. Friedland, W. H., *Vuta Kamba*, op. cit., p. 57.
35. See Table 6.1.
36. ARLD, 1960, Table 5, p. 66.
37. The following figures for the year 1960 are illustrative of the point.

Sector	No. of adult African male employees	No. of employers	Average no. of employees per employer
Agriculture, forestry, hunting & fishing	199 021	1 245	160
Mining & quarrying	11 061	102	108
Manufacturing	16 954	941	18
Construction	9 093	133	68
Electricity, gas, water & sanitation	1 395	42	33
Commerce	12 835	2 200	6
Transport (excl. E A Railways), storage communication	6 076	229	27
Services (excl. domestic service)	14 804	715	21
Government services, E A High Commission & Local Authority	86 237	999	86
Total	357 476	6 606	54

Source: ARLD, 1960.

38. Scott, R., op. cit., tends to exaggerate the role of TANU in the trade union movement. For a critique of his sources see Friedland, W. H., *Vuta Kamba*, op. cit., pp. 118ff.
39. Friedland, W. H., *Vuta Kamba*, op. cit., p. 169.
40. See above, Table 4.1, p. 108.
41. Friedland, W. H., *Vuta Kamba*, op. cit., p. 169.
42. ibid., p. 166
43. ibid., pp. 76–7.
44. ibid., pp. 174–5.
45. ibid., pp. 78–9.
46. ibid., pp. 175–6.
47. ibid., pp. 192–5.
48. Scott, R., op. cit., and Patel, L. R., 'Trade Unions and the Law in Tanganyika' in *Law and the Commonwealth* (Delhi: National Publishing House, 1971), pp. 598–603, make exaggerated claims as regards the political role of trade unions on the one hand and the role of TANU in the trade union movement on the other. Friedland (*Vuta Kamba*, op. cit.) argues that while trade unions were in sympathy with TANU and the two movements co-operated on occasions, there was no *organizational* link between the two nor could Tanganyika's trade unionism be described as *political* trade unionism. This is certainly

true when one examines the *strike* movement. Not a single strike between 1954 and 1964 could be described as *political* in the sense of being explicitly against the state for a political purpose.

49. See, for instance, Nyerere quoted in Friedland, W. H., *Vuta Kamba*, op. cit., p. 119, and Davies, I., *African Trade Unions*, (Harmondsworth: Penguin, 1966), p. 110.
50 Friedland, W. H., *Vuta Kamba*, op. cit., p. 117.
51. Davies, I., op. cit., p. 191.
52. Tandau, A., *Historia*, op. cit., p. 18.
53. See above, pp. 198–9.
54. Friedland, W. H., *Vuta Kamba*, op. cit., pp. 137–8, p. 254 n. 5.
55. Davies, I., op. cit., pp. 192–6.
56. ibid., p. 195.
57. ibid., p. 194.
58. See Friedland, W. H., *Vuta Kamba*, op. cit., pp. 120–1.
59. Davies, I., op. cit., p. 194.
60. Bhoke-Munanka to Miss Nicolson, 27 July 1954, FCB 121/2/11, RH.
61. F. E., Omedo to Miss Nicolson, 6 April 1954, FCB 122/2/34, RH, Fabian Colonial Bureau to F. E. Omedo, 28 May 1954, FCB 122/2/35, RH.
62. Kawawa to Miss L. S. Clarke, 19 May 1955, FCB 122/2/39, RH.
63. Fabian Colonial Bureau to F. E. Omedo, 28 May 1954, FCB 122/2/35, RH.
64. Omedo to Nicolson, 12 July 1954, FCB 122/2/38.
65. Davies, I., op. cit., pp. 44–5.
66. Fabian Colonial Bureau to H. Beer, 26 July 1956, FCB 121/4/8.
67. Tandau, A., *Historia*, op. cit., p. 9.
68. Friedland, W. H., *Vuta Kamba*, op. cit., p. 123.
69. ibid.
70 See above, pp. 199-200.
71. *Tanganyika Standard*, 25 February 1959.
72. Friedland, W. H., *Vuta Kamba*, op. cit., p. 120.
73. ibid., p. 117.
74. Marx to F. Bolte, 23 November 1871, in Marx, K. and Engels, F., *Selected Correspondence* (Moscow: Progress Publishers, 1955), pp. 270–1 (emphasis in the original).
75. *Tanganyika Standard*, 10 June 1959.
76. Wedderburn, K. W., op. cit., pp. 298–9.
77. See generally Shivji, I. G., *Class Struggles in Tanzania* (London: Heinemann, 1976).
78. Marx, K., *The Poverty of Philosophy*, op. cit., p. 150.
79. Marx, K. and Engels, F., *Selected Correspondence*, op. cit., p. 271.
80. Lenin, V. I., 'Lecture on the 1905 Revolution', in Lenin, V. I., *On Trade Unions* (Moscow: Progress Publishers, 1970), p. 299.
81. ARLD, 1951, Tables VIA and VIB, p. 76. Quarterly Bulletin of the Labour Department, 1953, App. A, TNA 215/1969/II.
82. ARLD, respective years.
83. ARLD, 1959, p. 11.
84. Quarterly Bullentin of Labour Department, April–June 1953, October–December 1953, TNA 215/1969/II.
85. The data in this table are collected from Form LDG 164 to be found in various under-taking files in the Ministry of Labour Headquarters, Dar es Salaam. The file numbers are as follows (MLH):
In the 4/19 series
6/II, 8/II, 9/II, 11/II, 18/II, 19/II, 20/II, 22/II, 26/II, 53/II, 66, 69, 74, 80, 88, 96, 100, 102/II, 104, 115, 130, 136, 137, 146, 148, 156, 157, 182, 184, 195, 198, 241, 256, 276, 281, 349, 401.
In the 4/29 series
73, 77, 75/II, 117, 124, 127/II, 206, 638.
Other
4/5/1/I, 4/15/2/III, 4/23/1/VI.

86. See above, p. 20.
87. See above, pp. 208–9.
88. MLH 4/19/198.
89. MLH 4/29/127/II.
90. MLH 4/29/281.
91. MLH 4/29/2/III.
92. ARLD. 1962, p. 8, para. 64.
93. MLH 4/19/146, MLH 4/19/241, MLH 4/19/401, MLH 4/29/75/II, MLH 4/19/276.
94. MLH 4/19/194, MLH 4/19/137.
95. The account of the 1956 strike is summarized from the following sources: ARLD, 1957, pp. 13–14; Quarterly Bulletin of the Labour Department October–December 1956 and January–March 1957, TNA 215/1969/II; Tandau, A., *Historia*, op. cit., pp. 25–34; Friedland, W. H., *Vuta Kamba*. op. cit., pp. 24, 124–5, 135.
96. Quarterly Bulletin of the Labour Department, October–December 1956, p. 6, para. 29, TNA 215/1969/II.
97. ibid., pp. 6–7.
98. ibid., p. 7.
99. Tandau, A., *Historia*, op. cit., p. 28.
100. See s. 33 and reg. 5.
101. Tandau, A., *Historia*, op. cit., p. 12.
102. Friedland, W. H., *Vuta Kamba*, op. cit., p. 135.
103. Tandau, A., *Historia*, op. cit., pp. 31–2.
104. Quarterly Bulletin of the Labour Department, April–June 1957, para. 25, TNA 215/1969/II, and Friedland, W. H., *Vuta Kamba*, op. cit., p. 125.
105. Tandau, A., *Historia*, op. cit., p. 34. Quarterly Bulletin of the Labour Department, April–June 1958, TNA 471/LI/3/I.
106. Statement reproduced in Tandau, A., *Historia*, op. cit., p. 37. Information on the beer strike is from this source.
107. *Tanganyika Standard*, 10 June 1959.
108. Friedland, W. H., *Vuta Kamba*, op. cit., p. 125.
109. ibid., p. 218. Tandau, A., *Historia*, op. cit., p. 41.
110. Jack, D. T., *Report on the State of Industrial Relations in the Sisal Industry* (Dar es Salaam: Government Printer, 1959), p. 2.
111. Quarterly Bulletin of the Labour Department, April–June 1957, p. 8, para. 36, TNA 215/1969/II.
112. Korogwe District Annual Report, 1958, TNA 304/R.3/1.
113. Quoted in Friedland, W. H., *Vuta Kamba*, op. cit., p. 97.
114. ibid., p. 220.
115. Jack, D. T., op. cit., p. 13.
116. Tandau, A., *Historia*. op. cit., p. 43.
117. Situation Report of Senior Labour Officer, Tanga, 22 January 1959, para 4. MLH 4/19/110.
118. Friedland, W. H., *Vuta Kamba*, op. cit., p. 221.
119. See Jack D. T., op. cit., pp. 14ff.
120. Friedland, W. H., *Vuta Kamba*, op. cit., p. 125. Information on the railway strike is from this source unless otherwise indicated.
121. *Tanganyika Standard*, 22 March 1979.
122. Friedland, W. H., *Vuta Kamba*, op. cit., p. 226.
123. Tandau, A., *Historia*, op. cit., p. 46.
124. ibid., p. 47.
125. Friedland, W. H., *Vuta Kamba*, op. cit., p. 229.
126. *Tanganyika Standard*, 24 June 1960.
127. ARLD, 1961, p. 95.
128. Minutes of the 5th meeting of the Central Joint Council of the Sisal Industry, 26, 27, 28 November 1959, Nihill Papers, File 1/121–2, RH.

129.   *Tanganyika Standard*, 23 October 1960.
130.   Friedland, W. H., *Vuta Kamba*, op. cit., p. 36.
131.   No. 15 of 1951.
132.   No. 1 of 1953 dated 16 February 1953, TNA 41/L 1/1.
133.   Friedland, W. H., *Vuta Kamba*, op. cit., p. 30.
134.   Minutes of a Joint Conference between Management and Employees of the Sisal Industry, 10 April 1958, Nihill Papers, File 1, RH.
135.   Friedland, W. H., *Vuta Kamba*, op. cit., p. 39.
136.   See, for instance, the Constitution of the Joint Staff Consultative Committee of the Tanga Town Council, MLH 4/19/146; Branch Secretary, Tanganyika Local Government Workers' Union, to LC, 17 November 1958, 4/19/146; Minutes of the PC Conference, January 1959, p. 10, EAF.
137.   Proceedings of the Legislative Council, 14 December 1956, 31st Session (1956-7), 2nd vol., p. 793.
138.   Section 25(2) as amended by s. 8 of the Trade Union (Amendment) Ordinance, 1959, No. 17 of 1959.
139.   Quarterly Bulletin of the Labour Department, 1956, TNA 215/1969/II.
140.   Kawawa, R., op. cit., p. 14.
141.   Trade Dispute (Arbitration and Settlement) Addition to Schedule Notice, 1956. GN No. 343 of 11 December 1956.
142.   Trade Disputes (Arbitration and Settlement) (Amendment) Ordinance, 1958, No. 56 of 1958. Section 6 repeals and replaces the schedule. See also Proceedings of the Legislative Council, 1958-9 Session, Vol. 2.
143.   Section 48.
144.   See above, pp. 199-200.
145.   Monthly Report of Ag Senior Labour Officer, Tanga, June 1957, MLH 4/19/98.
146.   MLH 4/19/146.
147.   ibid.
148.   MLH 4/29/27/I.
149.   Regional Secretary of the Senior Labour Officer, 31 January 1959, and Labour Officer's reply, 2 February 1959, MLH 4/19/198.
150.   Kifile, H. O., 'Labour Relations in Tanzania', *International Labour Reviev*, Vol. 88, October 1963, p. 357.
151.   ARLD, 1956, p. 77.
152.   Quarterly Bulletin of the Labour Department, July–September 1954, TNA 215/1969/II.
153.   Minutes of Motor Employers with the Senior Labour Officer, 28 November 1958, MLH 4/19/200. Sutton to LC, 20 January 1959, MLH 4/19/110.
154.   'Report of Committee on Proposed Employers' Organization', 3 September 1958, Nihill Papers, RH.
155.   ibid.
156.   ARLD, 1960, p. 66.
157.   Guillebaud, C. W., op. cit., p. 90.
158.   Friedland, W. H., *Vuta Kamba*, op. cit., p. 189.
159.   Memorandum No. 14, Appendix M, Minutes of the PC Conference, January 1957, EAF.
160.   Minutes of the PC Conference July 1957, p. 19, EAF.
161.   Jack, D. T., op. cit., p. 3.
162.   Tandau, A., *Historia*, op. cit., pp. 40-1.
163.   Quarterly Bulletin of the Labour Department, July–September 1957, TNA 215/1969/II.
164.   Quarterly Bulletin of the Labour Department, January–March 1958 and April–June 1958, TNA 471/L1/3/I.
165.   Tandau, A., *Historia*, op. cit., pp. 41-2.
166.   Quarterly Bulletin of the Labour Department, January–March 1958, TNA 471/L1/3/I.
167.   Tandau, A.,*Historia*, op. cit., pp. 41-2. Jack, D. T., op. cit., p. 4.
168.   Friedland, W. H., *Vuta Kamba*, op. cit., p. 218.
169.   Nihill Papers, File 1, RH.

170. Reproduced in Jack, D. T., op. cit., p. 18.
171. See above, p. 205.
172. Nihill to Le Meitre, 21 August 1958, Nihill Papers, File 4 folio 55, RH.
173. ARLD of respective years.
174. Friedland, W. H., *Vuta Kamba*, op. cit., p. 219. Korogwe District Annual Report, 1958, TNA 304/R.3/1.
175. Friedland, W. H. *Vuta Kamba*, op. cit., p. 220.
176. Korogwe District Annual Report, 1958, TNA 304/R.3/1. Jack, D. T., op. cit., p. 13.
177. Jack, D. T., op. cit., p. 12.
178. ibid, p. 23.
179. ibid., p. 7.
180. Friedland, W. H., *Vuta Kamba*, op. cit., p. 222.
181. ibid., pp. 223–4.
182. *Tanganyika Standard*, 4 June 1962; Guillebaud, C. W., op. cit., p. 96.
183. *Tanganyika Standard*, 5 June 1962.
184. *Tanganyika Standard*, 12 June 1962 and 24 August 1962, and *Sunday News*, 10 June 1962.
185. Guillebaud, C. W., op. cit., p. 96. Mascarenhas, A. C., op. cit., p. 212.
186. Quoted in Guillebaud, C. W., op. cit., p. 96.
187. *Tanganyika Standard*, 11 January 1963.
188. Guillebaud, C. W., op. cit., p. 97.
189. ibid.

7

The Fall of the
Trade Union Movement

During the nationalist struggle of the 1950s a kind of non-contradictory relationship between TANU and the trade unions had been worked out. The division between economics and politics functioned well so long as both the nationalist and the trade union movements were in *opposition* to the colonial state. Once the independent TANU government was formed the *modus operandi* between trade unions and TANU broke down.

TANU was dominated by the urban intelligentsia and small traders with a mass peasant base. One section of the intelligentsia — civil servants — did not participate directly in TANU activities because the colonial government prohibited them from doing so. They formed the vociferous leadership of the white-collar trade unions of government employees. This section of the petty-bourgeoisie found their base in the trade unions. The first few years of independence were marked by an intense political struggle among the various factions of the petty-bourgeoisie as each one vied and jockeyed for power. But this process also involved the transformation of the state and the emergence of the nascent bureaucratic bourgeoisie's organizational hegemony over the working class. It is this aspect of the struggle which directly concerns us here.

In this chapter we discuss the three main issues around which a significant section of the trade union movement came into direct confrontation with the state.

These three issues were as regards the future of the East African High Commission, Africanization and trade union autonomy. Each one of these issues, although originating from economic struggles of workers, pulled the unions into a direct political confrontation with the state and finally spelled their death.

East African High Commission

Two major strikes against certain High Commission services helped to crystallize the trade union opposition to the commission. The first was the postal strike which took place in December 1959 and lasted fifty-five days. The second was the railway strike which occurred in February 1960 and lasted eighty days.[1] In both these strikes the employer was able to keep the essential services running by using European and Asian employees. As we saw in the last chapter, the commission's management based in

Nairobi was totally insensitive to the territorial unions and tended to be outside the pale of even territorial governments. This made the Tanganyika African Postal Union and Tanganyika African Railway Union extremely hostile to the commission. In a memorandum presented to the visiting UN Mission, TRAU said: 'We abhor the High Commission and the sooner we are emancipated from it the better for us. Under the High Commission Tanganyika has become economically Kenya's satellite because the economic life-line is controlled from Kenya.'[*2]

In the meantime, TANU had moved to a different position. In June 1960, while in Addis Ababa, Nyerere made a proposal for the formation of the East African Federation.[4] Increasingly, TANU began to think in terms of using the commission as a structure on which the federation could be constructed. The commission was not bad, Kambona, the organizing secretary of TANU, argued. The people who ran it were bad. 'It is not that the house is bad; it is the people inside the house that are bad. But if you live in a house and there are vermin in the house, does that mean that you burn it down? The house has to be rid of vermin but that doesn't mean that the house itself is bad.'[5] But that could convince no one for the trade unionists had seen in practice the type of house it was, always prone to vermin of one kind or another. Both Namfua of the postal union and Tumbo of TRAU vehemently opposed the commission, and their respective conferences in July and August 1960 passed resolutions calling for its destruction.[6]

The TFL itself was divided on the issue. As independence drew closer, pro- and anti-government factions, led respectively by Kamaliza and Tumbo, began to crystallize within the TFL. The first open manifestation of the split came when the TGWU under Kamaliza passed a resolution at its August 1960 conference adopting a conciliatory position towards the High Commission. It called for restructuring of the commission and only if such restructuring failed would it support its abolition.[7] The public hostility between unions that this gave rise to was patched up only by a compromise resolution adopted by TFL at the end of August 1960 in which it put forward five conditions† which, if not fulfilled, would force the TFL to demand the breaking up of the commission.[8]

This was only a compromise for swords were drawn. With the establishment of the first TANU government on 1 September 1960, Rashidi Kawawa became Minister of Local Government and Housing and this sparked off a succession crisis in which the Kamaliza and Tumbo factions came out in the open. The whole dispute has been summarized by Tandau and Friedland and we need not go into details. Suffice it to mention a few important features.

According to Friedland the anti-government group included mostly unions of workers employed by the government, that is, white-collar unions, the railway union (TRAU), the postal and telecommunications union (NUPE), the public employees' union (TUPE) and the Local Government Workers' Union (TALGWU). The pro-government group included the TGWU and the Domestic and Hotel Workers' Union. There was the wavering or the so-called neutral group which consisted mainly of the

---

* In this TRAU and its leader Tumbo were far-sighted. Subsequent events were to prove them right. Some seven years later a similar argument was adopted by the Tanzanian government and its academic spokesmen against Kenya's domination of EACSO. This led to the Kampala Agreement and the formation of the East African Community to allocate equitably the benefits of the union.[3]

† These were: (1) that the reports of enquiries into salaries and conditions would be satisfactory; (2) that responsibilities regarding the commission would be vested in the heads in Tanganyika; (3) that Africans will be given responsible positions; (4) that Tanganyika will be given its deserved share in the EA economy; and (5) that the government will secure satisfactory terms on all claims.

plantation workers' Union, the two dockworkers' unions, and the African mine workers' unions. 'These Unions varied their stance depending upon the relevance of any given issue to their own interests. In many cases, these unions took a neutral stance between the pro-TANU and anti-TANU Unions; in other cases individual Unions took anti-TANU stand when some action was taken that affected their interests.'[9]

Besides the issue of the High Commission, there were two other main issues which divided the TFL at this stage. These were the proposed new structure of the TFL and the question of TFL–TANU relationship. The Kamaliza group favoured a much more centralized TFL with control over the finances of its constituent members. The TFL would also have the final decision-making power to approve calling of strikes. They also argued in terms of TANU and TFL being one thing. The Tumbo group bitterly opposed this on the ground that such a structure would destroy trade union autonomy. They argued that the trade unions — even while having close relations with a political party — should not be controlled by the party.[10] This dispute was only a precursor to the simmering question of the independence of trade unions that we deal with in a later section, 'Trade union autonomy'. A temporary solution to the Kamaliza–Tumbo dispute was to appoint a committee under the chairmanship of Chief Adam Sapi.

At the special congress of TFL called to discuss the Sapi report, Kamaliza won a vote of confidence by a slender majority of one. A few months later, Nyerere tried to diffuse the crisis by appointing Kamaliza as the Minister of Labour and sending off Tumbo to Britain as his High Commissioner. But the contradiction was deeper than personalities, as the subsequent events were to show.

Africanization

On the eve of independence the state machinery in Tanzania was predominantly manned by Europeans and Asians. Africans filled low clerical posts at best. 'In the civil service Africans held 1,170 of the 4,452 senior and middle grade posts in 1961. The position in the professions was worse. In 1962 only 16 of 184 physicians, one of 84 civil engineers, and 2 of 57 lawyers were Africans.'[11] Pressure for rapid Africanization had begun to build up within TANU even before independence. The issue had become a hot debating point at the party's annual conference in January 1958 with respect to racial parity in the forthcoming general elections. Soon after the conference Zuberi Mtemvu left TANU and formed his African National Congress whose motto was 'Africa for the Africans'.[12] Although Mtemvu's ANC never really threatened TANU, the issue of Africanization kept rearing its head. Thus for example the TANU back-benchers were among the most militant and vociferous opponents of the citizenship Bill.[13] Another quarter from which persistent pressure for rapid Africanization continued to be applied was the trade unions.

Among these, it was the white-collar trade unions consisting of government and High Commission employees who led the demand for Africanization.[14] Whereas the government had accepted that African citizens would be given preference over non-Africans in the recruitment of the civil service,[15] the trade unions concerned felt that the pace of Africanization was not rapid enough. Worse was the situation in the postal, railway and other services administered by the East African Common Services Organization (EACSO), the successor of the East African High Commission. As late as March 1963 Africans constituted only 8 per cent of the administrative and professional grades and only 12 per cent of the executive and high technical grades of EACSO compared to the 75 per cent of Africans who filled the lower scales of clericals and artisans.[16] No wonder that most militant spokesmen on Africanization was Tumbo, the secretary-general of TRAU.

TRAU even threatened to call a strike to force the issue. Around February 1962 it declared what it called a 'master plan' which, among other things, would have involved a procession with 'begging bowls' to houses of responsible people. The plan was to be put in operation in five stages, the last of which would involve putting selected Africans forcibly in the posts chosen for them.[17] The issue was apparently diffused temporarily by the appointment of an Africanization commission. Yet, such threats continued to pose a danger to the TANU regime which it could not ignore. Before we deal with the final resolution of the conflict in the ensuing section we need to look deeper into the issue of Africanization.

What was the social and material basis of this demand? First, the colonial state and employer, by their overtly racial policies, had created built-in racial biases in the employment structure. This in turn faced the trade unions as an objective condition which they had to come to grips with. Secondly, the colonial state and employer used the racial divisions among employees effectively to divide them. This was particularly the case in strike situations. As we saw above, European and Asian employees were again and again used as blackleg labour to break the strikes of African workers. It must be noted, however, that these divisions were not simply racial but also class divisions. As a matter of fact much of the European and Asian blackleg labour consisted of *supervisory* and *office* workers — the petty-bourgeoisie.[18] Nevertheless, their ready response and loyalty to the colonial employer[19] left a deep imprint on African trade unionists and further fuelled their demands for Africanization. Thirdly, and this is the most important level, the demand for Africanization was essentially a *sectional* demand of the predominantly white-collar unions and workers — the lower African petty-bourgeoisie. However militantly expressed, the demand did not go beyond asking for replacement of the European and the Asian by an African. This aspect is brought out in bold relief when compared with the contemporaneous struggles of the predominantly blue-collar unions: those of the plantation workers and the mine workers. In 1962, for instance, there.was a spate of strikes in the sisal industry against oppressive supervisory and managerial staff, many of whom happened to be Europeans and Asians.[20] But they were not confined to Europeans and Asians. The newly recruited or promoted African staff also came under heavy attack. Suffice it to cite one incident which illustrates the point rather dramatically. The TPWU called a strike at the expatriate-owned Lugongo Sisal Estate on 25 February 1962 to force the reinstatement of a nurse who had been dismissed. In the course of the strike, the African personnel officer, who had been appointed to the post just a year before, came under heavy criticism. In a subsequent letter to the general secretary of TPWU he narrated the incident as follows:

At the Public meeting of the Tanganyika Plantation Workers' Union held at Maramba on the 18th June, 1961 in which the Branch Secretary Mr Rashidi Mhando and the Regional Secretary Mr Ali Hassani were the principal speakers, the following statements inter alia were issued: That the Trade Union has fought for the promotion of Africans to higher grades in the Sisal Industry, but the Africans promoted in this area are the ones hindering the rights of the lower Africans (*sic!*). He went on to give an example of a hunter who went out hunting with a dog. The dog chased and caught an antelope. The antelope asked the dog to free him because they were both animals and the hunter was a human being. The dog refused and took the antelope to the hunter. The hunter killed it and gave the dog the legs and bones to eat. He then expounded his example as follows: That the Africans in the responsible posts are being used as dogs to catch their fellow Africans and what they get is nothing but a few hundred shillings.[21]

The personnel officer described the speech as 'most irresponsible, destructive and inflammatory' and that he did not expect such a thing from the trade union. 'I expected that the union would back me up as one of their few leading Africans in responsible positions so that the progress of the Africanization scheme would mean that eventually Africans will take over all responsibilities of the country.'[22]

The differing conceptions and practice of Africanization of the white- and blue-collar unions arose from the different class character and the corresponding material conditions of their membership. Objectively, the workers fought a *democratic* battle against the oppressive and humiliating supervisory staff while the African petty-bourgeoisie wanted to replace them. The demand for Africanization was essentially a partial demand objectively representing the sectional interests of the petty-bourgeois salariats. The struggle for trade union autonomy was, however, of a different character.

Trade union autonomy

The new TANU-government inherited the Three Year Development Plan drawn up by the colonial authorities.[23] Based on the World Bank Report of 1960, its main thrust was the creation of favourable conditions to attract foreign capital and allow local commercial capital to enter into the industrial sector. In the first years after independence, therefore, the new government did not have its own economic policy. Rather, it concentrated on political consolidation. However, even the limited objectives of the first plan implied, among other things, disciplining of the working class which in effect meant curbing of the strike movement. At the political level, the autonomous trade union movement posed a threat to the stability of the new regime. Outside the state structures, trade unions were the only well organized 'centre of power'. So for both economic and political reasons, the trade unions came into direct conflict with the TANU government.

The strike wave described above continued unabated after independence. In 1962 there were 152 strikes involving 48,434 workers with a loss of 417,474 man-days. This was nearly a four-fold increase over 1961 in the number of man-days lost.[24] Nearly half the strikes involved demands for better pay and opposition to oppressive management. Both as an employer itself and as the protector of capital generally, the state, now run by the TANU government, was affected and it began to step in. The new TANU ministers, who only a couple of months ago were supporting strikes, now began to threaten striking workers with dismissals (for example, during the Mwadui strike).[25] Workers' struggles were condemned as being destructive.[26] Nyerere described strikes as 'evil things', as 'the law of the jungle'.[27] One trade unionist appropriately retorted that only a few years before, during the breweries strike, Nyerere had described strikes as the workers' last weapon and now he called it 'the law of the jungle'.[28]

The government adopted the 'stick-and-carrot' method to deal with the unions. On the one hand, it made certain concessions to trade union pressure by increasing minimum wages and providing for other fringe benefits.[29] Simultaneously, it set into motion three Bills to curb strikes and bring the unions under further state control. These Bills involved an amendment to the Trade Union Ordinance, the repeal and replacement of the Trade Disputes (Arbitration and Settlement) Ordinance, and the establishing of a negotiating machinery for civil servants under the Civil Service (Negotiating Machinery) Bill. Before we discuss these pieces of legislation in some detail, it may be mentioned that the Bills invoked bitter opposition from virtually all trade unions. This opposition was expressed publicly at rallies and in press statements as well as in Parliament.

Rwegasira, one of the directors of TFL, described the policy behind the Bills as 'abominable'. 'It is a policy which the trade unions in this country will oppose relentlessly, if that be the last thing they do for the worker — the architects of our country's destiny.' He added: 'It is hard to believe that some of the Ministers who struggled and built up the labour movement . . . now in a position with legislative powers should be the ones to formulate such bills. This is incomprehensible.'[30] Another TFL leader, C. P. Kapungu, said in a statement that the 'forcible way of treating the trade unions will show how much the Government is scared of well-organized bodies in the country. These proposals are a national shame — and the TFL is ashamed of the Government's desire to oppress workers.'[31] A statement from the TPWU said that if the Bills were passed 'a perpetual war between the Government and the workers will start — a war which will cut Tanganyika completely from foreign investment'.[32] The union promised full support to the TFL, which it called upon to appoint a day of prayers against the Bills in no uncertain terms as a denial of 'human rights to the working people of this country'.[33] The general secretary, D. M. S. Mdachi and the president, P. Mwambele, of the union told a press conference that reading the Bills one could not escape the conclusion that 'we have come out of the clutches of colonialism and are fast moving into totalitarianism'. They said: 'Our uhuru seems to mean more and more uhuru for Ministers to assume dictatorial powers, instead of getting more and more democratic. Why force employee trade unions to join puppet 'designated federation', controlled by and bending to the whims of a minister?'[34]

The Tanganyika Union of Public Employees, the TGWU, the local government workers' union, the railway union and the dockworkers' union all condemned the Bill in the strongest possible terms.[35] At a rally called by TRAU just two days before the Bills were presented to Parliament, the union leaders, including the general secretary of TFL, J. R. Magongo, called upon the Minister of Labour (Kamaliza) to resign. At the same rally Victor Mkello, the president of TFL, appealed to his TANU counterpart: 'As President of the TFL I appeal to my fellow President of the TANU, to see that the country is not divided into two by the passing of these Bills. I want it to be clearly understood that the rule of the gun in Tanganyika will not work.'[36]

When introducing the Trade Unions Ordinance (Amendment) Bill to the Parliament, the Minister of Health and Labour, M. M. Kamaliza, argued that the aim of the Bill was to introduce unity in the trade union movement and to do away with splinter groups by having one designated trade union. Further, the government would introduce a compulsory check-off system so as to strengthen the unions financially. The area commissioners, the regional commissioners and some elected members who rose to support the Bill elaborated on these arguments, emphasizing that the government was a workers' government and could not possibly legislate against workers. But workers formed only a small minority and that the government had to look after the interests of the majority.

The only opposition came from Mkello, the president of TFL and a nominated member, who made a spirited and at times vitriolic speech in the morning session opposing the second reading of the Bill.[37] Mkello argued that 'if passed into law the Bill would place the trade union movement in Tanganyika under the control of Government, would destroy its independence and would take from the workers their right to determine and pursue their own policy and freely to utilize their own finances'.[38] He said it was true that the unions had sought the government's assistance to curb splinter unions but the government was seizing that opportunity to control them. 'We have never asked for Government protection, and if our friends cannot cooperate with us they should say so. But why come out with designation and non-designation and the power to suspend union leaders, and the control of our finances?' It was entirely absurd for the government to have powers to suspend union leaders elected by its members, Mkello forcefully argued. But despite his militancy and the spirted defence of trade union autonomy, he was in little doubt that he was talking in the chambers of the state and to the people who wielded state power. His final submission deserves quoting at length:

Mr Speaker, Sir, as we are one party Government in Tanganyika, the Government here is in a better position to pass any Bill into law without any difficulty. But I must, as a labour leader in this country, take this opportunity to convey to the Government and to all honourable Members, that the moment this Bill becomes the law of the country, there shall have been established a permanent division between the Government and the workers. I am quite sure about that.

You are the Government. You have the power to do as you like. You have the police, you have the Tanganyika Rifles and you can even get help from outside Tanganyika. But we are not going to sell our movement to the Government because they are powerful in that way. I am sure it is not the intention of the Government to create a state of emergency, or a civil war in Tanganyika.[39]

It was undoubtedly a principled stand of a trade union leader, but a stand not backed by any efforts to mobilize the class whose interests it represented. No wonder, when Mkello returned to the debating chambers after lunch he was not the same man. It seems a lot of pressure was brought to bear on Mkello during the lunch break. Supporting the second reading of the Bill, Mkello made a remark in passing pregnant with many questions: 'I seem to be a good boy this afternoon, Sir.'[40] Although it is clear that efforts were made at 'reconciliation' during the lunch break by one Mr Laxman (a Member of Parliament), it is possible there had been some arm-twisting as well. Next day, when the Trade Disputes (Settlement) Bill and the Civil Service (Negotiating Machinery) Bill were discussed, Mkello supported them, referring to the reconciliation efforts of Mr Laxman 'last night'.* He made a very short speech, the gist of which is summarized in the following paragraph:

I have indicated in this House several times that the labour movement of a country is very much concerned with the unity and we do appreciate that the present Government is a Government of the people including the workers. We do appreciate that the Hon. Prime Minister R. M. Kawawa and the Hon. Minister of Labour, M.M. Kamaliza they all come from the movement and we have every confidence that whatever they do it must be in the interests of the workers and on the whole I think we have a very good Government Sir. But Sir, I think even a good Government can sometimes make bad laws and I think here we are making a start . . . I am going to support this Bill with the hope that the Government will take into consideration the amendments we here submitted to them . . . .[42]

Mkello had undergone a metamorphosis. The roaring lion of the previous day predicting a civil war and a permanent division between the government and the workers had been reduced to a supplicating deer begging the 'good government' and hoping for a change of heart. This reflected not only the power of state but also certain fundamental weaknesses of the trade movement itself. Suffice it to mention that in opposing the Bills the trade union leadership had thrown themselves on a *political* battlefield for which neither their history of *economic* struggles nor their bureaucratic organization and petty-bourgeois ideological orientation had prepared them. But we are jumping ahead of our story. We shall return to these issues in our final section. For the moment

---

* 'Lastly . . . I would like to express my sincere thanks to the Hon. Mr Laxman who has played a considerable part as it were behind the scenes and brought about this happy reconciliation and I am sorry I made him stay late last night.'[41]

we need to look more closely at the three controversial Bills which were eventually passed into law.

Hitherto the state had sought to control workers' trade unions by various powers vested in the registrar. The Trade Unions Ordinance (Amendment) Act, 1962,[43] introduced an innovation to further consolidate that control. First, it empowered the minister concerned to *designate* a federation of trade unions, which federation would be the only one allowed to exist (ss. 7A and 13(1A)). Secondly, all trade unions were obliged to affiliate to the designated federation if they wanted to exist legally (ss. 7A(2) and 14(2A). The federation had to admit to its membership every registered trade union 'unless the Minister in writing otherwise directs' (s. 7B(a)). Furthermore, the federation could not cancel or revoke the membership of a registered trade union without the prior consent of the minister (s. 7B(b)). This gave the minister ultimate power to decide which trade union would be allowed to exist. As a matter of fact, the original Bill not only gave the minister power to designate a federation but also to revoke such designation. As a result of trade union pressure, the government made a minor concession and the powers of revocation were vested in the registrar in case the federation did anything contrary to law as stipulated in the provisions of the Ordinance (ss. 9(2) and 14).

Thirdly, having created a centre of its liking, the state sought to control this centre by giving the minister powers over its finance over and above the numerous control mechanisms over trade unions wielded by the registrar. Section 41A empowered the designated federation, with the approval of the minister, to require its members to pay it a specified amount of money every year or a specified proportion of the dues collected by member unions (s. 41A). Where a member union failed to remit the forcible subscription imposed on it, the union and its officers 'shall be guilty of an offence and shall be liable on conviction to a fine not exceeding one thousand shillings' (s. 41A(2)). Together with the provisions on compulsory check-off,* this would ensure a stable source of finance for the designated federation and help to create a strong centre. Only then would it make sense for the state to control the centre. The centre's own finances in turn were placed under the control of the minister. 'The Minister may in writing give directions . . . to the designated federation as to the purposes to which any moneys received by the designated federation . . . shall be applied and to the proportion of such moneys which shall be assigned to each of such purposes, and the designated federation shall give effect to such directions' (s. 41B(1)). This was a draconian measure which would have almost completely destroyed the autonomy of the federation. Even the colonial state had not attempted to control a union's finances and funds to this extent. (Nyerere himself had described the colonial state's relatively moderate provisions to control union's finances as 'ridiculous'.)[45] The trade unions bitterly opposed this 'interference in our internal organization',[46] and Mkello argued that they were prepared to forgo the check-off system if it came 'with strings attached to it'.[47] On this the government conceded. The Trade Unions (Revocation of Special Powes) Act, 1962,[48] revoked the powers of the minister 'to give directions to a designated federation as to the purposes to which any moneys received by such shall be applied,' (s. 2).

Nevertheless, the registrar's powers over the funds of a union, including the designated federation, remained intact. To be sure, two further weapons were added to the

---

* Under the amended section 52 (2) (hh), the minister was empowered to make regulations requiring employers of not fewer than ten employees, who were members of a registered trade union, to collect union dues by deductions from their salaries and to remit the same to the relevant union. Such regulations were made under the Trade Unions (Collection of Union Dues) Regulations, 1962.[44]

registrar's armoury in this respect. Section 47A empowered him to suspend the officers of a trade union, either indefinitely or for a specified period, if he was satisfied 'that the funds of trade union have been or are being expended in an unlawful manner or on an unlawful object or on an object not authorized by this Ordinance', or if a trade union failed to keep its accounts in accordance with the provisions of the Ordinance. The only concession that the government would make on this was to allow a suspended officer to appeal to the minister against the registrar's decision[49] (s. 47A(5)). This was neither here nor there for it was like complaining to Peter against Paul. Worse still, instead of suspending a union's officers, the registrar under section 473 could even apply to the High Court for the appointment of a receiver of the assets of a trade union under any of the two situations prescribed in section 47A.

Together with trampling on trade union autonomy, the state sought to curb the workers' most important weapon, the strike. The Trade Disputes (Settlement) Act, 1962,[50] set up a standing dispute-settlement machinery consisting of conciliation and arbitration. True, the parties were not obliged to use this machinery. They could settle their dispute themselves through negotiation or other means. But such 'collective bargaining' outside the statutory machinery and procedures had no teeth. For neither the employer nor the workers could ultimately resort to lock-out or strike in case of failure to reach agreement through negotiations. Section 13(3) made participation in strikes and lock-outs an offence punishable by a fine or imprisonment or both unless all the conditions stipulated therein had been fulfilled. These conditions required that the statutory dispute-settlement machinery should have been fully exhausted (s. 13(2)). In effect, therefore, strikes and lock-outs were made illegal, for if the machinery was exhausted the dispute would have been 'settled' and there would be no trade dispute to strike about. The most important feature of the statutory dispute-settlement machinery was that it was under the supervision of the state and its outcome had to be to the liking of the state. The first step was conciliation by a labour officer appointed by the Labour Commissioner (s. 3(2)). If no settlement was effected by the conciliator, the minister could take one of the following courses: (a) if the dispute was in essential service, refer it to a tribunal for settlement (s. 8(1)(b)); (b) if the dispute was not in an essential service, refer it to a tribunal if the parties consented (s. 8(1)(a); but if the parties did not consent, refer it to a board of enquiry to inquire into the causes and circumstances of the dispute and 'after considering the report of the Board, the Minister may then refer the dispute to a tribunal for settlement' (s. 8(1)(c)). Thus the minister could impose arbitration by a tribunal on the parties regardless of the parties' wishes. The 'essential services' provisions of the earlier colonial ordinance had now been generalized to all sectors with only one spurious distinction: the dispute had to go through one more stage of a board of enquiry before being sent to a tribunal in case the parties did not consent straightaway for it to be sent to a tribunal.

The tribunal themselves were *ad hoc* bodies in whose composition and decision-making powers the dominant actor was the state. Section 18(1) provided:

A tribunal shall consist of either:-
  (a) a sole arbitrator appointed by the Minister; or
  (b) an arbitrator appointed by the Minister, assisted by one or more assessors nominated by or on behalf of the employers concerned and an equal number of assessors nominated by or on behalf of the employees concerned, all of whom shall be appointed by the Minister; or
  (c) one or more arbitrators selected from a panel nominated by or on behalf of the employers concerned and an equal number of arbitrators selected from a panel nominated by or on behalf of the employees concerned, and an independent chairman, all of whom shall be appointed by the Minister.

In case (a) or (b), the award of the tribunal was to be made by the arbitrator and in case (c), if there was no agreement, by the independent chairman. In each case, therefore, it was the appointee of the state who made the final decision. Even then the state took no chances. The award had to be confirmed by the minister before it was brought into effect (s. 22(2)(a)). The minister could refuse to confirm it and refer it back to the tribunal with his own statement of objections in which case the tribunal had to reconsider its award and make a new one (s. 22(4)). If the minister was still dissatisfied with the new award he could scrap the tribunal and appoint a new one (s. 22(b)). The whole machinery was to ensure that it did not get out of the hands of the state at any point and that the final outcome was to its full satisfaction.

Outlawing of strikes and the imposition of compulsory statutory arbitration virtually abolished the free collective bargaining that the trade unions had won from the employers through their struggles. The trade union movement itself was so centralized and controlled by the state that it was a short step from being part of it.

There was a further right that the working class lost through this legislation without much fanfare. This was the right of striking in sympathy — a right to show solidarity with their comrades. This came about almost surreptitiously by changing the definition of the term 'trade dispute'. In the 1950 Ordinance, 'trade dispute' had been defined as 'any dispute or difference between employers and workmen . . . or between workmen and any authority or body, connected with the employment or non-employment, or the terms of the employment, or with the conditions of labour, *of any person*' (my emphasis). It was therefore recognized that a trade dispute could exist between certain workers and their employer (or even any other authority or body) not connected with *their own* conditions of employment but connected with the conditions of employment of other employees with another employer. This was an important legal recognition that the workers had won. The 1962 Act defined 'trade dispute' as 'any dispute between an employer and employees *in the employment of that employer* connected with the employment or non-employment, or the terms of the employment, or with the conditions of labour, *of any of those employees*' (my emphasis). The definition was narrowed in two respects. First, a legitimate trade dispute could exist only with one's own employer, not with any other authority or body; and secondly, the dispute had to be in connection with the conditions of employment of the employees involved in the dispute. The most important effect of this change, as we have already said, was to withdraw legal recognition from disputes arising in or as a result of solidarity with fellow workers not in the same enterprise.

Finally, the 1962 Act did not apply to those in the service of the government (s. 1(2)). Separate legislation was passed to cover civil servants. The Civil Service (Negotiating Machinery) Act, 1962,[51] set up a joint staff council on which the government and the relevant trade union were represented (s. 3). This was the negotiating body. Failure to reach agreement in this body resulted in a dispute, which had to be referred to the minister (ss. 2(1) and 8). The minister would then appoint a board of enquiry and ultimately make a final and binding award following the board's report (ss. 11 and 13). Participation in strikes was made a criminal offence unless the statutory procedure described above had been fully exhausted (s. 17), which practically made strikes illegal. The most controversial provision was that the Act applied only to junior civil servants, who were defined as those earning less than £702 per annum (s. 2(1)). Furthermore, no senior civil servant (that is, those earning above £702 per annum) 'shall be or become a member of any trade union or any body or association affiliated to a trade union' (s. 25). The trade unions put up a stiff resistance to this distinction between junior and senior civil servants for they realized that it would mean depriving the unions of their most articulate leadership. When the Bill came up for debate in Parliament, Mkello, although by now cowed down, argued that the division between junior and senior civil servants was not even in keeping with the aim of building a socialist country: 'if the country is divided up into two . . . how can we attain this socialism we are aiming at?'[52] He also cogently questioned the power of the minister to make the final award because the minister was part of the government, and the government was the employer of these employees. The then Prime Minister, Mr Kawawa, minced no words. Rhetoric of socialism apart, Kawawa argued that senior civil servants were in the shoes of management, in the place of an employer, and therefore they could not be members of a trade union. 'It is not that we are trying to create classes of people, not at all, Sir. It is only a division of labour.'[53] With regard to the minister making the final decision, Kawawa replied emphatically that the government must have the final say and could not leave the matter for an arbitrator to decide. In the language of all class governments, Kawawa argued that the government had a wider outlook and took into account national interests rather than just those of the civil service.

The passing of this legislation had one immediate effect: the number of strikes fell dramatically. In 1963 there were only eighty-five strikes involving 27,207 workers with some 77,195 man-days lost.[54] Yet the simmering conflict between the trade unions and the government had not quite subsided. Around December 1962, Victor Mkello, the general secretary of the plantation workers' union and the president of the TFL, and Shehe Amiri, the organizing secretary of the former, were rusticated to Sumbawanga following strikes in the sisal industry. When Mkello came out of restriction he only reluctantly and after pressure signed the sisal agreement. Tumbo had resigned his post as the High Commissioner within a few months of appointment and returned to form his People's Democratic Party.[55] Public attacks on the government for passing the hated legislation, for lack of Africanization and other matters continued unabated, and the most vociferous critics were the trade unionists.[56] Meanwhile, within the TFL itself internal conflicts continued, TANU and the government trying to pressurize and use some moderate leaders against the more militant.[57] The upshot was that in September 1963 the Minister of Labour, Kamaliza, circulated secret proposals for reorganizing the TFL as a national workers' union to be integrated in the ministry.[58] In spite of their relative weakness and fear that had been struck by Mkello's earlier rustication, the TFL (except the Transport and General Workers' Union and the Domestic and Hotel Workers' Union) rejected Kamaliza's proposals. Once again the conflict was given vent in vitriolic public debates.[59]

A few months later the state delivered the final blow. In January 1964 the soldiers of the Tanganyika Rifles mutinied, demanding higher pay and Africanization of the officer corps.[60] The mutiny was eventually suppressed with the help of British troops, but some 200 trade union leaders, including many members of the TFL executive committee, were detained on the alleged ground that they had attempted to make contact with the mutineers.[61] Among the detainees were all the important critics of the government, including the top leaders of TUPE, TRAU, TMU and the dockworkers' union.[62] Within a month of the detention, and while the leading trade unionists were still in gaol, the government rushed through Parliament the National Union of Tanganyika Workers (Establishment Act), 1964,[63] establishing one union and dissolving the TFL and its member unions (s. 7).

The NUTA (Establishment) Act was contrary to virtually every principle of voluntary organization of workers or trade unions known to the history of working classes. The law established the union and gave power to the president of the republic to disestablish it if he was satisfied that the union had failed to carry out its objects (s. 5(1)).

He could go ahead and establish some other body representative of employees which, again by law, was *deemed* to be a trade union (s. 5(1)(b)). Members themselves had no say whatsoever in all this. As a matter of fact, the membership itself was constituted by law, and such membership had no power to dissolve their own union (s. 5(2)). Section 11 made the members of the former unions members of the new union. The Act provided for union shop as well. Where 50 per cent of the employees of an employer were members of the union, the minister could apply the provisions of union shop under which the rest of the employees (except those earning not less than Shs. 14,040 per annum and performing managerial functions) would be obliged to become members of NUTA on the pain of being otherwise dismissed from their employment (see s. 6). The membership of the union was open to any employee employed in Tanganyika (rule 4(3)), which meant that the former ban on senior civil servants (that is, those earning more than £702 per annum) from becoming union members was lifted.* Now that the former unions were abolished, presumably there was no more a need for such a distinction.

The Act itself was a very short piece of legislation, consisting of only fifteen sections out of which almost one-third were transitional provisions relating to the property, rights, liabilities and other obligations of the former unions (ss. 8–10, 11–13). But the state also provided the rules by which the new union was to be governed. These were appended to the Act as its First Schedule. The rules gave the objects of the union, its structure, including various organs and officers and their functions and duties. Among its objects was to be affiliated to TANU, to promote policies of and to encourage its members to join TANU (rule 3(2)). A hierarchical structure of organs was established from branch to national level. At the national level there were three main organs: the annual congress, the general council and the executive council. Each of these organs was directed by appointed officers. (The chairman of the annual congress and the general council were elected by the general council — rule 33(2).) At the headquarters of the union, the administration was divided into departments and industrial sections. Eight departments (rule 15(1)) and nine industrial sections (rule 12(1)) were established. The departments were headed by directors, while each industrial section was headed by an assistant general secretary.

The general secretary and the deputy general secretary were appointed by the president of the republic. The general secretary in turn appointed the financial secretary, the assistant general secretaries, the director of organization and the director of economics and research who held office at his pleasure. These officers, known as the general officers of the union, constituted the executive council chaired by the general secretary. The executive council appointed regional secretaries and branch officers. Thus, virtually the total leadership of the union at all levels consisted of *appointed* officers, appointed either by the president or the president's appointees. They owed their existence to the state rather than membership of the union. The state in turn ensured that these officers did not develop ambitions of their own, by cutting off structural links between them and the grass-roots of the working class. Thus, for instance, although the industrial sections more or less coincided with the former unions,† they were

---

* The Trade Unions and Trade Disputes (Miscellaneous Provisions) Act, 1964,[64] amended the Civil Service (Negotiating Machinery) Act, removing the £702 limit and instead prohibiting only some named senior officers from joining trade unions.
† There were nine industrial sections: dockworkers and seafarers, agricultural workers, domestic and hotel workers, transport and general workers, government workers, local government workers, EACSO workers, mines and quarry workers, and teachers (rule 12(1)).

administrative departments rather than organs representing particular sections of the working class, and they had no structural or organic links with the membership. To put it differently, the assistant general secretary of dockworkers, to take one example, was not a *leader* of dockworkers, but an *administrator* shuffling files connected with dockworkers.

With the NUTA Act, the state had at one stroke accomplished two things: first, it destroyed the existing opposition from trade unionists and ensured, legally and structurally, that such opposition would not arise in future and have a base in the mass of workers; secondly, it established its *organizational* control over the working class. The Act pronounced the death of autonomous trade union movements in Tanganyika. NUTA was nothing but, for all intents and purposes, part of the state apparatus; it had in fact to be 'deemed' to be a trade union by law. The first secretary of NUTA was also the Minister of Labour, M. M. Kamaliza — and the majority of general officers were from the former pro-government trade union, the TGWU.[65]

There was no organized or spontaneous resistance from the working class to the smashing of the trade union movement and the formation of NUTA. This is probably understandable. Virtually the whole of the militant leadership of the movement was in gaol. Those who remained outside were essentially 'yes-men'. Furthermore, the context and circumstances in which the attack came, that is, as the immediate aftermath of the mutiny, allowed the powers-that-be to whip up nationalist phobia, making it most inopportune for any resistance or opposition. The working class was organizationally leaderless and ideologically defenceless. Smashing of independent trade union organizations was the first sign of the state's subsequent actions which destroyed in effect all organizations outside the state-party structures. Such an ominous turn of events passed without much fanfare or comment. Yet it ended one of the most important chapters in the history of the Tanzanian working class.

Conclusion: strengths and weaknesses

The relatively swift and easy dissolution, without much resistance, of what was once a strong and massive trade union movement leaves a big question mark: what were the factors which made this possible? We suggest that some of the same factors which accounted for the movement's strength and successes during the 1950s contained within them the germs of weakness which facilitated its downfall.

First, let us quickly recapitulate the historical origins of the working class. Until the 1940s it was predominantly semi-proletarian with very little experience of collective struggle and collective organization. Lack of industrial development meant that it fell to such permanent workers as dockworkers and domestic servants to lead the way. The first grass-root experience of the working class at collective organization among the dockworkers was brutally smashed, thus ending the most promising development of working class organization. In sum, the working class was relatively young and inexperienced when it faced the onslaught of the state in the 1960s.

Secondly, the development of trade unions which began in earnest in the mid-1950s was essentially 'from the top'. Compared to the first phase of the 1940s, there was a marked double-shift in the later phase: the dominance of white-collar unions within the movement on the one hand, and the dominance of petty-bourgeois leadership within the unions, on the other. These tendencies were nurtured, helped and encouraged by state policy and legislation. The formation or the centre — TFL — from the top, which was responsible for massive unionization, further consolidated these tendencies. The relatively undifferentiated and super-exploited working class in turn allowed rapid trade union growth with a mass base. The result was a highly bureaucratic and centralized organization heavily dependent on the leadership with minimal genuine participation in decision-making of the rank and file membership. Such organization, to a large extent, was well suited for *economic* struggle — collective bargaining, strikes, and so on with individual or a group of employers. Yet it harboured serious weaknesses. The trade union organization did not strike deep roots in the working class; it did not become part of their culture, in other words. There grew a distance between the leadership and the membership without any organic links, and the bureaucratic structure militated against democratic organization. This weakness became a decisive shortcoming when in the immediate post-independence period the movement was drawn into political confrontation with the state.

Thirdly, the so-called 'division of labour' between TANU and the trade union movement, between politics and economics, may have helped the trade unions to escape suppression of the colonial state in the short run. But in the long run, it bred the ideology of economism — which Lenin called bourgeois politics within the working class. This no doubt strengthened the hand of the trade union petty-bourgeois leadership *vis-à-vis* the mass of the working class, but in turn it weakened it as against the TANU-based petty-bourgeoisie. The latter's virtual monopoly of the leadership of the nationalist struggle and ideology gave it a legitimacy which was combined shrewdly with the use of state power to crush all opposition on the morrow of independence. So far as the mass of the working class was concerned, it was deprived of the experience of explicitly *political* struggles against the colonial state. As we have seen, there was not a single *political* strike during the strike wave of the 1950s. Thus ideologically and politically the trade unions were not equipped for the essentially political struggle that unfolded after independence.

Fourthly, immediately after independence, the struggles that ensued involved the transformation of the state and state power within the framework of imperialist domination. It involved the nascent bureaucratic bourgeoisie attempting to fill the role of a compradorial class *vis-à-vis* imperialism on the one hand, and establishing its hegemony over the working people, on the other. This reorganization was patently threatened by the trade unions, and inevitably they were drawn into a political struggle. The EA High Commission and the Africanization issues represented at best only sectional interests of the petty-bourgeoisie within the trade unions; but they were political issues nevertheless involving questions of state policy and orientation. The issue of trade union freedom, however, objectively represented the interests of the working class as a whole and was a political question *par excellence*. Yet the trade union movement was not prepared politically, organizationally or ideologically for an explicitly political struggle. Both the content and form of the struggle was dictated by the petty-bourgeois leadership. It consisted of public statements, vitriolic debates, militant language and *ad hoc* actions. But at no point was any attempt made to link it with working-class action. Political unionism was unknown to these trade unionists. It may also be true that the trade union leadership itself was too estranged from the working-class membership to feel comfortable to appeal to them. When some trade unionists did realize that the question of trade union antonomy was essentially a political question and could not be solved through the trade unions themselves[66] they resorted to either joining or forming splinter political parties. But these parties were petty-bourgeois and provided no alternative to the existing neo-colonial situation. Thus the trade unions could not withstand the onslaught of the state. Once the leadership was decapitated and the organization smashed, the working class appeared to have accepted its fate without a stir — at least for the time being.

NOTES

1. Friedland, W. H., 'Co-operation, Conflict and Conscription: TANU–TFL Relations, 1955–64', in *Boston Papers on Africa*, Vol. III (1966). (The page references are of the mimeo-graphed copy of the University of Dar es Salaam in my possession.)
2. *Tanganyika Standard*, 24 April 1960.
3. Rweyemamu, J. *Underdevelopment*, op. cit. pp. 45–6.
4. Nyerere, J. K. *Freedom and Unity* (Dar es Salaam: Oxford University Press, 1967), pp. 85–98.
5. Quoted in Friedland, W. H. 'Co-operation, Conflict and Conscription', op. cit., p. 7.
6. *Tanganyika Standard*, 7 July 1960.
7. *Tanganyika Standard*, 10 August 1960.
8. *Tanganyika Standard*, 29 August 1960.
9. Friedland, W. H., 'Co-operation, Conflict and Conscription', op. cit., p. 9.
10. See Tandau, A., *Historia*, op. cit., pp. 65–8. Cf. Magongo, R. J., 'Co-operation not domination', *Spearhead* (January 1962), Vol. I., No. 3, pp. 12–13. (Magongo was the general secretary of TUPE.)
11. Iliffe, J., *Modern History*, op. cit., p. 573.
12. Kaniki, M. H. Y., 'TANU: The Party of Independence and National Concilliation'. in Ruhumbika, G. (ed.), *Towards Ujamaa: Twenty Years of TANU Leadership* (Dar es Salaam: East African Literature Bureau, 1974), pp. 11–12.
13. Bienen, H., op. cit., pp. 162–3.
14. See, for instance, *Tanganyika Standard*, 9 February 1962, 7 March 1962 and 10 May 1972.
15. Nyerere J. K., op. cit., pp. 99–102.
16. EACSO, *Report of the Africanization Commission*, March 1963, Table I, p. 7.
17. *Tanganyika Standard*, 9 February 1962.
18. See, for instance, MLH 4/29/75/II.
19. Opening the Annual General Meeting of the Railway Asian Union, the acting Regional Representative of the Railways Administration said: 'The way in which your members behaved in the strike was an excellent example of how public-spirited servants of a national transport system should carry out their responsibilities in times of crisis' (*Tanganyika Standard*, 26 June 1960).
20. ARLD, 1962, pp. 8, 58. MLH 4/15/2/III, MLH/4/19/9/II, MLH 4/19/27/II, MLH/19/20/II, MLH 4/19/18/III, Monthly Report of the Labour Officer, Tanga, December 1963, MLH 4/19/55/II.
21. MLH 724/121/C.
22. ibid.
23. Rweyemamu, J. *Underdevelopment*, op. cit., p. 39.
24. ARLD, 1962.
25. Ofunguo, A. C., op. cit., pp. 111 ff.
26. Kawawa, R. M. op. cit., p. 15.
27. *Tanganyika Standard*, 23 June 1962.
28. *Tanganyika Standard*, 25 June 1962.
29. See above, Chs. 4 and 6.
30. *Tanganyika Standard*, 22 June 1962.
31. *Tanganyika Standard*, 21 June 1962.
32. ibid.
33. *Tanganyika Standard*, 17 June 1962.
34. ibid.
35. *Tanganyika Standard*, 15 June 1962, 20 June 1962 and 23 June 1962.
36. *Tanganyika Standard*, 25 June 1962.
37. The whole debate is in Tanganyika Parliamentary Debates (Hansard), 1st Session, 5 June–3 July 1962.
38. ibid., pp. 1023, 1026.
39. ibid., p. 1027.

40. ibid., p. 1052.
41. ibid., p. 1071.
42. ibid.
43. No. 51 of 1962.
44. GN No. 446 of 26 October 1962.
45. *Tanganyika Standard*, 10 June 1959.
46. Tanganyika Parliamentary Debates, 1st Session, p. 1026.
47. ibid.
48. No. 44 of 1962.
49. Tanganyika Parliamentary Debates, 1st Session, p. 1023.
50. No. 43 of 1962.
51. No. 52 of 1962.
52. Tanganyika Parliamentary Debates, 1st Session, p. 1080.
53. ibid., p. 1082.
54. Jackson, D., *The Disappearance of Strikes in Tanzania: Incomes Policy and Industrial Democracy* (Working Paper Series, No. 117, University of Aston Management Centre, November 1978), p. 2.
55. Bienen, H., op. cit., p. 58.
56. Friedland, W. H., 'Co-operation, Conflict and Conscription', op. cit., pp. 18–19.
57. Ibid., p. 2.
58. Guillebaud, C. W. op. cit., p. 98.
59. See Friedland, W. H., 'Co-operation, Conflict and Conscription', op. cit.
60. Listowel, J., *The Making of Tanganyika* (London: Chatto & Windus, 1965), App. III.
61. Friedland, W. H., *Vuta Kamba*, op. cit., p. 148.
62. Tumbo, N. S. K., 'Towards NUTA: The Search for Permanent Unity in Tanganyika's Trade Union Movement', Political Science Dissertation, March 1969, EAF.
63. No. 18 of 1964.
64. No. 64 of 1964.
65. Friedland, W. H., 'Co-opereation, Conflict and Conscription', op. cit., p. 23.
66. See, for example, Tumbo's remark cited by Friedland to the effect that whether an independent trade-union movement could exist in Tanganyika was not an economic issue but one which would be settled only through the political process. Friedland, W. H., 'Co-operation, Conflict and Conscription', op. cit., p. 28 n. 45.

Conclusion

This study has dealt with one area of law — labour law — and attempted to locate its development within the general social history of relations between capital and labour. Labour law is closely and immediately related to *capitalist* relations of production. We have had therefore to look into the development and the specific characteristics of wage-labour within the concrete context of the political economy of colonialism.

To be sure, the study has gone into a fair amount of detail and documentation. In this conclusion therefore we step back from the mass of details to paint an overall picture of the inter-relationships between law, state and society. In the language of an artist, we wish to depict the main relations in broad strokes on a historical canvass of some forty-five years.

Capitalist relations in Tanzania were not part of the process of organic development of the Tanzanian society. They were introduced as a result of imperialist invasion and subsequent colonization of the country. Finance capital partially destroyed the natural economy, introduced commodity production and integrated the Tanzanian social economy in the world capitalist market.

The first phase of capitalist penetration was characterized by the process of creation of labour power as a commodity. In this the colonial state played a central role. Various measures used to divorce the producer from his means of production were marked by administrative fiat and regulated by bureaucratic processes without much legal/judicial supervision. So far as labour law was concerned, the Master and Native Servants Ordinance formed the most important piece of legislation.

Although couched in legal language, the Ordinance was more of an embodiment of administrative directions to state officials rather than a result of any struggle between labour and capital. Its principal purpose was to facilitate and regulate the procurement of semi-proletarian labour for capital. The use of the instrument of 'contract' under the Master and Native Servants Ordinance was devoid of content. Contract as a legal vehicle reflecting the exchange of equivalents between 'free' agents presupposes the existence of 'free' labour. Semi-proletarian labour was not such 'free' labour; it was still tied to its means of production. Hence, even the remedy for breach of the so-called contract under that Ordinance was to be found in penal sanctions. (This further highlights the central role of the state during this phase of the development of wage-labour.)

Monopoly capital strives for not only average but super-profits. One of the ways in which it did this in the colonies was by creating the system of semi-proletarian labour which was paid ridiculously low wages. Thus the semi-proletariat lived in miserable conditions. In spite of that, labour could not put up much resistance because its semi-proletarian character militated against collective organization and resistance. On the other hand capital was extremely well organized, particularly in terms of minimizing inter-capitalist contradictions on the one hand and exerting pressure on the state, on the other.

None the less, 100 per cent monopoly is impossible in a capitalist mode of production. Inter-capital contradictions are inevitable. As we showed in Chapter 3, local big capital was closely allied with finance capital but having contradictions with local medium and small capital. If these contradictions did not manifest themselves in any serious fashion, it was partly due to the lack of opposition from the semi-proletarian labour which enabled capital to remain fairly united.

Although labour was predominantly semi-proletarian, it was inevitable that small nuclei of permanent wage-labour would develop within the interstices of the colonial economy. In Chapter 4 we discussed the various sources and origins of permanent wage-labour as well as its conditions. In that chapter we traced the history of the manufacturing industry and the development of the industrial proletariat.

The development of permanent wage-labour was reflected in law by the repeal of the Master and Native Servants Ordinance and the passage of the Employment Ordinance. Servant changed to employee. True, the Employment Ordinance still retained some of the features of its predecessor but this was transitional. The colonial state was too close to the settler and plantation interests to overcome their opposition to the abolition of migrant labour immediately. But the process had been set in motion. Within four years of its passage, and particularly after independence, the Employment Ordinance saw some major changes bringing the migrant system to an end. The new industralization policy of the post-independence state coupled with the intense trade union struggles of the working class made the change inevitable.

With the development of the proletariat, the struggle of the working class shifted from individual resistance to collective action, from rebellion and riots to strikes and from welfare societies to trade unions. The first salvoes of collective action were fired by the dockworkers in the early 1940s. Then the labour scene began to change, reflected in the labour legislation as well. The labour legislation that came in the wake of the struggles of the 1940s and the 1950s was of three types. The first type attempted to lay down minimum conditions and terms of employment. Such were the Minimum Wage Ordinances, the Factory Ordinance and the Workmen's Compensation Ordinance. The second type was to control and oversee the development of collective organization of labour. Such were, for example, the Trade Union Ordinances. Here the state came out as a collective capitalist to protect and ensure the long-term interests of the employing class by keeping track and control of working-class organizations. The third type laid down the standing machinery to settle industrial disputes arising from collective resistance of labour. This was the legislation dealing with trade disputes. Once again the state played a leading role in the process: ostensibly as a neutral referee between capital and labour but in reality in the interest of and on the side of capital as we have amply demonstrated in this study.

The legislation we just mentioned did not come about either fortuitously or as a result of benevolence or malevolence on the part of capital and its state. Rather it was part and culmination of intense class struggles between capital and labour. This point needs to be underlined if only to counter simplistic and mechanical notions which posit the relation between law, state and class in a mechanistic/economistic fashion. It is undoubtedly true that state and law ultimately serve the interests of the ruling/ dominating class. But this comes about in the process of complex social struggles. As a result of these struggles, undeniably the law comes to embody certain partial successes and concessions won by the dominated classes. But this should not be taken to mean that law has no class character or that it is a neutral arena of class struggle. Neither law nor legality *per se* is in the interests of the oppressed classes. Rather, it is the social struggles of the oppressed classes themselves which lend certain content to law and legality. Thus a lawyer has to look beyond law and discern its social character if he is to understand and explain it, a task beyond bourgeois positivism.

The relation between capital and labour is inherently contradictory with opposed interests. This contradiction is manifested in law at various levels. One manifestation of this contradiction goes under the name of industrial dispute in the language of industrial relations.

Two types of disputes may be distinguished: individual and collective. The relation between individual worker and employer in law is governed by the contract of employment, and the law treats individual disputes as essentially breaches of contract. This is only a partial reflection of the material relation of capital and labour. The contract of employment only encapsulates the market relation between labour power as a commodity and capital as money. But labour power is a unique commodity. Unlike other commodities, its use creates other commodities and it cannot be detached from its owner, the worker. Hence, its very use involves supervision and disciplining of labour which is beyond the pale of the market and behind the factory gates. Bourgeois law, however, has always been historically reluctant to enter the factory gates. That is the prerogative of capitalist management. It was only the collective resistance and organization of labour that forced through such legislation as the Factory law regulating conditions of work. Once again in Tanzania it was such struggles which forced the colonial state and the independent state to enact legislation dealing with minimum terms and conditions of employment.

But then the capitalist state is a custodian of the system as a whole. It must ensure that the system functions smoothly and the production process does not come to a halt. Hence its legislation on trade-disputes machinery which became a marked feature of the labour laws in the late 1940s and early 1950s. The state must also ensure that the working class does not overstep its boundaries of organization from demanding higher wages (trade union struggle) to fighting for the abolition of the wage-system (socialist struggle). Hence such laws as those which control trade unions, strikes and so on. Chapters 5, 6 and 7 dealt with these various aspects.

To be sure, the struggles described in the last three chapters have been about and organized around trade union demands. Yet at various points they have overflowed trade union boundaries into the overtly political arena. Working-class action, even if only in the form of a strike, has an inevitable *political* implication to the extent that it is an expression of a *class* (collective) will to withdraw labour power, the life-line of a capitalist system. To protect the system as a whole, the state invariably gets involved in such situations, whether through the force of its arms (such as the police and paramilitary to break strikes) or through its arm of force (law, bureaucratic directives and so on).

But the trade union organization is not ideologically nor politically nor organizationally armed to withstand the political intervention of the state which is the 'organization of the ruling class' (Lenin) *par excellence*. The two intensive periods of trade union struggles — 1939–50 and 1955–64 — dramatically illustrate these arguments.

Each of these periods was brought to a close, so to speak, by a decisive intervention of the state leaving the working class physically exhausted and organizationally decapitated. In the subsequent interval of relative 'peace', the state consolidated itself by adding to its legal armoury various pieces of legislation to control, supervise, 'channel in the correct direction', and so on, working-class resistance and organization. Yet in the absence of its own proletarian, political organization, the working class was not in a position to take stock of the past, learn from its 'mistakes', consolidate its experience and prepare for the next round. This is not to say that these struggles were totally lost and left no imprint on the development and consciousness of the class. Indeed, such separate economic movements and struggles are an indispensable means towards the development and consciousness of the working class and a first step in the growth of its political movement and organization. But there is no iron law that economic movement inevitably and necessarily grows into a political movement. For this, at a certain stage, political organization of the proletariat becomes absolutely necessary.

This study also illustrates our initial proposition that law does not have a history of its own and, we hope, helps to cast off many illusions perpetrated by lawyers themselves. Lawyers do not make or change laws. It is the social forces locked in struggle which really supply the content of what the lawyer shapes. He should therefore at least know what interests he serves in the process and, it is to be hoped, chooses his side accordingly.

Appendices

Appendix A Types of Labour

Table A.1 *Types of labour, 1947*

Type of labour	General No.	General %	Eastern No.	Eastern %	Lake No.	Lake %	Northern No.	Northern %	Southern No.	Southern %	Southern Highlands No.	Southern Highlands %	Tanga No.	Tanga %	Western No.	Western %	Total No.	Total %
Attested	—	— / 0.0	2 319	11.4 / 5.23	485	2.4 / 3.4	4 970	24.5 / 15.1	32	0.2 / 0.2	—	0.0 / 0.0	12 466	61.5 / 20.8	12	0.1 / 0.1	20 284	100.0 / 10.0
Local (non-attested)	2 074	2.1 / 88.0	25 283	25.6 / 56.7	8 464	8.6 / 60.2	10 204	10.3 / 31.1	11 835	12.0 / 63.0	8 858	9.0 / 45.0	25 966	26.3 / 43.3	6 145	6.2 / 65.5	98 829	100.0 / 49.0
Non-attested	282	0.3 / 12.0	16 991	20.6 / 38.1	5 111	6.2 / 36.4	17 664	21.4 / 53.8	6 916	8.4 / 36.9	10 808	13.1 / 55.0	21 506	26.1 / 35.9	3 225	3.9 / 34.4	82 503	100.0 / 40.9
Total male	2 356	1.2 / 100	44 593	22.1 / 100.0	14 060	7.0 / 100.0	32 838	16.3 / 100.0	18 783	9.3 / 100.0	19 666	9.8 / 100.0	59 938	29.7 / 100.0	9 382	4.7 / 100.0	201 616	100.0 / 100.0
Women	47		1 749		168		845		1 603		2 227		4 078		145		10 862	
Children	25		3 493		237		4 371		858		7 533		7 310		248		24 075	
Total workers	2 428		49 835		14 465		38 054		21 244		29 426		71 326		9 775		236 553	

Public services	60 037
Domestic service (est.)	25 500
Late returns (etc.)	2 443
Grand total	324 553

Source: Native Employees' Census, 1947, Table 1, TNA 32679.

Appendix B Female and Juvenile Labour

Table A.2 *Distribution of female and juvenile labour by economic sectors, 1947 and 1951 (in regular employment)*

	1947				1951			
	Female		Juvenile		Female		Juvenile	
	No.	%	No.	%	No.	%	No.	%
Agriculture	9 947	86.0	22 320	91.0	14 277	80.8	27 277	85.6
Mining and quarrying	110	1.0	385	2.0	233	1.3	425	1.3
Infrastructure	602	5.0[b]	379[b]	2.0	180	1.0	450	1.4
Manufacturing	485[a]	4.0	428[b]	2.0	227	1.3	847	2.7
Commercial & professional	n.a		n.a		1 593	9.0	1 295	4.1
Public service	—		—		160	0.9	31	0.1
Domestic service	n.a		n.a		641	3.6	957	3.0
Miscellaneous	479	4.0	1 021	4.0	353	2.0	578	1.8
Total	11 623	100.0	24 533	100.0	17 664	100.0	31 860	100.0
Total labour force	348 500				381 048			

Notes: [a] Includes trade and transport. [b] Includes public service.
Source: ARLD, 1948 (Table 11); ARLD, 1951 (Tables 1E and C).

Appendix C   The Industrial Proletariat: Skilled wage labour

Table A.3 *Distribution of employment of all adult African males by skills and industries, 1949*

Industrial classification	Clerical staff	Shop, office,[a] store boys, etc.	Total white-collar (service) workers	Mechanics fitters, etc.	Carpenters, joiners, etc.	Masons, bricklayers, etc.	Drivers	Total craftsmen	Other skilled workers	Unskilled workers	Grand total
Agriculture	2 078	1 501	3 579	2 363	1 328	2 207	2 316	8 214	5 935	99 200	116 928
Mining & quarrying	382	316	698	738	309	401	645	2 093	2 377	13 341	18 509
Manufacturing	304	322	626	664	533	574	309	2 080	2 019	15 607	20 332
Transport	784	487	1 271	673	437	408	831	2 349	1 804	16 867	22 291
Building & construction	724	405	1 129	846	1 792	3 649	1 216	7 503	1 852	19 971	30 455
Government employment	3 991	3 768	7 759	944	1 124	1 745	958	4 771	10 144	26 253	48 927
Commercial & professional	733	4 046	4 779	773	456	420	654	2 303	2 807	10 639	20 528
Educational	1 304	171	1 475	257	391	672	71	1 391	1 645	2 126	6 637
Miscellaneous	526	702	1 228	314	433	287	302	1 336	2 370	9 572	14 506
Total	10 826	11 718	22 544	7 572	6 803	10 363	7 302	32 040	30 953	213 576	299 113

Note: [a] Strictly speaking, some groups like office boys do not fall within the white-collar category, but from data available it is not possible to separate them.
Source: Calculated from ARLD, 1949.

Table A.4 *Distribution of employment of all adult African males by skills and industries, 1956*

Industrial classification	Headmen	School-teachers	Clerical staff	Shop, office, store boys, etc.	Total white-collar (service) workers[a]	Mechanics, fitters, etc.	Carpenters, joiners, etc.	Masons, brick-layers, etc.	Drivers	Total crafts-men	Other skilled workers	Unskilled workers	Grand total
Agriculture	8 270	94	2 181	1 352	11 897	2 597	1 285	2 242	3 016	9 140	9 199	134 289	164 525
Mining & quarrying	596	6	345	306	1 253	268	177	281	345	1 071	1 873	9 533	13 730
Manufacturing	388	–	493	537	1 418	1 052	718	161	732	2 663	2 127	9 931	16 139
Transport	483	–	1 383	524	2 390	709	346	206	1 355	2 616	6 721	13 240	24 967
Building & construction	214	47	154	155	570	186	1 018	1 992	329	3 525	606	7 881	12 582
Government employment	6 339	1 267	5 558	4 148	17 312	789	1 665	2 079	1 931	6 464	13 512	43 891	81 179
Commercial & professional	153	3	587	1 998	2 741	264	108	69	553	994	1 015	3 592	8 342
Educational	105	3 434	228	71	3 838	73	421	647	49	1 190	814	3 850	9 692
Miscellaneous	133	158	225	182	698	108	104	137	148	497	780	2 506	4 481
Total	16 681	5 009	11 154	9 273	42 117	6 046	5 842	7 814	8 458	28 160	36 647	228 713	335 637

Notes: [a] Strictly speaking, some groups like office boys do not fall within the white-collar category, but from data available it is not possible to separate them.
Source: Calculated from ARLD 1956.

Table A.5 *Distribution of employment (African adult males only) by skills (%)*

Year	White-collar service workers	Craftsmen	Other skilled workers	Unskilled workers	Total
1949	6	9	9	75	100 (349,239)
1956	11	7	10	72	100 (383,433)

Source: Calculated from Tables A.3 and A.4

Appendix D   The Industrial Proletariat: Manufacturing Sector

Table A.6   *Industrial establishments and employment, 1921–45 (selected years)*

CODE ISIC	Industrial activity	1921		1931		1939		1945	
		No. of establishments	Nos. employed	No. of establishments	Nos. employed	No. of establishments	Nos. employed	No. of establishments	Nos. employed
20–21	Food & beverage industries	10 (20%)	n.a.	103 (38%)	1 055 (14%)	246 (46%)	3 532 (4%)	813 (69%)	16 985 (15%)
22	Tobacco manufacture	1 (2%)	102	1 (0%)	11 (0%)	4 (1%)	565 (1%)	4 (0%)	325 (0%)
23	Textiles	12 (24%)	n.a.	40 (15%)	4 877 (64%)	155 (29%)	77 099[a] (93%)	161 (14%)	88 057[a] (76%)
24	Footwear, wearing apparel & made-up textile goods	–	–	–	–	–	–	–	–
25–26	Wood, furniture & fixtures	2 (4%)	n.a.	40 (15%)	545 (7%)	70 (13%)	937 (1%)	60 (5%)	2 006 (2%)
27–28	Paper printing & publishing	2 (4%)	n.a.	10 (4%)	205 (3%)	10 (2%)	162 (0%)	11 (1%)	75 (0%)
29	Leather products	–	–	1 (0%)	1 (0%)	20 (4%)	111 (0%)	7 (1%)	520 (0%)
30	Rubber products	–	–	2 (1%)	13 (0%)	1 (0%)	4 (0%)	14 (1%)	5 418 (5%)
31–32	Chemicals & products	3 (6%)	n.a.	27 (10%)	109 (1%)	1 (0%)	20 (0%)	72 (6%)	590 (1%)
33	Non-metallic mineral products	5 (10%)	300	27 (10%)	688 (8%)	18 (3%)	725 (1%)	24 (2%)	1 816 (1%)
34–35	Basic metal industries & manufacture of metal products	–	–	–	–	–	–	–	–
36–37	Assembly & repair of machinery	–	n.a.	–	–	–	–	–	–
39	Miscellaneous manufacture	14 (29%)	n.a.	17 (6%)	144 (2%)	7 (1%)	75 (0%)	10 (1%)	10 (0%)
	Factories not classified elsewhere	–	–	–	–	6 (1%)	79 (0%)	6 (1%)	201 (0%)
	Total	49 (100%)	402	268 (100%)	7 648 (100%)	538 (100%)	83 309 (100%)	1 182 (100%)	116 013 (100%)

Note: [a] These figures are of doubtful validity. They probably include the whole labour force of the sisal estates and not simply those working in the decorticating factories.
Source: Honey, M., 'Asian Industrial Activities in Tanganyika', *TNR*, No. 74, 1974.

Table A.7 *Factory employment 1952–66 (selected years)*

CODE ISIC	Industrial activity	1952			1956			1960			1966		
		No. of factories	Nos. employed	Average employees per factory	No. of factories	Nos. employed	Average employees per factory	No. of factories	Nos. employed	Average employees per factory	No. of factories	Nos. employed	Average employees per factory
20	Food manufacture	451 (21%)	7 619 (15%)	17	871 (26%)	10 443 (17%)	12	1 850 (37%)	18 224 (22%)	10	3 109 (46%)	21 835 (24%)	7
21	Beverage industries	40 (2%)	612 (1%)	15	63 (2%)	746 (1%)	12	60 (1%)	766 (1%)	13	61 (1%)	1 019 (1%)	17
22	Tobacco manufacture	3 (0%)	817 (2%)	272	32 (1%)	1 554 (2%)	49	54 (1%)	1 891 (2%)	35	110 (2%)	4 894 (5%)	44
23	Textiles	242 (11%)	21 883 (42%)	90	296 (9%)	26 730 (43%)	90	306 (6%)	35 302 (42%)	115	297 (4%)	27 035 (30%)	91
24	Footwear & clothing	658 (30%)	1 646 (3%)	3	987 (29%)	2 310 (4%)	2	980 (20%)	2 380 (3%)	2	1 126 (17%)	6 203 (7%)	6
25–26	Wood, furniture & fixtures	259 (12%)	6 312 (12%)	24	376 (11%)	7 059 (11%)	19	497 (10%)	7 273 (9%)	15	566 (8%)	8 098 (9%)	14
27–28	Paper, printing, publishing	22 (1%)	651 (1%)	30	26 (1%)	595 (1%)	23	40 (1%)	845 (1%)	21	48 (0%)	1 240 (1%)	26
29	Leather products	31 (1%)	488 (1%)	16	38 (1%)	482 (1%)	13	45 (1%)	574 (1%)	13	44 (0%)	489 (1%)	11
30	Rubber products	2 (0%)	49 (0%)	25	7 (0%)	87 (0%)	12	8 (0%)	90 (0%)	11	15 (0%)	211 (0%)	14
31–32	Chemical, and products	58 (3%)	950 (2%)	16	104 (3%)	1 290 (2%)	12	151 (3%)	1 959 (2%)	13	186 (3%)	2 519 (3%)	14
33	Non-metallic mineral products	21 (1%)	816 (2%)	39	22 (1%)	672 (1%)	31	46 (1%)	1 533 (2%)	33	53 (1%)	1 579 (2%)	30
34–35	Metals and products	23 (1%)	327 (1%)	14	30 (1%)	417 (1%)	14	36 (1%)	489 (1%)	14	43 (1%)	1 123 (1%)	26
36–37	Repair of machinery	108 (5%)	2 892 (6%)	27	124 (4%)	2 140 (3%)	17	213 (4%)	3 312 (4%)	16	263 (4%)	3 764 (4%)	14
38	Assembly and repair of transport equipment	150 (7%)	5 891 (11%)	39	237 (7%)	6 808 (11%)	29	333 (7%)	7 525 (9%)	23	406 (6%)	7 286 (8%)	18
39	Miscellaneous manufacture	41 (2%)	670 (1%)	16	51 (2%)	841 (1%)	16	66 (1%)	631 (1%)	10	102 (1%)	1 199 (1%)	12
	Factories not classified elsewhere	69 (3%)	422 (1%)	6	113 (3%)	487 (1%)	4	232 (5%)	689 (1%)	3	284 (4%)	1 695 (2%)	6
	Total	2 178 (100%)	52 045 (100%)	24	3 377 (100%)	62 661 (100%)	19	4 917 (100%)	83 483 (100%)	17	6 713 (100%)	90 189 (100%)	13

Notes: These figures are helpful only in showing the trend. Since a factory owner is not required to report the cessation of his factory, the data may include factories which are not operative.

Source: Constructed from data in ARLD, 1952, 1956, 1960 and 1966.

Appendix E Form LDG. 164

THE UNITED REPUBLIC OF TANZANIA   LDG. 164

MINISTRY OF LABOUR—LABOUR DIVISION

STOPPAGES OF WORK

File Ref. No..   Date...................................

Station...

1. Strike/Lock-out/Other stoppages.   (Delete whichever are inapplicable.)

2. Industry..I.S.I.C. Number..

3. (i) Undertaking...(ii) TOTAL LABOUR FORCE.....................

    (iii) Address...

4. Number of employees involved by occupation:

Occupation	Directly involved	Indirectly involved	WAGE RATES	
			Before stoppage	After stoppage
....				
....				
....				
....				
....				
Women and Juveniles....				

G P Dsm   13467/11–66/10m/2up

5. (i) Stoppage began at.................a.m./p.m. on................and ended................a.m./p.m. on...............

    (ii) Total number of man-days lost..

6. Reasons for the stoppage:

    (a) Wage rates..

    (b) Hours of work or tasks..

    (c) Other conditions of service (i.e. leave, bonuses, etc.)..

    (d) Joint consultation or negotiation...

    (e) Job security;

        (i) Length of notice...

        (ii) Monthly rates vice daily or kipande...

        (iii) Provident funds, pension or gratuity...

    (iv) Supervisors or supervision...

    (v) Other..

(f) Trade union recognition...

7. What joint consultative or negotiating machinery exists at this undertaking? Give brief details and state whether formally constituted...

....

....

8. Was use made of this machinery for the settlement of this dispute?   Yes/No.

9. Intervention by authorities:

    (i) Nature of (a)..

    (ii) Reason for (b)...

10. Method of settlement (e.g. conciliation by Labour Office, by negotiation, discharge of strikers, etc.)...........

....

11. Terms of settlement...

....

....

12. Comments..

....

....

NOTICE: (a) Labour Officer, Area Commissioner, Police.

      (b) Requested by employer, by strikers, own initiative.

                                              ....
                                              Senior Labour Officer

Bibliography

Note: This bibliography contains only those works which are actually cited in the text.

A. Official — unpublished sources

1. *Tanzania: Tanzania National Archives*

Over 200 files were examined from this source. These are mainly Secretariat and District files. In the notes this source is cited as TNA. Only those files actually cited in the text are listed below.

(a) Secretariat files
10218/I–II.1927–38. Recruitment of Labourers for work outside the Territory.
10286/II. Magisterial Powers for the officers of the Labour Department.
10922/I–III.1927–39. Labour camps.
10953/I–II.1926–54. Powers to force Communal Labour Under Native Authority Ordinance.
11127/I–II.1927–47. Labour Matters — Northern Province.
11168/I–II.1921–45. Labour Matters — Tanga Province.
11523/I–II.1927–32. Conditions of Labourers employed on Railways Construction.
11625/I.1928–31. General Information regarding Native Labour in Tanganyika Territory.
11803/I–III.1928–51. Labour Matters - Bukoba Province.
11850/I–III.1927–47. Employment of Child Labour.
12289.1928. Enquiry into the Deaths of three Native Labourers on the Mbugua Roads in the Arusha District.
13343/II.1946–51. Medical Examinations of Labourers.
18679/III.1932–6. Revision of Master and Native Servants Ordinance.
19335/I.1930–3. Trade Union Legislation.
19368/II.1939–45. Labour Matters — Eastern Province.
20217.1939–52. International Labour Convention concerning the creation of Minimum Wage Fixing Machinery.

21097/I–III.1931–3. International Convention concerning Forced or Compulsory Labour.

22938/I.1935. Outbreak of Scurvy in the Lupa Area Southern Highlands Province.

23047/I–II.1945–52. Recruitment and Supply of Labour for the Mines.

23202. Labour Commission Information and Statistics.

23217.1935 Provincial Administration — Annual Report 1935 — Labour Section.

23435/I–II.1936–37. Evidence and Memorandum for Labour Commission.

23544.1936. Labour on Sisal Estates — Reports by Mr F. Longland.

24693/I.1936–7. Labour for Sisal Industry.

25201.1937. African Labour Union.

25233/I–II.1937–43. Labour Conditions in Ginneries.

25468/I.1936. Factory Inspection Legislation.

25911/II.1940–7. Conciliation Machinery for Settling Labour Disputes.

25912.1939–40. Labour in Dar es Salaam Township.

25931/I.1938. Labour, Medical Survey in Sisal Estates, Northern, Tanga and Eastern Provinces.

25950/I–II.1939. 1951–2 Labour Officer's Report on Geita Gold Mine.

25956.1939. Labour Disturbance at Lanzoni Estate — Tanga.

25971.1940. Labour Conditions in Tanga. Report by Mr R. C. Jerrard.

27259/I–II.1939. The Labour Trade Union of East Africa.

27284.1939. Native Labour Riot in Kidugalo Estate, Morogoro.

28285.1940–50. Mining Accidents.

29002.1940–1. Feeding of Labour on the Lupa.

29619. Children under fourteen years of age accompanying labourers seeking work in Districts other than their own.

A 23217. Administration — Annual Reports — 1935. Labour Section — Provincial.

A 24829. Asiatic Labour Union.

A 25905. Advisory Board — Minutes of Meetings of Labour.

A 27336. Arusha Chini — Labour disturbance at the Tanganyika Planting Company's estate.

30136.1941. Employment of Children in Domestic Services.

30178.1941–5. Labour for Increased Production.

30336.1942. Labourers System of Payment 'by Results'.

30598.1942. Cost of Living for Africans in Townships.

32679.1944–7. Census of Labour.

32744.1949. Domestic Servants.

36490.1947–53. Strikes by Government Employees.

37680.1948–50. Annual and Other Reports — Northern Province Labour Utilization Board.

41111.1950. Select Committee on the Factories Bill.

(b) District files

Tanga: 304/R.3/1 Reports — 1958, 1959 and 1960.

Tanga Regional Office: 4/25/6/IV.1946–8. TSGA.

4/652/70.1947. Labour Strike Dar es Salaam.

4/962/9.1948–9. Labour Reports, Annual.

Mwanza: 41/L1/8.1936–61. Labour — Annual Report on Requisition Labour.

41/L1/2.1946–57. Provincial Wage Committee.

41/L1/1.1951–60. Labour Policy.

215/511/V.1948–50. Labour Reports and Returns.

215/511/VII.1954–7. Labour Reports and Returns.
215/1969/II.1951–8. Labour Quarterly Reports and Bulletins.
Arusha Regional office: 69/316/24/II.1946–47. Labour — Northern Province. Labour
  Allocation Board — recruitment.
  69/332/1.1928–47. Death and Accident Reports.
Mbulu: 305/3/5/14.1939–53. Labour Rations.
  471/L1/3/I.1953–60. Labour: Periodical Reports.
Dar es Salaam: 54. Dar es Salaam District Office.

2. *Tanzania: Ministry of Labour headquarters*

In the Dar es Salaam Headquarters of the Ministry of Labour and Social Welfare there
are files on each undertaking. These files contain mainly inspection and accident
reports and also strikes reports. I examined files for over 700 undertakings, some 600
from Tanga (numbered 4/19) and over 60 from Dar es Salaam (numbered 4/29). A few
files from Mwanza (numbered 4/15), Chunya (numbered 4/13) and Moshi (numbered
4/23) were also examined. The trade dispute files which begin with the number 724
were also looked into. In the notes this source is identified by the tag MLH.

3. *Great Britain: Public Records Office, London*

I consulted mainly the series marked CO 691, Vols. 1–192. Some 36 volumes have been
actually cited in this work. This series contains original correspondence from
Tanganyika.

4. *Other manuscripts: in the University of Dar es Salaam*

Hartman, F. F. and Wilmot, B. C., 'Translated extracts from the files of the German
  East Africa administration in connection with labour matters' (Dar es Salaam:
  Tanzania Ministry of Communications, Labour and Works, Labour Division,
  1969). F20K in University of Dar es Salaam Library.
Tanganyika, Annual Reports 1900–1910. (Typescript of translation in Professor A.
  Sheriff's possession).
—— Minutes of the Provincial Commissioners' Conference, July 1952 (EAF).
W. D. R., 'The Nutrition of Sisal Labour' (Medical Laboratory, Dar es Salaam, August
  1940).
Wilson, D. B., 'Report on a Medical Survey of Sisal Estates' (n.d.).

B. Unofficial — unpublished sources

1. *Great Britain: Rhodes House Library, Oxford*

I consulted mainly the private papers of Sir Barclay Nihill, Major Orde-Browne and the
correspondence of the Fabian Colonial Bureau (FCB) boxes 121–3.

2. *Unpublished theses*

All these except one marked * are to be found in the East Africana section of the University of Dar es Salaam Library.

Graham, J. D., 'Changing Patterns of Wage Labour in Tanzania: a history of the
  relations between African labour and European capitalism in Njombe District,
  1931–1961' (PhD thesis, Northwestern University, 1968).

Honey, M., 'A History of Indian Merchant Capital and Class Formation in Tanganyika, c. 1840–1940' (PhD thesis, University of Dar es Salaam, 1982).

Mascarenhas, A. C., 'Resistance and Change in the Sisal Plantation System of Tanzania' (PhD thesis, University of California, LA, 1970).

Ofunguo, A. C., 'History of Labour on the Mwadui Diamond Mine: 1940–1975' (MA dissertation, University of Dar es Salaam, 1977).

Tambila, A., 'A History of the Tanga Sisal Labour Force, 1936–1964' (MA dissertation, University of Dar es Salaam, 1974).

Tumbo, N. S. K., 'Towards NUTA. The Search for Permanent Unity in Tanganyika's Trade Union Movement' (Political Science Dissertation, March 1969), EAF.

*Walji, S. R., 'Ismailis on Mainland Tanzania, 1850–1948' (MA dissertation, University of Wisconsin, 1969).

3. Unpublished articles and materials

These are mainly to be found in the form of mimeographed material produced at the University of Dar es Salaam and usually in my possession.

Depelchin, J. and **LeMelle, S. J.,** 'Some Aspects of Capital Accumulation in Tanganyika, 1920–1940' (paper presented to History Seminar, University of Dar es Salaam, 1979).

—— 'Research Materials on Companies registered in Tanganyika' (in the possession of the authors).

Freyhold, M., 'On Colonial Modes of Production' (paper presented to History Seminar, University of Dar es Salaam, August 1977).

Hirji, K. F., 'Accidents at Work: The Case of Motor Vehicle Workshops' (Dar es Salaam: National Institute of Transport, 1980).

[Iliffe, J.,] 'Supplementary Statistics and Documents' (University of Dar es Salaam, n.d.).

Kautsky, K., 'The Agrarian Question' (University of Dar es Salaam, trans. J. Banaji).

Lubetsky, R., 'Sectoral Development and Stratification in Tanganyika, 1890–1914' (paper delivered at the 1972 East African Universities Social Science Conference, Dar es Salaam, August 1973).

Patel, L. R., 'East African Labour Regimes: Kenya and Tanganyika' (Dar es Salaam: 1972).

—— 'Labour and Law in East Africa' (Dar es Salaam: mimeo, n.d.).

Rweyemamu, J., 'Major Trends of Macro-economic Aggregates of the Tanzanian Economy since 1954' (Department of Economics, University of Dar es Salaam, n.d.).

C. Official — published sources

Charron, K. C., *The Welfare of the African Labourer in Tanganyika* (Dar es Salaam: Government Printer, 1944).

EACSO, *Report of the Africanization Commission*, March 1963.

East African Statistical Department (Tanganyika Unit), *The Pattern of Income, Expenditure and Consumption of African Workers in Tanga, February 1958* (Dar es Salaam Central Statistical Bureau, 1958).

Gulliver, P. H., 'A Report on the Migration of African Workers to the South from the

Southern Highlands Province, with special reference to the Nyakyusa of Rungwe District' (Dar es Salaam: Government Printer, 1955).

Jack, D. T., *Report on the State of Industrial Relations in the Sisal Industry* (Dar es Salaam: Government Printer, 1959).

— *Report on Methods of Determining Wages in Tanganyika* (Dar es Salaam: Government Printer, 1959).

Mitchell, P. E., *Notes on Labour in Tanganyika* (Dar es Salaam: Government Printer, 1933).

Molohan, M. J. B., *Detribalization* (Dar es Salaam: Government Printer, 1957).

Orde-Browne, G., *Report on Labour in Tanganyika Territory* (London: HMSO, 1926).

— *Labour Conditions in East Africa* (London: HMSO, 1946).

Tanganyika, *Report of the Committee Appointed to Consider and Advise on Questions Relating to the Supply and Welfare of Native Labour in the Tanganyika Territory* (Dar es Salaam: Government Printer, 1938).

— *Annual Reports of the Labour Department 1928-1930, 1944-1963* (Dar es Salaam: Government Printer).

— *Report of the Commission Appointed to Enquire into the Disturbances which occurred in the Port of Tanga during the month of August 1939* (Dar es Salaam: Government Printer, 1939).

— *Annual Report of the Provincial Commissioner, Eastern Province, 1947* (Dar es Salaam: Government Printer).

— *A Preparatory Investigation of the Manpower Position, 1951* (Dar es Salaam: Government Printer, 1951).

— *Annual Report of the Provincial Commissioner, 1952* (Dar es Salaam: Government Printer).

— *Report of the Territorial Minimum Wage Board* (Dar es Salaam: Government Printer, 1962).

— *Report of the Non-Plantation Agricultural Workers Minimum Wages Board* (Dar es Salaam: Government Printer, 1963).

Tanzania, *Survey of Employment and Earnings, 1965* (Dar es Salaam: Central Statistical Bureau).

— *Economic Survey, 1968/69* (Dar es Salaam: Government Printer).

D. Unofficial — published sources

Arrighi, G., 'International Corporation, Labour Aristocracies, and Economic Development in Tropical Africa', in Rhodes, R. I. (ed.), *Imperialism and Underdevelopment* (New York: Monthly Review Press, 1970).

Baran, P. A., *The Political Economy of Growth* (New York: Monthly Review Press, 1968).

Barker, C. and **Wield, D.,** 'Notes on International Firms in Tanzania', *Utafiti*, Vol. III, No. 2, 1978 (University of Dar es Salaam).

Bienen, H., *Tanzania: Party Transformation and Economic Development* (Princeton: Princeton University Press, 1970).

Brett, E. A., *Colonialism and Underdevelopment in East Africa: The Politics of Economic Change, 1919-39* (London: Heinemann Educational Books, 1973).

Buruku, D. S., 'The Townsman: Kleist Sykes', in Iliffe, J. (ed.), *Modern Tanzanians* (Dar es Salaam: East African Publishing House, 1973).

Clayton, A. and **Savage D. C.,** *Government and Labour in Kenya, 1895-1963,* (London: Frank Cass, 1974).

Davies, I., *African Trade Unions* (Harmondsworth: Penguin Books, 1966).

Encyclopaedia Britannica, Vol. 26 (11th edn).

—— Vol. 15 (1962 edn).

Engels, F., *Ludwig Feuerbach and the End of Classical German Philosophy,* in Marx, K. and Engels, F. *Selected Works,* Vol. III (Moscow: Progress Publishers, 1970).

—— *The Peasant War in Germany* (Moscow: Progress Publishers, 1965).

Frankel, S. H., *Capital Investment in Africa* (London: Oxford University Press, 1938).

Friedland, W. H., 'Co-operation, Conflict and Conscription: TANU–TFL Relations, 1955–64', in *Boston Papers on Africa,* Vol. III (1966).

—— 'The Institutionalization of Labour Protest in Tanganyika and some Resultant Problems', *Sociology,* Berlin, Vol. 2, No. 2, 1961.

—— *Vuta Kamba: The Development of Trade Unions in Tanganyika* (Stanford: Hoover Institution Press, 1969).

Guillebaud, C. W., *An Economic Survey of the Sisal Industry of Tanganyika* (Welwyn: James Nisbet, 1966) (3rd edn).

Hill, M. F., *Permanent Way: the Story of the Tanganyika Railways,* Vol. I (Nairobi: East African Railways and Harbours, 1957).

Hirji, K. F., 'Colonial Ideological Apparatuses in Tanganyika under the Germans', in Kaniki, M. H. Y. (ed.), *Tanzania Under Colonial Rule* (London: Longman, 1979).

Hitchcock, E., 'The Sisal Industry of East Africa', *TNR,* No. 52, March 1959 (Dar es Salaam: The Tanzania Society).

Honey, M., 'Asian Industrial Activities in Tanganyika', *TNR,* No. 74, 1974.

Huberman, L., *Man's Wordly Goods: The Story of the Wealth of Nations* (New York: Monthly Review Press, 1968).

Iliffe, J., *A Modern History of Tanganyika* (Cambridge: Cambridge University Press, 1979).

—— 'A History of the Dockworkers of Dar es Salaam', *TNR,* No. 71, 1970.

—— *Agricultural Change in Modern Tanganyika,* Historical Association of Tanzania, Paper no. 10 (Nairobi: East African Publishing House, 1971).

—— *Tanganyika under German Rule, 1905–1912* (Nairobi: East African Publishing House, 1969).

—— 'The Spokesman: Martin Kayamba', in Iliffe, J., (ed.), *Modern Tanzanians* (Dar es Salaam: East African Publishing House, 1973).

—— 'Wage Labour and Urbanization', in Kaniki, M. H. Y. (ed.), *Tanzania Under Colonial Rule* (London: Longman, 1979).

Jackson, D., *The Disappearance of Strikes in Tanzania: Incomes Policy and Industrial Democracy* (Working Paper series No. 117, University of Aston Management Centre, November 1978).

James, R. W. and **Fimbo, G. M.,** *Customary Land Law of Tanzania: A Sourcebook* (Nairobi: East African Literature Bureau, 1973).

Japhet, K. and **Seaton, E.,** *The Meru Land Case* (Nairobi: East African Publishing House, 1967).

Kaniki, M. H. Y., 'TANU: The Party of Independence and National Conciliation', in Ruhumbika, G. (ed.), *Towards Ujamaa: Twenty Years of TANU Leadership* (Dar es Salaam: East African Literature Bureau, 1974).

Kawawa, R. M., 'The TFL, TANU and Unity', *Spearhead* (The Pan-African Review), Vol. I., No. 2, December, 1961.

Khamisi, L., *Imperialism Today* (Dar es Salaam: Tanzania Publishing House, 1983).

Kifile, H. O., 'Labour Relations in Tanzania', in *International Labour Review,* Vol. 88, October 1963.

Kjekshus, H., *Ecology Control and Economic Development in East African History: The Case of Tanganyika, 1850–1950* (London: Heinemann, 1977).

Lawrence, P. R., 'Plantation Sisal: the Inherited Mode of Production', in Cliffe, L., *et al.* (eds), *Rural Co-operation in Tanzania* (Dar es Salaam: Tanzania Publishing House, 1975).

Lenin, V. I., *Imperialism, the Highest Stage of Capitalism,* in Lenin, V. I., *Collected Works,* Vol. 22 (Moscow: Progress Publishers, 1964).

—— *The Development of Capitalism in Russia* (Moscow: Progress Publishers, 1967).

—— 'Lecture on the 1905 Revolution', in Lenin, V. I., *On Trade Unions* (Moscow: Progress Publishers, 1970).

Leslie, J. A. K., *A Survey of Dar es Salaam* (London: Oxford University Press, 1963).

Leubuscher, C., *Tanganyika Territory: a Study of Economic Policy Under Mandate* (London: Oxford University Press, 1944).

Listowel, J., *The Making of Tanganyika* (London: Chatto & Windus, 1965).

Magongo, R. J., 'Co-operation not Domination', *Spearhead* (January 1962) Vol. I, No. 3.

Mandel, E., *Marxist Economic Theory* (London: Merlin Press, 1968).

Manson, P., *Manson's Tropical Diseases* (London: English Language Book Society, 1972).

Marx, K., *Capital,* Vol. I (Moscow: Progress Publishers, n.d.).

—— *Pre-capitalist Economic Formations* (New York: International Publishers, 1965).

—— *The Poverty of Philosophy* (Moscow: Progress Publishers, 1955).

Marx, K., and **Engels, F.,** *Selected Correspondence* (Moscow: Progress Publishers, 1955).

—— *The German Ideology in Collected Works,* Vol. V (Moscow: Progress Publishers, 1976).

Mbilinyi, M. J., 'African Education During the British Colonial Period, 1919–1961', in Kaniki, M. H. Y. (ed.), *Tanzania Under Colonial Rule* (London: Longman, 1979).

Morgan, M., 'The Rise and Fall of Malayan Trade Unionism, 1945–50', in Amin, M. and Caldwell, M. (eds), *Malaya, the Making of a Neo-colony* (Nottingham: Spokesman Books, 1977).

Morton, A. L., *A People's History of England* (Berlin: Seven Seas Publishers, 1965).

Nkrumah, K., *Neo-colonialism: the Last Stage of Imperialism* (London: Heinemann Educational Books, 1968).

Nyerere, J. K., *Freedom and Unity* (Dar es Salaam: Oxford University Press, 1967).

Patel, L. R., 'Trade Unions and the Law in Tanganyika', in *Law and the Commonwealth* (Delhi: National Publishing House, 1971).

Po-ta, Chen., *A Study of Land Rent in Pre-Liberation China* (Peking Foreign Languages Press, 1966).

Rigby-Jones, E., 'Sisal Production in East Africa', extracts in *Kenya Sisal Bulletin,* No. 63, February 1968.

Rweyemamu, J., *Underdevelopment and Industrialization in Tanzania: A Study of Perverse Capitalist Development* (Nairobi: Oxford University Press, 1973).

Sabot, R. H., *Economic Development and Urban Migration: Tanzania 1900–1971* (Oxford: Oxford University Press, 1979).

Sayers, G. F. (ed.), *The Handbook of Tanganyika* (London: Macmillan, 1930).

Saul, J., 'Marketing Co-operatives in a Developing Country: The Tanzanian Case', in Cliffe, L. and Saul, J., *Socialism in Tanzania,* Vol. II (Nairobi: East African Publishing House, 1973).

Schadler, K., *Crafts, Small-scale Industries and Industrial Education in Tanzania* (Munich: Weltforum Verlag, 1968).
— *Manufacturing and Processing Industries in Tanzania* (Munich: IFO–Institut für Witschaftsforschung, 1969).
Scott, R., 'Trade Unions and Nationalism in East Africa', *Proceedings of East African Academy*, Vol. III, 1965 (EAF).
Seidman, A., *Comparative Development Strategies in East Africa* (Nairobi: East African Publishing House, 1972).
Shivji, I. G., *Class Struggles in Tanzania* (London: Heinemann, 1976).
— 'Semi-Proletarian Labour and the Use of Penal Sanctions in the Labour Law of Colonial Tanganyika (1920–38)', in Sumner, C. (ed.), *Crime, Justice and Underdevelopment* (London: Heinemann, 1981).
— 'The Exploitation of the Small Peasant', in Das, A. N. *et. al.* (eds.), *The Worker and the Working Class: A Labour Studies Anthology* (New Delhi: Public Enterprise Centre for Continuing Education, 1983) and also in *Human Futures*, No. 4, Vol. 4 (New Delhi: PECCE).
Singh, M., *History of Kenya Trade Union Movement to 1952* (Nairobi: East African Publishing House, 1969).
Stalin, J., *Economic Problems of Socialism in the USSR* (Peking Foreign Languages Press, 1972).
Sumner, C., *Reading Ideologies: an Investigation into the Marxist Theory of Ideology and Law* (London: Academic Press, 1979).
Tandau, A. C. A., *Historia ya Kuundwa kwa TFL 1955–1962 na Kuanzishwa kwa NUTA 1964* (Dar es Salaam: Mwananchi Publishing Co. 196?).
Tschannerl, G., 'Periphery Capitalist Development — A Case Study of the Tanzanian Economy', *Utafiti*, Vol. I., No. 1, 1976 (University of Dar es Salaam).
TSGA *Determination of Tasks and a Study into Improvement of Methods in the Production of Sisal* (International Land Development Consultants, Arnham, The Netherlands, July 1966).
Vestbro, D. U., *Social Life and Dwelling Space: an Analysis of Three House Types in Dar es Salaam* (Stockholm: University of Lund, Report No. 2, 1975).
Wedderburn, K. W., *The Worker and the Law* (Harmondsworth: Penguin, 1965).
Woddis, J., *Africa, the Roots of Revolt* (London: Lawrence & Wishart, 1960).
— *The Lion Awakes* (London: Lawrence and Wishart, 1961).

E. Newspapers and magazines

Tanganyika Standard (Dar es Salaam).
Economist, 24 December 1938 (London).

Index

absenteeism, 30, 32–3, 51, 63, 98, 116, 118, 122, 169, 174
Accidents and Occupational Diseases (Notification) Ordinance (1953), 143
accidents at work, 75–7, 142, 143, 144–6
compensation, 166, 167
see also industry: safety; Workmen's Compensation Ordinance
African Commercial Employees' Association (ACEA), 185, 186, 191
African Cooks, Washermen and House Boys' Association, 120, 162–3, 164–5
African Labour Union, 162
African National Congress (ANC), 225
African Railway Union, 185
African Staff Association of the Landing and Shipbuilding Co. of East Africa, 186
African Tailors' Association, 162, 164–5
Africanization, 202–4, 223, 225–7, 233, 236
agriculture, 5, 6, 77, 85, 87, 89–90, 107, 176
employers' organizations, 209–11
labour, 18–19, 20, 28, 35, 118–19, 246, 247, (female and child) 65, 70, 71, 245, (proletarian) 2, 107, 108, 109, 115–19, 149, (semi-proletarian) 84, 115, (white-collar) 119
legislation, 125
nineteenth-century, 5–6
products, (exchange of surplus) 5, (export) 18, 27
strikes, 194, 195, 196
trade unions, 211, 212, 234n.
tribal and headmen's councils, 184
wages, 48, 117, 136
see also crops, cash; mechanization; plantations
All-Line Joint Staff Advisory Council (JSAC), 202
alluvial diggers, 48–9, 52, 54–5, 57, 90
Amalgamated African Motor Drivers' and Commercial Road Transport Workers' Union, 163
American Federation of Labour-Congress of Industrial Organizations (AFL-CIO), 189,190, 198n.
Amiri, Shehe, 233
apprenticeship, 114–15
Apprenticeship law, 114
Arnautoglu, George, 89
Arusha, 15, 18, 43, 46, 50, 99, 100, 120, 138, 173
Asians, 88–9, 109, 111, 115, 119, 159, 160–2, 175, 203–4
Asiatic Labour Union, 160–2
Aureole Mines, 55, 66

bakeries, 111; see also food industry
Baldwin, Stanley, 91–2
banking, 85, 86
Barrett, David, 212n., 214
bartering, 6: see also commodity exchange
beverage industry, 111, 112, 249, 250
Bhoke-Munanka, 184–5, 190

Bird and Co., 61, 87
breweries, 19, 113, 191, 199–200, 201, 208
Britain, 84, 87, 123, 192n; see also Fabian Colonial Bureau; Trade Union Congress
British colonization
permanent wage-labour, 106–50
semi-proletarian labour, 7–36, 42–78, (and capital) 87–97, (resistance of) 97–102.
trade unions, 156–78, 182–217, 223
British Ropes Ltd, 113
Building and Construction Workers' Union, 187, 195, 197
building/construction, 89, 90, 107–9, 117, 129, 141, 246, 247
trade unions/strikes, 160, 184–5, 186, 187, 193–7 passim; see also infrastructure; railway construction/operation
Byatt, Governor, 9, 119

capital
foreign finance, 2, 7, 8, 11, 18, 23, 24, 26–7, 33–4, 36, 42–3, 78, 84–8, 89, 90, 91–2, 96, 97, 107, 112–13, 144, 150, 227, 239, 240
local, 24, 85, 86, 227, (big) 85, 86, 88–9, 96, 97, 240, (medium and small) 85, 86, 89–90, 240
state, 85, 86, 90–2
capitalism
imperialism 27, 84

261